qual or Different

= =

Equal or Different

Women's Politics
1800–1914

Edited by Jane Rendall

Basil Blackwell

First published 1987

Basil Blackwell Ltd
108 Cowley Road, Oxford, OX4 1JF, UK

Basil Blackwell Inc.
432 Park Avenue South, Suite 1503
New York, NY 10016, USA

British Library Cataloging in Publication Data
Equal or different: women's politics 1800-1914
  1. Women in politics—Great Britain—History
  I. Rendall, Jane
  323.3′4′0941   HQ1236.5.G7

ISBN 0-631-14522-2
ISBN 0-631-14523-0 Pbk

Library of Congress Cataloging in Publication Data
Equal or different.
  Includes index.
  1. Women in politics—Great Britain—History—
19th century. 2. Feminism—Great Britain—History—
19th century. I. Rendall, Jane, 1945-
HQ1236.5.G7E68 1987   305.4′2′0941   87-13844
ISBN 0-631-14522-2
ISBN 0-631-14523-0 (pbk.)

Typeset in 10 on 11½ pt Plantin
by DMB Typesetting
Printed in Great Britain by Billing & Sons Ltd. Worcester

Contents

Preface

This book takes its place in a series of studies of different aspects of women's history, and is intended to be related to them. It is not possible to separate easily the private and public lives of women, integrally related as they were and are; and although this volume is centred on women's political experience it seeks throughout to see women's politics in relation to their lives as a whole. My own understanding of this has been greatly strengthened by the work of colleagues and students in the History Department at the University of York and by my colleagues and students in the Women's Studies Centre there. I should like to thank the editors of the first two volumes, Angela John and Jane Lewis, for their assistance at an early stage; and Sue Corbett, Virginia Murphy, Gillian Bromley and Alison Kelly at Blackwell. The contributors to this volume made it possible, not least by the promptness of their deliveries, and by their collective assistance in the writing of the introduction.

List of Contributors

Louis Billington is a lecturer at the University of Hull, where he teaches in the Centre for American Studies and the Department of History. He is the author of many articles on eighteenth and nineteenth century British and American history and has a particular interest in the social history of religion. He is currently working on a study of popular evangelicalism in Britain and North America between 1730 and 1850 which is due to be published in 1988.

Rosamund Billington teaches sociology and socio-history, with particular emphasis on gender, culture and ideology, at Humberside College of Higher Education, where she is also Course Leader of the BA (Hons) Social Science. She completed a Ph.D on the nineteenth century women's education and suffrage movements and has published articles on nineteenth century feminism.

Lucy Bland teaches sociology at Hatfield Polytechnic. She is writing a book on feminism and sexual morality 1885–1918, and has written several articles on the subject, including one in Jane Lewis (ed.) *Labour and Love* (Blackwell, Oxford, 1986).

June Hannam completed her Ph.D thesis on women's work in Leeds in 1984, and lectures in American and British social history at Bristol Polytechnic. She is currently writing a biography of Isabella Ford.

Patricia Hollis is a senior lecturer in history at the University of East Anglia. She is the editor of *Women in Public 1850–1900* (Allen & Unwin, 1979) and the author of *Ladies Elect. Women in English Local Government 1865–1914* (Oxford University Press, Oxford, 1987) as well as other books on Victorian radicalism. She is also active in local government herself, is leader of Norwich City Council, and serves on various national local government committees.

Jane Rendall is a lecturer in history at the University of York, with interests in eighteenth and nineteenth century political ideas, and the history of feminism. She is the author of *The Origins of Modern Feminism. Women in Britain, France and the United States, 1780–1860* (Macmillan, 1985).

Dorothy Thompson is a lecturer in modern history at the University of Birmingham. She is the author of a number of books and articles on popular politics in nineteenth century Britain, the latest of which is *The Chartists* (Temple Smith, 1984).

Deborah Valenze is a research associate at the Centre for European Studies, Harvard University, and a visiting lecturer in History at Smith College in Northampton, Mass. She is the author of *Prophetic Sons and Daughters: Female Preaching and Popular Religion in Industrial England* (Princeton University Press, Princeton, 1985) and is now working on a study of women and the industrial revolution.

Linda Walker has a Ph.D from Manchester University on the women's movement in the late nineteenth and early twentieth centuries. She has taught history and women's studies in Manchester where she currently lives.

Acknowledgements

I should like to thank the following: Calderdale Museum Service, Shibden Hall, Halifax, for kind permission to reproduce the photograph of Anne Lister on p. 77; the Hull Central Library for the photograph on p. 89; the University of Glasgow Library for permission to reproduce the photograph of the *Waverley Journal* on p. 117; the British Newspaper Library, Colindale, for the photograph of *Shafts* on p. 144 and the portraits from the *Leeds and Yorkshire Mercury* on p. 233. Permission to cite the journal of Anne Lister was kindly granted by the Calderdale District Archives, Shibden Hall Muniments (SH:7/ML/E/20).

Introduction

Jane Rendall

No article in this book deals directly with the suffrage movement. The symbolic importance of the vote to generations of feminists and subsequent historians has meant the obscuring of women's broader political culture and history.[1] The possession of the suffrage qualified women finally by the end of our period to enter that purely masculine and public world of national politics from which they had been so long formally debarred. In taking up citizenship in 1918, as the National Union of Women's Suffrage Societies turned itself into the National Union of Societies for Equal Citizenship, women over thirty won a formal equality in the public sphere, though a sphere defined in male terms. Liberal and democratic ideals of the equality of individuals were extended to incorporate the claims of women. Yet it is possible to approach the study of nineteenth-century politics with different categories in mind. The political journey for women should not be seen simply as a steady and unimpeded progress for a fortunate few, from the private life of home and family to the public world of pressure groups, trade unions, parties, Parliament. The political language and the objectives of both women and men were structured partly by their class, partly by their gender. This volume tries to illustrate and explore some of the specific and practical tensions that women in different political situations experienced, and evoked. These essays attempt to recover, from the cottage religion of Primitive Methodism to the local government councillors of the early twentieth century, the character of women's political language, and to understand how that language was structured by gender as well as by class.

In the study of political activity, we are looking at the ways in which authority and resources in particular societies are allocated, at the recognition of moral agency, at individual and collective patterns of action to change existing structures of political authority. Women had little formal part in the institutional and masculine world of parliamentary and national politics for most of this period. Around 1800, in common with the majority of men, they could neither elect nor were they eligible for any constituted authority, except for a few ratepaying women possessing the parish vote. Their absence may seem to suggest the limits of a study of this kind. Within those movements which successively challenged the political elites, in Chartism and the Anti-Corn Law League, their participation, only recently recovered by historians, may be judged by the objectives of those movements as supportive and secondary.

The division between private life and the public world has been extended into an argument for the 'universal structural opposition between domestic and public domains of activity', an opposition which carried with it the lower status of the domestic sphere and women in it. Michelle Rosaldo, in a key article some years ago, suggested that the status of women was lowest in any society where there was firm differentiation between domestic and public spheres, where women were isolated in their homes. In nineteenth-century England, such a differentiation undoubtedly had come to exist as a prescriptive model, for the middle and upper classes, and as an aspiration for those below them. Rosaldo suggested that women could challenge male rule either by seeking to enter a male world, or by stressing their own different and unique sphere:

> More commonly, in those societies where domestic and public spheres are firmly differentiated, women may win power and value by stressing their differences from men. By accepting and elaborating upon the symbols and expectations associated with their cultural definition, they may goad men into compliance, or establish a society unto themselves.[2]

There are here two propositions relevant to this volume: firstly, that the status of women will vary with the extent of the divergence between private and public worlds, and secondly, that there were two possible routes for women excluded from the world of authority and activity, in the claiming of equality or the assertion of difference.

The distinction between public and private worlds is an extremely relevant one to the study of women's situation in nineteenth- and early twentieth-century Britain. It has been a fundamental category of Western European thinking about politics, used to order the contrast, and sometimes the parallels, between close, familial relationships and the distant, abstract, ordered structure of authority in society.[3] But it is also a concept which must be seen in particular historical, and changing, contexts. The contrast may be between the Greek household and the *polis*, or between the seventeenth-century weaving household and the monarchy. Yet a growing and powerful model in the English political tradition was that of a politics based on the propertied individual, the head of the household, the moral and rational individual. That too could change in different contexts. Where in the late seventeenth century a political theory which awarded citizenship to that male individual had emerged, by the nineteenth century in England the prescriptive liberal distinction implied that the public world encompassed both the limited role of the state and the wider arena of the market place, and the withdrawal of the private world of home and family from both.

That model could of course be far removed from reality. In nineteenth-century England, for instance, much has been written on the survival of patterns of political deference, which rested on links of land, patronage, and employment. In rural society the territorial influence of the landed classes remained considerable: and in the new industrial world employers might parallel that in their influences over all aspects of the lives, including the family lives, of their workforce. Paternalist or philanthropic employers could perpetuate a hierarchical structure which left little scope for the politics of individual political judgement.[4] English common law exemplified that patriarchal structure within the family. Throughout English society for much of the nineteenth century, for most women and men, there was no firm differentiation between public and private worlds. Women did a great deal of paid work, much paid work was still carried on within the home, and much household labour might still be undertaken by women together. We shall want to consider how far such an intermingling of private and public meant a higher standing for women in their own culture.

The liberal perspective, and its distortions, is a constant theme within this volume, though the term is used here without party political implications. That perspective could be extended to contain the granting of individual and equal public rights to women: yet such rights did not include the reordering of the family model. In *The Subjection of Women* (1869) John Stuart Mill writes with eloquence of the oppression of women and the need for their legal and political emancipation, but he is silent as to the reordering of the inequalities of private life, of divisions of labour and their consequences for power within the family. He offers a liberal ideal of the companionate marriage of intellectual equals, yet hardly confronts the real relationship in his own mid-nineteenth-century society between the private and public worlds for women.[5] We need to challenge, as Dorothy Thompson has done in this volume, the liberal myth (of which Mill was one of the founders) of continuing progress for women along egalitarian and individualist lines.

There is a need to step away from the dominating themes of nineteenth-century political history and recover a different perspective. We need to understand in what many and varied ways women of all classes perceived the structures of authority in their own worlds: as mothers, consumers, and housewives, as workers, as philanthropists. In that way, this volume cannot be separated from its predecessors in this series, which considers women's domestic and working lives. Some historians have posed an opposition between 'women's politics' and 'women's culture', and argued that too much attention to the separateness of women's concerns, to their domestic, religious, and philanthropic lives, must detract from what should primarily be the political history of the challenge to oppression, organized, conscious, identifiable, always with a particular stress on the history of feminism.[6] The essays in this volume suggest rather that it is impossible to recover the language which women used, and the meaning of their politics, unless we consider that separate viewpoint. Without entering into women's private worlds it is impossible to grasp the range of women's political activities. And unless we expand our definition of what is properly political, as in very different ways both Deborah Valenze and Lucy Bland in this volume have done, then we shall be dependent on that nineteenth-century view of the public sphere. The history of women's political activity is not identical with the history of feminist movements, though at many points the two must overlap.

Gender was not necessarily the primary factor determining women's loyalties and interests. There were other loyalties, most obviously to class and community. Nineteenth-century England was a society in which class boundaries were increasingly complex. A landed class which maintained its personal hold on the institutions of national government nevertheless acknowledged and compromised with the in-dustrial strength of the manufacturing middle classes. The professional and upper middle classes grew in importance as shapers and leaders of public opinion. Yet the expansion of the middle classes at all income levels down to that of the suburban clerk or salesman confused both social aspirations and political loyalties for women and for men. And the pace of agricultural and industrial change was experienced dif-ferentially throughout the country, as the leading sectors of the early nineteenth century, textiles and iron, gave place to the new heavy in-dustries, and the sweated trades of the great cities. Such shifts in class dimensions meant the erosion of long-established community patterns: they could mean the creation of new ones, but with different male and female patterns of political and social association. They could mean too new and dynamic forms of political culture, as in a nonconformist and dissenting liberalism, and in the new kinds of labour and socialist politics.

The essays in this book suggest that nineteenth-century women did employ the language of their own experience, of motherhood, of domestic labour, of religious commitment, whether their links were primarily with other women or whether they were operating in more formal mixed institutions, or political movements. There is no doubt that the women described here did not ultimately challenge the sexual division of labour, though they did question the different forms which it took: many, while challenging injustice, drew their considerable strength from what they regarded with pride as their most fulfilling tasks, as wives and mothers. Yet many, whether working women within the Independent Labour Party, or the middle-class campaigners of the mid-nineteenth century, felt the justice also of the call for an equality which recognized them as political beings. They could still be torn by the need to identify with the needs of their class, whether in a socialist demand for a transformed society or in acceptance of middle-class values. A reading of the political history of the nineteenth century which incorporates the category of gender as well as that of class should help us to identify 'why at some moments . . . sexual difference and division take on a political significance'.[7]

In the first part of this book, the essays consider themes that are especially relevant to the period around 1800–60, a period of early industrial growth, of dislocation and transition. Historians have in these years identified working women's participation in movements of social and political protest. The essays here consider working women's part in the collective lives of their community, and their own authority within their families: that authority declined as the household economy was increasingly disrupted. A further theme is the way in which religious language and experience could provide the means by which women might actively express their grievances and win authority, as female preachers were able to do. In a different setting evangelical religion could provide the dynamic and model of organization for the participation of middle-class women in movements of moral reform, such as the anti-slavery and abolitionist movements. But Unitarian and Quaker dissent, rooted in a long history of dissenting egalitarianism, was in Britain as in America to dominate the more radical sections of the movement, especially those most in sympathy with women's rights. And from similar dissenting and politically radical middle-class families came the writers of the *English Woman's Journal*, a network of women, mainly single, who argued for the distinctive contribution which women should make to the ordering of the new industrial society.

Deborah Valenze puts the case for a new approach to the political history of working women, one to be removed from the masculine politics of the propertied individual, and the assumptions behind the separation of public and private worlds. Working women were oriented to the collective life of the family and the community, where the domestic sphere was intimately related to the public, where the notion of a separate private life had little meaning. Working women were involved in the labouring of the household, in meeting the family's daily needs, in the rituals of birth, marriage and death within the community. Dorothy Thompson too stresses the involvement of working women and their authority within the labour and the domestic responsibilities of the family economy. We know very little about the role of women in rural or recently urbanized communities: no historian has yet embarked on any discussion as to the kinds of informal power which the women of the community might together exert, as Martine Segalen has powerfully done for French peasant life.[8] Women were actively involved in crowds demonstrating against those who contravened local patterns of morality, by the nineteenth century as likely to be against regular wife beaters as scolding wives.[9] Food and enclosure riots, and women's participation in them, lasted long into the nineteenth century. These were areas where women might be thought to have a particular concern – but they should not be separated from other areas of conflict and protest.

Religious language and experience was one way through which the responses of women to the threat to their familiar pattern of life could be translated. The growth of small communitarian sects led by women such as Ann Lee, Luckie Buchan, and Joanna Southcott, has been described by J.F.C. Harrison.[10] Deborah Valenze here portrays female preachers from within the evangelical and Methodist tradition – Primitive and Quaker Methodists, Bible Christians and others – accepted by their communities as speaking in the language of the family and household economy, expressing in biblical terms their sense of grievance and threat. In the industrializing Black Country of Staffordshire, the new industrial villages of Derbyshire, and in the depressed agricultural areas of the south west, female preachers, bold, assertive, travelling, placed the values of family life against the individualistic harshness of the market economy.[11] Some preached in the open air or from their own or others' homes, away from churches and chapels. Some, as in the Bible Christians of the south west, were young and single, some even under twenty, and they transformed the meaning of their preaching into the serving of an extended family. Yet at the same time within the new industrial setting such preaching, recalling the order of the past, could also restate the desirability of family values within the new setting. Female preachers did not accept the 'separate' values of family life, but their message could seem to overlap with it.

Women's participation in movements of protest cannot be traced according to the familiar timetable of masculine demands for incorporation within the constitution. We know nothing of any female involvement in radical politics in the 1790s, though it is clear that women did form their own Female Reform Societies after the Napoleonic Wars, especially in Lancashire.[12] Perhaps such activity has to be seen not just in moments of particular political crisis, but in the light of continuing community reactions to a threat to livelihood and the familiar ordering of life. Women participated in significant numbers in the resistance to the New Poor Law of 1834, and in the Chartist movements of the late 1830s and early 1840s. In the manufacturing communities of the north, in areas where men and women worked together in textiles, or in continuing domestic industry there remained a close relationship between domestic and public lives. In Bradford, for instance, the Female Radical Association formed in March 1839 included factory operatives as well as woolcombers, weavers, and the wives and daughters of male Chartists in other employments.[13] Women Chartists raised funds, took part in political demonstrations, organized Chartist schools and Sunday Schools and used their control over family resources to deal only with sympathetic shopkeepers. Yet the force of the Chartist campaign was directed towards a political remedy, the Six Points of the Charter, including universal manhood suffrage, and employed a political rhetoric against a state which was seen as legislating against working-class interests. Some male Chartists did support women's suffrage, at least as a future goal, and a few women, like Susannah Inge of the City of London Female Chartists, not only looked for women's suffrage, but even questioned the purely domestic role of women. But the great majority of women Chartists gave greater priority to more immediate issues, arising out of what was seen as the oppression of employers and Poor Law Guardians, and did not identify their own interests as being in conflict with those of their husbands.

Though the Owenite movement appealed to relatively small numbers of women and men, compared to Chartism, it offers some insight into the specific appeal of utopian forms of socialism against a background of economic disruption in the domestic and working order. Robert Owen's 'New Moral World' offered a way of meeting the new industrial order, in transforming not only the political, but the social and economic future. He called for a 'moral revolution' and a new kind of communitarian ideal, which could transform not only the workplace but the household. Barbara Taylor, in one of the most distinguished recent works of women's history, has shown how the Owenite creed appealed to women in challenging the rigidities and inequities of the patriarchal common law and Anglican versions of marriage, and yet also by providing a route for many women to assert the importance of family relations. The difference between Owen and female Owenites such as Frances Morrison, Margaret Chappellsmith, and their audiences, on sexuality, points to a consistently different view of sexual politics, one which echoed Mary Wollstonecraft's rejection of the 'animal appetite' fifty years earlier.[14] Egalitarian in theory, the practice of the Owenite movement was not always so, either in its communities or its governing conference. Yet this secular sect also permitted men and women to turn the language of evangelicalism into a powerful and mystical expression of female superiority, in a vision of a truly complementary social order of the future which united male and female principles. But that vision could not survive for long.

Dorothy Thompson in this volume has amplified her earlier view of the 'withdrawal of working-class women' from the history of working-class movements, in her discussion of the transformation of the family economy.[15] Even by the mid 1840s the declining participation of women in Chartist organizations has been noted. Women were more likely to retain their commitment to chapel and temperance organizations than to the formal associations or the demonstrations of earlier years. Patterns of labour were changing, so that the household was no longer the focus of work, uniting the interests of all its members. Though women might continue to bring in a supplementary income, their financial rewards were no longer related to the central earnings of the household. Both women and men might place their hopes in the wages which the masculine breadwinner could win for the family, as its economy took a new shape. Women might retain considerable authority within the family, yet had no public role. Even within the family, where parents had once held responsibility for the training or education of their children, the educational policies of Church and state were gradually usurping that power. There must have been informal networks of women in the streets and courts of the new urban communities, able to exercise some kinds of local sanctions on behaviour: Ellen Ross has traced their existence in late nineteenth-century London.[16] Such relationships between women, however, clearly did not parallel the growth of more formal masculine institutions, based particularly on the workplace but also on shared patterns of leisure.[17]

Landed and upper-middle-class women in early nineteenth-century England could exercise certain political rights by virtue of their property and their family influence. Many, like Anne Lister, described by Dorothy Thompson, were likely to participate in elections by canvassing in the family interest. More generally, political hostesses in the world of London politics might well be in a position to affect political alignments and policies. Acceptance into the Holland House circle, for instance, might depend on approval by the powerful Lady Holland.[18] Electioneering in a husband's interest may have been affected by mid-Victorian standards of propriety, though it certainly continued. In the 1870s Evelyn Lady Stanhope was a successful political hostess, who organized her husband's electoral campaigns, supported and advised him: though her work could not ultimately counteract her husband's weakness as a politician.[19] Nevertheless the extending powers of state organization may have seen a diminution in the extent of informal influence such women could exercise: the New Poor Law of 1834, for instance, meant that the new workhouses were less likely to be patronized and visited by such women than the homes of the poor.[20]

For middle-class women the separation of the spheres of home and work pervaded the prescriptive literature of the first half of the nineteenth century: though there is much that we are still ignorant of as to the reality of that separation. Were there more of those successful businesswomen whom Mrs Oliphant has described in several of her novels, the Catherine Vernon who headed a bank, the successful single dressmaker, than prescriptive models allowed?[21] Dorothy Thompson describes the devaluing of women's skills and family authority within the middle classes by such a separation: though at the same time indicating their new tasks as household managers, administrators of the consumption of the new material wealth. Yet the middle classes were as a whole expanding greatly, from the trading, shopkeeping and mercantile sectors of the eighteenth century, to encompass a new range of incomes, from the industrial manufacturer to the London clerk. And in doing this, they were of course throughout the nineteenth century to challenge the social and political power of the landed classes. The participation of middle-class women in a variety of activities apparently crossing from private to public life must be seen in the light of that challenge, as well as being a defiance of gender prescriptions. Mary Wollstonecraft's demands for a moral and rational role for women were directed against the luxury and decadence of a tyrannical, aristocratic and clerical *ancien regime*, just as middle-class women participated in the work of the Anti-Corn Law League to support the claims of their class to participate in the making of national policies.

Women played a notable part in the development of those evangelical forces which from the mid-eighteenth century onwards were the most dynamic elements in English religious life. The language of evangelicalism emphasized individual salvation, the discipline of the self, the moral powers of women. That language was to have a powerful meaning for women of the middle and working classes. Such a movement was felt within all denominations, inside the Anglican Church, through Old Dissent, Independents, Baptists and Congregationalists, and most of all in the many varieties of Methodism. Many historians have stressed how evangelical theology and social prescriptions stressed the limited sphere of women, as did Hannah More and many others. The theme of the God-given 'domestic constitution' stressed by evangelical clergy like John Angell James from the 1820s and 1830s seemed to revive an older parallelism between the family and the state. Yet at the same time such evangelical doctrine brought with it a zealous missionary force. The sense of mission could be interpreted in the literal sense, in the new organizations established by all denominations to carry the word of Protestant salvation to many other peoples, in which women as organizers and fundraisers played a major part. The language of mission could be extended in other directions: the evangelical legacy was by no means clearcut in its implications for women's lives.[22]

At the same time those small but influential denominations, the Unitarians and the Quakers, though influenced by the evangelical movement, retained something of an older, egalitarian outlook towards the relations between men and women. This should not be overstressed, since the quietism of so much Quaker doctrine and the effective exclusion of women from much part in church government still remained. Many, perhaps the majority, of members of these denominations, had little sympathy for the cause of women's rights. Yet Unitarian and Quaker names constantly recur in this volume, and there is a need for a history of the consistent association between these denominations and the nineteenth-century movement for women's rights. Together, according to the 1851 Census, their total numbers were no more than 75,000.[23] Unitarian families mentioned here, besides such well known individuals as W.J. Fox, Harriet Taylor, Harriet Martineau, and Elizabeth Reid, include the Estlins, the Carpenters, the Courtaulds, the Leigh Smiths, the Davenport Hills, the Ashursts. Leading Quaker families like the Lloyds, the Sturges, the Peases, the Fords, appear as well as Anne Knight and Anna Richardson. Many of these families were dominant in centres of provincial trade and industry, like the Peases of Darlington, the Courtaulds of Essex, the Rathbones of Liverpool. Such families dissented not only on religious but on social and political grounds from the authority of the landed and Anglican establishment. They fought in many causes, from the battle against church rates to the Anti-Corn Law League and the case for secular education. Their battle was for ascendancy, and the struggle to improve, progressively, the rights of women, could make one part of the liberal ideology.

From the 1790s onwards evangelicalism across a broad denominational spectrum saw the growth of missionary and philanthropic activity: the two overlapped, the same methods of organization and fundraising being used for both. Women's philanthropic societies increasingly made their appearance in the first quarter of the nineteenth century, often in charitable activities with particular reference to poor women's health, or the education of their children.[24] By 1830, it has been argued, a sense of 'Woman's Mission' which rested on the unique qualities of women, could be extended to allow women to claim a part in movements of 'moral reform': in the anti-slavery and Anti-Corn Law League movements, in peace and temperance campaigns.[25] Radical and nonconformist pressure groups – of considerable political importance between the Reform Acts of 1832 and 1867 as the channels of middle-class opinion – drew very considerably on women's support. Women in such pressure groups had at all times to observe the conditions of female propriety. They were unlikely to speak in public to mixed audiences or to act as delegates, more likely to participate in bazaars, fundraising, tea-parties. Nevertheless such action pointed to the possibilities of the language of moral reform.

In their article on women's role within the anti-slavery movements in this volume, Rosamund Billington and Louis Billington have described the characteristic structure of such organizations, the emergence of women's separate auxiliary societies, the presence of women's committees, the likelihood of control by and conflict with overseeing male officers. They have illustrated too the significant splits after 1840 between the predominantly evangelical wing and those who stood for a more radical position, mainly Unitarians and radical Quakers, following the American Garrisonians, with a commitment to women's rights, though the split was never a clear-cut one. The contrast with the American movement remains an important one. The absence of personal experience of slavery, and perhaps also the very different social and political setting of the English movement, meant that it did not directly lead to an autonomous movement among women. Though a moral issue of great importance, offering important parallels to other movements of moral reform, it was not as it was in the United States, a political movement of immediate relevance to the struggle for national authority. Women's participation in anti-slavery movements shared the quality of these movements of moral and charitable reform. Women's societies could take a more radical stand on some issues, as did anti-slavery reformers when they argued for immediate solutions, and could prove resistant to the control of parallel male organizations. Yet they contained within themselves a critical dilemma: they drew their very rationale from a sense of difference and separatism, which was central to their rhetoric of mission and rescue. Was that rationale to reinforce the authority that stemmed from their class, or could it bring a more radical challenge to masculine authority?

The recent work of F. K. Prochaska has traced such a challenge even in the first half of the nineteenth century, in, for instance, the work of prison reformers, whose claims to care for female prisoners were not generally welcomed. After 1834, women came to demand a part in the administration of the new workhouses, as did Louisa Twining by the 1850s.[26] These claims were based unflinchingly on the demand to extend domestic values and domestic expertise into the management of institutions. They rested on the right to extend the practice of visiting, with its origins in eighteenth-century evangelicalism, into the prisons, hospitals, schools, workhouses of a state which though nominally adhering to a minimalist role, was already beginning to expand its governing powers. Such demands could be made against masculine resistance, yet entirely within the context of a unique moral mission for women. That could mean the assertion of conservative domestic values, of a harsh and moralistic regime, exercised by middle-class women over those seen as morally delinquent, in, for instance, refuges for prostitutes and fallen women.[27] It could incorporate too a call for a single moral standard for men and women. Anna Jameson in her writing on the 'communion of labour', a concept in some ways not so far from that unity of male and female principles desired by some Owenites and utopian socialists, was to call for the ending of male hypocrisy on sexual issues, and the recognition of the evil of prostitution.

It is not easy to locate the significance of the reforms sought by middle-class women's movements, in relation to both gender and class. The campaign of the mid-1850s for the reform of the marriage laws was certainly rooted in the recognition by women like Barbara Bodichon of the injustices created by the antiquated and patriarchal structure of the common law of marriage. That common law had been irrelevant for many years to the landed and upper middle classes, who used legal trusts under the law of equity to protect married women's property, though it was by no means irrelevant to those below those income brackets, and above the level of the working population. Such a campaign coincided with the aims of those who sought to rationalize and simplify English law, and eliminate the overlapping of the different systems of common law and equity.[28] It must be remembered that it was the protest against the patriarchalism of the common law, not that law itself, which was the product of Victorian liberal ideology. As Mill was to argue, the reform of the law of marriage could be seen as one further stage in the dismantling of the feudal legacy of the past era, moving yet another step towards the legal and political equality of all individuals.

The *English Woman's Journal*, whose brief career is described in my essay, was coloured by philanthropy and by profound though diverse religious commitments. It nevertheless moved beyond the purely philanthropic towards demands primarily rooted in the experience of single women, for education and for employment. Such demands began to cross an apparently new barrier for middle-class women, that which divided the home from the market place: they even suggested the possibility of married women's work. They raised different issues, not necessarily to be accommodated within the liberal vision of the freeing of old restraints on the individual. Mill and his supporters could cope with the shift towards equality: but they could not accommodate the recognition of difference. Women from such backgrounds felt divided loyalties. Some, like Millicent Garret Fawcett, wrote on popular political economy, and worked throughout their lives for political equality for women. Others preferred to continue to identify with their gender, as in work for the repeal of the Contagious Diseases Acts, and other areas of moral reform. Many did both.

Middle-class women might act together in the 'Ladies' Committee' based on the charitable model. But there were other less formal ways of association. In early-nineteenth-century Britain young women of upper- and middle-class families were allowed little freedom in relation to the opposite sex: but friendship between women did not contravene prevailing controls on sexuality. Such permitted friendship could unite personal affection and political commitment, and provide the kind of informal network that might be found in the common educational experiences and male clubs of their fathers, sons and brothers. Friendships of this kind were certainly not confined to unmarried women, and could last a lifetime. They could provide the basis for the choice of a single life. The founders of the *English Woman's Journal* enjoyed such a circle of friendship, which may be related to many others. Liz Stanley has traced those networks of friendship which linked together over-lapping groups of women in nineteenth-century England. Martha Vicinus has studied those communities in which single women might choose to establish their lives with other women, and in which perhaps they might exercise power as headmistress or matron, within a female hierarchy.[29] There was nevertheless a class dimension in the way such relationships were understood. Though young middle-class women were denied sexual feelings, for men or women, that was not the case for those beyond the pale of the respectable middle classes, whether working-class women, actresses, or those leading what was regarded as a Bohemian life.[30]

There were of course other kinds of informal networks: and those formed by the intermarriage of leading families of similar political views allowed to many women the chance to form continuing female friendships. They shared a common familial experience, and access to the shared political interests of their husbands, fathers and brothers. At the highest levels of politics, there was a tendency of families with similar political interests to mix, and to intermarry. Marriage itself could have among other purposes a political one, as was noted of Sir William Harcourt's second marriage to Elizabeth Cabot Ives: 'a good Liberal, and I hope will do her duty to the party and its leaders'.[31] Some women might of course bear the political future of their prospective partner in mind when choosing their husband, as Margot Tennant clearly did in marrying a man marked out as a future Prime Minister.[32] Upper-middle-class families, of liberal or radical views, including both provincial manufacturing groups and the intellectual aristocracy, might be united in their sympathy for women's participation in politics. Among the Unitarian families of Samuel Courtauld (1793–1881) and his nephew Peter Alfred Taylor (1819–91), were Clementia Taylor, secretary to the first women's suffrage committee, Elizabeth Malleson, a teacher in Barbara Bodichon's school and Secretary of the Working Woman's College, and Louisa Jeffrey, companion to Harriet Martineau.[33] Their network of Unitarian friends and associates extended far more widely, beyond W.J. Fox's London circle to the national network of Unitarian contacts. The Quaker family of the Brights of Manchester was similarly linked: though John Bright was himself opposed to women's suffrage, his brother and sister-in-law Jacob and Ursula Bright were among its most prominent supporters, as well as actively supporting the repeal of the Contagious Diseases Acts. So were Ursula Bright's mother, Mrs Blackburn of Stockport, and Jacob Bright's two sisters, Margaret Bright Lucas, and Agnes Bright McLaren of Edinburgh. Female networks of kinship and friendship were very apparent on the committee of the Ladies' National Association for the Repeal of the Contagious Diseases Acts.[34]

By mid-century it is possible to gain some idea of the ways in which women perceived the constraints which divided public and private spheres. For married women, there were the practical burdens of managing a home and caring for a large family. Working-class women had to ensure the family's survival by whatever means they could. These burdens were constant ones throughout our period and could leave little time, or energy, for anything not closely related to the family's struggle. Robert Moore's portrayal of Durham mining communities suggests a considerable difference between the part played by young women and married women in the life of the chapel, the only respectable source of activity for women outside the home.[35] The politics of survival might seem to require attendance at chapel, perhaps even participation in the temperance movement: concerns not integrally related to survival could seem secondary. And survival could equally seem to be associated with a positive withdrawal from public life, defined in terms of family respectability. Working-class women could be attracted to the values attached to privacy, where a husband with above-average income could secure it. For the middle-class married woman, with servants, the potential may have seemed greater, yet her responsibilities to house and family were still considerable and any indications of neglect likely to be censured. Few feminists were to criticize the assumption that the married woman's first responsibility was to the care of her family. Older and affluent married women were most likely to dominate the women's pressure groups of mid-Victorian England.

Gender constraints were a constant reality for single middle-class women, both imposed by parental authority and internalized by young women themselves. A young, unmarried woman could not mix freely with men, nor could she travel easily alone. The social demands on her time could be considerable, her own sense of frustration great. Single women too were assumed to have family responsibilities, to the care of parents, that would outweigh all other calls upon their time. Contrasting educational patterns for men and women limited the confidence of young women to participate in masculine areas of concern. Few middle-class women enjoyed secondary education of any quality, and only those fortunate enough to enjoy tuition through the initiative of a father or through sharing with brothers were likely to acquire such confidence. Nevertheless, single women did play a considerable part in political associations. Olive Banks' study of 98 feminists active in the women's movement between 1800 and 1930 has suggested that though married women were in a majority, single women were a large and significant minority.[36]

The maintenance of sexual propriety was a matter of overwhelming concern for such women. Few – with some exceptions such as Elizabeth Wolstenholme Elmy – were personally prepared to challenge the sexual conventions, though they would, in the interests of moral reform, discuss the taboo subjects of prostitution and venereal disease. Working directly with men, speaking in public, especially in mixed audiences, therefore presented immediate problems. Powerful and older women could finally escape the constraints imposed upon them, often only through wearing and exhausting battles, such as those Florence Nightingale successively fought. Though much attention is necessarily focused on the few who broke such conventions, their power should not be underestimated. A recent study of the eight sisters of Beatrice Potter (later Beatrice Webb) suggests how one prosperous Victorian upper-middle-class family, by the end of the century, still limited the lives of its daughters, who themselves reinforced its precepts. Only Beatrice, and to a lesser extent one other sister, seriously questioned the exclusive centrality of family life for married women.[37]

The physical constraints on young working-class women could be less, though domestic servants were of course equally under the rule of the head of the household. Deborah Valenze has noted how bold and assertive female preachers seemed to contemporaries and how that was indeed accepted by those within their congregations and communities. Working-class women might well in the early nineteenth century use the pubs, for meetings of, for instance, Female Friendly Societies, or for mixed meetings. Middle-class reports, and cartoons of working-class women in early-nineteenth-century riots and protests note and mock those qualities. Some hostile representations of working women speaking in public played on their sexuality, combining both ugliness and lustfulness, as did some cartoons of Female Reform Societies. But within such political movements, and within Chartism too, the public presence of women, dressed in white with appropriate sashes, as at Peterloo, in processions and on the platform could rather take on a symbolic quality, a quality which suggested the supportive role of women.[38] There is much to suggest that middle-class comment on the public behaviour of working-class women was shaped by their own convention, defining by its contrast: the Unitarian Elizabeth Gaskell, writing in Manchester, could contrast the difference in behaviour of factory women and the middle-class Margaret, and their different view of public space:

> Until Margaret had learnt the times of their ingress and egress, she was very unfortunate in constantly falling in with them. They came rushing along, with bold, fearless faces, and loud laughs and jests, particularly aimed at all those who appeared to be above them in rank or station. The tones of their unrestrained voices, and their carelessness of all common rules of street politeness, frightened Margaret a little at first.[39]

Yet there were changes too in what was acceptable. Barbara Taylor has described how Owenite meetings and social festivals might be channelled away from the pub, and the cruder areas of male dominance and spending, into temperate and respectable forms. Such shifts could still confirm a narrow view of women's role, a view shared with many proponents of moral reform, as 'alcohol and respectable womanhood came to be seen as wholly incompatible'.[40] Within such movements, and among the self-improving artisans whose autobiographies David Vincent has analysed, the particular educational failings of women were fully recognized. Those autobiographers noted the inferiority of their wives, their inability to share all their concerns: working women's literacy was markedly lower than that of working men, for most of this period.[41] Within the respectable working-class family, by the late nineteenth century, disciplines could also be strict and gender conventions enforced, as we know from the oral histories related by Elizabeth Roberts for the Edwardian period.[42]

Literature might satirize most effectively the participation of women in public life: and the powerful representation of Mrs Jellyby by Charles Dickens in *Bleak House* (1853) may indeed have had a significant impact on the way in which subsequent generations have regarded female philanthropy. The anonymity assumed by so many early- and mid-nineteenth-century women writers suggests both the social constraints and the critical standards applied to their attempts to enter the literary market-place, let alone their attempts to comment on public issues.[43] At the same time, best-selling novels such as those of Charlotte Yonge might strongly reinforce the confinement of women to a domestic role, even strictly limiting philanthropic involvement. In *The Daisy Chain* (1856), Yonge contrasted the failings of the Ladies' Committee in attempting to run a local school, with masculine good sense. But she still betrayed a certain personal ambivalence, in both satirizing and evoking sympathetically the spirited aspirations of young women for an alternative way of life, as in her portraits of Ethel, who might have been a fine classical scholar, in *The Daisy Chain*, and of Rachel, secretary to the FUEE (Female Union of Englishwomen's Employment) in *The Clever Woman of the Family* (1865).

For many women, one way to breach these restraints lay in imaginative writing. Fiction could be deployed to different purposes. Frances Trollope's *Jessie Phillips* (1842–3) attacked the 'bastardy clause' of the New Poor Law. *Eliza Cook's Journal* (1849–54), in particular in its fiction, advocated legal reform of the position of married women, urged sympathy for unmarried mothers, and suggested that the common interests of women 'cut across the conventional barriers of class and respectability'. Such a journal, with a circulation slightly larger than Dickens's *Household Words*, could reach a lower-middle-class audience.[44] Harriet Martineau's *Deerbrook* (1837) highlighted the lack of employment for single women, as did so many novels on the theme of the governess. Anne Bronte's *The Tenant of Wildfell Hall* (1848) depended for its plot on the patriarchal structure of the common law. And the finest writers were able to explore, both directly and indirectly, through metaphor and style those subjects otherwise barred: women's sexual initiation and feelings, rape, abortion. Such novels could indeed be interpreted as political statements. *Jane Eyre* (1847) could be branded by reviewers for its 'moral Jacobinism'.[45] The significance of Elizabeth Barrett Browning's poem *Aurora Leigh* (1857) for mid-nineteenth-century feminism is often underestimated. In this volume, Lucy Bland has shown how, by the 1890s, the novel might be used by women writers to question sexual convention, to point a way forward for the 'new woman'.

There was a considerable class differential in the nature of such conventions. Working-class women did speak in public to mixed audiences, as preachers, in the first half of the nineteenth century. Working-class women spoke to other women in the Female Reform Societies of the post-Napoleonic period, recognizing the novelty of what they did. A few freethinkers like Anna Wheeler and Eliza Sharples breached convention in the lecture halls, as well as in the Unitarian South Place Chapel, of the late 1820s. The Owenite movement saw a considerable expansion of women as lecturers in the 1830s and early 1840s, to mixed and crowded audiences, about marriage reform and the New Moral World, often in debate with an orthodox clergyman. Some like Emma Martin took the direct route, from preaching in a Baptist congregation to lecturing in the Owenite movement. There were Chartist women lecturers too. The decision taken by the World Anti-Slavery Convention in 1840 not to permit women speakers was therefore taken in a context where women of a different background did in fact speak in public. Some of those present, whose career spanned both Chartism and the anti-slavery movement, like Elizabeth Pease and Eliza Ashurst, must surely have been aware of this.[46] Yet by the 1860s and 1870s as the family ideal and its gender restraints were more generally adopted, women preachers had become unacceptable to sects such as the Primitive Methodists and the Bible Christians, as they had already become by 1803 for Wesleyan Methodism. Those women preachers active in the very different revivalist movements of the 1860s were drawn from a higher class than the Primitive Methodists, and were profoundly conscious of propriety and convention, fully accepting a subordinate role for women in religious and family life.[47]

Middle-class women were only beginning to breach this barrier by the 1850s, as some used the National Association for the Promotion of Social Science from 1857 to 1884 as a platform on which to try their powers of public speaking.[48] Women like Elizabeth Fry, Florence Nightingale, and Emily Davies, who chose to give evidence before parliamentary committees and Royal Commissions had a sense of their temerity and of the absence of precedents. So too as late as 1868 did Lydia Becker in the first Manchester suffrage meetings. Such speakers were most likely to be dismissed as either young and frivolous or elderly and spinsterish, in such establishment papers as *Punch* or the columns of the *Saturday* or *National Review*. To avoid such criticism, women had of course to pay attention to their appearance, and they did identify with the need to conform, in the political interest. One pioneer recalled many years later:

> My first suffrage meeting at St James Hall was a real *sight* – Becker to make the chief speech (and a magnificent one too, from a voice like a peacock) boiled down and poured into tight black satin (tight to bursting point – and hair scragged off a hideous forehead and Miss Blackburn and Miss Biggs one each side the platform, Miss Biggs in grey ringlets) holding up a long banner with a noble sentiment on it. . . . But it was a good and enthusiastic meeting – it must have been to have weathered such a sight! We laughed over it for years after, at home.[49]

By the 1870s women were speaking, though rarely, to mixed meetings of all kinds, including meetings for women's suffrage, where the preponderance of male speakers was still a matter for comment. And although the need for moral reform might justify the broaching of previously taboo subjects such as prostitution and the sexual abuse of children, women still could not easily, without cost to themselves, explore broader issues of sexuality, or question the very framework of their private lives.

Yet issues of sexuality and the reform of the structure of marriage were an essential part of the political arena for many women. That liberal approach which separated public and private worlds allowed little place for a different spectrum of feminist debate, one which examined, and sometimes challenged, the existing nature of marriage and the standards of male sexuality. Mill's denunciation of women philanthropists as a 'sentimental priesthood' illustrates the distance between two distinct strands of nineteenth-century feminism. In the campaign against the

Contagious Diseases Acts Josephine Butler and the Ladies' National Association (LNA) had challenged sexual proprieties, and built an alliance on the basis of their identification with their gender.[50] It was an alliance which could encompass a rejection of the double standard of morality, liberal rejection of state intervention, and nonconformist working men's support. Many women from leading manufacturing families, many Quaker and Unitarian women, supported it. They supported too the principle of separate organization by women on this issue. Few working women participated, though they did give informal support. But ultimately the challenge of the LNA rested on a sense of moral outrage, well within the limits of moral reform. It was to be carried further, by the advocates of social purity, by Ellice Hopkins, and the White Cross League.[51] Such moral reform could co-exist with profoundly conservative social and domestic values: though such work continued to proclaim the unity of women's interests.

Lucy Bland's essay in this volume suggests the relationship between the freedom which such women were using to discuss such themes, and their application to personal relationships. In the second half of the nineteenth century the law of marriage slowly saw some improvement: the ending of married men's rights to control property and earnings, to enjoy automatic custody of children, to chastise their wives, and control their residence. By the 1890s, a period when some single women could begin to support themselves, radical and liberal feminists challenged the existing basis of marriage. They went beyond such patterns of legal reform, in defending the right of women to control their own bodies, and to voluntary and spaced childbearing. They pointed to the effects upon women of venereal disease. They did not reject the heterosexual ideal of marriage and their arguments ultimately fell within liberal orthodoxy in presenting marriage as the companionship of equally moral individuals. But, like the utopian socialists of the 1830s and 1840s, most feminists would not be drawn into the endorsement of 'free love', fearing the damage it would do to their movement, and the abandonment of the legal protection which women might claim. Their new vision was of a transformed sexuality, of one which was primarily spiritual, which would 'banish the brute' of selfish masculinity for a new and more altruistic kind of love, which met the needs of women.

From a different perspective, social purity feminists identified their campaigns against prostitution, venereal disease and child abuse with the cause of all women: and they endowed the suffrage movement itself with a strong sense of the need to campaign against the evils consequent upon male sexuality. Yet at the same time, new definitions of normality in sexual relationships, formulated in the late Victorian and Edwardian periods, were profoundly to affect these attempts to redefine and restrain a masculine version of sexuality. In the work of Havelock Ellis and others, heterosexuality was set against its opposite, homosexuality. Sheila Jeffreys's work has pointed to the possibility of a new perspective upon the campaigns which centred around women's sexuality in the 1890s and the pre-war years. It would be misleading to identify progress in sexual matters simply with a sense of growing individual sexual freedom for women, and a changing heterosexual ideal, for much was to be lost to the feminist movement in later years by the labelling of homosexuality and by attacks upon spinsterhood. Nevertheless in the prewar period, such a polarization had not yet taken place, with a few exceptions such as Dora Marsden's paper *The Freewoman* of 1913, which did assert the argument for free and heterosexual relations.[52]

In the social and political climate of late-nineteenth-century and Edwardian Britain, much was apparently changing as women, mainly but not exclusively middle-class women, made an appearance in some of the institutions of public life. The electoral structure was gradually expanding to incorporate the majority of men by 1884, though universal male suffrage was not achieved until 1918. The issue therefore remained a live one, unlike those European countries where universal manhood suffrage was already a reality. Liberal and Conservative political parties began to create forms of national organization which absorbed a variety of provincial political associations. By the 1890s the Independent Labour Party also claimed a national voice. The pressure group, voluntarist and flexible, was to give way to a much more formalized and national structure of politics, though one with many regional variations. The history of women's participation in the new national organizations has only recently begun to be written.[53]

Linda Walker has compared the participation of women in the Conservative and Liberal parties before the First World War. More specifically she has contrasted the practical contributions of Conservative women in the mixed Primrose League with the separate identity of the Women's Liberal Associations. Women were admitted to the League in 1884 a year after its foundation, as Dames (the female equivalent of the Knight) or, if of lesser social standing, as associates. They worked in the mixed local Habitations: the Ladies' Grand Council for the League, subordinate to the male Grand Council, failed to develop any very clear stance of its own. Local Women's Liberal Associations were first founded after the election of 1880, but only in 1886 welded into the national Women's Liberal Federation. Liberals tended to come from a more socially mixed background, dominated however by nonconformity, and with a higher proportion of women already engaged in organized philanthropic activity. The Liberal Federation was locally responsive and less hierarchical than the Primrose League: but both organizations undoubtedly effectively deployed the talents of women.

There was a difference, however, both in outlook and policies. Both Conservative and Liberal women shared a concept of women's separate responsibilities. The Dames of the Primrose League disclaimed unfeminine assertiveness, and held fast to a 'womanly' ideal. At the same time they demonstrated effective and practical organizing abilities. They were particularly strong in rural areas where the politics of deference still had a powerful hold, where philanthropic work was linked to the influence of property. Yet their role as unpaid canvassers and organizers was an important one, extending the boundaries of what was acceptable for upper-middle-class women, as they entered into electioneering and canvassing, were instructed in political issues, and even, as some did, showed themselves to excel in public speaking. The Liberal Federation and its active Executive, which shared a similar commitment to the separate sphere of women, were both assertive and determined. They claimed that women too should shape and define policy, especially in areas of their special concern. Much sprang from that nonconformist and liberal 'moral arrogance' which Linda Walker notes as characteristic, already tested in campaigns for the repeal of the Contagious Diseases Acts, for social purity, and other moral causes. Liberal women aimed not only to draw in others to serve a party cause, but to preserve their own separate moral and political voice.

The Liberal women deliberately encouraged women to acquire political power, both directly and indirectly. They campaigned only for candidates whose policies they supported, and increasingly their Associations enjoyed a degree of independence. In contrast, most of the Primrose League's active canvassers took much less interest in matters specifically affecting women – with the exception of the women's suffrage issue, on which members were split, and actively debated. The Liberal Federation began to develop its own annual conferences, which covered many issues of interest to women: though they split on the women's suffrage question, the Federation was by 1902 calling on the Party to accept adult suffrage. Perhaps as significant, the Federation worked with many other women's pressure groups and trade unions to achieve their common objectives: labour legislation, legal reform, national insurance provisions. These differences between the political activities of women involved in the two parliamentary parties suggests perhaps that Liberal roots in nonconformity, in pressure group politics, in the politics of moral reform, offered women a basis for feminist claims.

In their study of the women's suffrage movement in France, Kenny and Hause have powerfully analysed the ways in which its regional strength was related to local political structures, and patterns of employment, and to regional cultural differences.[54] Though the essays by Patricia Hollis and June Hannam in this volume are not focused specifically on the issue of women's suffrage, they are intended in part as a contribution to such a map of England. Patricia Hollis has indicated the strength of middle-class women in local government in the great industrial cities of the North and Midlands, reflecting the dominance of the political structure by the liberal middle classes, and women's activities there in suffrage societies, philanthropy, and liberalism.

In her study of women's role in local government, she has stressed how 'invariably and inevitably' such women deployed the 'language of separate spheres'. Philanthropy was still the first public interest for many such women, from the Charity Organization Society to the many settlement associations to be found throughout the major cities. As women entered local government from voluntary philanthropy and suffragist societies, they defined a different version of the responsibilities of local government, one which saw its responsibilities as being to the community. Women councillors saw certain areas of concern as properly theirs, and their intervention made a marked impact on the standards of care in workhouses, education, and finally on town councils. They were interested in the quality of education received by the Board School child, and in the participation of parents in their children's education. Like earlier generations, they were committed to the improvement of sanitation and housing, to a town planning which took into consideration the practical needs of housewives and families.

Their values were those of domesticity and the family, yet they could see their task in local government not so much as extending the private sphere into the public, but as defending a proper female domain against the extension of masculine concerns. Just as Dorothy Thompson suggested in an earlier essay, they were defending their own authority, born both of class and gender. Such values could imply a conservative approach – but it could also mean a radical critique of local and party orthodoxies. Regardless of party, women staked out these interests as their own. Their relationships with their political parties, and male colleagues, were not always easy: and this was particularly evident within the Liberal Party. By 1907, as women were formally permitted to stand for town councils, their task had become more difficult, their success far more questionable. Here of course they were no longer limited to those separate spheres in which they might manipulate their especial claims, and faced the same hostility to their claims to political authority as suffrage campaigners faced.

In the lives of working-class women, neither employment nor domestic values offered such a route to the assertion of authority. The largest single group of working women of course remained that of domestic servants, in isolated and individual households, subject to the authority of middle-class women, unchallenged throughout our period. Hierarchical values and gender segregation could be as important in the workplace. Both Judy Lown, in her study of the Courtaulds silk mills of Halstead, and Patrick Joyce in a broader study of the political culture of northern industrial districts in the third quarter of the nineteenth century, have noted the paternalism of employers, their incorporation of deferential and familistic values. Joyce found that the deferential culture of the factory, which was also a social and political community, overseen by employers, left little space for women to play much part in its political and social associations, since women were mostly in segregated and inferior work of lower status. He suggested that within the factory, given the parallelism between the paternalism of the workplace, the employer's family, and the operative's family, women's work may even have helped to maintain such patterns of deference.[55]

This parallel, between the values of the household and those of employment, is one of great relevance to the study of women's political activities. Outside cotton textiles, trade unionism was slow to draw in working women, and the Women's Trade Union League founded in 1874 was to draw much of its dynamic for organization from middle-class women.[56] There were, of course, changes by the end of the century, especially as women's trade unionism gained strength in Lancashire. Yet even in the course of the First World War, Gail Braybon noted the extent to which employers might share male employees' concept of the secondary nature of women's employment, and the primacy of family values, even if these conflicted with economic priorities.[57]

Working-class culture was not necessarily rooted only in work. In the north the third quarter of the century saw the emergence of the first generations of working men's political clubs, Liberal and Conservative, in which women had no part. Other studies suggest the importance of that masculine culture centred on the institutions of leisure, on pubs, clubs and music halls, yet which looked inwards also to the family. The growth of the working men's club movement, and organized commercial forms of leisure, including sport, had little to offer women, yet they reinforced the division of space between private and public worlds.[58]

Questions which most appealed to working women were those which related to their immediate needs. The formal women's temperance movement which drew on the current of moral reform was never as strong in Britain as in the United States, nor did it attract working-class support. Yet within a denominational framework, commitment to temperance might prove a support to women's struggle for respectability. In the Methodist mining communities of the Deerness valley of Durham, where the Peases were the mineowners, 'temperance work was an integral part of chapel activities', which appealed particularly to women.[59] The Women's Co-operative Guild was similarly initiated by middle-class women like Alice Acland and Margaret Llewellyn Davies: but it could draw upon organizers like Sarah Reddish, whose life had begun in the Bolton mills, and a membership made up largely of the wives of artisans and skilled workers. It enabled such women to contribute their views to the debate in Edwardian Britain on women's health care, infant mortality, marriage and divorce. Its leaders were responsible for innovative ventures intended to take the principles of co-operation to the poor, as in the People's Store and Settlement founded in Sunderland.[60]

The participation of women in the labour and socialist movements of the late nineteenth century raised new issues. In Britain labour politics owed most to the trade unionism of skilled men, in areas of work in which women played no part. For them the route to an improved standard of living was the maintenance of a division of labour within the family which entrenched a separation of spheres, with husband and father as breadwinner, wife and mother as household manager. That, if not a reality, was still a most powerful aspiration shared by women and men. In socialist and Marxist theory too, there was little space for the reproductive role of women, little recognition of inequality in family relationships. Practically, the movement drew its strength from the workplace as the primary place of association among men. Unlike the utopian socialism of an earlier period it was the product of a more advanced industrial society, one in which the separation of home and work was already entrenched.

Jill Liddington and Jill Norris have greatly contributed to our knowledge of late-nineteenth-century women's political culture in their description of that range of activities which fed working-class women's suffrage campaigns in Lancashire. From the Methodism which nourished the nonconformist socialism of a Selina Cooper, to the trade union and co-operative activities of so many other women, we gain a sense of an area where women's employment and a long-established community life could to some extent unite the interests of men and women. It must be remembered that within the weaving towns of northern Lancashire women workers, married and unmarried, could win an unusual degree of status from their skill. By the 1890s the Northern Counties Amalgamated Association of Cotton Weavers, a mixed union, represented 65,000 workers, two-thirds of whom were women. In such a context, the socialist and labour movements could appeal to both men and women: though even there the limitations on women's activities must be remembered. Selina Cooper, as a paid lecturer and organizer for the NUWSS, needed the childcare and domestic help for which that organization was uniquely prepared to pay.[61]

In this volume, June Hannam has charted women's participation in labour and socialist politics in the West Riding of Yorkshire. In a period which matches that explored by Liddington and Norris, she has found marked differences in working women's political interests. West Riding socialists from the beginning showed interest in questions relating to the reform of marriage, and to women's employment. They noted the sexual contempt with which both Liberal and Tory employers treated women who dared to join their union. Socialist ideas brought working-class and middle-class women into politics from a new direction, though they still shared something in their approach with women from other parties. In local government they, like their Liberal women colleagues, spoke the language of separate spheres, and concentrated on the same issues in a Progressive alliance. However, they were especially involved in the conditions of women's employment, and specific needs in the factory. Socialist colleagues retained their view of women as marginal in this context, a view of family life in which men were breadwinners, women stayed at home. Such a conflict between interests was no new one: it had engaged the debates of the TUC since its foundation in 1875, and bedevilled women's emergent unionism. And it was at the heart of the difficulties of much 'scientific' socialist analysis. June Hannam describes how the Labour Party in the West Riding was nevertheless deeply interested in the question of the reform of marriage and family: but its solution, to be challenged by only a few, was the familiar and sentimental restatement of a family life still withdrawn from the world of production, yet strengthened by the changes which socialism could bring to the distribution of resources.

The suffrage issue in the West Riding brought more women to the ILP and saw the growth of a socialist and feminist campaign for women's suffrage: though many including Isabella Ford gave priority after 1906 to the suffrage question, there was sufficient local flexibility for them to remain under the labour umbrella. Still, to campaign for the vote was to lay the stress on liberal political goals, which meant the neglect of those issues of difference, at work and in the home. Ultimately the weakness of women's trade unionism in the West Riding, compared to its strength in Lancashire, accounted for the failure of any strong initiative in Yorkshire. Real conflicts of interest were sidestepped, while the ILP gave sincere support to the goal of political equality, and many individual socialists, both men and women, meditated on and debated family and work roles for the future.

For most women the First World War, in spite of war work and the acquisition of the suffrage, saw no dramatic shift in the relationship between public and private life. The twentieth century saw the formal achievement of the framework sought by many liberal feminists, but the real relationship between family and work still remained to be analysed and the claims of equality and difference resolved. Neither socialists nor liberals yet met that challenge. Many of the women described in this volume were profoundly committed to the ideal of equality: but almost all in some way used the language of difference, of separate spheres arising from their own experience. There still remains a question as to whether such separation was a sign of weakness or of strength. Perhaps the strength of women in the political arena should be correlated not only to the distance between private and public worlds but also to the relationship between gender and class. For many middle-class women, the claims that could be made on behalf of their gender were also the claims of class dominance. Working-class women's powerlessness was also the weakness of their class. Status, class and gender were confusingly intertwined in the political culture of nineteenth-century women.

Part I

Citizenship and Conscience

1

Cottage Religion and the Politics of Survival

Deborah Valenze

Several generations of social historians have struggled with the problem of identifying the consciousness of the English working classes. E. P. Thompson's exhortation, to rescue the poor labourer 'from the enormous condescension of posterity,' no longer requires a footnote when it appears in prefaces to historical treatments of the subject. For historians of women, such rescue work has presented some of the same tribulations, while posing the vexing but inescapable question of gender difference. Should historians of working-class women follow in the footsteps of Thompson, charting an analogous struggle for political rights, economic freedom, and autonomy among women? What have been the results when this approach has been tried? What is our alternative?[1]

Contemplating a wholly different sphere of activity can shed new light on these questions. At first glance, female preachers of the Methodist sects suggest an utterly conventional expression of domestic ideology; their ministry might even signal the 'feminization of religion' among the labouring classes.[2] But this interpretation ignores the salient plebeian character of their religion, an aspect which points to important features of labouring life at the beginning of the nineteenth century. According to their contemporaries, female preachers were heretics and rebels. Their public addresses to members of both sexes, solitary travel, and outspoken and sometimes offensive behaviour set them apart from more typical Victorian women occupied by philanthropy and private piety. As members of the labouring classes, they also challenged codes of paternalism and deference. They turned to religion to affirm a particular combination of domestic and community concerns, values they found threatened by the evolving industrial culture and only indirectly addressed in other working-class organizations.[3]

And yet these brazen evangelists, unsuited to the category of conservative religion, did not embrace the radicalism of their time. Though
they broke convention and overturned assumptions about the proper
sphere for women, female preachers remained silent on the subject of
feminism, radical politics, and their political and social oppression in
general. Despite similar experiences of displacement and poverty in the
first half of the nineteenth century, women preachers emphasized
distinctly different concerns from those expressed by Chartists,
Owenites, or trade union activists. From their marginal perspective,
women labourers may provide insight into social and political ideals that
were never incorporated directly into any political programme.

Women preachers of the labouring class call into question the larger
conceptual construct connecting politics to religion, and religion to
reactionary movements. Historiography has tended to place religion
and politics within a hierarchy running from primitive to modern,
attributing to religion an embryonic consciousness.[4] In this interpretation, religious language and belief strive towards expression of
something of greater import, struggling to escape the bondage of 'traditional' or pre-political conceptualization. Such a teleological view tends
to exclude those who were untouched or uninspired by radical political
ideology, often overlooking the peculiar needs of marginal groups
– women and the poor – most in need of recognition. More common
interpretations of Victorian religion employ theories of social control,
which argue that evangelicalism was the preserve of the middle and upper
classes and a tool with which they extracted deference and suppressed
revolt. Victorian radicals certainly took this view, and many historians
since Halévy have concurred. Nevertheless, though particular forms of
evangelicalism did represent the interests of established powers in the
Victorian age, especially in the later half of the century, religion also
proved to be a creative force in the hands of plebeian preachers even
while 'belonging' to others.

I

In a definitive essay on women in nineteenth-century radical politics,
Dorothy Thompson traced the involvement of working-class women in
Chartism in the 1830s, arguing that women shared in the general activity
and optimism of the movement. Male and female Chartists alike strove
to attain the vote for the working classes and change 'the structure of
power and authority in British society.' But, she admits, 'the moves
towards a more equal and cooperative kind of political activity by both

men and women, were lost in the years just before the middle of the century.' Working-class women disappear from radical politics in the 1840s; they 'seem to have retreated into the home.'[5] Putting aside the specific circumstances surrounding women in the Chartist movement, we can identify a related development within Owenism, the socialist movement founded in the 1820s by philanthropist and factory owner Robert Owen. Barbara Taylor's brilliant analysis of the feminist strain within Owenism ends on a similar note of lament. Though women contributed essential ideas and energy to the movement, their vision of a 'new moral world' did not survive in later years, when freedom and self-fulfilment for women vanished from the programme of socialism.[6]

These examples of labouring women's aborted political effort suggest not that women's performance was inadequate, but that the formal political discourse of radicalism had difficulty accommodating the aims of women. Even in its most outspoken challenges to conventional politics, radicalism (with the exception of Owenism) never called into question fundamental divisions between the sexes which often excluded female contributions to political ideology. Radical working men associated women with the aim of securing domestic well-being, and insofar as women shared that goal, they joined in ultimately silencing their own voices. But radical discourse need not have marginalized the viewpoints of labouring women in their struggle for domestic security. In its growing concern with constitutional rights and political representation, radical politics became implicated in the prevailing individualistic and contractual framework of liberalism and thus made the ultimate inclusion of labouring women all the more unlikely. Gareth Stedman Jones has argued persuasively that Chartism and earlier forms of English radicalism employed a specific political discourse rooted in eighteenth-century notions of power, rights, and property. As it evolved in the nineteenth century, that programme retained its links to the propertied individual. Given this basis, women may not have been allowed or been able to penetrate the effort at all.[7]

If we are aiming to characterize the activity and consciousness of a broad range of labouring women, the somewhat exceptional instances of Owenism and Chartism cannot tell us all that we need to know. Outside formal radical organizations, one is struck by the absence of labouring women struggling for such typical working-class goals as individual autonomy, 'moral goodness', and liberal political rights. As David Vincent has pointed out in his study of working-class autobiography, the silence of women 'cannot be explained merely by differentials in literacy,' (which were between ten and fifteen points behind male rates) or by lack of opportunity for a basic education (most working-class autobiographers had only a minimal amount of formal training, which was often available to girls as well).[8] Excluded from more and more forms of working-class organizations, denied access to skills that had, in the eighteenth century, improved their earning power and status, and occupied by family concerns that were theirs owing to their sex, women may have exhibited a different political orientation socially constructed and enforced. Whatever labouring women sought or achieved, it was seldom visible in terms of individualistic political and moral identity.

The explanation for this lies in a reconstruction of the earlier eighteenth-century world of labouring families. One might argue that this context depended on collective rather than individualistic assumptions. The family or household economy of the labouring classes, based upon 'the interdependence of work and residence, of household labour needs, subsistence requirements, and family relationships,' set the stage for such thinking. Within this setting, women were crucial to the survival of a household based on collective values. Seen in a yet broader context, the labouring family was shaped by specific political and economic factors, and thus was not simply a 'natural' or 'private' institution. The actual work of providing subsistence that women performed – growing and gathering food, collecting fuel, tending animals, carrying on domestic industries, as well as supplementing family income with waged labour – also depended upon collective principles built into the social and political foundations of eighteenth-century society.[9] For the labouring poor, survival depended upon a 'community' orientation. Common rights provided land for grazing cows, squatting rights enabled landless labourers to utilize wastes and sometimes commons; and gleaning rights could supply a family with enough grain for several months. All these activities necessitated a mutual understanding among landowners, tenants, and labourers that commanded an elaborate set of rules and regulations. By assuring subsistence through the poor laws and regulation of trade, the state also recognized a form of justice distinct from individual rights. Commonly acknowledged 'intrusive moral imperatives' governed eighteenth-century agrarian society; promoted by the state, sanctioned by landowners, they were necessary to the labourer's existence.[10]

While the eighteenth-century state and society had acknowledged the necessity of labouring women's work and aimed to assist them and their families, however imperfectly, later conditions were much less favourable. The rise of a new system of political economy, which the English state gradually embraced at the turn of the century, promised to marginalize labouring women even more acutely than men. Its vigorous emphasis on the needs of commercial agriculture meant that the rights of property and contract would prevail over community values and substantive need. Those aspects of rural society which permitted women to labour in the margins were destroyed. Deprived of access to various meagre means of subsistence, such as regular employment in agriculture, the opportunity to own and graze a cow, or sources of free fuel, labouring women had to resort to limited forms of employment, almost all underpaid and irregular. Outside the family, their collective orientation seldom had a social dimension.[11]

But their productive and social activity still displayed evidence of a mentality that was not precisely individualistic. Faced with the ever-changing nature of family needs owing to fluctuations in the new industrial economy, women (married and unmarried) adapted their earning skills to constant waves of male unemployment. Their wages made the crucial difference between survival and suffering. In agricultural areas, they combined field labour with raising produce on wasteland and allotments; in pastoral and proto-industrial regions, women worked in cottage industries while keeping cows and pigs. Similarly, fluctuations in male employment in mining or shipping meant that women doubled their efforts in local cottage industries. They were also poised to mobilize what Olwen Hufton, in a French context, has called 'an economy of expedients.'[12] This often entailed borrowing or begging, and sometimes pilfering, in order to make ends meet. Men, too, may have shared this non-individualistic outlook on their social and economic activity. But as they were drawn more fully into an economy based on the individual male wage-earner, as well as political activity based in theory on the individual property-owner, their identity perforce assumed a different character. We must ask how closely male labourers adhered to truly collective ideals during the transformation of working-class politics in the nineteenth century.

As pivotal figures in the family economy of labourers and as crucial providers of subsistence, labouring women occupied an important place in this world – not simply as oppressed victims, but as active agents who struggled to maintain and uphold imperatives and principles related to community, family and survival. Female preaching, appearing first in the late eighteenth century and continuing for more than half a century, was just one manifestation of their effort. As it evolved in villages and towns in the nineteenth century, female preaching presented a truncated form of its broadly based eighteenth-century social origins. The contrast with working-class radical politics suggests distinctly different aspects of labouring life at work, which force us to take into account more than just the history of religion.

II

Far from embodying the pleasing feminine virtues ascribed to middle-class women, working women of the early industrial age were often cast as aggressive and shrewish. Most eighteenth-century commentators saw labouring women as creatures close to nature, in need of suppression and control. In his *Commentaries* on common law, Blackstone pointed out that among the middle classes, a husband's power of correction over his wife had fallen out of favour by the eighteenth century; but 'the lower rank of people, who were always fond of the old common law,' he added, 'still claim, and exert their ancient privilege: and the courts of law will still permit a husband to restrain a wife of her liberty, in case of any gross misbehaviour.'[13] Their mythic image as devouring and demonic vixens survived in popular literature and folkloric accounts well into the nineteenth century, until it collided with more exhortatory representations of piety and goodness in the Victorian period.[14] Certainly women were believed incapable of the civic virtue required of men, as their unruly public behaviour confirmed. 'Women are more disposed to be mutinous,' Robert Southey observed in 1808, 'they stand in less fear of the law, partly from ignorance, partly because they presume upon the privilege of their sex, and therefore in all public tumults they are foremost in violence and ferocity.'[15] Forcefully assertive in personal matters, such as marriage and family finances, at times women were just as aggressive in the public sphere.

Historians have related such 'mutinous' behaviour in the eighteenth century to the political aims of the common people, arguing that women and men together engaged in 'collective bargaining by riot' to protest at changes in the English state that were undermining a moral economy. The more general behaviour of labouring women, however, has remained unanalyzed, along with a consistent pattern of female participation in certain kinds of popular demonstrations. Women often risked their reputations and safety in order to satisfy substantive needs for their families and communities; what was from one perspective unseemly behaviour was, from another, moral. As Edward Thompson has pointed out, the 'initiators of [food] riots, were, very often, women.' Redressing the injustices of high prices and unfair trading practices, they set out in search of offenders armed 'with knives stuck in their girdles' and 'using very ill language all the while.' In matters of subsistence, women capitalized on their role as providers of food and care; violating codes of propriety, they protested vigorously at social and economic injustices, establishing themselves as upholders of a rough popular form of justice.[16]

This is precisely the light in which female preachers of the early nineteenth century appear. The concerns expressed through their religion sprang from lives spent on the margins of subsistence. In no way did they emulate the manner or habits of evangelism of conventional ministers. Fond of face-to-face confrontations, female evangelists were shockingly forthright, often violating polite codes of behaviour to earn reputations for inquisitorial zeal. They demonstrated similar talents in the pulpit, expressing themselves 'too vehemently' and 'unguardedly,' and seldom apologizing for unmitigated 'candour'. Their notion of the religious life contrasted sharply with the prescriptive emphasis of middle-class evangelicalism, which they sought to contradict. Schooled in the lessons of poverty and economic insecurity, all preachers, male and female, sought to exemplify a distinctively plebeian version of the sacred life.[17]

Only the context of labouring life and the labouring family can explain the appearance of female preachers in early industrial England, justifying their assumption of power as well as their distinctive style. Interdependence and a certain degree of sex equality – crucial to the emergence of a female ministry – were fundamental to the daily life of followers. It was in the interests of family and community solidarity that these women advocated sinners being saved by grace. In this instance, grace was neither simply other-worldly nor individualistic. As labourers, female preachers contributed to a family economy that depended upon joint effort. Their evangelism, moreover, promoted a meshing of public and private interests that materially and socially aided followers in sustaining themselves. In the villages where sectarian Methodism flourished, members assisted one another through gifts, advice, work, and care. They also observed and commented upon every aspect of each other's lives in order to promote piety and ensure fidelity to the cause. The reproving 'village saint', most often an intrusive, assertive woman, became a well-known symbol of popular evangelicalism and an important distributor of mutual aid.

Through sectarian forms of religion, labouring women consciously addressed problems generated by the advent of liberal industrial society. The brief life of female preaching within the context of cottage religion, lasting only from the 1790s to the 1860s, suggests that it was intimately related to the economic instability and political and social unrest that marked the first half of the nineteenth century in Britain. The expansion of a capitalist agrarian economy, the uneven advance of industrial capitalism, particularly following the Napoleonic Wars, and the impact of the French Revolution on radical democratic movements in Britain set in motion popular religious, as well as political, traditions. Though overshadowed by established evangelicalism, sectarian religion none-theless responded to new conditions and widespread distress. Embracing aspects of popular culture, the sects often mobilized local customs and alliances. Agrarian hardship brought unemployment and homelessness, and expanding industrial villages and new factory towns were the scenes of unprecedented crowding and misery. Against these dif-ficulties, part and parcel of the dominant liberal political economy, female preachers held up their own solution of familial and community responsibility.

In the context of contemporary movements, female preaching could be seen as retrogressive. Certainly most political radicals would have had a hard time embracing the obviously pious orientation of the female preacher's aims. But certain aspects of female preaching and popular religion nevertheless had revolutionary implications, possibilities that warrant exploration from a new perspective. The religion of female

SARAH KIRKLAND.

Sarah Kirkland (1794–1880), a Primitive Methodist Preacher.
From *The Origin and History of the Primitive Methodist Church* by
H. B. Kendall (London n. d.).

preachers eschewed individualism as it appeared as a symptom of modern industrial society. Labouring women obviously derived part of their vision from the context of the family, which can hardly be cast as revolutionary. Yet paradoxically, within that normative context, one might conceive of relationships based on radically different criteria. Posed against the social relations of industrial capitalism, the family could provide the template for correct relations between 'unequal members of a society, relations based on dramatically different contributions to the group and equally dramatically different and incomparable needs':

> Such relations [are] asymmetrical, tender rather than passionate, helpful rather than experiential. They are the fundamental social example of compassion: that is, of the correct moral relation of the strong to the weak. No other unit regularly provides for helplessness, whether in childhood or old age, or for the temporary helplessness of illness. . . . The family is the one social unit that in political terms validates the entire life span, whereas most societies based on reason, prowess, or action validate only the middle span of life, roughly between 18 and 50.[18]

By affirming ties binding people within interdependent relationships, rather than addressing individual morality; by emphasizing substantive needs of followers, in place of contractual and procedural goals within politics; and by providing a community within which physical experiences of birth, illness and death could be ritualized, popular preachers addressed issues left out of contemporary politics. Without accounting for these needs, the state, politics, and the dominant form of liberal ethics would continue to exclude marginalized women, and, in fact, the substantive needs of everyone.

Female preachers were asserting a morality that had, in their eyes, a wider significance than simple private piety. For them, the domestic sphere was intimately related to the public; their dissatisfaction concerning the hardships of their lives was testimony to the withdrawal of the state, as well as the upper classes, from the 'moral imperatives' characterizing eighteenth-century English society. Their homelessness, poverty, and isolation resulted from changes in the assumptions binding together social classes as well as the transformation of the British economy. It is this larger context that unites in protest the voices of female preachers with those of their contemporaries, radical and feminist alike.

III

The origins of female preaching lay in the role of women in popular evangelicalism at the end of the eighteenth century. Early Methodism tapped a rich source of plebeian piety when it established a tradition of cottage-based meetings and preaching services. Cottagers organized and ran these rather informal religious societies, and women were quick to take the initiative in opening their homes, visiting their neighbours, and inquiring into the state of their kinfolks' souls. Widespread popular evangelism eventually led to schisms and the formation of the Methodist sects at the turn of the century. A chief force causing these rifts was female preaching; sectarians found the ministry of women indispensable, and in the face of official Wesleyan opposition culminating in 1803, refused to curb their activities. Primitive Methodists, Bible Christians, and other groups began their existence with dozens of women enrolled as public speakers; the number of female preachers rose to hundreds within the next twenty years.

The urgency of new needs within the labouring community warranted a wholehearted mission using unconventional forms of evangelism in the first half of the nineteenth century. Like the riotous protest against the demise of the moral economy, popular evangelicalism responded to the new notions of civic morality embedded in recently applied principles of political economy. Cottage religion could register a generally felt indignation over the loss of common rights, customary aid, and reciprocity characteristic of eighteenth-century rural life. As the transformation of agrarian society continued in the nineteenth century, the activities of the Methodist sects uncovered a panoply of popular grievances related to the advent of capitalism in the countryside. Expressed through democratic forms of worship, this distress formed the basis of the lamentations of female preachers.[19]

A well-rehearsed set of circumstances framed followers' lives. Capitalist agriculture brought a final wave of enclosure and new social relations to the countryside in the post-Napoleonic War period; the loss of employment, particularly for women, and a shortage of cottages, meant low wages and repeated displacement for most labourers. At the same time, cottage industries experienced extreme instability. Some, like spinning, nearly vanished during the early part of the century owing to mechanization and factory-based industry, while others rose and fell in relation to market demand and entrepreneurial whim. Labourers and humble farmers adopted 'dual economies' which combined earnings from agriculture with various small trades and industries . All of these activities constituted a precarious means of survival, for the economic fluctuations typical of the period often brought ruination to those living on the margins of rural society. Though changes varied regionally, preachers and followers everywhere shared a familiarity with uncertainty and privation.[20]

Such developments powerfully magnified the perennial hardships of labouring life that constituted the female preachers' chief concerns. Illness, disease, and death of family members scarred followers' and preachers' lives with frightening frequency; colouring these occurrences were poverty, unemployment, and repeated moves to new locales. Solitude posed a continual threat to be combated, encountered through the loss of parents, spouses, and children. Family strife, including marital difficulties and separation, brought perilous social and economic isolation. Contemporary solutions to these problems offered little to labourers. Benefit and friendly societies required an instrumentalism, as well as time and money, rare among the uneducated poor, and even radical politics demanded too great a devotion to self-improving activities like reading, discussion, and planning for the future. To many marginal labourers, political and institutional language did not always make sense of the inexplicable buffetings of their lives. An immediate need for recognition of their sufferings and for supportive association brought them to cottage religion instead.

The life of preacher Mary Porteus (1783–1861) offers a vivid account of the experiences leading a working woman to popular evangelicalism and eventually a preaching career. Born in Newcastle, Mary Porteus was an exception among female preachers, the majority of whom were of village origin. Her experience in various forms of female employment, however, as well as the hardship she faced, enabled her to speak for village concerns when she ventured into the countryside as an evangelist. More significant are the ways in which Porteus managed to survive, drawing upon the mutual good will of friends and followers for shelter, clothing, education, and of course, her understanding of religion. Her intellectual and spiritual development, rooted in the social experiences of poverty and womanhood, inevitably led to a position of greater importance within the popular evangelical movement. Mary Porteus began preaching in her forties, leaving her family in order to travel in the north of England for fourteen years.[21]

Noticeably absent from Mary's early life in Newcastle were the influences of schooling and organized religion. Though her father, a joiner and cabinetmaker, was a Presbyterian, his death soon after Mary was born deprived the family of financial security and religious affiliation. Mary's mother proved to be a staunch taskmaster, superintending the family and its earnings while working to support a considerable number of children. Mary was taken from school at seven because of the expense; at eleven, she was sent to work in a factory. Her contribution to the family economy, though trifling, was essential; her account of her childhood made clear that no one's earnings were stable, and for that reason, all were necessary, particularly within a female-headed household. When the entire family was 'afflicted with fever', a brother, their 'chief support', died. Eventually all her siblings married and left home, leaving Mary, then a spinner in a woollen factory, alone with her mother. Hard work provided formative training that welded Mary's experiences in waged labour to family survival.[22]

Though Mary's origins might have brought the cultivation and respectability typical of artisan families, the penury of her widowed mother and the narrow range of experience open to girls promised that she would follow a different route to self-fulfilment. Whatever help she received from friends and neighbours guided her in the direction of religion, despite the vigorous protests of her mother. A man at her factory gave her a copy of a catechism; a family nearby invited her to join their Presbyterian chapel. And when Mary propped reading material in front of her spinning wheel, she chose a religious tract found among her father's former belongings. Against her mother's 'flood of persecution', Mary followed the prophetic encouragement she gleaned from the first sermon she ever heard:

> Do not fear what you are about to suffer; behold the devil is about to throw some of you into prison, that you may be tested, and for ten days you will have tribulation. Be faithful unto death and I will give you the crown of life. Revelation 2: 10[23]

The prophecy rang true: loss and isolation, forging the crucial link between the female preacher's experience and nascent religious consciousness, characterized the following few years of Mary's life. In 1801, when she was eighteen, her mother died. Significantly, her biography referred to the bereft woman, well on the threshold of adulthood, as 'an orphan'. Though Mary was old enough to be her own mistress, her self-image and the image commonly held of quintessential female preachers, was that of 'a pilgrim and a stranger' without earthly ties. 'Be faithful unto death and I will give you the crown of life': loss following traumatic personal struggle, and isolation born of loss often became the seedbed of religious awakening. In her new state of 'orphanhood', Mary experienced conversion.[24]

For a brief period, Mary next worked as a domestic servant. As a solitary, vulnerable young woman with no power or means, her experience gives testimony to both practical and oppressive aspects of servanthood. She accepted a situation with an aged woman in the neighbourhood, who apparently offered her the job out of kind concern and quickly became 'a second mother' to her. Nevertheless, Mary left the position within a year, and in a sequence common to many domestic servants, secured a second situation that turned out to be less congenial. Distressed by a mistress who was 'difficult to please', it was only a matter of time before Mary began to contemplate marriage. With remarkable frankness, her journal revealed her doubts about the worthiness of her suitor and her weakness regarding the onerous decision she had to make. He seemed to have 'tender feelings' towards her; her mistress, besides, was exceedingly disagreeable. 'I yielded to my own carnal reasonings,' she confessed, and married him in 1803.[25]

For a moment – indeed, a crucial one – the spirit yielded to the flesh. Mary's rush into marriage was neither uncommon nor hard to understand, and upon closer examination, shows remarkable consistency with her previous life. Marriage quickly restored Mary to a familial context, but more precisely, provided the medium through which she created and expressed her self-awareness. Her identity related directly to a role in a corporate entity; her conception of self was not of a solitary 'individual', but of someone embedded in a nexus of relations. Though promising a limited number of options, and doubtless oppression, familial relationships offered life-giving ties. Bearing and raising children, managing a household, and earning small amounts in various ways, Mary built upon that mixture of hardfast endurance and individuality evident in her life since childhood. Though in one sense she accommodated herself to an oppressive situation, she did so with a dual consciousness that recognized the value of her activity within the context of necessity.

The difficult early years of marriage put Mary's fortitude to the test. Under the added hardship of her husband's lack of religion, she soon lost interest in chapel-going and 'confidence in God'. As a seaman, her husband went into hiding to avoid impressment during the war. In order to support themselves, the couple opened a small shop that soon failed. Two children, born within three years, added to the precariousness of their finances. They then moved to Ballast Hills, not far from Newcastle, the first of many short migrations punctuating their lives. Mary's husband returned to sea, and she faced months alone with children and the prospect of scraping together various means of survival.[26]

That paradoxical form of isolation originating in marriage and child-rearing brought forth Mary's second religious awakening. Particularly in poor families, where wage-earning fathers were often absent or deceased, and servants were non-existent, women faced enormous responsibility alone. Sectarian memoirs were rife with accounts of single or abandoned mothers seeking explanation of their predicament and encouragement in their struggles. More common were women like

Mary, whose husbands worked at jobs that necessitated long hours or travel. In some forms of employment, such as agricultural labour or shipbuilding, seasonality required intense, irregular periods of work. Then women would be left to manage households and augment unsteady income with their own wage-earning efforts in domestic industry, which was often solitary and relentlessly demanding. When frequent migration deprived them of familial and community ties, their isolation increased. No amount of gender socialization prepared women for this peculiar sequestering of their lives taking place after marriage. It is clear that pious working women were as aware of these strains as their radical feminist contemporaries, but the solutions they chose were markedly different.

For help, Mary turned to the Bible. She heard her downstairs neighbours, who were Methodists, pray one evening when she was alone, and she felt her solitude more keenly. She visited a Presbyterian chapel, but still felt unsatisfied longings, a mixture of curiosity and impatience. Expecting a solution to come from religious truths, she vowed to open her Bible at random for a direction or sign; providentially, she came upon 'I will heal thy backslidings, and will love thee freely.' 'The work was done,' she recorded simply in her journal. Whether by providence, or more likely, by her own determination, Mary's faith was restored. When her husband returned, she persevered, despite his 'slight reproof' when one day she suggested family prayer. Another turn at the Bible supported her wish to join friends in sick-visiting: 'Now therefore go, and I will be with thy mouth, and teach thee what thou shalt say' (Exodus 4: 12). Not long after, when the family moved to North Shields, Mary began to attend the local Methodist chapel and joined a class meeting. Her active career as an evangelist had begun.[27]

With her entrance into popular evangelicalism, Mary's daily social relations shifted perceptibly towards a sustained form of mutuality. In addition to visiting the sick, she hosted weekly prayer meetings at her house, and eventually organized a class of young women. Participation in both groups entailed conversation, shared experiences, and relationships that extended into other activities. Her efforts were matched by others' generosity; an elderly class leader taught Mary how to write, and with her new skill, Mary was able to open a school in order to supplement the irregular income of her husband.

Such mutual relations became an essential means of survival for the Porteus family during hard times, and later, the post-war depression. Mary's husband gave up his job as a seaman and bought a small boat in order to support the family by 'his stray earnings on the river, which, for a long time amounted to not more than six shillings a week.' Mary recorded grim prospects for the holiday season that year (1808?), until her husband rescued a ship's longboat the day before Christmas and was rewarded with a 'large lump of beef.' Less fortuitous aid came regularly from friends when Mary was about to deliver her fourth child and the family was still impoverished. Another move, this time to Gateshead, held out the hope of improvement. Shortly after, however, an accident tore the Porteus boat to pieces; compounding the tragedy, their eldest boy, now earning a sizable two shillings a week, was laid off, and Mary became ill. The family appeared ruined. Yet visits and gifts seemed to lift the gloom surrounding their household. Without the regular aid that came from the people they knew, the Porteuses would have been unable to feed and clothe their five children and pay the rent.[28]

The struggle to survive entered into a powerful relationship with crucially important religious connections, sometimes seemingly through 'Providence' and 'providential deliverances', but more often according to a carefully elaborated domestic theology. Sectarians stressed the significance of ties that bound together families, neighbours, and congregations. In the metaphorical language of sermons and hymns, as in labouring life, the distinction between such associations receded in importance. The belief in the equality of all believers, which the Methodist sects inherited from seventeenth-century sectarianism, suggested a less individualistic notion of the society member. Breaking down the barriers between public and private became the goal of most hymns, as in the following, shared by Primitive Methodists and Bible Christians:

> Haste again, ye days of grace,
> When assembled in one place;
> Signs and wonders mark'd the hour!
> All were fill'd and spoke with power;
> Hands uplifted, eyes o'erflowed,
> Hearts enlarged, self destroy'd!
> All things common now we'll prove,
> All our common stock be love.

At the core of this theology lay a recognition of the utter destitution of believers, not merely in spiritual terms (for most followers were 'destitute' before they were converted), but in material ways. Sectarian hymns often referred to the 'stock' of the congregation, playing upon the dual meaning of ancestry and supply; in both senses, followers were assumed to have little or none. Hence family – and sectarian – solidarity became ever more essential in the battle against the 'wilderness below'.[29]

This domestic-based theology instilled potent conviction in women, who occupied key positions in implementing sectarian principles and witnessed their effectiveness. Not surprisingly, many felt the call to preach, and sectarian Methodists gave women not only permission, but encouragement. The official Primitive Methodist defence of female preaching, written by founder Hugh Bourne, shows astonishingly little awareness of middle-class objections, proving how embedded in plebeian consciousness this role of women was. 'I have not been accustomed to study this controversy,' Bourne demurred, 'for the following reasons, which have been established among a few of us [:]'

> 1 If persons who exercise in the ministry are of good report, and the Lord owns their labours by turning sinners to righteousness, we do not think it our duty to endeavour to hinder them; but we wish them success in the name of the Lord, without respect to persons.

Though not above worrying about the personal reputations of prospective preachers, Bourne used the language of equal opportunity. Amazingly, Bourne feared for the souls of unconverted sinners, not brazen female preachers':

> 2 We do not think it right to be the cause of any one's going to hell through a proud and fond desire of establishing our own (perhaps vain) opinions.

His third and fourth reasons, most of all, reflected his inner resistance to bourgeois concerns:

> 3 Instead of stopping to reason about various things, we find it best to be pressing on.
> 4 In general, instead of engaging in useless controversy, we find it more profitable to continue giving ourselves to God, and spending the time in prayer.

Bourne spent the remainder of the defence outlining biblical precedents for public speaking by women in the church, a decidedly traditional sectarian tactic and one that would convince no one outside sympathetic circles.[30]

Yet Bourne's exegesis yields germane evidence of the same struggle for survival within a popular theology of the oppressed. Inevitably, Bourne was forced to reckon with 1 Corinthians 14: 34: 'Let your women keep silence in the churches.' 'I have heard it stated further,' added Bourne, 'that he there says, "If they will learn any thing, let them ask their husbands at home."' The egalitarianism of sectarian theology, however, intruded upon and altered such traditional domestic power relations; it also implicitly recognized the possible absence of marital harmony from working-class marriages. 'All those who have ungodly husbands' should not be 'restricted from learning any thing from any but their husbands,' Bourne objected.

> If also this must be stretched out so as to exclude women from teaching men religion, it would reach too far, – it would break the order of God, – it would interdict mothers from teaching their sons; and I believe that I owe my salvation, under God, in a great degree, to a pious mother.

In the labouring household, female piety carried weight. Bourne was aware of the class as well as the gender dimensions of his concluding text which he significantly cited only by chapter and verse. 'I think all the objections that can be brought may be confined to this, that the woman is the weaker vessel. But this is so far from making against, that it is strongly in favour of it. See 1 Cor. 1:27.' Such indirection was always a sign of deflected aggression within theological debate, and Bourne indeed intended an attack: 'But God hath chosen the foolish things of the world to confound the wise; and God hath chosen the weak things of the world to confound the things which are mighty.' Elsewhere, Bourne cited Acts 2:18 ('And on my servants and on my handmaidens I will pour out in those days of my Spirit; and they shall prophesy'), pointing out that the passage referred to 'persons of the lowest condition, such as male and female slaves.' To Primitive Methodists, labouring women were quintessential prophets owing both to their gender and their class.[31]

By the time Mary Porteus felt compelled to preach, the Primitive Methodist cause was far advanced; indeed, her call came from witnessing a woman speak near Newcastle around 1820. 'After hearing the Primitive Methodist missionary, the Lord, with a peculiar force, laid souls near my heart,' she recorded in her journal. Gradually, her conviction directed her attention outside her household to the people around her:

> Many a time, when in the street, if I saw a sinner do evil, or heard him speak sinfully, my heart recoiled, and I got home as fast as I could, to engage in prayer for him. . . . This anguish, I found, was the result of a tender regard for the honour of my Lord, and was produced also by such views as I had never experienced of the dreadful state of sinners and of the torments of the damned.[32]

Once a woman had begun to 'wrestle' with God in this way, her move into the pulpit was imminent. Through her anguish, Mary entered into communication with God and obtained instructions:

One day, in this state of agony, I was laid wrestling on my face on the ground, crying, "Lord, I cannot bear it. Men and women, in this Gospelland, are dying every day and going to hell."

She presented God with a typical ultimatum, a self-made prayer composed in characteristic language: 'O wilt thou not either stretch out thine hand of power to save them, or take me home to thee?'

Instantly it was as powerfully impressed on my mind as if the words had been pronounced audibly, "Why liest thou there as if prayer were in itself sufficient to snatch souls from woe? Go forth, and preach the Gospel."

After several disclaimers of her abilities, and several dismissals from on high, Mary raised the critical issue:

. . . I tremblingly replied, "I am a woman; and I never could see it right for a woman to preach." Again, with power, it was answered, "Woman was the first that brought sin into the world – woman ought not to be the last to proclaim the remedy."

Such self-deprecating reasoning, a mixture of apology and promotion, served as a common justification for preaching among women. Subscribing to the doctrine of the Fall had a strangely liberating aspect: with responsibility, and even culpability, came the obligation to speak out.[33]

Missing from Mary's call, however, was a liberation of the individual, who was still thoroughly implicated in the fate of others, including that of men. The heavy worldly responsibilities assigned to working women explain why sectarians rarely if ever elevated women's moral mission to a position of superiority that would place them on a par with their middle-class counterparts; doing so would have removed them from their own 'proper sphere' in the labouring family and community. Instead, by focusing on the familiar passage 'your sons and your daughters shall prophesy', sectarians argued for a somewhat limited notion of equal rights. 'Whatever may be the meaning of praying and prophesying, in respect to the man, they have precisely the same meaning in respect to the woman,' argued a Primitive Methodist defence of female preaching.[34] Women themselves were loath to press their cause beyond equality, as 'The Female Preachers' Plea', by a Bible Christian woman, illustrated in a lighter way:

By sweet experience now I know,
    That those who knock shall enter in;
God doth his gifts and grace bestow,
    On Women too, as well as men.

The sacred fire doth burn within
  The breasts of either sex the same;
The holy soul that's freed from sin,
  Desires that all may catch the flame.

This only is the moving cause,
  Induc'd us women to proclaim,
"The Lamb of God." For whose applause
  We bear contempt – and suffer pain.[35]

The limitations of this spiritual equality were not, evidently, a concern of female preachers; no evidence exists of protest against their exclusion from positions of administrative power, or against their continuing social and political disabilities. Their goals differed dramatically from those of socialist infidels like Emma Martin and Catherine Barmby, who attacked modern institutional religion for its subjugation of women and its overpowering patriarchalism.[36] Indifferent to a notion of self-determination rising from rights associated with the state, female preachers inhabited a world cut off from a formal political sphere.

Though markedly different from that of an emancipated woman, Mary's new-found voice nevertheless rose from a sense of individuality. But in this case, individual identity depended upon material circumstances that persistently intruded into her considerations. Furnished with an inward call, she waited a full two years before recognizing that the time to preach had come. 'My lips were sealed on this subject till the door was opened,' she recalled matter-of-factly.[37] Self-knowledge had not yet come into alignment with other factors, for she was still affiliated with the Wesleyans, who did not permit female preaching. She recoiled from the Primitives, whose manners and appearance were decidedly lower-class. 'The light tunes they sang rather disgusted me, and the disorderly conduct and indifferent aspect of several persons deeply affected me,' she wrote in her journal.[38] The distinction between the two denominations often represented a divide between respectable and unrespectable poor, one which both groups had a stake in maintaining in their competition for sanctity and souls. Ironically, Mary's straitened circumstances led her deeper into the Primitives' camp. As a source of income, in addition to needlework and her children's wages, Mary took in a Primitive Methodist preacher as a lodger. Other preachers soon congregated at her house. Conversing with them, she received an invitation to preach at Wreckenton, a nearby village. 'Now this is the door Providence has opened for you,' Mary said to herself. 'Remember your promise, and deny it if you dare. Alas, I durst not.' And so she spoke twice on the designated day, two sermons 'neatly and beautifully arranged', thus marking her first appointment as a local preacher.[39]

Mary's new career was more remarkable for the continuities it affirmed than for any change it brought to the rest of her life. As a local preacher, she continued to live at home, work during the day (she still kept a school and did needlework), and care for her family; her appointments required that she travel short distances at weekends, often spending Saturday nights with families of neighbouring village societies. The move into preaching depended on the same connections to neighbours and friends, associations of women, and care of others, including children, that had characterized her earlier activities. Yet the extraordinariness of preaching was a means of sanctifying everyday relationships, lending an aura of importance and profundity to the lives of labouring women and galvanizing them to awareness and action. Except for the stimulus of an indigenous popular religion, there was little to inspire them to consider their ordinary existences as anything but humble and insignificant. Through the female preacher, women and their families could locate themselves within traditions and a community.

An equally short distance separated pious concerns that had once been private and even secret, and the formalized message of Mary's sermons, prayers, and correspondence. Primitive Methodists seldom preserved and reprinted sermons of common preachers; their evocations were, by definition, impossible to capture in written form, and in any case, the connexion preferred to de-emphasize the hierarchical relationships created by the pulpit. Correspondence, however, carried a more accessible, practical import, and often appeared in connexional literature. Owing to the conversational style of most sermons, letters could also appropriate prayer included within popular preaching. Mary's correspondence was immediately singled out as exemplary and published in the *Primitive Methodist Magazine* only months after her first public appearance. Like her preaching, which was praised for its 'perfect naturalness,' Mary's letters mixed mundane and sacred with simple ease. Her domestic responsibilities were readily visible, but without the suggestion of their being in conflict with her preaching commitments.

> Dear Brother and Sister H.,
>   Please inform Bro. Gilbert that, God willing, I shall be at Morpeth on Saturday evening; but shall only be able to speak morning and afternoon, as my family concerns require me to be at home on Sunday evening. I rejoice in the prospect of seeing you again in the flesh. I trust I shall find you happy in the Lord, and on full stretch for glory.

The combination, and even confusion, of public and private interests gave striking evidence of how the mentality of the preacher was linked to that of the family member; in this case, preaching was not so much a 'profession' as a way of life. Mary's view of her work was little different from that of a mother, and the one role clearly informed the other:

> Glory be to God! he has restored my family to health again. Help me to praise him. I am still going on bearing the burden of the Lord. I never saw the value of souls so clearly, nor felt so much sorrow and love for them as I do at present. The Lord save them!

The health of her family and the welfare of 'souls' in general were hardly distinguishable in Mary's prayers. She sincerely personalized the fate of humanity, generalizing from the microcosm of her own experience. 'My life will not be comfortable without this [salvation] – it will only be labour and sorrow,' she lamented.[40]

'Sorrow and love', 'labour and sorrow' – these were key phrases in the language of women preachers. As Carolyn Bynum has argued, the complex identification of women with the Christ figure as sufferer enabled them to experience a compelling faith related to specifically female experiences of menstruation, childbirth, and lactation.[41] Combined with the actual physical labour and hardship of working life, the travails of female preachers clearly corresponded to the metaphors of the Bible, restoring the language of the book to its original, vibrant literalism. Their limited exposure to other ideas – indeed, other books – ensured that the Bible would remain as an essential touchstone and tool in their intellectual development.

Labour and sorrow were also the daily realities that brought labourers to religion: poverty, sickness and death punctuated the lives of all followers and intensified the female preacher's interest in fusing together families and the sectarian community. Mary's journals reported numerous incidents of men and women 'finding true religion' by recognizing obligations that took precedence over their individual impulses. Converted drunkards shunning the public house, women dashing their straw bonnets to pieces, and fellow members giving away clothes and food fill the pages of her journal as her travels increase. 'Our wives and families reap the advantage of our wages,' a group of men reportedly said to her after giving up drink; whether apocryphal or not, the story reveals the 'works of God' Mary believed worthy of celebrating.[42] Such 'sacrifices' were not self-abnegating, but in an important sense, self-affirming; they were more akin to gift-giving than forfeiture, based on a relational identity. Mary's own life demonstrated the amazing frequency of acts of generosity within a religious community that saved her family from hunger and cold. Though impossible to quantify, such gift-giving constituted an essential part of the social life of the poor.[43]

Death was perhaps the most common experience of labouring existence calling for some form of collective understanding and support. The demographic facts of the period were inescapable: infant and occupational mortality rates left their imprint on Mary's life, for example, every few years. Two of her children died, her son and his wife lost at least one child, and later on, her husband was killed in a mining accident. Historians have paid close attention to the economic costs of death within the working classes; what must be added to this is an account of the ineluctable grieving that accompanied the loss of family members. Clearly, dealing with grief was the business of sectarian preachers, male and female, who did not regard this aspect of their work as 'private', and might have come close to understanding their activity as 'political' in view of the competition between the Established Church and Methodists for rituals such as baptisms and funerals. In the years after the New Poor Law came into operation, political concerns came to be implicated more overtly in the ordeal of death for the poor, as pauper funerals loomed as an awful fate to be avoided. In all instances, sectarian religion aimed to unite followers on the basis of viewing death as a common experience requiring a collective response.[44]

Death could also act as a catalyst within the personal life of a female preacher, marking a turning point in her career. After the loss of two of her children, and the troubled behaviour of a third, Mary found consolation in Matthew 16: 24: 'If any man will come after me, let him deny himself, and take up his cross, and follow me.' Through self-denial of 'company, conversation, dress, food, sleep, and desire', she transformed deprivation into an empowering form of discipline; henceforth, she herself would determine the occasion and extent of her deprivation. It was in this heightened state of consciousness, typical of ecstatic forms of religious ritual, that she first experienced her conviction to preach. Weaning oneself from worldly concerns as a means of attaining grace became a unifying goal in her life, a pursuit which, since the time of Augustine, provided a sure antidote to individualistic impulses. Only a year later, she received another conviction, this time to itinerate. She thus resolved to give up her family life, the cornerstone of sectarian domestic theology, in order to become a travelling preacher in January 1825.[45]

Such an appointment, far more influential than that of local preacher, enabled a woman to affect a wider sphere, while providing her with an extended familial structure in the form of a network of sectarian societies. An entire region (in Mary's case, a large area of the North

Riding of Yorkshire) became a community writ large; the female preacher performed a crucial function, nurturing and strengthening the various circuit societies through her repeated visits, her talents in healing and advice, and her correspondence. Methodist sectarians were conscious of this larger role available to women, which merited the distinctive title of 'Mother in Israel'. Derived from the Old Testament, the maternal image referred not to acts of procreation or child-rearing, but to a role as community leader. In another sense, the title suggested a besieged city or place of refuge. Both meanings departed from the typical notion of motherhood pertaining to the nuclear family and private activities. That no analogous title of 'Father' existed within the sects (all men were called 'Brothers') underscored a significance ascribed only to women. Through the 'Mother in Israel', sectarian Methodists attempted to transcend a public/private boundary by assigning a distinctly female form of leadership to a social entity larger than the family or household.[46]

Mary thus perceived no contradiction in having to leave her husband and the children who remained at home in order to tend the families of followers as an itinerant preacher. She was, at the age of forty-two, a grandmother, and though her youngest child was only eight, Mary had enjoyed considerable freedom in combining her family responsibilities with a local ministry. Her husband, though still unconverted, encouraged her in what was a totally absorbing religious career; once she left home to travel, his presence became but a shadow in her active life. Mary would visit her family frequently in years to come, taking time from her appointments to nurse a daughter when she became ill, and living with different children after she gave up travelling. But she clearly wished to devote her greatest energies to a larger circle of people who, in turn, supported her. She set out for her first circuit assignment at Whitby and Guisborough, with clothes, boots, and train fare as far as Sunderland provided by friends. There she spent the next two and a half years, travelling 260 miles on foot within her first six months, speaking sixty times each trip around the circuit. By the end of her life, she had travelled for fourteen years, and served twenty-two more years as a local preacher. Mary Porteus undoubtedly earned the title of 'Mother in Israel', boldly imprinted on her biography when it appeared in 1862, a year after her death.

IV

Nineteenth-century religion may have been an unlikely vehicle of change for labouring people living at the margins of society. Given the alliance of Church and state in England, and the decidedly liberal ideology of established dissent, organized religion did not present a radical or transcendent alternative to the *status quo*. But sectarian religion was able to subvert the hegemonic power of established religion and give expression to needs and goals of otherwise inarticulate or silent members of the labouring classes. While political movements were based on a social definition of human nature that addressed primarily economic needs, popular religion could give as much attention to needs stemming from physical experiences and limitations of human existence – weakness and sickness, childbirth and child-rearing, aging and death.[47] Interwined with material struggles, these aspects of labouring life formed the basis of collective action within sectarian Methodism. Getting a living, through hard labour, repeated migrations, and often by expedients such as borrowing and sharing, hawking and gleaning, became ritualized in cottage religion. Societies also performed collective rituals in association with birth, illness, and death. Women who were otherwise doubly marginalized, by class as well as gender, were rendered quintessential prophets of this world. Their job was to tap the common concerns of local labourers and generate some form of collective activity.

Female preaching among the Methodist sects should not be confused with the evangelical activity of middle-class women characterized as work in a 'separate sphere' in the nineteenth century. The doctrine of separate spheres was based on a liberal interpretation of the place of woman: male property-owners and heads of households presided in the public sphere, exercising political rights and freedoms and providing material needs in the interests of their families, while women attended to emotional and spiritual matters, as district visitors, mothers, governesses, or companions. Even within the extraordinary groups of professional 'philanthropic' women, such as nurses and the Anglican sisterhood, the class component was decisive in establishing the relations between these women and men, and women and the working classes.[48] Female preaching demonstrated the absence of a separate sphere for labouring women, and pointed to the difficulty and even impossibility of imposing a liberal framework on working-class culture. With such clear recognition of weakness and need, regardless of gender, questions of equality and freedom faded in importance. Even the realm of the private was thrown into question; claims to privacy, so cherished by liberal society, and undeniably desirable in many instances, were unaffordable in labouring life – both materially and spatially. Women labourers provide a reminder that in the late eighteenth and early nineteenth centuries, the fundamental work of production and reproduction required more than the privatized efforts of a nuclear family rigidly divided according to sex.

A larger supportive context was necessary for this struggle for survival. As the moral economy of the English state was dismantled at the end of the eighteenth century, and the folds of what had been a relatively enhancing context for labouring women dropped away, female labourers were less able to provide a subsistence for themselves and their families. In this context, female preaching implied a critique of the liberal individualism embodied in the laissez-faire policies of early industrial England. Substantive issues separated the religion of labouring women from that of the middle classes; and as concerns less and less often defined as labouring men's immediate political goals, a 'politics of survival' represented a set of values and goals that fit into neither category of religion or politics. Female preaching may have given voice to an eighteenth-century mentality that was not sustained in radical politics and was lost entirely from nineteenth-century political discussion.

The early industrial age marked a critical period in the development of modern individual rights language associated with the rise of capitalism; the contrast with the language of labouring women would have critical importance for the future of radical politics, and politics in general. As Michael Ignatieff asserts in an eloquent critique of this political heritage:

> Rights language offers a rich vernacular for the claims an individual may make on or against the collectivity, but it is relatively impoverished as a means of expressing individuals' needs *for* the collectivity. It can only express the human ideal of fraternity as mutual respect for rights, and it can only defend the claim to be treated with dignity in terms of our common identity as rights-bearing creatures.

In obscuring such needs, the new political movements of the nineteenth century only partially represented the panorama of labouring life, and marginalized the struggle for survival carried on by women. Female preaching by labouring women provided only a passing form of expression: by mid-century, the increasingly prosperous Methodist sects were moving into chapels and gradually shedding many of their earlier tendencies. Female preaching occurred rarely after 1860, and virtually vanished after 1880; in the changing context of Victorian England, female piety perforce assumed a different face. Silenced by chapel hierarchy and convention, women would reappear in the pulpit only in the twentieth century, when education and professionalization had moulded them into an acceptable form.

The associative activity of women, within a changing family economy and local community, carried little weight in later nineteenth-century evaluations of labouring women. Their presence and behaviour in the labour market were noted, scrutinized, and criticized. Seen through the lens of the new individualism of the Victorian age, labouring women appeared lacking in morality, as well as in every virtue of womanhood. Parliamentary commissioners, philanthropists, and Victorian social commentators and artists trained their gaze upon the individual female figure – the solitary seamstress, the agricultural labourer, the factory girl – and debated questions of individual morality defined by terms irrelevant to labouring life. Many important considerations were lost. Even today, we can profit from the warnings of the female preacher, and ponder the question of whether those fundamental activities, production and reproduction – or work and love, as Freud would have it – can in fact be carried out in tandem without the more explicit, formal recognition of society.

2

Women, Work and Politics in Nineteenth-Century England: The Problem of Authority

Dorothy Thompson

The nineteenth century in Britain saw a great expansion of population, an apparently irreversible concentration of population in large urban centres, an expansion and mechanization of most areas of industrial production, and many changes in the institutions by which the economy was controlled and the country governed. It was a century of social and political change, in which customary and traditional behaviour and institutions were being superseded and replaced by new forms, based on different perceptions, located in different places and in many cases subject to rational re-assessments based on the needs of the larger, richer, more expansive society of the period. Many of the changes that occurred involved the moving of authority from the private sphere of household and family to the public one of local or national government. The magistrate's court in the country house was replaced by the official court building, the school room moved from the home to the school or college, work moved into workshop or factory away from the home or home-based workshop.

The changes stimulated intellectual enquiry and provoked movements which demanded greater changes or which resisted change. Institutions came under scrutiny and were subject to criticism; established custom and tradition lost much of its power and in many areas became subject to rational critiques and to movements for reform. Among the most vigorous movements for change was that made up of a number of different but associated campaigns for the emancipation of women which was gathering momentum during the second half of the century.

This movement, or movements, highlighted the inequalities and injustices under which women lived. These are well-known. The legal restrictions imposed by the concept of *feme covert* on married women, limitations on the ownership of property and the legal custody of children, the limited range of paid employment open to women and the meagre pay for what work was available are part of nineteenth-century history which has been recorded in all accounts.[1] The changes which were gradually brought about and the culminating organized campaign for the suffrage which saw in the twentieth century are historical events which have not been hidden from history.

Many of those who took part in the campaigns of those years, and many who have written about them, saw the age as an age of enlightenment coming after centuries of darkness. This view has, of course, an element of truth. The nineteenth century did allow wide public questioning of ideas about class and gender which had been based on centuries of tradition and doctrine, and which had long reinforced patterns of male authority. But in many ways the situation of the oppressed in British society had been worsening – relatively if not absolutely – in the early part of the century. The rationalization and centralization of institutions and the over-riding of traditional and customary practices had in many cases closed off or marginalized activities which had given meaning and authority to social groups in spite of overarching legal definitions. The demand for the vote and for admission to public life and public office by hitherto excluded sections – of which women were one, but not the only one – became more insistent as public policy increasingly took over functions of authority and decision-making which had earlier lain in various institutions and structures many of which were local, familial and private rather than public.

Some degree of power and authority may reside in personal qualities which override theoretically imposed legal rights and status. Thus in individual households a woman may exercise authority even where she is legally powerless. But beyond this is an area in which public recognition of power and authority may derive not only from legal definitions but also from customary expectations within the community. In the course of the nineteenth century many such customary expectations were being replaced by new legal and administrative forms, as communities were changing in size and location and new forms of authority were developing to control them. In these processes women were particularly disadvantaged, and the women's movements of the latter part of the century were in part a response to this, as well as to quite new ideas about the possibility of improved status for their sex.

Rarely have subject peoples, classes or genders in history totally accepted and internalized their subjection. Alternative cultures have been developed and areas carved out in which authority can be exercised and a degree of self-determination and choice opened for some of the under group. In the complex history of gender relations this process can be clearly seen. The poor of both genders have always been limited in the choices open to them or in the authority they possessed. But women of wealth and status, although in the final analysis of second rank to men, have exercised considerable authority in many ways over both men and women of lower rank, and in some areas of equal rank. Changes taking place in the early nineteenth century were eroding some of these areas of women's authority, providing part of the impetus for the demands of the later movement. Some of the changes were changes in the definition of the public and the private spheres. The polarization of the 'public' (male) and the 'private' (female) spheres is part of Victorian ideology, but is also part of nineteenth-century experience. Women's desire for a greater public role without relinquishing their private or family role accounts for much of the real and the rhetorical argument surrounding the women's movement, and also for much of the tension within the women's movement itself.

From Hannah More at the opening to Eliza Lynn Linton at the close, the nineteenth-century feminist and women's rights movement had its share of apostates. They were not alone, however, in the fear that gains in public and political rights might only be made at the expense of loss of authority in the private sphere of family life and morality. These doubts can be found in many of the century's women pioneers. Mrs Linton engaged in a rancorous argument with feminists of a younger generation, but her defence of the traditional role of wife and mother was one which she shared with her greater literary contemporary, George Eliot. Although neither experienced the role in the form in which they advocated it, both women distrusted an ideal of independence which rejected traditional marriage.

Without minimizing the extent to which women were undervalued and in law regarded as second-class citizens, it is possible to demonstrate areas in which some women did exercise considerable power and authority. I want to look, necessarily briefly, at three of these – work, charity and politics.

'As a woman', declared Maria Edgeworth, declining on one of many occasions to write a biographical preface to one of her works, 'my life, wholly domestic, can offer nothing of interest to the public.'[2] Miss Edgeworth was not subject to false modesty. One of the outstanding writers of her day, held in high critical regard by contemporaries of the rank of Scott and Thackeray, she had in addition an active life as manager of her father's estates in Ireland, where she exercised control, both personal and political, over a large body of tenants.[3] With her father she worked and wrote in the field of education, watched and read by a worldwide audience. She lacked neither determination nor self-confidence; indeed hers was one of the most successful literary careers of the century, and her role in the family and on the estates carried prestige, authority and power. Her denial of any public interest in her life shows perhaps more about the concepts of 'public' and 'private' which were held in her time than about her own self-assessment.

This question of the public and private spheres is essential to an understanding of many of the problems involving women's status and self-image.[4] The nineteenth century saw a number of changes in the perceptions and in the location of activity. Many things moved from the private to the public area including, for the lower classes, such basic activities as work, the education and training of children and young people, as well as much of the cooking, brewing, sewing and recreational activities. The male breadwinner and the children increasingly pursued the main part of their lives away from home, leaving the role of the woman in the house changed and in many ways lessened in importance. The increasing middle class was characterized by the emergence of a growing number of women for whom neither the private, domestic, sector nor the public sector of paid work and political activity seemed to have any place. For women of this class, their domestic role appeared increasingly to be lacking in scope and in opportunities for decision-making. To a certain extent their problems were specific to the nineteenth century.

Then, as in all earlier centuries, the majority of the population, male and female, worked all day and every day. Different patterns of work and leisure were followed by different trades and in different localities but, with the exception of the small elite of property-owners who could live on their rents, and whose households employed a full retinue of servants, the whole population was subject to the curse of Adam. Agricultural pursuits and the manufacture of goods for the household and the market occupied the waking hours of men, women and children.

As well as unremitting toil, women were likely to be involved for a large part of their lives in a series of pregnancies, births, abortions, miscarriages and babies. Some women chose not to marry, others would have liked to marry but did not. Some were widowed, some were married but childless. But most women in the century were involved in heterosexual marriages and in the resulting pregnancies. Like the Duchess of Richmond, whose early death Horace Walpole ascribed to her having been with child twenty-seven times, most women experienced the child-bearing years as years of uncertain and unpredictable health. So the physical and financial support of marriage was essential to any woman who wanted a heterosexual relationship. Throughout the century, however, an unmeasurable number of women who were wives and mothers also contributed to the family income. Although the ideal of a man's wage that could support his wife and younger children without the need for them to work was increasingly aimed at during the century, it was an ideal that was probably only achieved for a small section of the working people, and not necessarily for the whole of the working lifetime even of that section. The changes that took place in the work done by women in the course of the century were in the location of her work and in the centrality of that work to the main source of the family's income.

When the nineteenth century opened, much of the productive work of Britain's major industries was still being carried out in the home or in the small workshop. 'Public' work in factories still had for many a slightly unrespectable aura, an association with prison or workhouse.[5] A famous account of a typical (or perhaps ideal) example of domestic industry is given in an eighteenth-century poem about the woollen workers of West Yorkshire. The poem shows the master clothier, his wife, children, maids and apprentices taking their part in the work and in the running of the household. When the master announces the plans for the next day, on which he intends to go into the country for fresh supplies, he allocates some of his work to his wife. She protests

> Mistress: "So thou's setting me my work
> I think I'd more need mend they sark, *
> Prithee, who mun sit at t' bobbin wheel?
> And ne'er a cake at top o' th' creel!
>
> And we to bake, and swing, to blend,
> And milk, and barns to school to send,
> And dumplins for the lads to mak',
> And yeast to seek and 'syk as that!'
> And washing up, morn, noon and neet,
> And bowls to scald and milk to fleet,
> And barns to fetch again at neet!"
> Master: "When thou begins thou's never done!
> Bessie and thee mun get up soon,
> And stir about and get all done,
> For all things mun aside be laid –
> When we want help about our trade."[6]

* sark = shirt.

She, of course, agrees, and after their evening meal master and missus go out together to visit neighbours, leaving the lads and girls to spend an hour smoking and talking round the fire before bed.

Idealized though it probably was, this picture and other similar accounts show households in which work was allocated according to gender, but where the work was understood by all and interchange and overlap were possible. Boy apprentices learned baby-minding as well as their trade, whilst maid or mistress could turn her hand to most of the processes when work was heavy or speed essential. The wife's contribution, which often included book-keeping, was vital to the organization of the trade. The pattern persisted in most artisan trades, even those debased by the increasing pace and commercialism of the nineteenth century. Francis Place described how he and his wife worked together at his trade of breeches-making at the end of the eighteenth century. After a period of enforced idleness following his part in a strike, his wife obtained work for them both, and they worked at sewing and stitching for sixteen hours a day or more, Saturdays and Sundays included. When things got a little better they managed a walk out together on Saturday afternoons and 'as we scarcely left our work for meals all the week, we had a hot supper on the Saturday, a beefsteak or mutton chops'. Since she was helping with her husband's work, it was worth Mrs Place's while to pay an old woman to do the washing and cleaning for them.[7] This picture could be repeated in the early years of the nineteenth century in many urban trades. With all the problems involved in the overlap of working and living space, there were positive aspects of the arrangements. Men and women shared a vocabulary of work as well as family, understood and respected each other's contribution, recognized the interdependence of their various jobs, and shared in the training and rearing of children. Many boy apprentices must have learnt female domestic tasks as young Robert Crowe did in the 1840s:

> I became . . . far more expert in cooking and nursing than tailoring, for my brother who was considered one of the best coatmakers in London, lived exclusively a dual life. One-half work night and day, when occasion offered; the other half, drinking his earnings and his wife's as well, for I never remember him to have spent one hour on the board that his wife was not by his side. She was remarkably gifted as a sewer. . . . Four or five pounds would slip through his fingers in one night, and so for the coming week we were put to the severest straits to live.[8]

The young apprentice brother clearly took on some of his sister-in-law's work at busy times, while she had an essential part, like Mrs Place, in her husband's work. John Bedford Leno, successful small master printer, recalled in his autobiography the help given by his wife: 'How she laboured at the press and assisted me in the work of my printing office with a child in her arms, I have no space to tell, nor the many ways she contributed to my good fortune'.[9] Such cooperation was becoming less and less the norm as the century went on.

Compare an account written in 1869, a century and a half after the description of the woollen workers. Here the author describes the workman leaving his job at a regular time, coming home to his tea, and facing the question of how to spend his evening:

> What can our artisan do? It is still winter and he can hardly bring himself to think that taking a stroll is the right thing to do. He cannot for shame turn in at seven o'clock. He is not a Methodist, or if he is it is not his class night, or his singing night, or his prayer-meeting night. He is in a building society, but that meets only now and again. He belongs to the Union of his trade, but there is no strike or other important movement in prospect, and meetings are few and far between. He is a tolerably sober man, but not a teetotaller, or if he is one, there is neither lecture nor lifeboat rescue tonight. What is he to do for the next two hours? . . . he argues to himself that there are three courses open to him. One is that he should tumble into bed forthwith, but that he is decided against. . . . . He can stop where he is, dozing. But that is of doubtful practicability, for the bairns have to be undressed and got into bed, and then the wife has more than one hand's turn of washing to finish. The third and last course open to him is to retreat to the 'Three Pigeons'. . . .[10]

The piece is in fact arguing for the setting up of working men's clubs to which men could go in the evenings. But the striking thing about the passage is the sense of an absolute divorce from home and family – no sense at all of shared occupations or interests. All the possible ways listed of spending his evening totally exclude both wife and children except for the quickly dismissed one of staying at home while his wife finishes her domestic chores.

Was the authority of women in the working-class communities lessened by this separation of work and home? Such questions are very difficult if not impossible to quantify and, like the examples I have chosen, illustrative evidence is bound to be highly impressionistic. I have suggested elsewhere that the participation of women in popular politics during the first half of the century was related to their activities as workers and as members of radical families. In the Chartist and general union movements of the 1830s and 1840s, the main centres of political activity were the manufacturing communities in which whole families worked in the same industries. The association in work and in a community of workers with shared experience and shared vocabulary encouraged some women to take part in the public arena of political demonstrations and meetings in a way which had not happened earlier and was not to happen again for more than a generation.[11] Although oral and other evidence suggests that the women of the working class still had considerable authority within their individual families in the later nineteenth century, they took little or no part in the public institutions of trade unions, friendly societies, cooperative societies and political organizations in the mid-Victorian years.[12]

We know remarkably little about the lives of married working-class women in the second half of the nineteenth century. Census returns have tended to distort historians' views of the extent to which women contributed to the family income. It seems increasingly clear that, although the percentage of married women in full-time work outside the home decreased, and with the decay of the domestic system proper the number who assisted their husbands in skilled trades declined, very many, probably most, married women earned small supplementary incomes from such jobs as charring, laundry work, clothes dealing, sewing, child-minding, taking in lodgers, or from the vast range of sweated domestic work from cardboard-box making to various finishing processes done at home for the increasingly mechanized and factory-based ready-made clothing industry. But work of this kind carried little authority, either on its own account or in the production of a substantial proportion of the family income. In fact, compared with the confident, rough, sometimes vociferous wives of the Chartists, urban working-class women later in the century seem subdued and self-effacing, joining in semi-public activity like Sunday schools, mothers' unions or even the later Cooperative Women's Guild under the guidance of men or of women of a higher social class.

If women's authority among the lower classes was lessened by the move of work from the private to the public domain, the effect of the removal of the parental function as educator must have been even greater. In the early years of the century the responsibility for the child's social training and education rested with its parents. They could choose outside educators within their means, or rely entirely on their own resources. But from the Chartist period onwards the movement for church-or state-provided education gathered momentum, and by the final quarter of the century compulsory education was becoming a reality. This has sometimes been seen as the triumph of enlightenment over ignorance and illiteracy, but it was as much the triumph of respectable mores over the rough and idiosyncratic customs of the poor. In school children were taught not only the three Rs but such things as punctuality, obedience, cleanliness, proper eating habits, respect for authority and for the institutions of the state. A reading of the statements of educators of nearly all political persuasions shows this to have been so. It may well have been an admirable programme, but it certainly involved the creation of new centres of authority for children outside the home, and lessened the authority and control of the parents, particularly the mother on whom in earlier years most of the responsibility had fallen. It is true that many of the elementary school teachers were women, but headmasters, school board chairmen and the major authority figures were men. Although education was a field in which women began to engage in public activity in the later years of the century, most of these women were unmarried or childless ladies of the middle classes, as much wedded to the conflict of values and authority with parents as their male counterparts.

As workers and as educators, married women were being displaced as the century progressed. There was another form of public activity in which women of the lower orders had taken an active part in the eighteenth century and earlier; that was in marketing and in control of the market. At its most dramatic this could take the form of riots against unfair or exploitative practices in times of food shortage and high prices. As large towns developed more sophisticated forms of retail food marketing this form of protest and control by crowd action became less common, though it persisted in some parts for longer than has always been recognized. Where it did persist, it seems to have been in areas in which women still worked in manufacturing and proto-industrial trades, and women appear to have played a leading role.

During the bitter winter of 1855, and again in 1867, food riots occurred in a few places on a considerable scale, mainly in areas in which older industrial forms persisted. There were riots in Nottingham among lace-makers and stockingers, and in Buckinghamshire among lacemakers and straw plaiters. Middle-aged women and women with young children, precisely the groups most absent from most kinds of public activity, were the leaders in these events. In Crediton in January 1854 two hundred women and children armed with sticks and stones smashed the windows of bakers' shops and stole bread and cakes. Not until the second day did male rioters join them, and in several days' rioting that followed in Devonshire, women appeared everywhere to be in the lead, attacking unpopular bakers whom they accused of profiteering, and impounding and destroying bad grain.[13] In the food riots which took place in 1867, women were still to be seen among the leaders of the crowds.[14]

These food riots and crowd activity in the market place may seem like hangovers from an earlier age, when communities were smaller and customary practices more generally recognized. In the more conservative atmosphere of the nineteenth-century countryside too, women, although part of a depressed trade, may have retained greater authority and initiative in some ways than their sisters in the cities. Although agriculture remained the greatest single employer of labour throughout the nineteenth century, the proportion of the population engaged in it fell steadily. Changes in technology and in certain kinds of customary practice clearly forced out and marginalized in many ways the work of countrywomen. An important feature of the depopulation of the countryside in the later years of the century was the departure of the girls to work in service and other jobs in the towns, leaving in many villages a population imbalanced by a superfluity of men. For those women who stayed in the villages as labourers' wives, the decline of traditional crafts and the loss of customary occupations such as harvest work and gleaning must have added to the burden of poverty to which the labourers were becoming accustomed. But among the slightly higher groups – the smallholders and smaller tenant farmers – older patterns of shared work persisted, with women still controlling the production and marketing of poultry and dairy produce in many parts of the country. In a debate in the House of Commons on women's suffrage in 1873, Jacob Bright, a Liberal member and a strong supporter of the measure, asserted that in England and Wales some 22,708 women were tenant farmers in their own names.[15] Such women clearly exercised considerable authority as workers, employers, buyers and sellers in the economy of the countryside.

In the towns, however, the households of skilled workmen changed their nature in the course of the century, as did those of the artisan, craftsman and small shopkeeper. Suburban villas away from industrial districts provided homes for non-working wives of the middle classes. The process did not go unnoticed by contemporaries. The emergence of a new model middle-class woman whose virtue lay in her idleness and whose domestic role was quite divorced from that of the working members of her household (both the servants and the menfolk) was a major concern of reformers and feminists. Bemoaning the development of 'ladyhood' as a vocation, one pamphleteer wrote in 1869:

> It was otherwise some thirty or forty years ago. At that time, especially in large towns and centres of occupation, there was not that difference between the avocations of men and women that now separates them for most of the daylight hours. . . . The house and the business, if not under one roof, were then generally not far asunder, so that the dinner hour and many an odd few minutes besides allowed the relaxation of each other's society and home arrangements, tending to a more true acquaintance on either side.[16]

It was from among the middle classes above all that the complaint was increasingly heard of the lack of opportunity for challenging paid work outside the home and of the boredom and trivialization of women's occupations within the home. It was from the middle and lower middle classes that the later nineteenth century women's movement largely arose. Were the grievances of this class greatest? Was there a retraction of status and opportunity for such women, or was it simply an absolute increase of numbers which put insupportable pressure on those possibilities for self-expression and self-fulfilment that did exist?

For the greater part of the century neither men nor women of the working class had a vote, or enough property to be much concerned with the laws relating to married women's property. The call for the reform of these laws came above all from women, and some men, of the middle class. The perceived injustices of the laws in this area were specific to the later nineteenth century. As the jurist A.V. Dicey commented, hitherto 'The daughters of the wealthy were . . . protected under the rules of equity in the enjoyment of their separate property. The daughters of working men possessed little property of their own'.[17] Settlements, private acts of Parliament, entail and testamentary dispositions and trusts of various kinds had long ensured that women of property were protected from the simple operation of the husband's property rights. Among the smaller property-owners, however, it may be that here, too, the rights of women had been eroded as the century progressed. Very little work seems to have been done on the common-law right of dower which was abolished by the Dower Act of 1833. Before that act women had a common-law right to a fixed proportion of their husband's property on his death, a right which seems to have included the right to a claim on property which the husband had owned at any time during the marriage but had disposed of without the agreement of his wife. This suggests a communality of property which went further than the nineteenth-century laws under the concept of *feme covert*. Many legal devices existed to bar the right of dower, and it may well be that by 1833 the system had become a legal fiction or a total dead letter. It appears to have been observed among the small landowning families in the West Riding of Yorkshire in the eighteenth century, however, where it clearly added to the status and authority of the women in the families.[18]

In practical terms, then, women of the middle classes were particularly disadvantaged by the laws relating to married women's property. They were also experiencing the rapid devaluation of traditional skills by the development of rigid career structures in business and professional life, and they were being excluded by spatial changes and by new ideological perceptions from concern with matters of business or with work outside the home. Participation by a woman in her husband's business or the need to earn money herself was increasingly seen as non-respectable, or an indication of failure of the husband in his duty to provide.

A home which is not also a workshop or business offers the possibility of greater comfort and beauty than either. To run a household consisting of two or more adults and a number of children, to produce regular meals, to furnish, clean, mend, see to the household linen and clothes of a whole family, to send husband to work and children to school, to care for the under-school-age children, to entertain family and friends, to take some part in the regular life of the parish – this activity at a time when cooking was done on coal fires, heating was by wood or coal, cooking in iron or copper vessels, washing in boilers and wash-tubs with clothes to be blued, starched and ironed with flat-irons, shopping to be done without the aid of telephone or the internal combustion engine – no one should suggest that the life of a middle-class housewife even where servants were employed, was necessarily one of idleness or boredom. It became understandably customary among feminists to denigrate the domestic arts of sewing, 'fancy work' and embroidery, but there is no doubt that a great deal of creative effort was involved in the domestic crafts which modern generations are beginning to recognize and value. Mabel Ashby recalled the linen box she inherited from a great-aunt, a working small farmer from the mid-nineteenth century:

> Here was a huge store of Victorian elegance – for example, some dozens, perhaps scores . . . of elaborate tea-table cloths. Some were mere ribbons of linen between broad lace "insertions", others of embroidered net, and others again of drawn-thread work and Richelieu work. Many were worn out with washing and starching but some are still worthy of acceptance by a modern bride. Besides these household cloths were ladies' under-clothes in a like style.[19]

The comfort and beauty of the home depended on the wife's skill, efficiency and good management. The novels of George Gissing illustrate, as does his life, the enormous difficulties of a professional man whose wife is not able or not prepared to support his work by her maintenance of his home.

Nevertheless, Gissing also saw what to many feminists was all too clear, that the option of being an efficient head of a household was not open to a great number of women. The middle-class household did not have the resources to maintain family members or unmarried daughters. It was this prospect of remaining in her uncle's household as an unmarried lady, permitted only to 'sew and cook' that appalled Caroline Helstone. Neither she nor her more spirited friend Shirley Keeldar objected to the domestic duties or to the subject status involved in marriage to the men of their choice.[20]

Literary evidence is misleading in many ways, and never more so than as a direct source of information about the lives of nineteenth-century women. It seems probable that more women of the middle classes, married as well as unmarried, worked for payment in the early years of the century than has always been recognized, but that opportunities for such work were declining in many trades and professions. Unique among professions for women was that of writer, for it could be followed exclusively in the home, with only the name and the product of the author being necessarily in the public domain. When Florence Nightingale developed her distressing determination to become involved in reorganizing the profession of nursing, her mother suggested that she should write books on the subject – an option which would avoid the need to enter the public world of practical medicine.[21] Writing – especially certain kinds of writing, such as works for children, remained acceptable even to the most ardent advocates of women's domestic role – indeed many such advocates were themselves professional women writers. But hack writing, editorial and journalistic work remained grey areas. Specifically women's journalism must have involved an increasing number of women in the later years of the century as a mass popular magazine press developed, but the extent to which women were involved in the expansion of journalism generally, especially in the higher echelons which were becoming for the first time respected professional occupations, is not clear. We do, however, have a recent insight into the lives of some of the less successful professional writers of the early years of the century in the fascinating study by Nigel Cross of the papers of the literary charity, the Royal Literary Fund.[22] He shows that between 1790 and 1830 six hundred men and one hundred women writers applied to the fund for help. Half of these women were novelists, of whom thirty were married women writing to support their families. Their often heart-rending stories show the fragility of the profession as a source of income, but their existence and that of the many other female novelists whose work is now being recovered and re-published suggests a strong female presence in late eighteenth- and early nineteenth-century Grub Street. Whether even this exceptional profession was providing fewer opportunities, comparatively, for women during the second half of the century remains unclear.

In other professional occupations, however, increasing professionalism was undoubtedly leading to masculinization at the higher levels, and so to the decrease and marginalization of the role of women. The nineteenth century saw the restructuring of education to provide technical and professional training in place of apprenticeship and home teaching. Although girls had never had the same access to apprenticeship as boys, opportunities had been found in more traditional systems of training for daughters, sisters, wives and above all for widows to practise the trades of their households, whilst a few occupations in the general areas of medicine and in the service trades had been regarded as largely the province of women. Increasingly, however, the professional jobs were being carried out by qualified persons trained in the all-male institutions, universities and colleges, which bestowed the qualifications required for practice. Among the poor the midwife retained her authority, but in the higher and better-paid classes qualified male doctors took over. The dame school gave way to the board school, the college or high school educated man took over all but the most junior positions. Women were marginalized into practices like private piano tuition or elocution instructing where, like their even more marginal sisters the fortune tellers or spiritualist mediums, they disguised their lack of formal qualification under the courtesy title of 'Madam'.

Participation in quasi-professional occupations seems traditionally to have been quite compatible with marriage and family commitments; indeed midwives and dame school proprietors seem mainly to have been married women. The new professions, however, initially practised only by men, became organized on the assumptions of a man's life and career expectations. Even when, later in the century a small number of talented and energetic women forced small cracks open and entered professional training, they had to accept a career structure already determined by men. By accepting the social role of men and choosing a career as an alternative to marriage, such pioneers distanced themselves from the aspirations and experience of the majority of their sex.

Middle-class women seem to have been losing the authority involved in some traditional professional or quasi-professional roles, and were certainly not obtaining a fair proportion of the expanding number of professional jobs, since these increasingly required qualifications available only in institutions from which women were specifically excluded. This exclusion was of a different order from that experienced by working-class women. For working people of both sexes work outside the home was usually hard, unpleasant and ill-paid. Workmen were subject to daily humiliations and to the often arbitrary authority of employer or overseer. A woman with young children was hardly likely to feel desperately anxious to join her husband in a coal mine or a factory if his income, with perhaps some occasional help from her own part-time employment, could provide. The pattern of two full-time workers in a marriage is mainly a development belonging to an era of planned families, supportive social services and the more civilized work practices in an age of greater trade union strength. Thus the problems of access to employment were very different for women of different classes and, within classes, for women of different marital status. Generalizations about a whole gender have to be treated with great caution.

The vigour of the movements for women's emancipation during the latter part of the nineteenth century derived largely from women of the middle and upper classes. It came partly from a perceived diminution in the authority exercised by women in many areas of life, as well as from demands for greater freedom and greater authority. A Fabian tract of March 1900 underlined another way in which women were being excluded and their role diminished:

> As the law stands at present, women can sit on Parish Councils, on Urban and Rural District Councils, on Boards of Guardians and on School Boards. They cannot sit on County Councils or Borough Councils; and in spite of the decision of the House of Commons that they should sit on the new Metropolitan Borough Councils which replaced the Vestries under the London Government Act, 1899, they were expressly excluded by the House of Lords . . . on 26 July 1899. . . .[23]
>
> Duties exactly similar to those of the educational and charitable bodies, on which they now sit unchallenged, are discharged by County Councils and Borough Councils.[24]

The last sentence is an important reminder. Just as the re-structuring of the professions was working to exclude women from traditional aspects of education, healing and pastoral work, so the taking over by the state and local authorities of many new concerns was moving authority and influence away from charitable provision, and so again reducing the power of women of the middle and upper classes.

English society in the nineteenth century was held together by complicated networks of charity. For the poor, survival would have been impossible without the daily patterns of reciprocal giving and lending within the family and the neighbourhood. State provision by means of the poor law was minimal and often administered with harshness and lack of human respect. Beyond the poor law and the mutuality of family and neighbourhood, lay an enormous variety of institutions, large and small, local and national, which served many of the purposes now covered by state welfare provision as well as some which are not. The administration and supervision of these charities provided an important focus for the social life of many middle- and upper-class women, and also an opportunity to enforce their canons of behaviour and personal morality on the recipients and potential recipients of their patronage. Powerful as was the influence of the parson in the lives of villagers, it may well be that in day-to-day matters affecting choices and decisions about family and personal life, the influence of his wife and daughters was even greater. Hannah More, feminist and blue stocking, pointed this out in her novel *Coelebs in Search of a Wife*. Mrs Stanley, his future mother-in-law, told Coelebs

> I have often heard it regretted that ladies have no stated employment, no profession. *It is a mistake. Charity is the calling of a Lady; the care of the poor is her profession.* Men have little time or taste for details. Women of fortune have abundant leisure, which can in no way be so properly or so pleasantly filled up, as in making themselves acquainted with the worth and the wants of all within their reach. With their wants, because it is their bounden duty to administer to them, their worth, because without this knowledge they cannot administer prudently and appropriately.[25]

The whole Stanley household was geared to this role, the tiniest daughters being brought up from infancy to trip along to deserving villagers as soon as their tiny hands could hold a basket of goodies or their infant lips transmit a moral message.

The authority exercised by charitable ladies over the lives of the lower orders, male as well as female, should not be underestimated. Much of this work was carried out with the highest motives, and it is perhaps churlish to see it too much as an expression of the desire to control the lives of others. But since the subject under discussion is authority, this aspect should be stressed. A recent valuable study of women's participation in philanthropic activities records a vast amount of work, much of it in the form of donations by women and of service on committees which must represent a very conservative measure of female participation since it cannot record the daily activities of charitable ladies in the observation and administration of charitable giving.[26] The Mendicity Society, for example, founded in 1818 to prevent street begging by offering beggars meals of bread and cheese to be eaten in the presence of officers of the charity listed 25 per cent of its supporters as women in 1830 and 34 per cent in 1895.[27] The Royal Society for the Prevention of Cruelty to Animals, a charity which was popular with women throughout the century, received 64 per cent of all its legacies, totalling £194,115, during the last seventy years of the century, from women, although women did not sit on its national council until 1896. The London Society for the Encouragement of Faithful Female Servants listed, perhaps not surprisingly, 56 per cent of its donors as women in 1820. Many other local and national charities whose subscription lists survive show a considerable proportion of their income coming from women subscribers. In an age in which property and distributable income was most likely to be in male hands, and the influence of wives over its charitable disposal must have been considerable, this information reinforces a picture of a very strong female presence on the charitable scene.[28] A glance at any local newspaper will confirm this:

> (7 January 1820) Mrs Thompson Corbett, of Elsham Hall . . . with her usual liberality, has just distributed beef to upwards of 80 families in that parish. - Visiting the sick, feeding the hungry and clothing the naked is this lady's delightful employment.[29]

This item may perhaps remind us of little Ben Brierley's being refused a dish of beef stew by the woman serving it out at the charitable feast laid on to celebrate the coronation of William IV, because 'thy gronfeyther's a Jacobin'.[30] A good moral and political character would certainly be required, as well as hunger, to qualify for much of the bounty that was available. As the *Stamford Mercury* stated, when urging charitable concern for the poor of the village of East Stockwith in the winter of 1845:

> We are credibly informed there are families there of good character and of industrious and sober habits, who are suffering severely, scarcely ever tasting animal food, their chief support being a little bread and potatoes.[31]

It was, indeed, one of the social duties of charitable ladies to watch the habits of poor families, and reward or otherwise in times of general dearth or particular family misfortune. All hospital provision other than that offered within the workhouse, any educational opportunity beyond the basic provision of the church or board school, and for many children the possibility of apprenticeship to a trade or admission to a post in a respectable firm or a reasonably paid domestic post in a 'good' household, depended on the patronage of people of quality - the supporters of the charitable bodies whose donations entitled them to nominate candidates for free medical treatment or admission to charity schools. Even a second go at the vicarage tea-leaves or permission to go for 'broken victuals' to the back door of a local gentry house depended on approval by - usually - the ladies of the vicarage and the manor house.[32]

Ladies, then, were the social observers and to an extent, the social workers administering such welfare provisions as were needed. Few among the poorer classes would have been unaffected by this particular form of authority, certainly not in the countryside. The century saw many attempts to extend this charitable surveillance to the growing cities, some more successful than others. But as the cities increasingly called for new forms of salaried social officers, women had to battle to be allowed to take up these posts. A great deal of the energy of the women's movement in the last twenty years of the century went into gaining the right to train for and practise such positions as factory inspectors, sanitary inspectors, prison officers and above all to serve on national and local councils to whom these officers were responsible. In doing this they were breaking new ground in public activity, but also attempting to regain forms of authority which were disappearing with the declining power of charity as a form of social authority.

Harriet and John Stuart Mill referred to women as 'a sort of sentimental priesthood' in 1851.[33] This description rests presumably on the growing popular mythology of the superior moral qualities of women which forms an important element in Victorian thought. As Alex Tyrrell has pointed out in an interesting study of the role of women in some of the mid-century moral reform movements, this elevation of women to a superior moral status is very much a nineteenth-century development.[34] It was to be used extensively by opponents of women's political and educational emancipation, although elements of the same argument could even then be found among some feminists. But the polarization of roles and values – the feminine private, morally uplifting, concerned with the affections and the family, the masculine practical, public, concerned with the rough realities of the wider world of forum and market place – meant that even women who did achieve some public status, women like Elizabeth Fry or Josephine Butler, were obliged to do so with a halo of saintly perfection hovering by implication around their heads. Tyrrell documents the considerable part played by women in some of the most important moral crusades, including the anti-slavery movement, but shows the very strict rules of behaviour, particularly public behaviour, under which they took part.

To the degree that the nineteenth century saw much charitable work, particularly in the cities, being undertaken by large bureaucratic bodies or increasingly by agencies of national or local government, women were being excluded from the practical activities which had formed a large part of the lives of women of the country house and the parsonage. In the very nineteenth-century phenomenon of the great national moral crusade, a few outstanding women emerged as leaders while many others undoubtedly worked anonymously as committee supporters and fund raisers. But this work was either inspirational or supportive. It was not the kind of practical daily control over people which earlier forms of charitable activity had provided.

Of course, rich women continued to exercise authority over poor men as well as over poor women, in their roles as employers, customers or landowners and in their control of the disbursement of charitable contributions. Nevertheless, women seeking a more clearly defined authority and legal equality with men found themselves up against both long-standing prejudice and the newer, specifically nineteenth-century ideology of the moral purity and superiority of women. The Mills had used the comparison with a priesthood in a semi-humorous fashion. By the end of the century the same image was being used in all seriousness.

> She fought for Woman, and for all the gifts
>> Which consecrate her priestess of mankind;
> Eternal priestess – she who leads and lifts
>> The man, who, but for her, crept dark and blind.[35]

The *locus classicus* of women's struggle for emancipation in the later years of the nineteenth century was the demand for the suffrage and thereby for entry into the political nation. But even here, although in the clearly defined public arena women had played little part, the shift from private to public activity, from local to national focus, was excluding women from the exercise of authority and influence. Since the exercise of the vote did not in any way conflict with domestic duties, it may seem surprising not simply that it was so long withheld from women, but that it was not put forward earlier as a major demand. The fact is, of course, that for most of the century the vote as such was not a powerful instrument for affecting governments or policies.

For all but the last few years of the nineteenth century the great majority of the population of Britain played no part in the election of members of Parliament. Women shared their exclusion from the franchise with most men and all people under the age of twenty-one. And since until 1872 voting was open and since there was no payment of MPs until after the end of the century, the exercise of the privilege of voting and the choice of candidates for whom to cast the vote did not have much to do with the political preference of the individual voter. Candidates were selected and elections organized in accordance with the prevailing system of influence and patronage. The system changed over the course of the century, and by its close the exercise of the vote had become more important. Nevertheless, real influence remained more closely tied to property and family than to the exercise of constitutional rights. The main areas of political action were clearly occupied by men. Not of course entirely so, since the highest office in government was held by a woman for two-thirds of the century, a fact which must be considered when looking at the place of women in British society in those years. But both Houses of Parliament were attended only by men. Even though British noble titles could be handed on by the female line and peeresses could hold titles in their own right, such titles did not carry the right to a seat in the House of Lords.

Nevertheless, throughout most of the century politics had an important and influential 'private' aspect outside Parliament. Patronage dominated all appointments and all offices, and in the exercise of patronage property rather than gender could be the determining factor.

Anne Lister was a Yorkshire landowner and property-owner, a competent business woman, a great traveller and a strong supporter of the Tory interest. She never had a vote, but probably exercised as much political influence as most of her male contemporaries. On Friday 4 August 1837, for instance, we find her and her friend Ann doing what might be called heavy canvassing in the Tory interest:

> Off with Ann to her tenants (Bottomley) at Shibden Mill to canvass the votes of the two sons. The oldest from home. Saw George. He would not vote at all. A simple looking young man, but he said it in such a way that showed he would not be persuaded by Ann. His mother evidently for not giving Ann his vote. I said what could they do; they had their trade to consider. Ann said not much but that she thought her tenants ought to vote on her side, which would otherwise not be represented at all. The young man looked sullen. I said well! you have refused your landlady the only favour she has ever asked. I hope you will not have any opportunity of refusing her many more favours. He answered I hope not. Came away. She determined to quit the people, and I quite agreeing she was right.[36]

The final word here clearly lay with the landlady, as it did in a number of other such encounters. In some cases Miss Lister asked for the pledge of a vote on her side before allocating tenancies, and she seems to have no problems of pocket or conscience when it came to actually buying votes directly.[37] In this part of the country at least the women in the family – in this case the miller's mother – regarded the vote as a family property rather than as being at the personal disposal of the nominal voter.

Miss Lister's type of 'canvassing' was only one of many. Ladies were prominent canvassers, and after the 1832 Reform Bill, which enfranchised many urban shopkeepers, their influence was important. Voters respected the wishes of their best customers, many of them of course women, and their exercise of the suffrage took account of their commercial interests. Woe betide the shopkeeper who dared to vote against the wishes of his customers. General Napier, supporter of the Radical candidate, J. A. Roebuck, in Bath on the occasion of the election of 1837 wrote:

> The Tories, especially the women, are making a run against all the Radical shops. Can we let a poor devil be ruined by the Tories because he

Anne Lister, a Tory canvasser in the 1830s.

honestly resisted intimidation and bribery? Nothing can exceed the fury of the old Tory ladies.[38]

The risk was too great for many shopkeepers to stand out. Where conflicts of 'loyalty' arose, as in the case of the Shibden miller, caught between Whig business men customers and Tory landlady, they were likely to be resolved on grounds of expediency rather than of political conviction.

Even in the realm of politics, then, family influence, money and property were the most important sources of power and authority. Political hostesses at the highest level of politics were considerably more powerful than politicians at the lower levels. The vote, for most of the century, was a fairly insignificant indicator of political power or influence. As the century went on, as more and more aspects of social life came under political control and more people came into the political nation, the vote increased in real and symbolic importance. Even at the end of the century, however, and certainly in the early years, there were radical and working-class politicians who actively opposed the extension of the existing property-based franchise to women on the grounds that the interests of property would be even more disproportionately represented if this were done. The interests of gender and those of class could be in contradiction.

It is also worth remarking that the main drive of the women's movement was towards admitting women to the public domain and training them for their part in it. The idea that a woman who was indeed totally preoccupied with family and domestic affairs could have something to contribute in her own right to public decision-making was rarely put forward. Donald Robinson, writing to the biographer of Jane Harrison, recalled:

> One of the few things that sticks in my mind was a remark of hers about polar bears at the zoo. She told me that they had been moved into a new cage or something of the sort, and that while the male bear at once explored his new premises, his wife refused to stir from the inner compartment. She said "It made me so unhappy about the Suffrage."[39]

Those who advocated women's suffrage in the earlier part of the century, as many of the Chartists did, usually confined the demand to unmarried women and widows, partly on the grounds of the unity of interest of man and wife, but partly also with the often unexpressed view that someone totally absorbed in domestic matters was not equipped to make judgements on public affairs. The token women included on committees concerned with such matters as the care and education of mentally retarded children towards the end of the century were also held to be there as a humane softener of public attitudes rather than as equal members of public bodies.

As late as the second half of the eighteenth century, British society had been controlled and administered very largely by the authority of local institutions. In spite of the laws relating to property, many women found for themselves areas of authority – for those of royal or noble family means to evade or modify the law were many and various, and their authority could be protected by settlements, entail or provisions made through private Acts of Parliament. For the women of artisan families, their essential role as family organizer was interwoven with an equally essential role in the productive work of the household. Among the intermediate classes of small farmers, tradesmen and the lower professions, women often worked beside their husbands or fathers, or sometimes as recognized practitioners of crafts or professions. This is not to suggest that there was anything like equality between the sexes in the public domain, but simply that there were opportunities for women in some areas and that there was a greater overlap between public and private. As the nineteenth century developed population increase, urbanization and industrial and social change led to the centralization of authority, the taking over by the state of many of the functions of local government and of charitable provision and personal intervention in peoples' lives. The move of manufacturing industry from home and small workshop to factory or large units, and the growth of provided and state schooling, transferred many previously domestic activities into public areas. The growth of professional education and required qualifications concentrated the higher professions and their administration in the hands of men. Women's work and women's occupations were by and large lowered in comparative status and reward, while women's activity as housewives and mothers was deprived of much of its practical authority.

The widening gulf between public and private domains had many different results. Florence Nightingale is the archetype of the woman who successfully made the deliberate choice of a public career. Her story documents the problems. For her the choice included the deliberate rejection of marriage, and a break with the women members of her family. In her career she found it easier to work with men, and indeed in her own family it was her mother who most passionately opposed her choice rather than her father. Her mother was a woman of talent with a strong personality who found satisfaction in the social and family life which her money and social rank enabled her to pursue. By leaving the social milieu occupied by her mother, Florence cut herself off from most of her women contemporaries. For most of the campaigners for women's admission to the public area of work and government it was still, at the end of the century, seen as an alternative to marriage for those for whom marriage and children were not possible.[40]

For working people the public area was that of non-domestic work. Women with families were still mainly seeking the right not to have to work rather than a right to work, although the later years of the century saw the growth of women's trade union organization to establish better standards of work and pay. But for the working-class family the second half of the century seems to have been marked by the exclusion of the man from the private areas of family life. The campaigns for shorter working hours often stressed this, and it was used in the arguments of philanthropists and middle-class supporters of the eight- or nine-hour day movements. Thus Charles Mark Palmer, Jarrow shipyard owner, spoke in favour of the Saturday half-holiday:

> There is nothing can be more gratifying to me or any employer of labour than to contemplate that you all cease your work at the end of the week, so as to allow you to accompany your wives to market and to have your full Saturday afternoon as a holiday and recreation before Sunday.[41]

A similar argument was used by E. S. Beesly:

> A diminution of the hours of work is felt by all the best workmen to be even more desirable than an increase of wages. . . . If the working day could be fixed at eight hours for six days in the week, and a complete holiday on the seventh, the workman would have time to educate himself, to enjoy himself, and above all to see more of his family.[42]

The masculinization of the public sector and the feminization of the private affected all classes. The strange ideology of the moral superiority of women rested partly on the concept of the home as a haven of purity, and, far from raising the status of women in any but the most marginal areas, it must, for those who subscribed to it, have lowered her authority, since women who worked outside home and family were in a sense automatically degraded by that very fact. At the nation's head for the last two-thirds of the century was a female figure who was required to bridge the public realm of government and the private one of home and family. She was used by politicians and by moralists, and in her own life experienced in a unique way the satisfactions and frustrations of both sides. At more than one point she made the deliberate choice to withdraw from public activity; the best-remembered occasion was following the death of her husband, but there were times recorded in her journals when her family concerns were of a happier kind. 'Really' she wrote in her journal, shortly after the birth of her third daughter,' when one is so happy and blessed in one's home life, as I am, Politics (provided my country is safe) must only take a 2nd place.'[43]

In striving for the admission of women to the public domain, feminists themselves often implicitly or explicitly devalued the private area of home and family. Inevitably this caused tensions between women with different or conflicting interests. The defence of the home, however, was made not only by women but by a strong ideological development many of whose leading exponents were men. In retrospect we have often dismissed this 'cult of domesticity' as a confidence trick designed to delay the achievement of women's right to a full place in society. In making such a judgement, however, it is easy to overlook the genuine conflicts of interest which existed, and still exist, between the private world of family and children and the public world of money and achievement. By the end of the nineteenth century many doors admitting women into the public world of commerce and the professions had been forced open, or partially open. But the recovery of the lost authority which had been exercised by women who had not given up the authority of the private zone of family and household was hardly on the agenda.

3

'A Burning Zeal for Righteousness': Women in the British Anti-Slavery Movement, 1820–1860

Louis Billington and Rosamund Billington

Mid-nineteenth-century feminism claimed the earlier anti-slavery movement as one of its antecedents, indicating that this movement contained the seeds of women's political education. Yet historians have hardly commented on women's involvement in the British movement, although their importance in American abolitionism is now acknowledged. Through this involvement, women appropriated an ideology of injustice, and valuable experience of tactics and organization. But here we intend to show that there are aspects of British women's abolitionist activity which necessitate revision of the view that feminism and anti-slavery were simply two sides of the same coin, while recognizing the process by which women have legitimized their own history.[1] Women's involvement from the 1820s in the movements to abolish Negro slavery in the British colonies and the United States evolved out of their already accepted roles in religious philanthropy and the religious societies aimed at the expansion of evangelical Christianity. Philanthropy and religious work were accommodated as extensions of women's caring and domestic functions, part of the *status quo* of gender relationships. However, to the extent that such activity was concerned specifically with the injustices of women and also allowed them some autonomy, it was one of the factors which heightened the consciousness of women as a disadvantaged group more generally.

From the late eighteenth century a growing network and variety of religious societies had been organized on a denominational and interdenominational bases, for foreign and domestic missionary work, religious publicity, propaganda, education and welfare. Based in

London, these societies had an interlocking directorate of prominent evangelical clergymen and laymen who usually employed a small group of male professionals as secretaries or editors. The national societies were supported by a network of county and local organizations. Evangelical clergy acknowledged that Christianity 'knew neither male nor female', and social convention placed aspects of religion within women's sphere. But women had no place at the power centres of the growing 'benevolent empire' of the evangelical societies, although they were vital to its expansion and functioning. In addition to supporting local auxiliaries, women organized separate 'ladies'' societies. These groups reflected evangelical prescriptions concerning the motivations and behaviour of women. Young women raised within evangelical families accepted their values of youthful seriousness, educational endeavour and emotional piety.[2] Some willingly volunteered for the arduous tasks of missionaries' wives, sustaining the work of their husbands and making a special outreach to heathen women. Few British women were called to make such sacrifices, but all were constantly reminded of the advantages they enjoyed through living in an evangelical Protestant society and, like their sisters in the mission field, were expected to take a particular interest in women oppressed by Popery, Islam or the 'savageness of the heathen'. Missionary literature regularly presented reports and provided illustrations of the 'degraded condition of women in heathen countries', a form of propaganda which the anti-slavery movement would quickly adopt.[3]

By the 1820s there were thousands of 'female societies' with overlapping membership, directed by ladies' committees and devoted to evangelical causes. In most of these, women worked only with women. If they addressed mixed-sex meetings, they did not speak in public but at 'drawing-room' or 'parlour' meetings of invited guests. Collecting donations from acquaintances and distributing literature, particularly to the lower classes, remained within the boundaries considered proper for women. A smaller number of ladies' organizations restricted themselves to special missions, such as working-class female education or aiding female prisoners. These groups used similar methods of organization and fund-raising, including missionary cards and boxes through which large sums were raised by tiny donations. These were the equivalent of American women's 'cent societies'. Other women paid annual subscriptions or made personal donations which could rise to sums as large as £50 per annum. All members could contribute to an annual sale of work organized on a local basis, or drawing on local support for a great national fund-raising effort.[4] These annual sales or bazaars often raised a substantial part of a national organization's annual income. One historian has recently estimated that by the 1820s women's auxiliaries were raising between ten and twenty per cent of this. Male officials frequently acknowledged women members' importance in this function, although some conservative churchmen opposed women's auxiliaries, accepting them only when the women stood their ground.[5] Opponents of evangelicalism were quick to ridicule 'female societies', and even some supporters were not uncritical, expressing dislike for ladies' societies which included 'officious, gossiping characters', overbearing in their solicitation of funds. To safeguard themselves against 'ostentatious' and 'amazonian' women and retain control over women's activities, some male committee members succeeded in grafting separate female societies on to the men's societies. Despite this opposition to women's increasing involvement, evangelical organizations were rivals in pursuit of funds, and the growing network of ladies' societies was indispensable in tapping a wide circle of contributors.[6]

From the 1820s this network provided a milieu from which the women's anti-slavery movement could develop. Quakers and evangelicals shared a dislike of slavery, and the dominant party within the Society of Friends had long been influenced by the wide beliefs and values of evangelicalism, with women members working for the Bible Society and other key agencies. Some Quaker and evangelical women had been involved in the earlier campaign, led by Wilberforce against the slave trade, which was abolished in 1808. When attention then turned to the abolition of the institution of slavery itself, these women quickly came to the support of the Anti-Slavery Society when it was organized in 1823, with the aim of bringing about the gradual emancipation of slaves in the British colonies and especially the West Indies.[7] From the start, women made a financial contribution to the Anti-Slavery Society. Of an income of £1,093 from donations and subscriptions in its first year, a Miss M. W. Smith contributed £50 and numerous other women contributed smaller amounts. Although modest compared to the major evangelical organizations, by 1824 the society's income had more than doubled. By 1825, printing, publishing and circulation costs made up the greater part of the Society's expenses, and by 1826 income had risen to over £2,933. Women must have contributed to this increase. The Society of Friends was by far the largest contributor, giving £1,500. Four ladies' anti-slavery societies had contributed over £100 each and this was only a fraction of what local women's groups were beginning to raise.[8]

By 1825 organization of ladies' anti-slavery societies was well under way. The Anti-Slavery Society distributed three thousand copies of their model rules for the creation of 'ladies' associations', and these were followed by an Address urging women to support the 'sacred cause' of abolition. Much of this outlined possible areas of action within women's 'own sphere of influence'. The Address also emphasized the broad purposes to be served by women's involvement. Greatest emphasis was to be placed upon the anti-slavery movement as a Christian cause: 'Should they, for His sake, actively engage in this labour of Christian love, they cannot fail, whatever be the issue, to inherit "the blessing of those who are ready to perish", and the richer blessing of Him who declares that even a cup of cold water given in His name shall not lose its reward'.[9] Distribution of literature and similar tasks and 'imbueing . . . the rising race with an abhorrence of slavery' fitted easily into the dominant evangelical model for the gender-based division of moral labour, 'without violating that retiring delicacy which constitutes one of . . . [women's] loveliest ornaments'. But petitioning Parliament in support of the cause was recognized as a legitimate political dimension of women's work.[10]

Among the earliest and most important of the women's anti-slavery organizations was the Birmingham Ladies' Society for the Relief of Negro Slaves, inaugurated at a 'large and respectable meeting' on 8 April 1825, over a year before a general anti-slavery society was organized in the city. The original aim of the ladies' society was 'the amelioration of the condition of the unhappy children of Africa, especially Female Negro Slaves . . . living under British laws'. While trying not to offend West Indian planters needlessly, the organization pledged to use every proper exertion in aid of 'our sisters, the Female Negro Slaves'. Many of the founder members came from prominent Quaker families like the Lloyds and Sturges, but key positions were taken by evangelical women such as Lucy Townsend, wife of the Vicar of West Bromwich.[11] In many ways the Birmingham Ladies' Society acted as a national rather than a local organization. Its district treasurers, responsible for collecting funds and arousing local interest, were scattered not only through the Midlands but further afield, and were frequently instrumental in creating women's anti-slavery societies in their own neighbourhoods. These often retained close personal, financial and operational links with the Birmingham society, which, as the mother organization, aided local groups with funds and publications.[12]

Although a local company acted as treasurer, the Birmingham society's affairs were entirely executed by women. Minutes of quarterly and annual meetings were kept, correspondence conducted, and a cash book of income and expenditure maintained. A steering committee met quarterly and organized an annual meeting at which accounts and an annual report were presented and a new committee selected. Initially, the subscription was to be twelve shillings, which was higher than the men's society, indicating perhaps recruitment from a narrow social class base, but the Birmingham ladies soon adjusted their rate to cover a range from five shillings to twelve shillings. Members were issued with collecting books for the receipt of subscriptions and donations, and were also expected to raise funds.[13] The second Annual Report, for 1826-7, shows that the society handled over £823 – more than half the sum received in subscriptions and donations by the national Anti-Slavery Society in 1827, which included donations from provincial and ladies' societies. In 1828 subscriptions and donations to the national society showed a marked turndown, partially attributable to the growth of local and provincial ladies' societies, like the Birmingham one, through which an increasing proportion of activities and funds for the anti-slavery movement were channelled.[14]

In 1827 the Birmingham ladies' society distributed nearly 35,000 items of propaganda, regularly forwarded £50 to the London Anti-Slavery Society and also spent more than £500 each year on abolitionist literature.[15] By 1831 there were more than forty societies engaged in similar work.[16] The Sheffield Ladies' Anti-Slavery Society, for example, claimed some eighty members and distributed a large number of cheap tracts, chiefly among the poor. But its annual budget was rarely more than £25 and it made no donations to the national Anti-Slavery Society from which it bought only £4 or £5 worth of literature each year. This was typical of the scale of operation of many local societies, although some, like Birmingham, operated on a larger scale.[17] By 1830 the major evangelical denominations were giving public support to the anti-slavery campaign, and ladies' anti-slavery societies had been organized in all large cities and in smaller towns, including those where Quakers were few. Women's groups were a major support of the London Anti-Slavery Society. Fourteen per cent – nearly £300 – of its income from subscriptions and donations in 1830 came from twenty-six ladies' societies and this proportion continued to increase. Women also gave generously as individuals and through the Society of Friends. By this date, too, ladies' societies purchased seventeen per cent of the Anti-Slavery Society's literature for distribution. The increasing importance of women's endeavours was rather patronizingly acknowledged by male abolitionists.[18]

In their work, women abolitionists faced a variety of discouragements, apart from male patronage. Local treasurers had to reconcile their work with domestic commitments, and treasurers changed frequently. Nevertheless, by 1827 the Birmingham Ladies'

Society was receiving letters and reports from women's anti-slavery organizations in many parts of the country. Many of these looked to the Birmingham society as a parent body which had provided initial encouragement, financial aid and literature. It could draw upon the resources of many wealthy Quaker families, whose male members too played an increasingly prominent role in the national campaign. Empowered by the Quaker network to which so many of their members belonged, women's anti-slavery societies regularly shared ideas and information concerning advancement of the cause. To keep up the momentum, societies arranged monthly meetings of key members, where literature was studied and strategies planned. Neighbourhoods were divided into small districts and 'visitors' appointed to distribute literature, obtain donations and press householders to support the movement. Some of these activities fitted neatly into conventional notions of 'women's sphere', while at the same time constituting political action.[19]

Since the eighteenth century, British and American Quakers had argued that the use of goods produced by slave labour was as indefensible as slaveholding itself, and many had boycotted West Indian sugar during the campaign to abolish the slave trade. From the inception of the national Anti-Slavery Society in 1823, abstinence from slave-produced goods as a means of damaging the planter interest had been widely advocated in Britain. Bringing moral pressure to bear on the public, in an area so closely concerning the household, was thought particularly suited to the growing network of ladies' anti-slavery societies. As early as 1824, Elizabeth Heyrick of Leicester was writing the first of a series of widely circulated pamphlets making a special appeal to the 'hearts and consciences' of British women and stressing that all abolitionists should abstain on principle from slave produce.[20]

Members of women's anti-slavery societies throughout Britain canvassed door to door, handing out pamphlets with such titles as *What Does Sugar Cost?* and *Reasons for Substituting West Indian Sugar*, arguing with housewives that use of East Indian sugar was a moral obligation to avoid complicity in the sin of slaveholding. It was not only middle-class families, like those who formed the bulk of membership, who were urged to avoid such complicity, but also working-class women. They were told that 'the money they can afford to expend on sugar during the year should be laid out in the purchase of that which is the produce of free labour'. Some district visitors reported success in this campaign, although they complained that it was difficult to guarantee the authenticity of East Indian sugar and also that it was often more expensive. To meet these problems, some ladies' societies organized the purchase of free labour produce, the endorsement of commercial suppliers or distribution through special depositories.[21] Attempts were also made to produce a national list of all individuals and families agreeing to abstain from use of slave-produced sugar. This was designed to show the extent of anti-slavery support, encouraging the smaller women's organizations that their modest work made an impact on the planter interest.[22]

Moral and economic consciousness-raising was a small part of the larger work of publicity and propaganda that women's anti-slavery societies were undertaking. They also used publicity methods which reflected women's conventional concerns and talents. Abolitionist literature was distributed through house-to-house visiting and sent as 'work bags' to likely women in communities without a female anti-slavery society, forming a basic resource around which a ladies' society, or informal group, could be organized. Some of these bags were 'exquisite bead and satin affairs', for which wealthy supporters paid twelve shillings and sixpence or more.[23] Women also put together carefully selected albums of anti-slavery propaganda aimed at women and children. In 1826-7 the Birmingham society spent over £31 on binding, paper and pictures for these albums or scrapbooks which were sold as useful gifts to raise funds. The albums contained copies of the annual reports of the ladies' societies so that women aroused by the material would have guidelines for conducting their own organization. A typical album contained illustrations emphasizing the brutal exploitation of slave women and children, including their semi-nakedness and exposure to the lash of overseers. Britannia was often shown as a 'Goddess-like Woman' intervening between the man with the lash and pleading female slaves, ultimately triumphing as the scourge fell from the man's bloody hands and pious female slaves prayed to the 'great massa' as their children were torn from their arms. Other material for the albums was taken from the planters' own newspapers in the West Indies, proof that female slaves were treated like cattle, bought, sold, whipped and branded.[24] These themes link the anti-slavery movement with the powerful evangelical missionary movement to which women gave so much support.

Between 1822 and 1830 the British anti-slavery movement generally limited its aims to the amelioration of slave conditions and gradual emancipation, with the achievement of this goal in the West Indies being the primary concern of the women's societies. As early as 1824, however, a growing number of women abolitionists, including Quakers, supported the idea of immediate emancipation, being vigorously argued by the leader of the Leicester Women's Anti-Slavery Association,

But soon as approaching the land,

That Goddess-like Woman he view'd ;

The scourge he let fall from his hand,

With the blood of his subjects imbrued.

Britannia enlisted in the anti-slavery cause.

Elizabeth Heyrick. In her pamphlet *Immediate Not Gradual Abolition*, Heyrick called for a 'holy war' against slavery, the 'deep entrenchment of the very powers of darkness'. She argued that opposition to slavery had been based on political calculation but should be a Christian crusade against sin, and she placed great emphasis on the need for a massive consumer boycott of West Indian products.[25] This pamphlet and others which Heyrick wrote were widely read, and Corfield argues convincingly that Heyrick's immediatism, with its emphasis on moral imperatives, was most influential amongst women abolitionists.[26] Heyrick's writing did much to persuade women abolitionists on both sides of the Atlantic towards the free produce movement and immediate emancipation, but she also persuaded some American male abolitionists.[27]

Although women were excluded from power in the national organizations dominated by men, historians are increasingly recognizing that women's anti-slavery societies were not simply passive auxiliaries. By the mid-1820s they were beginning to exert moral and financial pressure on the national movement to abandon gradualism. In Sheffield, the women's society called for 'total and immediate abolition' in its Report for 1826, and distributed two thousand copies of Heyrick's *No British Slavery* and *Immediate Not Gradual Abolition*. The men's society remained gradualist, but the women's society determined 'to take their stand against the united wisdom of the world'. Anti-slavery women in Wiltshire were equally resolute in calling for immediate emancipation in the face of male opposition. In April 1830, the Birmingham Ladies' Negro's Friend Society resolved that it would make its usual donation of £50 to the London Anti-Slavery Society only if that society gave up the word 'gradual' in its title.[28] This resolution antedated by six months the speech by the Reverend Andrew Thomson of Edinburgh, attacking slavery as a crime and a sin, which is usually regarded as the beginning of the 'immediatist' phase of the campaign against West Indian Slavery.[29] The Birmingham Ladies' Society withheld its donation to London in 1831 and switched its support to the more radical Agency Committee, a splinter from the national Anti-Slavery Society, promoted by abolitionists like Joseph Sturge. Thirteen women's groups soon supported the Agency Committee, and women provided nearly a third of its funds. The Agency Committee had a team of six professional lecturers who toured the country reinforcing and extending the network of anti-slavery groups.[30] Popular Agency lecturers such as George Thompson and Charles Stuart came to rely heavily on the friendship and financial support of a network of women, and in turn these men helped to establish the network of contacts between British and American women abolitionists.[31]

Drawing on the methods and organization they had developed in the previous decade, women's anti-slavery organizations played a major role after 1830 in the work of collecting signatures for petitions asking Parliament for immediate emancipation of the slaves. One petition of 187,000 signatures was largely the work of two women canvassers, and Parliament was deluged with petitions from women in many towns and cities. Such political activities foreshadowed those of the later women's suffrage movement.[32] More women were drawn into anti-slavery work, including petitioning, by the work of the societies and Agency lecturers, and also the widespread publicity given in the denominational press to the persecution of missionaries and mistreatment of slaves by planters after the Demerara troubles of 1823 and the Jamaican slave insurrection of 1831. Wesleyan Methodist and Nonconformist missionary societies working in the West Indies were already supported by a large number of women's auxiliaries. These were now drawn into the anti-slavery campaign, and for example, the overwhelming majority of Wesleyan Methodist women members signed their denominational anti-slavery petitions.[33]

Although primarily concerned with the abolition of West Indian slavery, some British women's groups had also taken an interest in the work of the American Colonization Society, which had long aimed at the gradual emancipation of the slave population of the United States and its re-settlement in West Africa. By 1830 this impractical and racist programme was difficult to reconcile with the growing emphasis on immediate emancipation by British women's anti-slavery organizations, and they supported Charles Stuart in a lecture and pamphlet campaign against the Colonization Society. This campaign alerted many British women abolitionists to the horrors of American slavery and the extent of colour prejudice and discrimination in the United States, especially against their own sex.[34] They also set up contacts with the beginnings of the American 'immediate emancipation' movement. With the passage of the Emancipation Act in 1833, which abolished slavery in the British colonies, some British women concentrated on the campaign to abolish American slavery, and the activities and organizations of British women were copied by their American sisters. It was recognized that women had played a major role in bringing the British abolitionist campaign to a successful conclusion: they had been the 'cement of the whole Anti-Slavery building'.[35] Americans had long grasped the importance of women in the British crusade, and in his pioneering anti-slavery paper, *Genius of Universal Emancipation*, the American Quaker, Benjamin Lundy had carried many reports of British women's abolitionist work, including the free produce campaign. Lundy's former associate,

William Lloyd Garrison, who had adopted immediate emancipation as the slogan of his new magazine, the *Liberator*, was especially anxious to involve women in the American anti-slavery cause:

> The ladies of Great Britain are moving the sympathies of the whole nation, in behalf of the perishing slaves in the British Colonies. We cannot believe that our ladies are less philanthropic or less influential. In their hands is the destiny of the slaves.[36]

American women were invited to communicate with the London Female Anti-Slavery Society for advice. By 1832 several ladies' societies had been formed in America, including some by black women. Many, like the Boston Female Anti-Slavery Society, corresponded with their older sister organizations in Britain and carried out similar activities. The Philadelphia society, headed by Lucretia Mott, endorsed the strategy previously used by British women of boycotting all but 'free' produce.[37]

In Britain, although many abolitionists came to regard the 1833 abolition bill, with its provision for planter compensation and apprenticeship system for freed blacks, as an unsatisfactory half-measure, it was difficult to sustain the previous level of interest and enthusiasm. Provincial anti-slavery organizations disappeared or became inactive, with some of the continuing women's societies being most interested in philanthropic schemes to aid blacks in the West Indies and elsewhere.[38] Some veteran British abolitionists doubted the wisdom of working against slavery in America, fearing an American nationalist backlash, but key women who had growing personal links with the American movement remained convinced that England should continue the campaign. In this they were supported by the more radical Scottish anti-slavery societies and their women's auxiliaries.[39]

Support of American anti-slavery activity did not distract British women from taking a major part in the campaign to end the apprenticeship system for blacks in the West Indies. In October 1837, for example, an *English Female Address* on behalf of apprenticed labourers was presented to the Queen, containing over 500,000 signatures.[40] In Darlington, a committee of fourteen engaged in a house-to-house canvass resulting in the collection of 5,315 signatures, a processs duplicated by other groups elsewhere.[41] The Sheffield women were more energetic than the men's anti-slavery society, to whom Mary Rawson sent a stinging letter, stressing that if the men did not act on the suggestions of the women then they would act alone.[42] Women's groups celebrated the ending of the apprenticeship system in 1839, and many became auxiliaries of the recently formed British and Foreign Anti-Slavery Society dedicated to overthrowing slavery and the slave trade throughout the world.[43]

Anti-slavery women were shocked by increasing reports of racial prejudice in the northern states of the United States, particularly cases which affected their own sex. In 1832, Prudence Crandall, a Quaker-educated teacher, admitted a black girl to her private school in Connecticut. White parents removed their daughters and Crandall changed her school into a residential one for black girls, resulting in the passing of a state law banning schools for out-of-state blacks. Backed by abolitionists, Crandall fought through the courts but the school was closed by mob violence in 1834. This case was an early catalyst of specifically feminist anti-slavery agitation, raising not only the issue of racial discrimination but also the right of a woman to engage in one of the few respectable middle-class occupations open to her.[44] Women's anti-slavery organizations in Edinburgh and Glasgow raised funds to help Crandall and presented her with gifts, as a mark of support and esteem.[45] Charles Stuart sent accounts back to Britain of his American lecture tours, emphasizing that the Crandall case was only one of many incidents of racial prejudice and the unprincipled means used against believers in racial equality. A fervent supporter of the American moral reform crusade and the purification of sexual mores, Stuart argued that most Americans ignored the worst example of sexual exploitation and injustice, the treatment of female slaves by their masters.[46] Similar reports were received from the anti-slavery lecturer George Thompson, touring the United States in 1834-5 with the financial assistance of Glasgow Ladies' Anti-Slavery Association and other British women's groups, but Americans were outraged by interference in their domestic affairs by a 'foreign agitator' like Thompson.[47]

Thompson and his American supporters faced violence from anti-abolitionist mobs, and publicity resulting from this strengthened ties between British women and their American sisters, who faced a physical hostility never shown against British women abolitionists (but later met by women campaigning against the Contagious Diseases Acts and later again by the women's suffrage movement). There was a revitalization of some British women's anti-slavery organizations, and new ones were formed.[48] These now aimed at universal abolition of slavery and the slave trade, but expressed particular concern for the 'noble minded and devoted women' in America making 'great efforts and painful sacrifices in defence of the sacred rights of freedom'. Although such resolutions had political overtones, most British women continued to define their anti-slavery involvement in religious and moral terms, working through prayer and giving financial aid to assist their American sisters.[49]

This subordination of politics within religious and moral reform motivated the work of women like the Quaker Elizabeth Pease, whose father had been a pioneer in the movement. Pease began a women's anti-slavery society in Darlington, encouraging work in the northeast and Scotland through a network of Quaker women. She organized an Address of sympathy and support from the women of Darlington, in response to a similar document from women in New England. Publicity from such exchanges mobilized additional women's anti-slavery societies in Britain. Leading American abolitionists like Angelina and Sarah Grimké and Maria Weston Chapman, with whom Pease corresponded, urged British women to provide material and moral aid.[50] By the time of the fourth American fund-raising fair in Boston, in 1837, British women were sending a wide range of goods for sale, and making financial contributions to the American cause.[51] Pease and her aunt, Sarah Beaumont, arranged for a British edition to be published of Angelina Grimké's *Appeal to the Christian Women of the South*, which among other points emphasized the importance of American women adopting the British women's tactic of petitioning.[52]

An increasing number of British women, like Elizabeth Pease and her sister Quaker, Anne Knight, became involved in the American women's anti-slavery network.[53] Efforts of women in the struggle were given greater publicity by the Unitarian Harriet Martineau. Already a well-known author and journalist when she visited the United States in 1834-6, she became friends with many leading abolitionists in Boston. On returning, Harriet Martineau wrote at length about American abolitionism, especially the heroism of women who faced verbal and physical abuse. In her *Westminster Review* article, 'The Martyr Age of the United States', Martineau emphasized that American women faced greater opposition than their British sisters because public sentiment here was more generally in favour of abolition. Prophetically, she also wrote that 'vindicating the civil rights of negroes' would take much longer than abolishing slavery.[54]

The British anti-slavery movement faced major ideological and organizational problems. Shocked by the reluctance of American churches to support the anti-slavery movement as evangelicals in Britain had done, British abolitionists nevertheless had difficulty in persuading British churches to criticize their American co-religionists or end their fellowship and co-operation with American Christians. This was especially so from the late 1830s, when indications were received concerning the 'infidelity' or unorthodoxy on key aspects of evangelical Protestant belief of radical abolitionists associated with American leaders like Garrison. Radical women abolitionists in Britain were disturbed to discover that even many American Quakers distanced themselves from these ultra-radical ideas.[55]

During the long campaign against colonial slavery, British women abolitionists stressed their avoidance of acting outside their 'proper sphere'. They reiterated this in the late 1830s, whether petitioning against the apprenticeship system or seeking support for the American anti-slavery movement, but they perceived this sphere to be wider than some of their critics believed it should be. In Darlington, for example, the group led by Elizabeth Pease stated that none of their methods were 'unbecoming to their sex'. Many women who had supported Thompson's politically provocative tour of America later insisted that their action did not go beyond the 'limits of feminine propriety' and that they were motivated by common feelings of humanity and the principles and precepts of Christianity, not politics.[56] This combination of sensitivity concerning their 'proper sphere' and sometimes uncompromisingly radical abolitionist sentiments has been emphasized by recent research on women in the anti-slavery movement.[57] By 1840, however, Pease and a few other women were aware that some American women were acting and arguing for the cause in ways which challenged conventional notions concerning women's behaviour.

In 1836 the Grimké sisters had lectured to large audiences of both sexes, a form of public agitation never adopted by the largely middle-class British women's anti-slavery groups.[58] Americans also moved towards the organization of large-scale regional anti-slavery conventions for women. At the first of these, in May 1837, emphasis was given to the repellent sexual immorality of slavery, and women were also urged to throw off the shackles preventing them from taking a full and equal part in the crusade against oppression.[59] In a period before the social purity movement altered popular opinion, sexual exploitation of women under slavery was rarely considered a topic for explicit public discussion in Britain, although American women abolitionists sometimes raised the issue.[60] Angelina Grimké's *Appeal to the Women of the Nominally Free States* was the first of a series of pamphlets emphasizing women's equal responsibilities and rights with men to decide contemporary moral and political issues. The majority of evangelical clergy, however, opposed women acting as 'public reformers' and 'usurping authority over men'. Drawing directly on their earlier campaign against women preachers, they used biblical sanctions to maintain the 'divine law of female subjection', and many conservative evangelical women argued in favour of their own subordination.[61]

Women like Harriet Martineau rejoiced that in pressing for the rights of slaves, women were 'coming at a conviction of their [own] rights', but by 1839 the American anti-slavery movement was bitterly divided over the 'woman question' and also over other issues of ideology and tactics. In 1840 the movement split, radicals retaining control of the American Anti-Slavery Society and their opponents forming the American and Foreign Anti-Slavery Society, modelled on the British organization. Some abolitionists, including women, attempted to transcend this division, and family and friendship ties spanned both 'camps'. But division was bitter, the more evangelical 'new' organization accusing its opponents not only of intruding the 'woman question' into abolitionism, but also of atheism, 'infidelity' and a host of other ultra-radical views.[62]

Most British women members, always more interested in the abolition of colonial slavery and already drifting away following the triumph of 1839, probably remained unaware of these developments until the Garrisonian radicals appointed women to the World's Anti-Slavery Convention in London, in 1840. Under the auspices of the British and Foreign Anti-Slavery Society, the convention was an Anglo-American gathering to celebrate the end of the apprenticeship system and focus attention on the scale of slavery and the slave trade elsewhere. Sending women delegates was a deliberate challenge by the 'old' American Anti-Slavery Society to the conventional denial of public platforms to women. The British and Foreign Society quickly identified itself with the 'new' American and Foreign Society, opposing admission of the American women to the floor of the convention. The women adjourned to a gallery, joined by Garrison and other male supporters.[63]

This group was already viewed with suspicion by many British evangelicals because of their largely Unitarian or unorthodox religious views, while the bulk of British Quaker abolitionists were disturbed because American delegates like James and Lucretia Mott were Hicksites, members of a schismatic neo-Unitarian group. The American women delegates and their associates were mostly supported by British radicals, Unitarians, and Scottish and Irish Quakers, often more sympathetic to radical American causes than their English counterparts.[64] A few English Quakers, led by Elizabeth Pease and Anne Knight, remained committed to both abolitionism and women's rights.[65] During the Convention new supporters of the women delegates came forward: Elizabeth Ashurst and her father William Ashurst, Elizabeth Reid and William and Mary Howitt.[66] Women like Elizabeth Pease, already identified with American radical abolitionists, skilfully argued for women's rights, and it was reported that John Scoble, secretary of the British and Foreign Society, was so overwhelmed in such a discussion that 'he took refuge under man's strongest weapon in contest with women – flattery'![67]

After the World's Convention many feminist delegates toured Britain, consolidating their support.[68] Anxious to retain the loyalty of surviving women's groups and form new ones, the British and Foreign Society employed Charles Stuart (previously supported by women's societies) to tour the country publicizing the views of opponents to women's equal involvement in the Convention. Stuart's feminist opponents reported that he was 'swallowed up in the littleness of putting down women', using the lecture platform, private correspondence and printed circulars to attack 'the Woman Intruding Anti-Slavery Society which stood for the principle that whatever is morally right for a man to do is morally right for a woman to do'.[69] Nevertheless, Stuart managed to retain the loyalty of the Birmingham Ladies' Negro's Friend Society and the recently founded Bristol and Clifton Ladies' Anti-Slavery Society.[70] Many other ladies' societies were moribund and others uncertain over the issue of women's rights. In Sheffield, Mary Rawson – not slow to criticize male colleagues, as we have seen – found that most favoured the British and Foreign Society, but she refused Stuart's request to hold a meeting in support of the British and Foreign Society and gather together the remnants of the women's organization. In a letter to Elizabeth Pease, Rawson admitted that her sympathy lay with the American Anti-Slavery Society.[71]

The Garrisonians sent John A. Collins to Britain on a fund-raising mission, where he launched a fierce verbal and printed attack on the British and Foreign Anti-Slavery Society and its provincial supporters. His *Right and Wrong among the Abolitionists of the United States* had an introduction by Harriet Martineau defending the Garrisonian feminist position. Collins's visit was a financial failure but strengthened the feminist wing of British abolitionism, while exacerbating conflict over women's rights within the movement.[72] In Edinburgh, the Ladies' Emancipation Society, headed by Jane Smeal Wigham, expressed loyalty to the Garrisonian position, but in Glasgow the Ladies' Society took the opposite position. Influenced by evangelicals, they argued that seating women at the World's Convention would have been acting in opposition to divine teaching and have obscured women's feminine character, 'a quality . . . as natural to one half the human race, as masculine is to the other'.[73]

In the resulting schism the Garrisonian Glasgow Female Anti-Slavery Society was formed, quickly issuing an *Appeal to the Ladies of Great*

Britain urging continued moral and financial support for the American Anti-Slavery Society. The *Appeal* avoided a statement on the 'extreme' subject of women's rights but welcomed the co-operation of everyone wishing to work for the abolition of slavery: 'What woman reflecting that nearly one and a half million of our sex are writhing in chains could throw a straw in the way of the effective pleading of Abby Kelly, Maria Chapman and of other of our American sisters'.[74] Failing to confront directly the women's rights issue, the Glasgow Female Society did little to challenge conventional ideas about gender roles. More than four years later its annual public meeting was chaired by a man and men read aloud the Annual Report, made resolutions and gave speeches. The American radical, Henry C. Wright, commented: 'Though it is a female society, they cannot act as Presidents . . . read reports or make remarks . . . Men must do all'.[75]

Conventions concerning gender, legitimated by the ideology of evangelicalism, ensured that feminism surfaced within the anti-slavery movement only amongst a minority of radical women. In many towns and cities there were only two or three women willing to support a Garrisonian organization. Such women subscribed to the *Liberator* or the *Anti-Slavery Standard* and corresponded with American sympathisers, but their activities were still largely of the domestic kind which did not challenge the *status quo*.[76] Much time and energy were spent making and collecting goods for the annual Boston Anti-Slavery Bazaar. In conjunction with the *Liberty Bell*, a gift annual to which some British women were invited to contribute, the bazaar gained great publicity and was a major fund-raising event. British supporters sent a wide range of manufactured products, together with a variety of handsome goods including beautiful examples of women's needlework and hand-painted gift albums.[77] After the first World's Anti-Slavery Convention, Lucretia Mott had cuttingly commented that many British 'Anti-Slavery Ladies' were fit only to be the 'drudges' of the movement.[78] Her comment underestimates the constraints which a more conventional British society imposed on women attempting to adopt 'feminist' action. It also undervalues the significance of regular meetings and programmes in widening the horizons of these women beyond the confines of domestic life, and the importance of such activity in keeping the British abolition movement alive. However, Mott's comment highlights British women's difficulty in finding appropriate anti-slavery work, as the non-Garrisonian wing of the American movement took up more political activity through the Liberty and Free Soil parties.[79]

Despite a second World's Anti-Slavery Convention, during the early 1840s interest in the movement waned, partly because Garrisonianism was increasingly seen as opposed to evangelicalism, creating further conflict and reducing support. Another factor was that many key women in the anti-slavery movement – for example, Elizabeth Pease and Jane Smeal Wigham – were, like many men, involved in other political reform movements, including the Anti-Corn Law League, Chartism, temperance, peace, and the reform of British India. Work for these movements required similar activities to anti-slavery, including attendance at public meetings, and for some abolitionists, women's involvement reinforced the importance of the women's rights issue.[80] Elizabeth Pease, Anne Knight and other women wanted to use the Chartist and Complete Suffrage organizations to press for women's political rights. They sought the support of Chartist leaders well known in anti-slavery circles, like William Lovett, Henry Vincent and Joseph Barker, but discovered that many thought it outrageous that women should speak in favour of the Charter. Despite the ambivalence of most male Chartists on the question of women's rights, Pease and other women used their publications as a forum. They also noted similarities between British conservatives' arguments that the mass of the people were unready for political equality, and slaveholders' insistence that blacks were unprepared for emancipation.[81] Increasing interest in women's rights by women on both sides of the Atlantic led some outside abolitionism to become interested in the work of American women like Maria Weston Chapman. While these radical Englishwomen acknowledged the importance of the struggle against slavery, they saw political and social injustices in Britain, including the position of women, as demanding the prior attention of women reformers.[82]

Although other campaigns attracted away many abolitionists, some women, mostly Quakers and Nonconformists, continued to support the British and Foreign Anti-Slavery Society and its American allies. In Birmingham, Bristol and a few other cities, women's anti-slavery societies continued to meet monthly or quarterly. Indeed, these women's societies often represented the sole activity, as men's societies became moribund. Visiting American abolitionists addressed these women's groups as did fugitive slaves supported by the British and American non-Garrisonian organizations. Birmingham Ladies' Negro's Friend Society and Bristol and Clifton Ladies' Anti-Slavery Society were the most important of these 'moderate' organizations, and continued to work for the cause in ways already indicated. They also lobbied MPs concerning questions such as British recognition of Texas, a slaveholding state; and the extradition clause of the Webster-Ashburton Treaty, which they thought would threaten fugitive slaves in Canada. The Birmingham and Bristol Societies also co-operated with smaller, often Quaker, groups and contributed handiwork to a rival Boston bazaar, held by the non-Garrisonian Massachusetts Female Emancipation Society.[83]

In 1846 the presence in Britain of Garrison, Henry C. Wright and the fugitive slave Frederick Douglass, reinforced the position of pro-Garrisonian women abolitionists. They campaigned against the Evangelical Alliance for failing to endorse a sufficiently radical anti-slavery policy and against the Free Church of Scotland for accepting slaveholders' money. Funds and energy were weakened by these campaigns and there was little support for the short-lived pro-Garrison Anti-Slavery League, which excluded women from membership, segregating them in the familiar ladies' auxiliary.[84] The Irish famine and other domestic problems reduced British women's ability to contribute to the Boston Bazaar, and simultaneously a growing number of evangelical women were influenced by continued reports of Garrisonian religious 'infidelity' and increasing criticism of him by British evangelical clergy and editors. The *Liberator* frequently aligned itself with radical causes, including feminism, and further alienated some women.[85]

In 1850, to the chagrin of stalwart Garrisonians like Jane Smeal Wigham and her daughter Eliza, the Edinburgh Ladies' Emancipation Society, attempting to disassociate itself from Garrisonianism and infidelity, refused to support the Boston Bazaar, creating considerable controversy. Simultaneously, a substantial number of evangelical women withdrew from the Glasgow Female Anti-Slavery Society and organized a New Ladies' Anti-Slavery Association which gave its financial support to the New York Vigilance Committee, a group which aided fugitive slaves.[86] By 1853, this New Ladies' Association was raising five times more money than the Garrisonian Female Society, and contributed £400 to the Vigilance Committee's annual income of just over £711.[87] As more fugitive slaves came to Britain after 1850, a group of women organized the Ladies' Society to Aid Fugitive Slaves, which provided food, lodging, education and employment for American blacks in Britain and assisted a few to move on to Canada. Like the work of the New York Vigilance Committee, such activity was seen by radicals as diverting funds away from the central objective of immediate emancipation. Garrison opposed the ransoming of slaves, arguing that it conceded slaveholders' rights to human property.[88]

Frederick Douglass had been ransomed through the fund-raising activities of Anna Richardson, a Newcastle Quaker, who with her friends supported the British and Foreign Society rather than the Garrisonians. Douglass increasingly distanced himself from Garrison, aided by an Englishwoman, Julia Griffiths, who returned with him to the United States, where she became his business manager and editorial assistant on the *North Star*. Griffiths devised a variety of fund-raising methods, including a large bazaar and a popular gift book. Through her female contacts, especially Anna Richardson, Julia Griffiths deflected towards Douglass and his paper some of the donations and bazaar gifts previously sent to the Garrisonian group in Boston. She was also supported by British Nonconformist leaders who regarded Garrison as a freethinker and rationalist. Griffiths agreed with the evangelical precept that women's activities should remain within the private sphere, constantly stating that she would talk herself hoarse on slavery 'in the parlour', but disapproved of women's rights and women as public speakers.[89]

Garrisonianism and feminism remained distinct minority positions within the British movement, but continued to create tensions, sometimes together and sometimes as separate issues. In the 1850s a major success for Garrisonianism and 'immediatism', was the switch in allegiance of the Bristol and Clifton Ladies' Anti-Slavery Society. The Bristol society had aided emancipated slaves in the West Indies, fugitives in Canada and a variety of American anti-slavery organizations approved by the British and Foreign Anti-Slavery Society. Interest in more apparently vital work was increased, amongst Unitarian women in particular, by visiting Americans who pressed the Garrisonian line and gained support from male and female members of the influential Estlin and Carpenter families, and the Unitarian minister, George Armstrong.[90] These Unitarians urged their American co-religionists to oppose slavery more strongly, although the Address from British Unitarians to the American Unitarian Association was signed only by adult male members of each congregation.[91] Mary Estlin, aided by her father, a prominent local doctor, persuaded the Bristol women to support the Garrisonian Boston Bazaar and advised against support of the free produce campaign favoured by many non-Garrisonian women's groups.[92]

In their struggle with the British and Foreign Anti-Slavery Society, the Bristol and Clifton women were supported by a short-lived local radical paper, the *Examiner* which also supported adult suffrage, the secret ballot, women's rights, temperance and similar causes.[93] Relations between the women's society and the national organization deteriorated, the crisis coming with the visit of Maria Weston Chapman and her family. These women convinced their Bristol sisters that the British and Foreign Society concentrated on marginal aspects of abolitionism and ignored the important work of American Garrisonians.

The Garrisonians accused the British and Foreign Society and its provincial allies of being little more than a paper organization, with a small clique of members led by Joseph Sturge. Although substantially true, this accusation underestimated the activity and membership of women's anti-slavery groups. After severing links with the British and Foreign Society, the Bristol women had some success in converting to the Garrisonian cause certain Unitarians, who were less alienated than orthodox Quakers and evangelicals, by Garrison's radical religious and social views.[94] No new women's anti-slavery societies were formed, but aided by American women like Sarah Pugh, a delegate at the World's Convention, Mary Estlin was influential in founding the Leeds Anti-Slavery Association. This was a largely Unitarian group whose secretary was Harriet Lupton, and membership and officeholding by both sexes was a contrast to the pattern in many towns of separate men's and women's organizations.[95] Sarah Pugh became a lifetime correspondent of many radical Unitarians, and it was such women, on both sides of the Atlantic, who were later involved in the feminist movement.[96]

Most Garrisonians had abandoned the free produce principle by the 1840s, but many other women's groups remembered the successful campaign against West Indian slave products, discussed earlier. The British and Foreign Society encouraged the idea, supported by Quaker-dominated groups within American abolitionism, although free produce manufacturing in Britain took place on the tiniest scale, until the movement was rejuvenated by Anna Richardson. Assisted by her husband Henry, and recalling the pioneer work of Elizabeth Heyrick, Richardson organized the Newcastle Free Produce Association, a women's group of which she was secretary. She published a series of pamphlets and also issued a monthly propaganda sheet, *Illustrations of American Slavery*, distributed free to newspaper editors. Anna Richardson's pamphlet, *To the Friend of the Slave in Great Britain*, attracted the attention of the Birmingham Ladies' Negro's Friend Society, many of whose members belonged to the Quaker women's network.

For rank-and-file abolitionists, unlike leading Quakers and Unitarians, American politics and movements seemed remote, and free produce principles provided a guide for practical action. Using the Quaker network, the Birmingham society established a country-wide chain of free produce committees, which defined the movement as one of politically non-aligned moral reform. Like their menfolk, the women were ardent free-traders and were convinced that, with sufficient demand, free labour textiles would prove as cheap and varied as goods made from slave-grown cotton. Manufacturers in general were sceptical, but a number of firms, predominantly run by Quakers, were persuaded to use cotton from the West Indies, the Middle East, or small non-slaveholding farmers in the southern United States, and manufacture it into cloth, hosiery, underwear and other goods stamped with a free labour symbol. The movement was on a smaller scale than the earlier one against West Indian produce, but the black American Presbyterian minister, Henry Highland Garnet, toured Britain to publicize the venture, and the Richardsons established a new monthly mouthpiece, the *Slave*. They also enlisted the support of the American, Elihu Burritt, who frequently toured Britain promoting peace, temperance and anti-slavery, through his League of Universal Brotherhood.

Despite its name, Burritt's League was open to both sexes, although women were channelled into separate Olive Leaf Circles, consisting of 'ladies of the first rank of the middle class and all trained in benevolent enterprises'. Olive Leaf Circles corresponded with each other, similar groups in Europe and America, and Burritt. They arranged bazaars and collected money, and attracted young idealistic middle-class women, especially, although not exclusively Quakers, whose activities, like those of evangelical women, were restricted to the 'private sphere'. A central Olive Leaf Circle was founded in London with an Anglican, Mrs Bessie Inglis as treasurer and general administrator. Encouraged by Henry Highland Garnet's tour, by the close of 1850, the one hundred and fifty Circles had joined the network of free produce committees. Harriet Beecher Stowe and her husband Calvin Stowe, visiting Britain in 1852 following the publication of *Uncle Tom's Cabin*, endorsed a free produce pledge similar to the temperance pledge.

The central offices of the Olive Leaf Circle became a free labour depot or warehouse supplying local groups too small to deal direct with manufacturers of free labour goods. Run by Bessie Inglis, the central depot sold goods direct to customers and also distributed hundreds of samples to prospective customers who then ordered direct from the manufacturers. At Street in Somerset, the Olive Leaf Circle organized a free produce store in the local temperance hall, leading roles being taken by women from the Quaker Clark family. Similar depots existed in other cities and towns, though many were short-lived. The free produce movement probably peaked about 1854, when Anna Richardson withdrew from an active role because of his husband's ill-health, and Burritt gradually became involved in grandiose and unviable schemes to obtain a regular supply of free labour cotton. Supply had proved unreliable and expensive, and manufacture more costly than commercially produced goods. Some unscrupulous drapers had their shirtings and calicoes stamped 'warranted free labour goods' and this type of deception disgusted and disillusioned many supporters.

Yet the free produce movement continued, the Birmingham Ladies' Negro's Friend Society remaining loyal to the principle until the Civil War. Condemned as impractical and irrelevant by Garrisonians, other abolitionists thought free produce activity particularly appropriate for women. Quakers, especially, favoured reform work emphasizing peace, sobriety and moral control and improvement. Although small-scale, the movement involved the time, energy and commitment of dozens of women. While its major emphasis was the moral power of the housewife, it focused, too, on women's power as consumers, widening the horizons of their role and keeping them in touch with other women and with more radical feminist ideas. At the private meetings of the Olive Leaf Circles, for example, feminism was discussed along with other radical reforms.[97]

Publication of *Uncle Tom's Cabin* and Harriet Beecher Stowe's visit to Britain in 1852-3 raised popular anti-slavery feeling to its highest level for a decade. Mrs Stowe attended many public meetings where her husband or brothers spoke, speaking herself only in private meetings of women. She was fêted by the aristocracy and the Stafford House Address appeared under upper-class sponsorship. Signed by more than half a million British women, it embodied a form of gradualist abolition more concerned with the dangers of emancipation than the right of slaves to be free. Most support for Harriet Beecher Stowe and the Address came from outside the organized anti-slavery movement.[98] Many Garrisonians dismissed the event as 'sentimental excitement', promoted by political conservatives with little sympathy for American democracy or radical social and political reforms. Abolitionists argued that some people had supported the Address as a form of anti-Americanism and that many more, especially women, had signed out of romantic pity for the slave.[99]

British abolitionists nevertheless attempted to harness the publicity generated by Harriet Beecher Stowe's visit: those allied to the British and Foreign Society, through the promotion of free produce for example, and Garrisonians by publication of the *Anti-Slavery Advocate*.[100] An anti-slavery conference in London, in November 1854, was attended by abolitionists of all parties. The Garrisonians insisted that two women were seated as delegates, but the Conference refused a vote of praise for Garrison's American Anti-Slavery Society, and conflict between the two wings of the British movement was exacerbated.[101] The Garrisonians continued to send to Britain ultra-radicals such as Parker Pillsbury, who was most successful with British vegetarians and 'universal reformers', where amongst others he could advocate the 'cause of woman in her condition'. But his fierce anti-clericalism, support for a whole range of radical reforms and apparent lack of social skills, made his visit as divisive of abolitionism as John A. Collins's, more than a decade before.[102] Less abrasive Garrisonians, like James Miller McKim of Pennsylvania, reached a slightly wider audience, mainly composed of Quakers and Unitarians.[103]

Garrisonian organizations became dispirited, questioning the utility of their efforts for the Boston Bazaar. Bristol and Clifton Ladies' Society feared it was becoming an isolated clique, viewed with suspicion by many evangelicals and orthodox Quakers.[104] Conventions still surrounding women in British society also rendered them comparatively powerless within the movement. At the close of 1853, the illness of John Estlin brought much of their work to a halt because they could find no other 'gentleman' to assist in organizing public meetings and other events 'beyond the scope of a ladies' society.[105] In Edinburgh, similarly, the efficacy of the Ladies' Emancipation Society was challenged by the formation of a 'Christian Anti-Slavery Society' for women, leaving Eliza Wigham and other radical women isolated. This new organization was largely composed of evangelical women from the United Presbyterian and Free Churches, and was part of the wider campaign against Garrisonians as 'godless anarchists'.[106] Such views were given new intensity by the interest of evangelicals in the American religious revivals of the late 1850s, dismissed by Garrisonians as further evidence that America was a religious but not a Christian country.[107]

Evangelicals replied in kind through writers like Isabella Bird (later Bishop), already popular as the author of *The Englishwoman in America*. In her *Aspects of Religion in the United States*, Bird emphasized the strength of evangelical Christianity. Although believing that hundreds of thousands of slaves were contented and happy, she favoured abolition on moral grounds, but its organization was to be in the hands of the evangelical clergy. Bird devoted considerable space to an attempt to destroy the reputation of the Garrisonians as serious abolitionists, arguing that they advocated revolution and dissolution of the union of states and should receive no support from the religious public in Britain. She also used the Garrisonian support of feminism to discredit radical abolitionism, in her caricature description of a visit to an anti-slavery meeting in a 'dark and dingy old theatre' in Boston:

> The gentlemen generally wore very long beards and very long hair, divided in the middle and frequently trained into elaborate ringlets which fell over the shoulders. The ladies were singularly ill-favoured, and all had long ago discarded any pretensions to youth or beauty. . . . Five Bloomers, in a costume which neither youth nor beauty could render picturesque failed to attract much attention. Many of the ladies, in-

cluding the Bloomers, belonged to the Women's Rights Society and con-
tended for perfect equality with the "lords of creation".

After more in this style, Bird linked the Garrisonians with the radical
Unitarian, Theodore Parker, whom she accused of advocating marriage
as a temporary contract which could be easily broken. Such accusations
concerning the ideas and morality of radical abolitionists and feminists
were refuted and regarded as gross prejudice by the groups of British
women who had close contacts with American feminists.[108]

By the late 1850s, many women abolitionists were increasingly active
in movements for promoting women's education and political and legal
rights in Britain. A younger generation of women like Barbara
Bodichon had grown up in a radical Unitarian, Quaker and abolitionist
milieu and absorbed the view that anti-slavery and women's rights were
interrelated:

> Slavery is a greater injustice, but it is allied to the injustice to women so
> closely that I cannot see one without thinking of the other and feeling
> how soon slavery would be destroyed if right opinions were entertained
> upon the other question.

During her American tour in 1857-8, Barbara Bodichon met not only
abolitionists like Theodore Parker, 'the noblest preacher in the world',
but also feminists – women doctors, lecturers and newspaper editors.
Although sympathetic to Garrisonian abolitionism, women like
Bodichon were only peripherally involved in the limited activities of the
small number of radical women's anti-slavery groups that survived in
Britain.[109] Even the loyalty of these groups and leaders like Mary Estlin
and Eliza Wigham was tried, when in 1858, Maria Weston Chapman
suddenly announced that the Boston Bazaar, for which British women
had laboured so long, had outlived its usefulness and direct financial
contributions to abolitionism were required.[110]

In spite of such discouragement, the few surviving Garrisonian
women's groups in Britain benefited from the growing political tension
in the United States which focused public attention on the slavery
question. After the divisive effects of Parker Pillsbury's British tour,
Garrisonian women's groups were wary of visiting radicals, and found
it difficult to promote public meetings under their own auspices. Yet
they needed to compete with the growing number of 'Christian'
women's anti-slavery organizations, often associated with the British
and Foreign Society, which sponsored a stream of black and white
American abolitionists.[111] British Garrisonians were able to invite over
Sarah Remond, a free black woman whose family had long been
involved in abolitionism. Black American women had spoken to British

women's groups and at parlour meetings, and at least one black woman preacher had conducted services in Methodist chapels.[112] But Sarah Remond was the first black woman to undertake a public lecture tour in Britain on the slavery question. Although sponsored by British radicals and friends of Garrison, Remond attracted support from many women's groups associated with the British and Foreign Society. She avoided old controversies, although disliking the aid given by the more conservative women's free produce groups to projects promoting the colonization of American blacks in West Africa.[113]

Remond was a feminist and a friend and protegée of Maria Weston Chapman. Her closest associates in Britain were largely radicals and Unitarians. At the close of her tour she became a student at Bedford College, boarding with the founder, Elizabeth Reid. Her career was publicized by feminists in the *English Woman's Journal*, and in an autobiography which she published at the request of Matthew Davenport Hill, and his daughter Rosamond, the Unitarian reformers.[114] In her lectures, Sarah Remond spoke about the plight of slave women and their families, the eight hundred thousand 'mulattoes' who were the 'fruits of licentiousness', and the high price as concubines commanded by pale-skinned female slaves. The publicity value of her sex and colour and her schedule of public lecturing – sometimes three times a week to audiences of two thousand – guaranteed that the tour was widely reported not only in anti-slavery magazines but in the general press.[115] Remond emphasized the extent of colour prejudice in the United States, and was quick to exploit publicity from the discriminatory treatment she and her sister received, travelling on the Cunard Line to Britain. Perhaps the widest press coverage she obtained was when the American Embassy in London refused to visa her passport, which it claimed should not have been issued, since Negroes could not be citizens of the United States! The long correspondence with American officials which followed was reprinted in many papers generally hostile to the United States on the slavery issue.[116] While in Britain, middle-class American blacks like Remond encountered much less racial prejudice than in the United States, and American visitors were often critical of the extent of interracial friendships and even marriage. Yet by the 1860s, a new style of 'scientific' racism, partially imported from America, was sufficient to worry black Americans, and Sarah Remond's friend, William Crafts, attracted much publicity by his attack on it at the British Association meetings of 1863.[117]

Apart from Sarah Remond, the most active woman abolitionist in Britain on the eve of the American Civil War was Julia Griffiths. After working with Douglass in America, Griffiths returned to Britain in

1855. With the aid of the British and Foreign Anti-Slavery Society, the Birmingham Ladies' Negro's Friend Society and influential Nonconformists, she founded or revived at least fourteen ladies' groups. One of these was the Edinburgh New Ladies' Anti-Slavery Society, which left in isolation the older Garrisonian group in the city.[118] The new or revived groups pledged to raise between £5 and £25 a year for Douglass's paper, and contribute goods for the Rochester bazaar until, like the Garrisonians, they found it more profitable to hold local fairs and send the money to America. Griffiths increased the number of subscribers to *Frederick Douglass' Paper* to the point where it became feasible to print a special monthly edition for shipment to Britain. Many of the anti-slavery groups with which she was involved consisted of only two or three dozen women each and were sponsored by evangelical churches, but their activities were encouraged by the crescendo of events leading to the Civil War.[119] Frederick Douglass visited Britain in 1859-60, staying in Halifax with Julia Griffiths (now Mrs Crofts), and lecturing throughout Yorkshire on current American politics and the slavery issue. His frequent clashes with the Garrisonians helped to fuel British interest. Ladies' Associations supporting Douglass existed in many major towns by 1860 and they worked in co-operation with the surviving free labour groups and the British and Foreign Anti-Slavery Society.[120]

Julia Crofts's views of women's role were mentioned earlier, and unlike Sarah Remond she was not a public speaker, but Douglass supported women's rights and had spoken in favour of women's suffrage at the Seneca Falls Convention in 1848.[121] In general, however, it appears that even at this late stage of abolitionism, non-Garrisonian women's groups in Britain remained closer to the evangelical notions of what was fit work for women. In Sheffield, for example, the revived Ladies' Anti-Slavery Society dwelt heavily on the question of slavery as a sin and on Douglass as a 'man of high Christian character' recommended by many evangelical ministers. The women emphasized that they had no intention of involving themselves with the politics of slavery or 'meddling' in American affairs. Their aims were more modest and befitting to women:

> We hope that by exciting sympathy for the slave, and diffusing an intelligent healthy moral sentiment concerning slavery in our own humber sphere . . . we may assist in gradually producing corresponding feelings in the Western world especially among professors of religion.[122]

Many women abolitionists followed closely the events of the American Civil War, impatient at the slowness of the North to abolish slavery. The Emancipation Proclamation of 1863, stirred surviving British women's anti-slavery societies into action promoting organizations to aid freed slaves. Although Garrisonians like Mary Estlin and Eliza Wigham were prominent in this movement, it took on many of the characteristics of the conservative style of abolitionism.[123] The Birmingham Ladies' Negro's Friend Society, the free produce circles and the 'Christian' anti-slavery societies did much to initiate the establishment of Freedmen's [sic] Aid societies in many cities. However, because this work lay more in the realm of public politics than the moral reform emphasis of the anti-slavery movement had done, it quickly became dominated by men and in many places there were separate ladies' associations. Freedmen's Aid societies aroused more popular interest than previous anti-slavery activity, and much larger sums were raised, a substantial part by women's associations.[124]

Through correspondence, visits and journal subscriptions, radical British women abolitionists took a keen interest in the developing American women's suffrage movement, including the split in 1869 over the tactical question of whether black male suffrage should take precedence over the enfranchisement of women. By this date too, many were involved in British feminism, including women's suffrage organizations and the campaign to repeal the Contagious Diseases Acts and promote 'social purity'. To this campaign women brought the same concern for moral principle which had characterized Garrisonian abolitionism in particular. Social purity was seen by many women (and men) as the 'new abolition movement', and veteran abolitionists involved in women's movement organizations pointed out both how far women had come since being excluded from the World's Anti-Slavery Convention of 1840, and how much further they had to go before they achieved emancipation.[125]

Abolitionism was essentially a movement of moral reform, in which political and economic issues were secondary to the strategy and aims of moral persuasion. It shared this ideology – as well as members and a repertoire of organizational tactics – with many other movements of 'social evangelicalism' in which women played a crucial part. Drawing on their experience in religious and philanthropic work, women developed skills as major fund-raisers, publicists and lobbyists for abolitionism. They emphasized the plight of their own sex at the hands of male slaveowners and overseers, but above all, they defined slavery as a sin calling for immediate emancipation of the slaves, a more radical anti-slavery position than that held by many men. Paradoxically, this 'moral radicalism' was a function of women's location within the 'private' sphere of society where they exercised their role as superior moral guardians of the nation.[126] Until the later part of the century women were largely excluded from the 'public' sphere of politics and religion, in which successful moral reform movements also needed to operate, and also from formal leadership of the anti-slavery movement. With a bourgeois membership drawn largely from amongst Quakers and evangelical Protestants, 'ladies'' anti-slavery groups harnessed traditional women's accomplishments to make goods for sale, but also distributed and produced literature and collected donations. Through their initiative in organizing the boycott of slave-produced goods and the supply and sale of 'free labour' products, anti-slavery women underlined women's role as household organizers, endowing this role with economic as well as moral significance.

In terms of funds raised, pamphlets distributed and general work undertaken, women formed the backbone of the Anglo-American abolitionist movement. With emancipation achieved in British colonies, British women provided an abolitionist model for their American sisters, but in a situation where slavery and racial prejudice were more central, American women faced greater opposition to their anti-slavery activity. Out of this opposition, and in a more democratic and fluid society, they developed ideas linking slavery with women's oppression, an ideology which grew more slowly within the relatively constrained atmosphere of the British anti-slavery movement. By 1840, that movement was already in decline, and for the next twenty years women's involvement consisted mostly of moral and financial support to American women's anti-slavery groups. American Garrisonianism, with its links to a wide range of ultra-radical causes, including free thought and religious unorthodoxy, attracted only a minority of British Unitarians and radical Quakers, and alienated evangelical Christian women's anti-slavery groups. It is misleading however, to draw sharp distinctions between radical women abolitionists, with their extensive correspondence and personal links with American feminists, and quietist groups of Quaker and evangelical women working in a limited and conventional way: in their private discussions and parlour meetings, they too, discussed women's rights.

The anti-slavery movement drew upon ideas and beliefs of a wider liberal humanitarianism as well as religious evangelicalism, but also upon more radical ideas held by numbers of Nonconformists, Quakers and Unitarians, concerning the perfectibility of individuals and social institutions. Within this radical milieu, parallels were drawn between the unfree Negro and other oppressed groups, including women.[127] Some women active within anti-slavery articulated explicitly feminist views concerning their role within the movement and outside. Other women, mostly motivated by evangelical Christian views, believed that women had an important moral and practical role within the movement but one which did not overstep the bounds of the private and domestic.

We cannot say that in some simple way women's anti-slavery involvement was a stage in the evolution of a separate feminist movement. Indeed, it could be argued that much of it reinforced their confinement within the private sphere. But as other papers in this collection show, throughout the nineteenth century this sphere was in fact widening, or at least its boundaries were frequently blurred enough for women to legitimize their involvement in non-traditional activities. Thus, feminism did draw upon the more radical elements of abolitionist ideology, and the experience of a network of women working within the reform milieu. In this sense, as later feminists recognized, the activities of their mothers, grandmothers and aunts in the anti-slavery movement laid the foundations of feminism.

4

'A Moral Engine'? Feminism, Liberalism and the *English Woman's Journal*

Jane Rendall

The *English Woman's Journal* was launched in March 1858 and lasted only six years. George Eliot regretted its mediocrity. The *Saturday Review* lambasted its feminism. The leading editor of the *Journal*, Bessie Rayner Parkes, however, looking back, saw its achievement differently: for the periodical, at the heart of a new range of women's campaigns and activities, 'had threaded the separate parts of the movements, brought the thinkers and the workers together'.[1] The origins, the politics and the decline of the *Journal* suggest in miniature some of the difficulties which middle-class women in mid-Victorian England could face, as they attempted to define, and to organize around their own needs. The *Journal* can, rightly, be seen as representing a 'liberal feminism', rooted in political individualism and political economy, a near contemporary of John Stuart Mill's *Subjection of Women* (1869). Yet to leave it at that would be to ignore the divergent experiences of nineteenth-century middle-class men and women, and their consequences.[2]

The founders of the *Journal*, Bessie Rayner Parkes and Barbara Leigh Smith Bodichon, came from that progressive and dissenting strand of middle-class political opinion which was at the centre of liberal political organization. Joseph Parkes, Bessie's father, had been a leading Radical in the 1830s, a most effective political manager, who in the 1850s still closely watched the political world. Her mother was the granddaughter of Joseph Priestley. Parkes was in touch with the manufacturing circles of Birmingham and the West Midlands, and was equally an old friend of the elderly radical Lord Brougham, who in 1857 presided over the founding of the reforming National Association for the Promotion of Social Science (NAPSS). Benjamin Leigh Smith, a radical MP like his father, supported actively and financially a range of progressive causes.

Both men were Unitarians: the Unitarian network which included the Parkes and Leigh Smith families was wide, including Harriet Martineau; William Johnson Fox, the Unitarian preacher, writer and radical MP; Samuel Courtauld, Essex silk manufacturer, and his relative, the radical politician Peter Alfred Taylor and his wife Clementia Taylor.[3] Such was the background from which the *English Woman's Journal*, like so much other feminist activity of mid-Victorian England, emerged.

The *English Woman's Journal* grew out of the friendship and shared political commitment of Bessie Rayner Parkes and Barbara Leigh Smith Bodichon. They came from similar social worlds: they had been intimate friends since 1847. Within that friendship they had explored their own concern and frustrations at their situation as young women, at first through letters, diaries, unpublished novels, all of which reflect a desire for occupation and action. They had jointly embarked on journalism in local papers and radical periodicals. Later they offered each other support, as Bessie committed herself to the writing of poetry, and Barbara to the serious study of art. Their friendship had been, and continued to be a close one, expressed often in the early years in passionate and emotional terms. As Lilian Faderman and Martha Vicinus have suggested, for these middle-class young women, barred from almost all friendly relationships before marriage with the opposite sex, fulfilment and self-expression came through their relations with other women.[4] Bessie Parkes's family was conventionally strict and she was never free to spend time alone with a man, even a potential suitor: she remembered her home life as one of 'conventual exclusion'.[5] She wrote in 1854 to Samuel Blackwell, a cousin of Elizabeth Blackwell, of the difficulties of a possible marriage:

> in all these years we have scarcely since 1847 been alone together, so as to gain that confidential knowledge of the intimacies of character which occurs with friends of the same sex. Nor have you seen me among my personal friends where I am quite free to speak and act.[6]

She was able to use her energies and find satisfaction only in the company of her many women friends. Such commitment to female friendship lasted throughout her unmarried life, perhaps later.

Given the family tradition of political activism, neither woman was content at exclusion from public debate. By 1854, Bessie had published her *Remarks on the Education of Girls*, and Barbara had studied the legal situation of women, on which she published the *Brief Summary* in 1854. In 1855 the two formed a committee to submit a petition on the legal position of married women to the Commons. They were aided by

Lord Brougham and the Law Amendment Society. The petition failed, yet it had demonstrated the possibilities of determined campaigning and organization.[7] Both women were influenced by the writer Anna Jameson, whose *Sisters of Charity and Communion of Labour* was republished in 1856 with a new introduction. Anna Jameson for a time played an almost maternal role in the lives of the two women: she advised Bessie Parkes on her poetry, counselled both of them on the Commons petition, and discussed new philanthropic ideas with them. Her arguments were for the expansion of women's sphere into the public life of the nation through the 'communion of labour' of complementary male and female responsibilities, and the acceptance of a single moral standard. She found the ideas of Bessie Parkes and Barbara Leigh Smith on marriage and divorce often too radical, but continued to offer help and advice in their work until her death in 1860.[8]

Between 1855 and 1857 there were also important changes in the personal lives of the two women. Their friendship was a unique one which lasted throughout their lives: but it was not exclusive. By 1857 Bessie Parkes had come to know in particular two women who were to play an important part in the *Journal*. One was Matilda Mary Hays, actress, novelist, translator of the works of George Sand, whom Bessie first met probably in 1855 in London in the company of Charlotte Cushman, the American actress. Hays had been for some time the companion of Cushman, but their differing abilities, and perhaps Hays's personality meant that the association was coming to an end. Bessie Parkes called Matilda 'Matthew' or 'Max', just as she wrote to Barbara Leigh Smith as 'Dear Fellow', or 'Barbarossa'. From 1855 to 1857 the friendship grew in London, and in Rome in 1857, on Bessie's visit there, especially in the circle around the studio of Harriet Hosmer, the American sculptress.[9] No letters between the two have survived: but to Barbara Bessie wrote in August 1855 of her 'greatest love' for 'Matthew', and in July 1856 she wrote to Barbara of 'one of the very happiest evenings of my whole life', spent with Matilda Hays.[10]

Another, very different, woman drawn into Bessie Parkes's circle of close friends was Mary Merryweather, Quaker, philanthropist, nurse. Since 1847 Mary Merryweather had been involved in philanthropic work for Ellen and Samuel Courtauld among women and men who worked in the silk mills of Halstead, in schools, a creche and a home for working women. Bessie Parkes visited Halstead, and from 1856 the two were in correspondence, as Bessie travelled and wrote. In 1857, while in Algiers with Barbara, Bessie wrote to Mary of the struggle that it had been to leave her, of how much she missed her and wanted to give her hugs and 'a shower of kisses'. She wrote of her gratitude to Mary, who had identified herself with Bessie's interests, supported and stimulated her in her work.[11] From Mary Merryweather, she learned about the possibilities of philanthropy and 'sanitary improvement' in a new industrial setting and from 1862 in Liverpool where Mary, a trained Nightingale nurse, was employed by the Unitarian William Rathbone to superintend a nurses' training school.

The network of interested friends was growing rapidly. Maria Rye, daughter of a London solicitor, had in 1855 become the secretary of the campaign to amend the Married Women's Property Acts. Adelaide Anne Procter, a minor poet, had been a friend of Bessie Parkes and Barbara Leigh Smith, since the early 1850s.[12] And in October 1856 on a visit to Edinburgh, Bessie Parkes met Isa Craig, orphaned daughter of an Edinburgh hosier, and a writer of poetry and journalism. They noticed a periodical called the *Waverley Journal*, 'published by ladies for the cultivation of the memorable, the progressive and the beautiful', whose chief editor was an Eleanor Duckworth: the fortnightly paper, annual subscription 10s 2d stamped, was in newspaper format and mainly literary, with some fiction and occasional articles on philanthropy of a strictly Protestant kind. In that month they contributed to the paper, and in 1857 joined the staff of the paper.[13] Bessie Parkes wrote on 'French Algiers', and on the 'Physical Training of Females', and Barbara Leigh Smith also contributed, in February 1857, articles later published as her *Woman and Work* (1857). Extracts from Anna Jameson also appeared.[14] Parkes and Leigh Smith became, however, impatient with the paper's trivialities and low quality, and began negotiations, with money from Barbara Leigh Smith, to purchase it. Bessie Parkes was offered the editorship in April 1857 and by May agreement was reached. Her first issue came out in July.[15] To Barbara, Bessie wrote of her determination to deal 'unsparingly' with 'everything connected with professional life for women'. The new editor saw the paper as a 'Working Woman's Journal':

> In the term "Working Woman" it is intended to include all women who are actively engaged in any labours of brain or hand, whether they be the wives and daughters of landed proprietors, devoted to the well-being of their tenantry, or are to be classed among the many other labourers in the broad field of philanthropy; – whether they belong to the army of teachers, public or private, or to the realms of professional artists; or are engaged in any of those manual occupations by which multitudes of British women, at home and in the colonies, gain their daily bread.
>
> This journal endeavours to collect all facts relative to the important question of Remunerative Employment for Women, and reports upon all legal questions affecting their welfare. It also devotes especial attention to

the great movements of social reform, and partakes of the character of a domestic Magazine, containing Literary Reviews, Fiction, Poetry, and Scientific Papers of a popular character.[16]

Bessie invited Matilda Hays, searching for a new life after parting from Charlotte Cushman, to be involved in the *Waverley Journal* project and at one time hoped that she might become its editor: she wrote poetry for it in the course of 1857, and with Bessie worked for the last months of that year in the small London office at 14A Princes Street, established by September 1857.[17] Isa Craig came to London in the middle of 1857, and became assistant secretary to the new National Association for the Promotion of Social Science. Mary Merryweather wrote a series of articles on factory life in Halstead for the *Waverley*: these articles were published separately, from the Princes St office, as *Experiences of Factory Life* (1857).[18] Unfortunately few copies of the *Waverley Journal* under the new editor can be located: those that have been suggest that it foreshadowed the *English Woman's Journal*, drawing on the same network of friends and contributors, and including an 'Open Council.' But to be editor and not the owner of the paper proved to be unsatisfactory: negotiations for the purchase of the *Waverley*, undertaken by the barrister and reformer George Hastings, with money from Barbara Leigh Smith, failed and its last issues appeared in January 1858. Hastings advised a fresh start with a new journal.[19]

The plans developing were not only for a new and better journal. In January 1857 Bessie had written from Algiers of the possibility of establishing a shop for books and stationery, employing women only, in London. By May the plan had developed further, for Bessie hoped that 'the Waverley can be got chiefly into friendly hands & *brought to London*,' and that 'we can have our own book shop & the beginning of a Club'.[20] She planned to devote herself to this from her return in June. What was involved was deliberately seen as a new co-ordinating centre for women's activities. Already in 1857, at the small office in Princes Street, guaranteed by a 'lady of rank', a small reading room for ladies was established and rapidly became popular, with over seventy subscriptions by 1858.[21] The project was already expanding beyond the periodical.

But these plans required capital and rested on the security of the finance which among this group only Barbara Leigh Smith, whose father had given her an annual income of £300 at twenty-one, and other capital sums, could individually provide. Bessie Parkes had no money of her own until she received a legacy in 1859, nor did the other women, all single, who worked for the *Journal*. In 1856 Barbara Leigh

The mast-head of the *Waverley Journal*, Saturday December 13, 1856.

Smith had met, in Algiers, Eugène Bodichon, whom in July 1857 she married. That was not to exclude her future involvement in all these projects. She was in most years to spend half her time in Algiers, half in England, renewing old friendships and committed to old and new political activities. She was however to be away on an extended honeymoon in the United States from December 1857 to June 1858, at the launching of the new *Journal*. Her financial as well as personal backing was still essential: her interest and support of the *Journal* was constant yet more detached than that of others involved in the daily work.

In contrast to the network of female friendship which created this new centre of activity, the formal history of the *English Woman's Journal* began with the formation under the new limited liability legislation of 1856 and 1857 of the English Woman's Journal Company Ltd. The Company was registered on 13 February 1858, and started with a capital of £1000, issued in 200 share lots.[22] There were the minimum necessary, seven initial shareholders of the first eighty-four shares. Bessie Rayner Parkes and Matilda Hays took five each, Maria Rye one. Anne Leigh Smith, the sister, and in this case to be assumed the representative of Barbara Leigh Smith Bodichon, was the major shareholder and financial support with sixty shares. There were three male shareholders, Samuel Courtauld, the Essex industrialist, who had already shown his interest in feminist activity by contributing to Bedford College, and James Vaughan, barrister, son-in-law of Jacob Bright, held four each: William Strickland Cookson, a leading Lincoln's Inn lawyer of progressive views and Unitarian background held five. Robert Wainewright, Cookson's partner, uncle by marriage of Bessie Parkes, was also present as a witness.'[23] These seven shareholders were the directors of the new company: Cookson was the chairman. The registered office of the company was at 14A Princes St, Cavendish Square, the *Waverley*'s old office. The formal articles of association of the new company laid down, as legally required, the procedures for the election of directors, for the annual meetings of shareholders, for the issue of dividends, and for annual audits. The use of the joint stock company may well have seemed an appropriately collective mode of operation, as well as being a safe way to raise more capital. Bessie Parkes and Barbara Leigh Smith, who read Mill's *Principles of Political Economy* together soon after its first edition in 1849, agreed with his views on the desirability of co-operative organization. Bessie Parkes later wrote:

> Mr Mill alludes to the formation of joint-stock companies, and partnership of various kinds, as becoming possible whenever people become morally capable of working together. The small means and more delicate

physical powers of women may thus be utilized, when each by herself would have failed.[24]

The new company rapidly expanded. By November 1858 the share capital had been doubled to £2000, and William Johnson Fox was appointed auditor. By February 1859 212 of the available 400 shares had been purchased. A new patron had been found. Helena Comtesse de Noailles, a widow, who had given substantial sums to help the medical career of Elizabeth Blackwell, purchased sixty shares.[25] The Courtauld-Taylor influence had grown, as three more family members, Peter Alfred Taylor, Catherine Taylor of Hampstead, and William Taylor of Bocking, Essex held shares. Others holding less than five shares included another Unitarian, Mary Myrtilla Sturch, the sister of Elizabeth Reid, founder of Bedford College; Bella Leigh Smith, Barbara's sister; Eugène Bodichon; and Mary Merryweather. Married women could not, of course, hold shares in their own right. Of twenty-three shareholders, ten were spinsters, two widows, and the rest men of varied professional and commercial interests. By December 1859 another patron, Theodosia Lady Monson, widow of a Tory peer, and an old acquaintance of Matilda Hays, who with her had been active in the Princes St office, had taken for them new and more spacious rooms, making it possible to move from the small office in 14A Princes St to 19 Langham Place where a reading room could be provided, and a focus for associated societies set up. In March 1860 she too was appointed a director: by then 271 shares had been purchased.[26]

Bessie Parkes and Matilda Hays were co-editors, though with Bessie very much in command. More supporters came to help. In November 1858 Emily Faithfull, the daughter of a clergyman, first came to work at the *English Woman's Journal*, before setting up the Victoria Press. Bessie Parkes described her as 'a most hearty young worker . . . who has brought us a host of subscriptions', and as 'rather strong-minded; carried her own huge carpet-bag'.[27] Jessie Boucherett, from a Lincolnshire landed background, first came to London in June 1859 with the deliberate aim, which she immediately discussed with those supporters she found in the reading room, of establishing the Society for Promoting the Employment of Women. Emily Davies first met the group in Langham Place in London in 1859, wrote for the *Journal* from her father's Gateshead parish, and after his death finally settled in London in January 1862.[28] Elizabeth Eiloart, later a prolific novelist, was also a frequent contributor, under the pseudonyms of 'Asterisk' and 'E'. Sarah Lewin was employed as secretary and book-keeper.[29] This group of women, all single except Bodichon, was to create both the *Journal* and a centre for middle-class women's activities. The two are hard to distinguish, and often overlapped with participation in the NAPSS: but here the *Journal* only will be considered, as offering an immediate route to both the politics and the structure of this group of friends and political workers. The editorial direction remained in the hands of Bessie Rayner Parkes: Hays resigned as co-editor in 1862. Parkes was the major single contributor, whose views shaped the policies of the journal. Emily Davies replaced her as editor for about six months from September 1862.[30]

The new monthly periodical retained a mixture of articles, fiction and poetry. Its character, however, had moved a long way from the *Waverley*'s origins as a 'domestic magazine'. Parkes saw it as 'a special periodical' by which she meant one which had an avowedly political purpose. In recalling the origins of the paper she stressed not its radicalism, but its breadth, never excluding diversity of opinion. As editor, the only subject she had refused to contemplate was the suffrage – as an impracticable aim. The *Journal* had originally been supported by those committed 'to investigate the great mass of female misery and indigence existing in England'. She believed such a journal should have an '*organic* character', 'not a mere machine used for the purposes of propaganda', to be 'worked out not by one but by many, under a certain supervision by one'. It provided a way of working together in an unpopular cause, in 'a humble but ceaseless struggle', by its nature one distinguished from the rest of the periodical press.[31] Barbara Bodichon thought that Bessie Parkes had a wildly exaggerated sense of the importance of her work. Bessie wrote to her:

> you were not judging fairly of the success of my work in the Journal and consequently of the changes of the Woman Cause here. It will probably *never* take in England the form of an abstract adhesion to justice & equality between man & woman, because such a form is wholly opposed to the very genius of our national intellect, but in practical results it is maturing & extending every day. . . .
>
> On all hands we have letters & testimonials of our success, new subscriptions thick as blackberries, & every reason to think that the judicious path has been chosen.

She believed that there was 'a deal of strong feeling gradually rising' to support their cause. Barbara Bodichon wrote to George Eliot, who agreed, that she was unconvinced by Bessie's 'pure enthusiasm'.[32]

The *Waverley Journal* had declared itself a journal for working women: and the outstanding characteristic of the *English Woman's Journal* is its driving concern with middle-class women's need for occupation and activity. Employment was the key issue of the periodical: associated were the necessity of education and training, and commitment to the philanthropic responsibilities of women. These themes were inseparable, yet raised further issues. The *Journal* had to consider the appropriate sexual division of labour between men and women, and face the issue of the employment of married women. The issue of class was inescapable. What employment might a 'lady' properly take, and how far could such a term have any relevance in the market-place? And how far did these feminists accept the gospel of industrial progress, and the science of political economy, so much a part of their own liberal middle-class background?

In a series of leading articles, Bessie Parkes spelt out the need for the widening of opportunities for middle-class women. Her policies were echoed by the work of Jessie Boucherett, and the Society for the Promotion of the Employment of Women (SPEW), founded in 1859, though their emphases were sometimes different. The first article of the *Journal*, on 'The Profession of the Teacher', pointed to the overstocked market in governesses, their poor qualifications, and their destitution in old age: all well-worn themes. The remedy was for young women of the middle classes 'the daughters of our flourishing tradesmen, our small merchants and manufacturers' to enter into the occupations of their class. One obstacle lay in their sense of caste:

> women will not manage washing and sewing machines, work electric telegraphs, keep tradesmen's books, or set up shops, so long as they think, and so long as society enforces the idea, that by so doing they forfeit caste and are rendered unfit to associate with "ladies" though their fathers, brothers and prospective husbands may each and all be engaged in some form of business.

The *Journal* constantly tried to enlarge the appropriate range of occupations for middle-class women, attempting to convince its readers that 'their social caste is dependent on what they are, and not on the occupation on which they may happen to be engaged'.[33] The writers, and certainly the readers, of the *Journal* found the topic of class unavoidable. A letter, perhaps a planted one, from 'A West End House-keeper' in 1861 suggested that paid employment of any kind was incompatible with the status of a 'lady'. The editorial reply, acknowledging the 'tender susceptibilities' which gathered around 'the word "lady" and the public and private estimation of woman's work', attempted to locate the origins of such feelings, in the mixing of two social worlds. In the landowning classes, in the army and Church, rank was absolutely defined: in the new world of manufacture such exclusiveness was rejected, yet the middle classes still adopted the practice and the vocabulary of classes above them. The advice of the writer is '*forget it*': for working women should create 'their own caste, their own social guild'. Yet Parkes also, clearly torn, wrote with great sympathy of the aspirations to gentility and refinement of women who came to Langham

Place looking for work. Their aspirations were not, she felt, in the light of their upbringing, altogether ignoble.[34]

While attempting to shift such perceptions of status, Parkes took care to fit such new kinds of employment to the separate constraints of gender. Following Anna Jameson, she set out the kinds of work which women might do in taking responsibility for the supervision and care of other women in institutions, in hospitals, prisons, reformatories, workhouses. In factories too there was an urgent need for the superintendence of working women by educated women. Yet even such employment would not be sufficient: young women had to enter the world of their class, the occupations of commerce and trade. Their fathers, as guardians and ratepayers, and as employers, had to be persuaded to recognize the needs of daughters, for work, for education and training, even for capital. Even in such circumstances, there would still be the need for separate conditions for young middle-class women, for the right 'moral tone':

> We must, therefore, exercise a little common sense in arranging all those workshops and offices in which girls work, and we must invariably associate them with older women; they must in all cases work in companies together and not intermixed with men, and so long as they are young they must be under some definite charge.[35]

The *Journal* was not concerned only with the range of employment which middle-class women, once educated, might undertake. The paper carried much material throughout its six years on the situation of needlewomen and seamstresses in London and elsewhere, and addressed itself to the overstocking of this market as it did that of governesses. Again as Barbara Bodichon had done in *Women and Work* (1857), the *Journal* recommended proper training so that women might acquire appropriate skills. SPEW aimed to help provide such skills. Jessie Boucherett wrote of the occupations which working-class women were prevented from entering, by their ignorance, and by prejudice against female employment. Work in shops, clerical work, semi-skilled manual work such as watch-making, jewellery work, and china-painting: all might help to free women from reliance on needlework. In a letter Bessie Parkes raised the possibility of women printers, one to be put in operation in 1860 by Emily Faithfull and the women compositors of the Victoria Press.[36] In a paper given to SPEW, though read not by her but by the male Vice-President, Parkes explored two problems:

> For what employments are women fitted by nature? and How is it possible to introduce them practically into new and remunerative spheres of labour?

In answer to the first question, she suggested that 'all the mechanical arts which demand perception and skill rather than strength' were suitable for women of average ability from the lower and middle classes. She included under such a heading some departments of all the major trades: metal works, nail factories, paper mills, and the more obvious tasks such as hairdressing, engraving, jewellery making. Again, work-shops should be organized so as to meet the needs of women workers, through rooms with 'female overseers' and hours of work adapted. By such means women might be persuaded into new arts and trades: though masculine opposition might still remain to be overcome.[37] Such a policy was followed at the Victoria Press, as those areas of work which did not require strength were taken by working-class women, supervised by Emily Faithfull and those few women she could find trained in printing. Of course, the commonest occupation of young working-class women was domestic service: and the importance and need of formal training for young girls in domestic service was by no means ignored in the *Journal*. Correspondents frequently raised the problem of recruiting good servants, and showed some nervousness that creating new areas of employment for women could hardly be in the interest of a middle-class readership. While accepting its importance, editorial policy did not stress this option for young working-class women, though it did emphasize the responsibilities of mistresses towards their servants.[38]

In exploring what occupations women were suited for, the *Journal* inevitably faced the accusation, from readers and hostile reviewers, that it was diverting women of all classes from properly domestic concerns. That accusation was rebutted in Parkes's article on 'Domestic Life'. She made it clear that questions relating to the life of home and family, 'the primary element of all true social life' were not seen as the subject matter of the *Journal*. But she never intended to challenge the primary commitment of married women to their families. Still there were employments, especially in literature and the arts, which middle-class women, depending on domestic servants, had undertaken and might continue to do. Above all, their obligation to social and philanthropic responsibilities was still present. The argument that young women were diverted from learning their domestic responsibilities was less tolerated: Parkes suggested that the reluctance of well-to-do young women to undertake any manual work should be reconsidered: 'our daughters would be immensely benefitted for being obliged to work in the house'. They should be able to choose professional occupations, or to take up domestic chores cheerfully. Marriage could be viewed, as the French saw it, as a working partnership to which each partner brought capital, the woman in the form of her dowry: this, though mercenary, was in many ways more effective than the view prevalent among the English middle classes reflecting a 'political economy which would throw the livelihood of all wives upon the earnings of all husbands'. A third viewpoint, using the same economic metaphor, was that 'the woman's power of household management is her natural capital': and this was clearly Parkes's preferred view.

It was, too, that which could be said to be true for the lower classes, in which 'the actual and constant superintendence' by wife and mother had a monetary as well as moral value.[39] The *Journal* reported as a matter of fact the widespread employment of working-class mothers away from home, whether as seamstresses in a London warehouse, in the Courtaulds' silk mills in Halstead, or in the factories of the north and midlands. Given that fact, different employments should be thrown open to them. The *Journal* regarded such employment, however, as an evil to be avoided, and one which it was the task of philanthropy to mitigate. Jessie Boucherett, for instance, pointed to the ways in which the temperance movement could help to increase the proportion of male wages reaching the working-class wife, making it less necessary for her to work, and leaving female occupations to the single.[40] Increasingly, Bessie Parkes came to condemn the work of married women outside the home. Writing of France, she commended the usual provision for female supervision in workshops, but condemned the widespread work of married women and the customary wetnursing of infants there. In her survey of the condition of working women in both Britain and France, and in her review of Jules Simon's *L'Ouvrière* (1861) she pointed to the similar effects, moral and material, of industrialization on family life in both countries. It was not feminists, but 'a mighty and all-pervading power, the power of trade' which took married women from their homes.[41]

By mid-1862 Parkes had begun to retreat a little from her earlier strong commitment to the opening up of new occupations. She stated that 'she never wished or contemplated the mass of women becoming breadwinners'. Her support for the Victoria Press had rested on its distinctive superintendence by a woman. She would not wish to see women working with men in printing offices under male supervision. The majority of women would always look to family life as their future; working women would be a minority. Yet these views were not those of all her colleagues. Emily Faithfull, in a letter to the paper, openly dissented: she was not prepared to view marriage as an inevitable destiny. She wished to see women, of all classes, with sufficient training and judgement in everyday affairs to have the choice of marriage. Moreover the work of household management should be seen and defended, as work, and that could best be done by raising the level of women's independence:

> every woman should be free to support herself by the use of whatever faculties God has given her. In this career I ask no favor for her because she is a woman, I ask only that she should not be obstructed, and that she should be paid for her labour the same wages that a man would be paid for the same work equally well done. When this position is attained the next will easily follow: that economical employments should be acknowledged to be as tenable a ground of independence as any other occupation. We should not then have a multitude of women working hard and efficiently and yet regarded as unproductive by those for whom they work.[42]

Jessie Boucherett too continued to advocate admitting 'women freely into all employments suitable to their strength', allowing the labour market to adjust itself. If men were more suited than women to the hard labour involved in the colonizing of new territories, then it should be young men who emigrated first, while women found their work at home among occupations previously perhaps done by men.[43] These differences between contributors point to underlying conflicts within the *Journal*.

The logical accompaniment of the argument for expanding employment lay in improved education and practical training for women of all classes. The leading contributors to the *Journal* all pointed, often from personal experience, to the poverty of middle-class women's education. Most contributors and correspondents rejected the view that women's education was desirable simply for its enhancement of a cultivated life. There could be no doubt of its fundamental importance for future employment.[44] Bessie Parkes surveyed the few existing colleges for girls. One contributor quoted the important work of John Duguid Milne, *Industrial and Social Employment of Women* (1857), on the gulf between the mental worlds of men and women, educated so differently, in those classes.[45] Both Barbara Bodichon and Jessie Boucherett pointed to the inequity of endowments for boys and girls of the middle classes across the country, and the need for an equivalent to the many grammar schools for boys. In such schools the younger girls should receive a good general education and the older ones learn appropriate skills for future employment, such as book-keeping.[46] One contributor expressed reservations as to whether examinations should be permitted in girls' schools, but most saw the case for examinations as unanswerable. Emily Davies wrote of her work to gain girls' admittance to local examinations, and ultimately to universities. For her, examinations symbolized the encouragement of girls to steady and orderly learning, and offered them a certificate, an objective measure of achievement, which would be the key to future employment. Ideally, it should not be SPEW which ran classes to introduce women to book-keeping, lawcopying, and basic clerical work: but schools which could offer such training and certification.[47]

Between the kinds of schools recommended here and those appropriate to the majority of women there was seen to be a gulf, not in standards but in social demarcation. The very suggestion that an educated woman might participate in teaching in elementary schools was seen as a daring one. For one contributor, educated women of gentility required quite different training, in separate colleges from those already established.[48] The lack of resources and expectations of girls' education were recognized from the first, in an article 'Why Boys are Cleverer than Girls', which contrasted the teaching of master and mistress in a small village school. Yet a further issue which roused some disagreement lay in the kind of training which such schools could provide: should they concentrate on the acquisition of basic skills – or should they provide a training programme for domestic servants, a training programme in what were misleadingly termed 'industrial skills'? Isa Craig argued that it was not the task of National Schools to create good domestic servants, but to encourage intelligence:

> Industrial practice in schools is an attempt to mix up two things which are quite distinct, to carry on two different trades under one management, and so to lead to the mismanagement of both. The school for lessons, the house for domestic work, appears to us the true principle. The lessons of a girl's school ought to have reference to domestic management, so as to teach on what principle a household should be conducted.

Bessie Parkes added an editorial note of dissent: she felt that there might still be a place for encouraging the 'declining' 'household arts' 'through industrial training'.[49] In these discussions, the need for higher, though still different, standards of education for all classes was maintained: yet the separate education of girls was largely assumed. Co-education was little discussed (though it was practised in the school founded by Barbara Leigh Smith).[50] More attention was given to the separate and domestic needs of working-class than of middle-class women: and it is impossible to separate this from the philanthropic issues raised in the *Journal*.

The social responsibilities of middle-class towards working-class women was a theme of the *Journal* from its first issue, in which 'The Profession of the Teacher' was followed by 'A house of mercy', an article on the London Diocesan Penitentiary for fallen women in

Highgate. The discipline described is not to a modern reader merciful, though it was admired by the author. The editors of the *Journal* were determined not to evade the issue of prostitution: Parkes wrote that the existence of prostitutes daily met on the streets of London was a fact not to be ignored, like the existence of so many working women. Her father, echoed by Anna Jameson, criticized the use, by unmarried women editors, of 'the *disgusting* term' 'prostitute', in a magazine circulating among women of 'delicate sensibilities'.[51] The editors' aim was to encompass not only the outcast and delinquent, inhabitants of workhouses, hospitals, prisons but also those of the factories, schools and cottages of the majority. The *Journal* was committed to Anna Jameson's theme of the 'Communion of Labour', the unity of male and female principles in the social order. Anna Jameson's words were invoked:

> all our endowments for social good, whatever their especial purpose or denomination, education, *sanitary*, charitable, penal – will prosper and fulfil their objects in so far as we carry out the principle of combining in due proportion the masculine and the feminine element, and will fail or become perverted into some form of evil in so far as we neglect or ignore it.[52]

Contributors never doubted that women's role would be a different one from that of men, and that it should be directed primarily to other women.

Many articles offered accounts of individual institutions, as examples of what might be achieved: industrial and ragged schools, cottage hospitals, local refuges. Mary Carpenter wrote of women's involvement in the reformatory movement, Louisa Twining of the necessity for women to become involved in the management of workhouses, Frances Power Cobbe described the 'preventive female mission' to working women in Bristol. Maria Rye gave an account of regular meetings of mothers, organized by a committee of ladies 'for the purpose of instructing them in habits of frugality and cleanliness', in Westminster.[53] The subject to which most editorial attention was given was that of 'sanitary reform': and in a series of articles the influence of Mary Merryweather on her friend Bessie Parkes is clear. Parkes wrote historically on the rise of the public health movement, suggesting that though legislation could undoubtedly reduce mortality, yet 'the grand political agencies of the Parliament with their Acts and their Boards must be narrowed down to a minute domestic application.' This could be done only through detailed domestic instruction given to poor women on cleanliness, on the importance of good water, and healthy habits. Only women could give such instruction:

> We want the action of *women* in every parish: we want the clergyman's
> wife and the doctor's daughter to know the laws of health, and to enforce-
> them in the perpetual intercourse which we hope and believe they main-
> tain with their poorer neighbours.[54]

The squire's wife and the parish nurse – all those in responsible
positions could play a part. Parkes wrote of the new Ladies Sanitary
Association founded in 1857 through the NAPSS, with plans to spread
the 'sanitary' message over the country through local associations,
through tracts and through the work of women able to teach the
domestic laws of health. Home visiting, maternal meetings, and the
distribution of tracts were to be used in a new secular mission. Mary
Merryweather contributed an article on 'Cottage habitations' in 1860,
which suggested what could be done in the cottages, however poor, of
Halstead. Such a cause could mean an onslaught on the absurdities of
women's dress and lack of physical exercise: it could mean careful
instruction on women's physiology, and demands for better housing
and water supplies. But above all it meant a carrying of an understanding of the proper conditions of domesticity to the homes of the poor,
according to contemporary middle-class 'sanitary' standards.[55]

By 1859 the *Journal* was announced, in a meeting at Willis's Rooms
addressed by Charles Kingsley, to be the official organ of the Association, which would continue to print its tracts first in the *Journal*, and
would share the office in 14A Princes St. Parkes had hopes that the
Journal would be able to support Mary Merryweather in a new career
as a missionary in 'a social and sanitary crusade' supporting local
associations to be founded in every town and parish. These ambitious
plans failed, perhaps overextending the workers on the *Journal*, but the
commitment in principle remained.[56] The magazine was sympathetic to
temperance and the movement for 'rational recreation'. It reviewed very
favourably a group of works by women active both in the temperance
movement and in the reforming of 'ragged homes'. Only Jessie
Boucherett wrote of a possible conflict of interest with such reformers,
but even for her such a conflict could be reconciled.[57]

What becomes clearer in the later years of the *Journal* is the
admiration of Bessie Parkes for the philanthropic work conducted in
France. Her detailed accounts of Soeur Rosalie in Paris, of the '*salles
d'asiles*' of Mme Pape-Carpentier, and of Mme Luce in Algiers, all
point to an increasing interest in French practice, and in the mixture of
state supervision and female religious orders.[58] In Paris, she deliberately
sought out information about the state of working-class women in
France: and was impressed by the mixed workhouse and hospital, the
Salpetrière, which she contrasted very favourably with English work-

houses, for its cleanliness, comfort, and female supervision. She visited a Maison de Secours run by Soeurs de Charité, which included a refuge for the aged, and an industrial school for girls, which she greatly admired 'of the kind for which we are crying out in England'. Part of Bessie Parkes's own attraction to the Catholic Church, to which she was formally converted in 1864, lay in its 'active well-ordered charity'.[59] Not all of these French philanthropists were Catholic: but the principle of trained and committed sisterhoods was one with which she strongly sympathized, as did other contributors. A new acquaintance, the Catholic Sarah Atkinson of Dublin, had drawn her attention to new institutions run by Irish religious orders. In 1858 Matilda Hays, following Anna Jameson, had written in an article on Florence Nightingale of the need for a sisterhood of nurses comparable to the Soeurs de Charité. 'A.R.L.' condemned the lack of training among English women compared to sisterhoods abroad.[60] It was a popular theme among correspondents. In 1860 'L' wrote of the growing movement for Anglican sisterhoods, which offered both a philanthropic purpose and a congenial home for single women, and 'A subscriber' suggested an Anglican sisterhood of women of all classes, with at least one-third educated women, to undertake work in a manufacturing town.[61]

Religious differences made explicit discussion difficult, yet 'sister-hoods', whose attraction Martha Vicinus has described, had a profound appeal to those still seeking some kind of separate women's sphere. Parkes asked whether religious orders or sisterhoods, or simply trained nurses, were the more effective in hospital work? This was partly a matter of religious commitment, partly to be judged by success. She compared Anglican and Irish Catholic sisterhoods with those training institutions for nurses which existed in England, which still drew nurses from the same classes as good domestic servants.[62] The issue overlapped with that of women's employment. One contributor proposed a survey of all women formally in paid employment in such work, because of its vital relationship to that question.[63] The writers of the *Journal* accepted that a wide variety of charitable or 'sanitary' activities could offer employment to working-class women. They were less clear on the extent to which middle-class women might enter into such professional capacities: did not sisterhoods offer single women more congenial surroundings and sense of religious mission? Should not married women continue to play a voluntary role?

These dilemmas paralleled others. The writers of the *English Woman's Journal* identified both with their gender and with their class, and inevitably there were conflicts. One lay in their treatment of the contemporary language of political economy, of the supposedly scientific authority of the market-place, orthodox and commonplace in mid-nineteenth-century liberalism. The competitive operation of the free market in labour was crudely invoked against the entry of women into the public sphere and the market-place. Charles Bray, Coventry ribbon manufacturer, had in 1857 read a paper at the NAPSS, later published as the *Industrial Employment of Women* (1857) which argued that the entry of women into the labour market inevitably competed with the labour and depressed the wages of working-class men. The *Saturday Review* labelled the writers of the *English Woman's Journal* ignorant of the laws of political economy which posed an absolute barrier to working women.[64] The charge was one which stung women whose families were from the very heart of middle-class radical politics. Aware of the complexities of the economic issues, the *Journal* turned to sympathetic writers whose work seemed to offer alternative answers, still within the bounds of orthodoxy. The brief references to women's work in John Stuart Mill's *Principles of Political Economy*, and the recent, detailed and attractive work of John Duguid Milne, *The Industrial Employment of Women* (1857) offered such answers.

The *Saturday Review* had charged that 'among all their studies, political economy has not yet presented itself to the reforming ladies'. In a direct reply, the *Journal* put it clearly: other factors besides the strictly economic influenced employers. Custom and prejudice operated:

> The Hindoo will not select the best workman, in spite of the laws of caste; . . . and so the banker will not pick the best bookkeeper in England, if the best bookkeeper should happen to be a woman, since the novelty of a woman-clerk would be likely to startle his customers, In fact, custom and prejudice are at work to exclude us from earning a living.

But the author followed Milne in the argument that the *Review* had its political economy wrong: no economist had argued for a 'fixed quantity' of employment, but rather for a wages fund which, while in the short term a fixed amount, also responded to increased production and profits.[65] Jessie Boucherett, Emily Faithfull, and Bessie Parkes in a number of articles followed Milne, suggesting that the new kinds of employment into which women were entering, were new and specifically female occupations and in no sense competed with or affected male employment.[66] Jessie Boucherett was prepared to face the logical consequence, nevertheless, of a free market in labour. If men and women were in competition, the advocates of women's employment should not accept the burden of suffering, but should stake their own claims. It might be that given such competition, and the readjustment of the labour market, men would have to take their share of hardship, perhaps be driven to emigrate. 'J.T.', too, defended the individual and temporary hardship caused by competition, 'the strongest instinct of our nature', on the grounds of ultimate and lasting good done to all.[67]

Some writers in the *Journal* met critics on their own ground. Some also challenged the exclusive claims to authority made by the science of political economy. Parkes wrote with respect of John Stuart Mill, yet noted inconsistency:

> The great laws which it defines stand up like rocks amidst the wild waves of theory and compel them to retire, yet natures in whom love and reverence predominate insist on supplementing their shortcomings by a higher principle. Nowhere is this tendency more clearly to be discerned than in the writings of John Stuart Mill himself: indeed he occasionally retreats upon the moral intuitions of the human heart in a way that exposes him to censure from those who are willing to push intellectual conclusions to their farthest limits.[68]

Other considerations than those of scientific economics had to enter into debate, where human distress was caused by decisions based on self-interest and the profit motive – as, for instance, the introduction of machinery. For Parkes, the operation of the scientific laws of political economy had to co-exist with Christian moral principles, centred in the personal relations of the domestic economy:

> the more completely society is infused with those ideas which modify the action of purely scientific laws, the easier it will be for women to work without being crushed by its machinery.[69]

Associations and co-operation offered a new kind of employment, which might challenge the harshness of the market. The *Journal* published several articles on the subject. Parkes wrote enthusiastically of Mill's work on co-operation, quoting extensively, especially from his chapter on 'The Probable Futurity of the Labouring Classes', that most influenced by Harriet Taylor. Utopian socialism had failed, she wrote, through its moral atrocities, by which she presumably meant its sexual radicalism. The joint-stock principle, and the new co-operative societies, however, were making headway. Co-operation was, she suggested, particularly suitable for female labour, whether among needlewomen or in a shop. 'M.A.''s 'Outline of a Plan for the Formation of Industrial Associations among Workwomen' in October 1860 was said to embody the principles advocated by Mill, and already proved successful in Rochdale and elsewhere. In 1861 Bessie Parkes discussed with the other members of the Langham Place group the enlarging of their small paper store, already run on shareholding principles into a larger, new co-operative stationery store, managed by and employing women, of the kind suggested in her article on 'The Opinions of John Stuart Mill'. Like many such projects, the idea was too ambitious, but she continued to support the principle in the *Journal*. Some proposals raised looked more like organized philanthropy than co-operation – as did Ellen Barlee's Institution for the Employment of Needlewomen. The dividing line was never clearly drawn.[70]

Not all Parkes's contributors, however, could agree with the opposition posed between political economy and Christian and female responsibilities. In January 1864 an anonymous contributor put the case for economic laws and economic progress as perfectly in accordance with the intentions of the Deity. The general use of the sewing machine, instead of causing ruin, would bring final relief to the poor London dressmakers. Emily Davies, too, was unhappy at contributors 'setting Political Economy at defiance'.[71] The *English Woman's Journal* had to meet an economic orthodoxy which was also a political symbol of middle-class strength: in so doing, they exposed their own differences, as well as those among economists. That mixture of missionary dynamism, of philanthropic commitment, of domestic morality, which arose from the experience of middle-class women, led some feminists to criticize, to doubt the unrelenting achievements of economic expansion, and to hope for different kinds of co-operative alternatives. Others found they could rather accept and deploy the arguments of radicals and economists in their own cause, that of employing, educating, organizing middle-class women.

Practically, however, the *English Woman's Journal* needed to sell. Successive editors wrote to Barbara Bodichon about its financial situation, and the personal, political and religious difficulties of the women involved. By January 1859 Bessie Parkes wrote that they had achieved nearly 400 annual subscriptions, and in addition the sale of about 250 issues a month, as well as back numbers. She felt 'amply satisfied' at the end of the first year's work, and wrote: 'the field of the Journal is just like a rich mine'. That January fifty-seven new subscriptions were received. By November 1859 circulation had risen to over 700.[72] When she attended the annual conventions of the NAPSS she always took a large number of current issues, and gained new subscribers. In January 1860 she still wrote optimistically of their situation. Twelve hundred and fifty copies were printed and their circulation was around 1000 a month, with an allowance of 250 a month for backnumbers. Both circulation and advertisements were rising steadily. In the following year, however, the situation did not look so healthy. Anne Leigh Smith had had to donate or lend £200 to the *Journal*, mostly to be applied to the payment of contributors. By April 1862 the circulation was still at around 1000 subscribers, but Bessie Parkes was worried:

> The Journal makes me anxious what to do for the best; the conditions of
> the periodical market have quite changed in the past 4 years. it has
> become the great field for *speculation*, each journal pitted against the
> other which shall buy the cleverest article; at the same time, the trade is
> very uncertain; the circulations of the different serials rise & fall, and it
> has become a race which seems to be unwholesome & foolish, & with
> which I cannot possibly cope.[73]

Emily Davies, who took over in September 1862, was also worried, for
a variety of reasons. She wrote a series of lengthy and detailed letters on
the finances and future of the *Journal* to Barbara Bodichon, who was
still injecting cash to meet immediate needs. By this time its continuing
existence was much discussed in Langham Place. In her projected accounts for 1863 drawn up in December 1862, Sarah Lewin estimated
future subscription income as £374, based on 624 subscribers, though as
recently as September there had been 697. She estimated sales receipts
at only £24. Total receipts were estimated as £598, expenses £550, leaving
only £48 for contributors for the year.[74] The shortfall lay in money for
contributions. Davies calculated that if she offered some of the weaker
contributors 4s a page, better ones 10s (still less than half that paid by
other periodicals), she was still left with the problem of filling thirty to
forty pages a month, out of a total of seventy-two, from those who
would contribute gratuitously. Davies painted a much blacker picture
than Bessie Parkes had done. The previous year's injection of £200 had
made little difference. Greater efforts to increase circulation in
Mechanics and Literary Institutes had failed. Emily Davies questioned
whether the *Journal* should carry on. Others believed that it should be
given one more year, and that argument temporarily prevailed. Emily
Davies may to some extent have exaggerated the financial weakness of
the paper: but the narrow financial margins help to explain the often
poor quality of contributions.[75]

By 1863 some changes had taken place in the company itself: because
of a legacy, Bessie Parkes had become the major shareholder, holding
123 out of 351 shares taken up. It was, perhaps, under her influence
that in May 1864 the share capital of the company was increased in a
new issue, from £2000 to £6000. But this final, desperate attempt to keep
afloat failed and a year later only 376 out of a possible 1200 shares were
taken up. At the shareholders' meeting of August 1864, the entire
management of the *Journal* was transferred to Bessie Parkes: but it was
resolved that it should be wound up as soon as possible. The company
was finally dissolved under the Companies Act in 1881.[76]

The financial failure of the magazine was not the only reason for the ending of the *Journal*. The internal debates and differences within the *English Woman's Journal* helped to bring this particular political enterprise to an end. These differences were personal, religious, political. There was, first, the personality of the first co-editor, Matilda Hays. It is clear that she was regarded by many as difficult and irritable, and that Bessie constantly defended her to Barbara Bodichon in Algiers. Barbara Bodichon heard much from others of the quarrels at Princes St and Langham Place. Even Bessie Parkes occasionally wrote of undertaking a *coup d'etat* against the rest. But in the main Bessie defended the enterprise, and the affection that underlay the quarrels and helped women working together:

> Remember the difficulties & disgraces of one's work have to be endured with the rest. It is very hard for women in England just now; men fail them & there is a terrible tacit division between the sexes. It is *no wonder* that the warm tender feelings cling too much to each other in *default* of natural ties. We must try to bring men & women more together in every way, & to have patience meanwhile. . . .
>
> The battle is won if the soldiers reckon their lives in the question. Our little band of faulty, stormy, clever warm hearted women are to me just representative of the dangers of the whole movement & I'll never desert them or it.[77]

By 1861, however, even Bessie had come to wish Matilda in a position elsewhere: that took a long time to achieve, probably finally only with the help of her patron Lady Monson.

Unmarried women editors faced particular problems. Joseph Parkes had advised his daughter to be extremely careful of the moral outlook of her fellow workers. Matilda Hays had a reputation for moral looseness, perhaps through being an actress, perhaps through her work on George Sand, perhaps her long friendship with Charlotte Cushman. Emily Davies wrote of the damage done to the *Journal* by her reputation for Bloomerism; and Bessie Parkes of her, like Emily Faithfull, being 'unsettled morally'. By January 1863 Emily Davies could refer to the *Journal* being known for its license.[78] Young unmarried women of their class still had proprieties to maintain: and powerful public ridicule fell on those who challenged such proprieties. The *Saturday Review* mocked the Ladies Club at Langham Place as an almost orgiastic venture: the impact and the stresses of moving even so far beyond convention should not be underestimated. There is a sense of stress too in the references to health of those most closely involved in the *Journal,* unused by convention to regular occupation. Bessie Parkes wrote frequently to Bodichon of her health and of the possibility of 'fits of exhaustion' under the 'incessant grind'. Not all fears were imaginary. Bessie Parkes caught diphtheria in 1859, and scarlet fever in Liverpool in March 1864, visiting an emigrant ship with Mary Merryweather. Adelaide Procter died of consumption in February 1864.[79]

There were other differences between fellow workers: most notably religious differences. Unitarian backing for the venture had originally been strong. Parkes had been attracted to the Catholic Church for some years before in 1864 she was formally converted. Adelaide Procter was also a Catholic. Maria Rye was a High Anglican, and Emily Davies also an Anglican whose father and brother were in the Church. Parkes's declared policy was to maintain a neutral position: but to both readers and contributors that was an unsatisfactory compromise. Elizabeth Garrett called the periodical almost 'atheistic'. Parkes wrote of her difficulties to Barbara Bodichon, who, remaining herself agnostic neither shared not sympathized with her own religious commitment. Parkes would not include articles by Bodichon's husband on anti-clerical French subjects which would offend her philanthropic contacts in France and her '*numerous* Catholic & High Church subscribers'.[80] She came to find cohesion of purpose almost impossible without 'the inward binding of a common religious principle:'

> I can work with Unitarians, because tho' I am not dogmatically a *Unitarian* I have been trained in and still retain in a great measure their view of life and its duties. And I could work with Catholics because of my intellectual sympathy with their doctrines, and the definiteness of their plans. But I confess that when I get hold of minds which have been trained (or not trained) in the Church of England, I don't know how to deal with them – Emily Davies, Jane Crowe, E.F. and to a certain extent my own dear little Isa, seem to me to have not floors to their interior domains! and one may talk with them by the hour without coming to a solid conclusion.[81]

From a different perspective Emily Davies complained of the same problems. She could not freely treat the question of sisterhoods, knowing Bessie's views – if she included an article by her brother on 'Christian Liberty', other workers or shareholders might have a right to complain that she was spreading Anglican views. Religious allegiance was a fundamental part of the personal identity and inspiration of these middle-class feminists of the mid-nineteenth century: it could not be easily set aside. Systems of belief could divide as well as unite. Emily Davies commented on Bessie's 'entire ignorance of the state of religious parties in England', each of which had their own information about their own philanthropic doings.[82]

Even more divisive, however, were the different concepts of the purpose of the *Journal* that surfaced among its workers by the early 1860s.

In 1857 Bessie Parkes had taken an exalted view of the creation for women of a new kind of focus for political activity by women: the *Journal*, with its reading room and club, and its associated societies, on issues such as employment, emigration, sanitary reform, was to offer women a rallying point for some form of action. Men were not, of course, excluded from contributing to and supporting the *Journal*, and many did. But the emphasis was on women's organization, to create such a centre. As Adelaide Proctor wrote, Bessie saw her work as a 'moral engine'.[83]

Barbara Bodichon had always expressed doubts of this vision. In the correspondence between herself and Emily Davies in 1862–3, Davies began a debate on the very ' "idea" of the *Journal*', and a new model appeared. Davies had little time for Bessie Parkes's claim that the Langham Place work demonstrated what women could do in association together:

> She [Bessie] says that if the EWJ were to die, it would be talked of "in America & Paris, to say nothing of our own towns" as one more failure in women's attempts at working together. In everything Bessie says I am struck with her amazing ignorance of what other people think & feel about things in general. If she had been brought up among either Church people or orthodox Dissenters, who between them constitute the great mass of English society, she would know that there is nothing at all new in women's working together. All over the country, there are Ladies' Associations, Ladies' Committees, Schools managed by ladies, magazines conducted by ladies &c &c, which get on well enough. The new & difficult things is for men & women to work together on equal terms, & the existence of the EWJ is not testimony with regard to that.

To Davies the *Journal* was *not* a rallying point because it was not being read. Its name should be changed – it was too like all the other ladies' journals, and it should become a 'good general magazine' assuming that men and women were interested in the same things, though noting any particular grievances which women suffered. Men as well as women were interested in working for such a cause, and to Davies any appearance of antagonism between the sexes was to be avoided.

> I know Bessie feels this too, perhaps even more strongly than I do, but when she begins to talk about centres & rallying-points & so on, & shewing that women *can* work together (at L.P. of all places!) it seems as if she had forgotten it.[84]

Emily Davies discussed a new periodical to replace the 'weak, poor Journal' with Frances Power Cobbe, agreeing that they needed to support one religious line of thought, and to raise the general standard of articles. But it was with Emily Faithfull that she came to agreement on a new kind of magazine, general in its outlook, written by men and women, though at first principally by men, till it had won a reputation and could press its special arguments. It would pay its contributors well and raise the general standard of articles, from the *Journal*'s reputation for dullness and triviality. With a change of name, a new policy and an injection of capital, a different kind of magazine, more attuned to the periodical market, able to compete with *Fraser's* and *Macmillan's*, could get underway. Emily Davies edited the *Journal* for April 1863, and then joined Emily Faithfull. She believed the company's management had failed and had been insufficiently businesslike. She and Emily Faithfull took care to define their relationship in a written agreement, which departed from the 'friendly vagueness in matters of business' at Langham Place. The *Victoria Magazine* was never, however, to fulfil these high hopes. Partly because of Faithfull's involvement in a scandalous divorce case, partly because of interest in other work, Emily Davies left it after a year as it too struggled, but survived till 1880.[85]

Bessie Parkes admitted many of the *Journal*'s weaknesses, yet she did not wish to abandon it. She returned as editor in May 1863, though in its final stages Elizabeth Eiloart temporarily took over as editor. Bessie Parkes wrote to Bodichon of the differences between herself and those she identified as the 'liberals', who wished to bury the paper 'like a veteran pioneer', rather than accept its failings. 'Still under the power of her old delusions', as Davies put it, Bessie Parkes started the new *Alexandra Magazine and Englishwoman's Journal*, cheaper than the old paper but with the same aim of providing practical help and advice to working women.[86] Under that name it failed, and Parkes herself gradually withdrew from feminist activity. But Jessie Boucherett in 1865 inherited the paper, which lasted till 1903 as the *Englishwoman's Review*.

The contrasting language of Bessie Parkes and Emily Davies suggests some of the dilemmas of mid-nineteenth-century feminism. The origins of their enterprise lay in personal friendships and networks, largely outside the public world of the market and its judgements. The struggle of the political magazine to survive was new only to these daughters of the middle classes: they rapidly learnt the difficult choices that had to be confronted. Some hoped to carry private values into the public sphere. The title of *The English Woman's Journal* was a deliberate attempt to proclaim its political purpose, one which was rooted in experience of a different sphere of life, to which domesticity and philanthropy were more central than the experience of earning a living. Yet coming from the progressive and radical families of their day, the women who ran the *Journal* were also entirely aware of the liberal ideals of those families, of the models for political action presented to them, of a political economy which represented the increasing power of such classes. Such models were persuasive. The debate over whether the magazine should be organized primarily by women or become a general magazine was to be duplicated in the formation of the first woman's suffrage committee, by Emily Davies, Barbara Bodichon, and Helen Taylor, and the arguments replayed again in the campaign against the Contagious Diseases Acts. Some identified most strongly with the particular political perspective of women, like Bessie Rayner Parkes: others, like Emily Davies, found a liberal model of political action, which identified the interests of middle-class women and men, to be more appropriate, and more successful. Such tensions, representing, though not simply, the claims of class and gender, continued to characterize the women's movement of late-nineteenth-century Britain.

Part II

Class, Party and Sexual Politics

5

The Married Woman, the 'New Woman' and the Feminist: Sexual Politics of the 1890s

Lucy Bland

The history of feminism has tended to ignore the 1890s. The period between the victory of the campaign against the Contagious Diseases Acts in 1886, and the rise of militant suffragism in the early twentieth century has largely been labelled a time of feminist quiescence. Yet this chapter will argue that rather than silence, the 1890s witnessed the increasingly voiced demand for a woman's right over her own person – in particular a *married* woman's right – a demand coupled with the 'speaking out' on marital iniquity. Both the demand for a woman's bodily integrity and the exposure of marital disharmony were expressed in the pages of newspapers, journals, feminist novels and through campaigns to change the law. In seeing the 1890s feminist 'new woman' novels as part of the wider women's movement, one is able to recognize the interlinking and cross-fertilization of ideas, actions and protagonists. The challenges raised by the far-ranging debate over marriage and marital sex fed directly into, and gave a particular moral cutting edge to, the militant suffragism of the early 1900s. The 1890s contributed an important heritage to early-twentieth-century feminism; it also raised issues of contradiction which still leave present-day feminists uncertain and confused. Can sexual 'freedom' ever be an equivalent freedom for women as for men? In demanding equality, and declaring our 'sameness', how are women to argue simultaneously for recognition of *difference*: our different procreative capacity and our different experience of sexuality? Feminists in the 1890s puzzled equally over such issues.

The Women's Movement of the 1890s

In relation to the struggle for the vote, the period from 1884 (the exclusion of women from the Third Reform Act) to 1897 (the formation of an amalgamation of different suffrage societies into the National Union of Women's Suffrage Societies) has been seen by various historians as one of low ebb.[1] Ray Strachey however, although agreeing that these years were comparatively inactive in relation to suffrage, argued that 'the real effort which the suffragists made was to introduce the idea into current political thought'.[2] The suffrage movement had dwindled somewhat with the rise of party political women's organizations, formed to carry out party electioneering once the hiring of paid canvassers became illegal under the Corrupt Practices Act of 1883. However, the experience and confidence consequently gained by women possibly contributed to their growing astuteness in tackling parliamentarians in the 1890s. For, indeed, during these years the issue of women's franchise slowly began to be taken more seriously by Parliament and press, and a suffrage bill looked close to victory in 1892 and again in 1897.[3]

Women were becoming involved in other spheres of public activity as well. The Local Government Act of 1894 confirmed rate-paying married women as eligible for election as Poor Law Guardians (widows and single women had been eligible since the 1870s), and the growth of schooling and of the Civil Service provided new employment opportunities for women. And it was not simply middle-class women who were becoming more active in the public world. The 1890s saw the expansion of the Women's Trade Union League and increasing numbers of working-class women joining the Women's Co-operative Guild.

However, apart from the struggle for women's suffrage, none of this public activity was necessarily feminist. Readers may object to my use of the words 'feminist' and 'feminism' in the first place, since the terms only arrived in Britain (from France) in 1895, and even then they were rarely used. I use the terms to refer to thoughts, actions and persons that challenged the existing power of men over women and its consequent inequalities. The corresponding contemporary terms included: 'the women's movement', 'the cause of women', (or simply 'the cause'), 'a worker for the cause', a 'woman emancipator'. It is important not to reduce feminism solely to suffragism. Feminist historians have rightly pointed to the role of earlier feminists in changing the law on married women's property or opening up areas previously closed to women, such as higher education and medicine, but they have been less ready to see fiction writing as itself a feminist activity. Yet with the rise of the 'new woman' novel, many women began to write literature that was explicitly didactic and feminist.

But what was the 'new woman' novel and who and what was a 'new woman'? The feminist novelist Sarah Grand apparently invented the term in an article in 1894.[4] The 'new woman' referred to the new generation of women who were entering higher education and new areas of employment. They were doing so in an atmosphere slightly less restrictive in relation to the discussion of sexual matters. Feminism had been central in breaking the taboo on mentioning anything sexual. The campaign against the Contagious Diseases Acts in the 1870s and 1880s, and the revelations around 'white slavery' (the exposure of juvenile and enforced prostitution) had raised the spectre of 'bestial' male sexuality.[5] By the 1880s feminists were united in desiring change in male sexual behaviour – although some feminists were more reticent than others in openly discussing such issues in case it should tarnish their image of respectability.

Although there has been a fair amount of recent consideration of this 'new woman' fiction, this has generally not been placed in the context of the contemporary women's movement.[6] I would argue however that we should not separate off this writing from other feminist writing of the 1890s. Not only were the female 'new woman' writers generally feminists (and many were involved in various women's rights campaigns), but they openly wrote as such and believed their 'first duty as women writers is to help the cause of other women . . . . In women's hands – in women writers' hands – lies the regeneration of the world'.[7] Feminist journals (and *not* exclusively literary feminist journals), extensively discussed 'new woman' fiction and 'new woman' writers. The liberal feminist journal *Shafts*, for example, gave over large amounts of space to extended reviews of certain 'new woman' novels,[8] and the feminist *Women's Penny Paper* interviewed certain 'new woman' writers.[9] Feminists drew on incidents or quotations from this fiction in their more overtly political writing.[10]

I have suggested that it was the unequal and undesirable position of married women in particular which was opened up for discussion and dissection in this period. Feminists were not in total agreement over the best tactics for tackling the married woman's predicament. For a start, the suffrage movement was divided over the question of whether or not married women should be included in a woman's suffrage bill. Although the championing of married women's suffrage was certainly a minority position (which had led in 1889 to the formation of the Women's Franchise League), the 1890s witnessed increased interest in

AUGUST 15.

PRICE 3d.

GIVEN AWAY, with every knitting CRYSTAL PALACE JOHN BOND'S GOLD MEDAL MARKING INK, 6d. and 1s. Bottle, a Vouch* purchaser to
Their Name in Full, or Monogram Rubber Stamp for Marking Linen or Stamping Paper. Sold everywhere, or direct from Works, 75, Southgate Road, London.

SHAFTS

A PAPER FOR WOMEN & THE WORKING CLASSES

LICHT COMES TO THOSE WHO DARE TO THINK

WISDOM
JUSTICE
TRUTH

CONTENTS

No. 8. Vol. II.

EDITED BY
MARGARET SHURMER SIBTHORP.

OH. SWIFTLY SPEED, YE SHAFTS OF LICHT,
WHILE HOSTS OF DARKNESS FLY
FAIR BREAKS THE DAWN: FAST ROLLS THE NICHT
FROM WOMAN'S DARKENED SKY.

Cover page of the liberal feminist journal *Shafts*.

the position of married women more generally. It appeared that gains for the married woman were lagging somewhat behind those of her single sister. The two Married Woman's Property Acts of 1870 and 1882 had indeed been important stepping stones and married women had gained limited guardianship rights over their children, but coverture clung on tenaciously: the condition of a married woman as legally under the 'protection' of her husband.

For the single woman, however, it was now becoming possible to exist outside the boundaries of the nuclear family. Various doors were slowly opening into higher education and into various professions (although not without a protracted struggle), while changing economic conditions provided job opportunities in new areas such as clerical work. Martha Vicinus has shown how single women, forced to redefine themselves in terms outside both the nuclear family and the institution of prostitution, transformed the passive labels of purity and goodness into 'active spirituality and passionate social service'.[11] They developed a new role for themselves in which they could operate in the public world as paid workers, while retaining their domesticity and femininity.[12] The single woman was gaining a new sense of herself, in which marriage was not necessarily the only desirable option open to her. As the feminist 'new woman' writer Sarah Grand expressed it: 'Thinking for herself, the modern girl knows that a woman's life is not longer considered a failure simply because she does not marry.'[13] Indeed, for many women it simply was not possible in the first place, given that the ratio of women to men was steadily increasing. In the 1851 Census there were 1,042 women to every 1,000 men; by 1901 it has risen to 1,068.

It was in the discussion of marriage in the press and in the 'new woman' fiction that the plight of the married woman began to be explored, in particular her experience of undesired sexual intercourse and involuntary childbearing. In this writing we can recognize the heritage of feminism from the 1880s – on the one hand the feminist wing of the social purity movement, on the other, radical liberal feminism. As already indicated, the social purity movement had begun the process of 'speaking out' about sexual immorality and exposing hidden sexual injustices through the campaign against the Contagious Diseases Acts and the 1885 'white slavery' revelations. Radical liberal feminism, with its long tradition from Mary Wollstonecraft onwards, stressed a woman's individual civil rights, including the rights of a woman over her own person. The 'marriage debate' and the 'new woman' fiction shifted the social purity focus from prostitution and into the heart of the marital home. Marital sex was now under scrutiny:

men's behaviour and women's experience. At the core of such writing was concern to argue for a married woman's right to bodily integrity.

The Marriage Debate

The so-called 'marriage debate' was instigated by an article in *Westminster Review* in 1888 by Mona Caird. Caird was on the brink of becoming a 'new woman' novelist; she was also a journalist, an animals rights activist, a committed radical liberal feminist, and influenced, on her own admission, by J.S. Mill, Herbert Spencer, T.H. Huxley and Darwin.[14] She was a member of the Personal Rights Association, with its roots in the campaign of the 1870s and 1880s against the Contagious Diseases Acts and its programme of radical individualism. Her anti-statism was clearly spelt out in her various writings on marriage. In the above-mentioned *Westminster Review* article Caird argued that marriage was a 'vexatious failure'.[15] In this and several subsequent articles in the 1890s she put forward a number of ideas on how marriage could be transformed for the better.[16] Having opened the doors on the issue, the next years witnessed a flood of articles and letters to the press. Much to its amazement, the *Daily Telegraph's* request for correspondence on the question 'Is Marriage a Failure?' prompted 27,000 letters.[17]

As the debate continued on through the 1890s, many feminists participated in the discussion and common themes started to emerge. The central claim was that the present practice of marriage was deeply immoral. There were several reasons for this. Firstly, marriage was immoral because sex was frequently non-consensual, as too was the consequent endless childbearing. The liberal feminist journal *Shafts* was one location for this debate over marriage. In existence from 1892 until 1899, it was initially subtitled 'Light comes to those who dare to think', then 'A paper for women and the working classes' and latterly 'A magazine for progressive thought'. The cover depicted the Greek goddess Artemis shooting her arrows of 'wisdom, justice and truth', 'into dark places of sin, injustice and ignorance'.[18] A correspondent to *Shafts*, reflecting on sex, remarked that 'the reason why many women learn to loathe its expression in marriage is because it is continually imposed on them'.[19] As for enforced maternity, to veteran feminist Elizabeth Wolstenholme Elmy (herself a subscriber and contributor to *Shafts*), it was 'a crime against the highest humanity'.[20] To many, marriage – at least loveless marriage – was nothing but 'legalised prostitution',[21] or seen as no better than slavery. The marriage market entailed the 'purchase' of women. Once married, a woman became effectively her husband's property, including his sexual property, given his irrevocable sexual rights over her. Marriage and prostitution were increasingly being seen as inextricably interlinked, the supposed 'purity' of the bourgeois wife existing at the expense of the working-class prostitute who sexually serviced the middle-class man. Further, many feminists recognized that the existence of prostitution affected men's view of *all* women.[22] To Mona Caird, marriage and prostitution:

> are the two sides of the same shield and not the deepest gulf . . . can prevent the burning vapours of the woman's inferno . . . from penetrating into the upper regions of respectability and poisoning the very atmosphere . . . the same idea – the purchase of womanhood – . . . rules from base to summit of the social body.[23]

Marriage's immorality was compounded by the current divorce law. At great expense, divorce had been available since 1857 to a husband on the grounds of his wife's adultery alone, while the wife had to prove not only her husband's adultery but additionally either his cruelty or desertion. It was argued that this vindicated the double moral standard by which unchastity was excusable in a man but totally unforgiveable in a woman.

Despite seeing present marriage as immoral, this did not lead most feminists to reject marriage *per se*. On the contrary, they held up an *ideal* marriage – a future vision – for men and women to aspire towards. A number of writers, including Mona Caird, followed the philosopher Herbert Spencer in assuming that human society was evolving gradually towards a higher stage in which love and permanent monogamy would prevail. Despite this (supposedly inevitable?) evolution, it was still thought necessary to push for marital reform in the here and now – rather than abandoning marriage altogether or waiting around until that future glorious day.

To reform marriage, one of the first steps necessary was to ensure that it was built on a true friendship which could gradually blossom into love.

> A perfect marriage should always begin by the two 'being friends', growing into the love which makes wedded life possible. Many a woman is married – and alone . . . the man she has loved . . . cased . . . in a hard shell of masculinity.[24]

For such friendship, let alone true love, to be possible, it was necessary to promote easier contact between young people.[25] Caird advocated co-education and for men and women to work together alongside each other.[26] First, however, it was necessary to obtain greater freedom for young unmarried women generally. One young woman reflected:

An increase in the number of unhappy marriages arises from girls plung-
ing into matrimony simply and solely to escape from a home life whose
restrictions they imagine less endurable than a loveless marriage of conve-
nience.[27]

All this was not enough however. To destroy the mercenary quality of
marriage, women needed full economic independence. The divorce law
also needed to be changed. Yet some feminists were against the
existence of divorce in *any* form. The Christian feminist Elizabeth
Chapman, for example, viewed divorce as 'an unmixed evil. . . . It
tends to undermine monogamy . . . it deliberately encourages hasty
choice, puts a premium on temporary liaisons'.[28] Yet given that divorce
was a current reality, she supported its equalization between the sexes
as one blow against the double standard of morality – against the con-
doning of a man's adultery.

Caird anticipated a gradually increasing resentment towards state
interference in private affairs. She argued that ideal marriage would
involve a private, free contract based on comradeship and equality in
which there would be 'a full understanding and acknowledgment of the
obvious right of the woman to *possess herself* body or soul, to give or
withhold herself . . . exactly as she will' [her emphasis].[29] Others were
expressing the same sentiments. In reply to the question 'What do
Women Want?', a correspondent to *Shafts* asserted: 'They want to *own
themselves*, to dispose of their bodies as seems to them best, not to have
maternity forced upon them' [her emphasis].[30]

By the mid 1890s two additional themes surfaced more and more frequently: firstly that equality within marriage and morality could only
finally come through changing the law, including the winning of the
vote; secondly, that young women needed to enter marriage with a basic
grounding in sex education, including an awareness of the potential
health hazards of marriage. On the one hand we find feminists working
to change the law on marriage, and on the other, women writers using
the vehicle of fiction both to expose matrimonial horrors and to suggest
alternative ways of living and relating.

Changing the Law: the Clitheroe Case and the WEU

Marriage has traditionally been the sanctioning by the Church, and
more recently by the state, of the one legitimate form of sex: sexual
intercourse between a man and a woman. Not only have sexual relationships between the sexes outside marriage been deemed illegitimate, but
sexual intercourse *within* marriage had been seen and is still seen as part

of a husband's 'conjugal rights', his 'right to consortium', namely the living together as husband and wife 'with all the incidents that flow from that relationship'.[31] One of these incidents has always been the husband's right to sexual intercourse.

Back in 1880, in a paper read before the Dialectical Society, Mrs Elizabeth Wolstenholme Elmy raised the issue of the non-recognition of rape within marriage.[32] She had been active in the women's movement since 1861 in a host of concerns including women's entry into higher education, the campaign for the Married Women's Property Acts, the campaign against the Contagious Diseases Acts, maternal custody and guardianship rights, and the struggle for women's suffrage. Eighteen years later the marital rape situation remained the same (as it does even today) and Wolstenholme Elmy reflected bitterly that 'the wife . . . is in a different position from any other woman, for *she has no right or power to refuse consent*. Anything more infamously degrading it is impossible to conceive' [her emphasis].[33] There had however been one important legal victory in the intervening period: the verdict of the Clitheroe case.

Edmund Jackson had left for New Zealand to establish a business in November 1887, immediately after his marriage to Emily, and she had gone to live with her sisters and brother-in-law. It had been arranged that she would join him about six months later, but she wrote asking him to return. He did so in July 1888 but she refused to see him. He began proceedings for restitution of conjugal rights, he wrote her letters, but still she would have nothing to do with him. Then one Sunday in March 1891, he, with two accomplices, grabbed her as she was leaving church in Clitheroe, dragged her backwards into a carriage, took her back to his uncle's house in Blackburn and locked her in. Her sisters immediately applied for *habeas corpus* on her behalf. The husband claimed that common law entitled him to his wife's custody, and although the lower court agreed, it was unanimously held by the Court of Appeal that:

> where a wife refuses to live with her husband he is not entitled to keep her in confinement in order to enforce restitution of conjugal rights.[34]

The verdict was heralded by feminists as a great victory.[35] Even the *Law Times* referred to the verdict as 'the charter of the personal liberty of married women'.[36] Mrs Wolstenholme Elmy gleefully wrote to her close friend Mrs McIlquaham:

> Let us rejoice together . . . "coverture" is dead and buried. . . . It is the grandest victory the women's cause had ever yet gained, greater even than the passing of the Married Women's Property Act. . . . by the law of England a husband has no more right over the person of his wife than over the person of any other woman.[37]

In another letter to Mrs McIlquaham she referred to the judgement as 'that glorious vindication of justice and equality'.[38]. She immediately wrote a series of five letters to the *Manchester Guardian* on the case, its future implications and the legal position of women generally. She reprinted these in pamphlet form, distributing 100,000 copies.[39] This led to numerous responses from people eager to work along the lines of the proposed reforms laid out in the letters. Thus she set up the Women's Emancipation Union (WEU) that autumn with the following programme:

The Union claimed for women:

1   equality of right and duty with men in all matters affecting the service of the community and the state;
2   equality of opportunity for self-development by the education of the schools and of life;
3   equality in industry by equal freedom of choice of career;
4   equality in marriage and equality of parental rights.[40]

The WEU was therefore linking the reform of different aspects of women's subordination into one overarching programme. It also explicitly took a non-political stand. Although small in size (its subscription figures indicate a membership of a couple of hundred, the vast majority being women), it held hundreds of meetings around the country, organized petitions and distributed feminist literature widely.[41] Under aim number four, the WEU committed itself to the reform of the divorce law. Wolstenholme Elmy and others were hopeful that all the publicity surrounding Mr Jackson's inability to get a divorce from his unwilling wife would help carry an amendment.[42] During its life-span (1891 to 1899) the WEU produced leaflets on the issue and circulated a petition demanding amendment, but all to no avail.

Mrs Wolstenholme Elmy had been pushing for a divorce bill since 1886.[43] Eventually in 1889 she succeeded in inducing a Dr Hunter to bring in a bill which equalized divorce between the sexes and proposed desertion as an alternative to adultery as grounds for divorce. But Dr Hunter seemed uncommitted to the project. Wolstenholme Elmy bitterly commented: 'For four years he merely played with it, never bringing it in . . . during which time *I* had circulated some 200,000 leaflets and worked hard to develop opinion'.[44] In 1892 the bill was before Parliament but Dr Hunter only told her at the last minute and it fell. The main argument put against it was that it was wrong for a Scotsman to be in charge of a bill addressing English law (divorce law in Scotland was different – and better). She found someone else (Sir Frank Lockwood) who promised to introduce the bill but he too made no effort.

Three years later she remarked cynically: 'It has often been said of Sir Frank "that he never broke a promise". I suppose this refers to promises made to men . . .'.[45]

'New Woman' Writings: the Exposure of Marriage and the Empowering of Women

Despite 'its flippancy, its garish crudity, its edification of selfishness' the social purity feminist Blanche Leppington felt that the 'new woman' novel was 'helping to carry the pressure of the moral question into the sacred enclosure of marriage itself, from which all questioning had been too long excluded'.[46] The feminist participants in the 'marriage debate' had begun the process of opening up marriage for public exposure; scrutiny was to continue and extend through the 'new woman' novel. The 'new woman' novels had as their subject matter the doubts and dilemmas surrounding the 'new woman': her experience of work and higher education and her challenge to conventional marriage and sex. But the novels were also largely written by women who themselves epitomized the 'new woman' stereotype – women who earned their own living, travelled widely and were unabashed to speak their minds. Most, if not all, were also feminists. Many of these novels, especially those by women, are today unknown, but at the time they sold in millions, far in excess of other books of the period which we today consider classics. The female 'new woman' fiction writers were markedly distinct from their male equivalents. While the male 'new woman' writers, such as Hardy, Gissing, Grant Allen and Moore, tended to focus on the sexual 'freedom' of a 'new woman' heroine, the woman writers concentrated more on the sexuality of men. It was male sexual behaviour which was singled out as the key problem: demanding, selfish, frequently injurious to its female 'recipient', it was seen as the central cause of many married women's unhappiness.

When Blanche Leppington wrote of 'new woman' novels 'forcing the morality of marriage out into the open' she was referring to the novels' depiction of the double moral standard at work within marriage, the non-consensual sex, the incessant childbearing and – previously unmentioned in the 'marriage debate' – the marital dangers of venereal disease. In other words, the 'new woman' novel was spot-lighting a host of horrors lurking behind the veneer of marital respectability – horrors already more than hinted at in the various marriage articles mentioned above, but unable, as yet, to be elaborated upon in anything other than a fictional form. Marriage as virtual slavery or prostitution was a common complaint, already familiar to the readers of the marriage debate articles. In *A Superfluous Woman* Emma Brooke informed her readers that 'lovely girls are bought and sold in the London marriage market very much as Circassian slaves are sold to a Turkish harem'. The book's heroine had been taught to think of herself as 'a dainty piece of flesh which some great man would buy'.[47] Bought like slaves, they nightly fared no better than prostitutes. George Egerton (pseudonym of Mary Chavelita Dunne) has one of her heroines bitterly remark:

> as long as man demands from a wife as a right, what he must sue from a mistress as a favour ... marriage becomes for many women a legal prostitution, a nightly degradation, a hateful yoke under which they age, mere bearers of children conceived in a sense of duty, not love.[48]

Another of the themes of the 'new woman' fiction was the prevalence of venereal disease. Its serious consideration had already greatly shocked London in 1891 at the first showing of Ibsen's *Ghosts*, a play focusing on the disastrous effects of congenital syphilis within the family. It was unanimously condemned by the press. To the *Daily Telegraph*, for example, it was nothing but 'an open drain, a loathsome sore unbandaged, a dirty act done publicly', to the *Daily News* it was 'naked loathsomeness'.[49] Despite such a verdict, venereal disease was a central theme of Sarah Grand's 1894 novel *The Heavenly Twins*. Venereal disease surfaces in the narrative in relation to two young brides, representing the 'old' and 'new' woman. Evadne refuses intercourse with her husband on the discovery of his pre-marital incontinence, but Edith, 'seeped in religion and feminine mystique', as opposed to Evadne's self-education in 'science, medicine and the works of J.S. Mill', marries and conceives by a debauched syphilitic.[50] The result is a diseased child and Edith's mental deterioration, culminating in agonizing death. As Nurse says: 'It's the dirty men who make the misery'.[51] Although *The Heavenly Twins* was denounced as 'a product of hysteria and wilful eccentricity', it became an immediate best-seller.[52] In Grand's obituary in 1943, the *Manchester Guardian* remarked: 'It is hard to realise now what a shock *The Heavenly Twins* gave the reading public in 1893'. One admirer reflected that Grand stood as 'the real pioneer of public enlightenment on venereal disease. Participants in the Ministry of Health's campaign today can only guess how much courage this took fifty years ago'.[53] Yet others continued to develop the theme. In one section of Ellis Ethelmer's annotated poem *Woman Free*, published in the same year, Ethelmer ominously comments: 'Vicarious punishment for manhood's crimes takes grievous toll of all her active prime'.[54] The footnotes inform the reader that reference here is to masculine excess and abuse as the cause of 'diseases of women' – diseases which lead to thousands of women being 'consigned to premature graves'. It was probably clear to everyone that the 'vicarious punishment' was venereal disease. The following year Emma Brooke's *A Superfluous Woman* also has as one of its themes the effects of congenital syphilis.

In an article in 1890 Mona Caird had pointed to women's nervous exhaustion and ill-health brought on by excessive childbearing.[55] Two years later she concluded that 'if the new movement (of women) had no other effect than to rouse women to rebellion against the madness of large families, it would confer a priceless benefit on humanity'.[56] In her novel *Daughters of Danaus* Caird's heroine reflects on how the appeal of the so-called maternal 'instinct' had been used to subordinate women:

> Throughout history ... children have been the unfailing means of bringing women into line with tradition. ... An appeal to the maternal instinct had quenched the hardiest spirit of revolt ... their (children's) helplessness was more powerful to suppress revolt than regiments of armed soldiers.[57]

In a debate the next year in *Saturday Review* between 'Woman of the Day' and Lady Jeune for the 'Old Woman', the former declared that the 'new woman' had exposed the immorality of indiscriminate breeding.[58]

On the whole, however, the 'new woman' writers were not opposed to maternity as such. Yet this did not mean that they believed that women should bear numerous children as part of their inevitable destiny and duty. Feminists tended to argue not only for voluntary motherhood but for 'purposed maternity': smaller planned families which would in turn mean healthier mothers and children.[59] Many at the same time tried to hold onto a notion of maternity as the most valuable attribute of femininity – *the* definer of sexual difference, even of women's superiority. As we shall see, this notion of motherhood formed a crucial part of the 'new woman' utopian vision. Before examining this future ideal it is worth considering one strategy implicitly presented in some of the 'new woman' fiction for changing the unequal marital relation here and now.

The marriage debate had made some mention of the dire effects of women's sexual ignorance. The need for a sex education which not only taught the physiological facts but also warned girls of sexual dangers, gradually became one plank in the feminist demand for transformed sexual relations. It was nothing new to want sex education for *boys*, but until the 1890s girls' sexual innocence-cum-ignorance had generally been believed to provide their 'protection'. The 'new woman' fiction writers focused on some of the consequences of the silence surrounding

sex. It contributed to the vulnerability of Sarah Grand's 'Edith';
Egerton's 'Florence' believes it is the key to her disastrous marriage.
She turns accusingly on her mother:

> "I say it is your fault because you reared me a fool, an idiot, ignorant of
> everything I ought to have known . . . my physical needs, my coming
> passion, the very meaning of my sex, my wifehood and motherhood to
> follow. You gave me not one weapon in my hand to defend myself against
> the possible attacks of man at his worst. You sent me to fight the biggest
> battle of a woman's life . . . with a white gauze" – she laughed derisively
> – "of maiden purity as a shield".[60]

Brook's heroine in *A Superfluous Woman* reflects: 'As to her nature, of
that she had heard nothing; passion, she had been taught, was an
offensive word'.[61]

Ellis Ethelmer was one of the first to write sex education material for
young people and children of both sexes. It is unclear whether Ethelmer
was the pseudonym for Elizabeth Wolstenholme Elmy or her husband
Ben Elmy. Sylvia Pankhurst claimed Ethelmer to be Ben Elmy; Sheila
Jeffreys believes it is a pseudonym for his wife.[62] In the letters between
E. Wolstenholme Elmy and her close friend Mrs McIlquaham there are
a number of indications that Ethelmer is her husband, for example
when she refers to his finishing a long poem.[63] It appears to be a
reference to *Woman Free*, and she mentions his writing *Phases of Love*
in several letters. Both are by Ethelmer. In relation to *Human Flower*,
she quotes *The Lancet* saying that it is evidently the work of a 'refined
and pure minded *woman*' [her emphasis]. This emphasis on 'woman'
seems to suggest that *The Lancet* got it wrong – that the book was by a
man or possibly their joint work. Interestingly, Sylvia Pankhurst does
refer to *Human Flower* as Mrs Wolstenholme Elmy's 'little text-book',
despite having just identified Ethelmer as husband Ben.[64] Possibly they
shared the pseudonym. In *The Human Flower* (1894) and *Baby Buds*
(1895) human reproduction was introduced through the initial description of reproduction in flowers. In *The Human Flower* the child was
to move through the chapters as she/he advanced in years into puberty.
As in all Ethelmer's writings, stress is made on a woman's right to complete control of her person, with knowledge of the dangers as 'the surest
safeguard':

> the function of wifehood and motherhood must remain solely and
> entirely within the wife's own option. Coercion, like excess, is in itself a
> contravention and annihilation of the physic nature of the sexual relation

... to inflict a grief or an injustice on a reluctant partner, and to submit her thus to the possibility of undesired maternity is a procedure equally unjustifiable and inhuman to the mother and the "unwelcome child".[65]

Ethelmer, like many feminists, advocated abstinence during certain periods, in other words contraception through use of the 'safe period'. (Ironically, right up until the Second World War the 'safe period' was wrongly thought to occur in mid menstrual cycle.) Few feminists were in favour of artificial forms of birth control (known as 'preventive checks') such as the sheath, cap, syringe or sponge. The sheath had long been associated with prostitution, and thus women tended to feel its use in the home reduced them to the status of a prostitute. Further, many feared that use of 'checks' would remove one of the few excuses open to women to refuse sexual intercourse: the threat of pregnancy. By demanding 'continence' – spaced, infrequent sexual intercourse – as the *safe* form of birth control, women were able to demand (if not always actually achieve) a lessening of both sexual intercourse and incessant childbearing.

Inspiring Visions

Nineteenth-century novels, particularly those by women, were conventionally the site for the exploration of love, marriage, family and (above all) the personal. For feminists to think about such issues, including the possibility of changing not only these institutions but also *themselves*, the fictional form allowed a safer means for the vicarious reflection of both writer and reader. Although the majority of 'new woman' novels and short stories adopted a social realist approach that laid bare the unpalatable reality of the present, a number opted for utopianism.[66] Arguably it was only in an ideal fictitious world that the woman writer could explore some of the different visions of what transformed sexual relations might mean – a utopian world in which women no longer face restrictions on their freedom of action and choice. For example in George Egerton's short story the 'Regeneration of Two', the finale sees the heroine and hero setting up some kind of free union in which either can come and go as they choose. The heroine announces to the hero: 'I ask you nothing ... for I am sure of myself, proud of my right to dispose of myself as I will, to choose'.[67]

The marriage debate and the 'new woman' fiction not only projected an image of an ideal marriage but on occasion hinted at a whole new world in which women had true equality in every sphere of their lives.

The lynchpin was a transformed moral order: a New Order in which men lived by the same high moral standards as women. Getting the vote was indeed seen as crucial, but the vote was only *one* of the various means for finally toppling the double moral standard. It was not until the twentieth century that the demand for the vote dwarfed all the other demands of the multifaceted women's movement.

Feminists had an inspiring vision of this new world. For Elizabeth Wolstenholme Elmy it was just around the corner:

> We believe and know that the time is fast coming when men having learnt purity and women's courage, the sexes shall live together in harmony, each other's helpers towards all things high and holy; no longer tyrant and victim, oppressor and oppressed, but, hand in hand, eye to eye, heart in heart, building up that nobler world which yet shall be. In this faith we have lived and worked; in this faith we shall conquer.[68]

To reach this new world, women and men needed to be regenerated: women to gain freedom and a sense of themselves, men to become – in the words of the social purity feminist Blanche Leppington – 'debrutalised': raised from the bestial physical plane to a higher spirituality.[69] As Sarah Grand rather righteously expressed it:

> The New Woman can be hard on man, but it is because she believes in him and loves him. She recognises his infinite possibilities. She sees the God in him, and means to banish the brute.[70]

Women might be set to 'banish the brute' but men had to work on themselves as well. The conversation between Florence and her mother in George Egerton's short story 'Virgin Soil' makes this point succinctly:

> "But men are different Florence; you can't refuse a husband, you might cause him to commit sin."
> "Bosh Mother, he is responsible for his own sins, we are not bound to dry-nurse his morality."[71]

To the 'new woman' this ideal world was not envisaged as asexual, but the sexual side of relations in this new world were radically transformed. They were about love, not lust, the spiritual rather than the mere physical. Here the picture becomes somewhat confusing for the reader of today. For example, Ethelmer suggested, as had Caird and Chapman, that we were evolving from the 'physical to a higher level . . . marriage will be then essentially a physic alliance'.[72] It is not quite clear – at least not to me – what role the physical would play in all this. The vision becomes rather more confusing when an ideal of motherhood is introduced. It is not merely the physiology of motherhood that is being referred to, but, like purified sex, an almost *spiritual* attribute.

Elizabeth Wolstenholme Elmy again: 'Let it be frankly granted that motherhood *in its largest sense* is the highest function of woman . . . a special dignity and worthiness superior to that of the mere male faculty of fighting'.[73] Margaret Shurmer Sibthorp, editor of *Shafts*, incited women to 'love and respect maternity . . . the highest and holiest function that our life holds, from its ordinary physical capacity to its wide and grand and full meaning in Universal Motherhood'.[74] But for a changed world, men too needed to respect the power of motherhood. In one article Wolstenholme Elmy approvingly quoted Frances Swiney's *The Awakening of Women*:

> It is only as men recognise the supreme unselfishness and sublime abnegation of motherhood that they will themselves rise to a higher plane of ethical evolution and emerge from self-centred masculine in-dividualism to a far loftier discipline of a tender sympathetic Altruism.[75]

Sibthorp took the argument a stage further in implying that true love *is* the maternal desire:

> Woman is not free from passion . . . only *more* free having put her foot on the further track which, developing the maternal, leaves the passional some paces behind. Eventually passion must cease and give place to the God-like love, universal . . . but *wholly* of the spirit. . . . With the death of passion will cease all desire on the part of man to dominate over woman. [her emphasis][76]

But it is misleading to imply that all feminists equated the sexual in women with maternity. Many saw it as an additional resource, unique to women, that mobilized them towards change – for personal *and* altruistic reasons. Thus to Wolstenholme Elmy:

> The mother risks her life for the perpetuation and progress of the race. It is because women are resolved to be mothers in the highest, and no longer in the ignoblest sense of that term, that they now demand for themselves and for each other, the fullest opportunity of self-development.[77]

Here we see the way in which the evolutionary ideas of racial (and here read 'human') progress became incorporated into a feminist vision of *women's* special and crucial role. By the early twentieth century, this stress on women's role in mothering the 'race' started to be deployed by imperialists, eugenists and even a number of feminists, and thereby took on different and more disturbing connotations. The feminist 'edge' to such ideas tended to disappear beneath a morass of jingoistic and racist rhetoric.[78]

Living out Alternatives

The feminist critiques of marriage and their visions of alternative ways of living clearly contributed to an increasing number of women being happy and prepared to stay single. However, few feminists wanted the abolition of marriage. If a woman was to be in a sexual relationship with a man, such a relationship should be sanctioned legally. 'Free love' was anathema to many feminists. Incidentally 'free love' in this period was generally used (at least by its advocates) to refer to monogamous long-term relationships outside the sanction of Church and state. 'Free lovers' tended *not* to countenance promiscuity. A 'free love' relationship was referred to as a 'free marriage', 'free union' or 'free alliance', the terms tending to be used interchangeably. Given that feminists were so critical of marriage, why did most of them oppose free unions? Firstly, it was argued that free love allowed men unrestrained sexual licence. Secondly, it rendered women more vulnerable. Many held that legal marriage, whatever its failings, did protect women to some extent. A 'trained nurse' feared that: 'It would be a bad day for my countrywomen . . . if a verdict should be given for free love. What would become of wives over 40 if they could be thrown on one side like broken toys?'.[79] However, not all feminists agreed. One correspondent to *Shafts*, in response to a 'modern woman' who argued that free unions would mean 'licence for the man and disgrace and desertion for the woman', suggested that 'surely the man has licence now? . . . the nobler man . . . is faithful to her because *he loves her*, rather than because he is tied to her. If a man ceases to love his wife, she is better without him' [her emphasis].[80] Thirdly, it was felt that in a free union the woman risked being left to fend not only for herself but for the children too. Further, many believed that 'the long period of helplessness of the human child is indication of the need for the *permanent* principle'.[81] However, there was disagreement here as well. A female correspondent writing in response to the *Daily Telegraph's* 'Is Marriage a Failure?' reflected that "free love" sounds like an excuse for licence, but I honestly believe that the children of a marriage in which the only ties were love and respect would be better cared for, better trained and . . . become better citizens than the offspring of a legal union where love and respect had become impossible'.[82] Nevertheless, generally feminists were opposed to free unions, feeling that given the double moral standard it was better to increase rather than decrease the taboo against non-marital sex. The most explicitly feminist wing of the social purity movement, the Moral Reform Union, took an uncompromising position: free love was a 'grave evil', 'which really means the substitute of lust for love against which we shall wage an unremitting warfare'.[83] The MRU's main objective was the distribution of moral and sex education literature, but such writings held marriage and the family sacred.

The Legitimation League and Free Love

Although most feminist bodies had no truck with free love, there was one small organization both formally committed to women's emancipation and also, by the late 1890s, pledged to the furtherance of free love. Set up in 1893, the Legitimation League's initial objective was 'to create a machinery for acknowledging offspring born out of wedlock and to secure for them equal rights with legitimate children'.[84] At its first annual meeting in March 1894, its president, Wordsworth Donisthorpe, refuted charges that the League advocated free love. Nevertheless, the following year it began to invite those 'willing to live together without the bond of state wedlock . . . to register their alliances before the notifying clerk of the Legitimation League'.[85] It also invited notification of illegitimate offspring. (Replies to both invitations proved disappointing, however, with only a few respondents.) The differences within the League finally came to a head in 1897 when it formally shifted its position by adopting as the second but primary aim the principle of 'freedom in sexual relationships' (relegating the issue of illegitimacy to second place). Free love was made to sound highly honourable: 'Free love is simple two of the noblest principles of human relations – freedom and love – merged together'.[86] A number of members promptly resigned, including the president. With its new aim blazened, the League launched its journal *The Adult* in the same year. It declared that 'while the League takes a purely theoretical standpoint in relation to sex matters . . . our united help will . . . be at the service of those on whom the law or its administration, or its abuse, presses harshly on account of their heterodox sex relationships'.[87] But the League was anxious to dispel any fears that support for free love would be at women's expense: 'One of the fundamentals of our position is the equal sex freedom of man and woman. "Free love" for one sex at the expense of the other means neither freedom nor love'.[88] Although it is clear from various articles in *The Adult* that not all members (who were of both sexes) were especially supportive of feminism, the League's formal commitment was explicit. In *The Adult's* first issue the editorial stated that, 'we protest . . . against the theory underlying laws, marriage settlements and popular practice that a women's person can be the "property" of her husband'.[89] It appears that about half of its members were women as, too, were the holders of official posts (or at least so *The Adult's* editor claimed).[90] Its president from 1897 was the American libertarian feminist Lillian Harman and its treasurers were both women.

If its officials were convinced that feminism and free love were reconcilable, not all the League's members were so sure. In *The Adult* a Mary Reed announced:

> To my mind "free love" offers no honourable or happy solution to the woman. It certainly leaves her freedom, but at the cost of what makes life endurable – the respect of the men and women of character whom she admires, while ... it absolves the man from all legal parental responsibility. . . . a woman who accepts a free union has now the choice of remaining childless or accepting the final responsibility of the children she bears. Is this the solution?[91]

At a League dinner one feminist League member, Edith Vance, hinted at the especial difficulty for women in suffering this loss of respect. In reference to Gladys Heywood, common-law wife of the League's founder Oswald Dawson, who had taken his name in 1893, she addressed the men:

> I did not know until I had a talk with Mrs Dawson afterwards what a very great deal she has to endure. It is very easy – perhaps it is fun for you gentlemen – to be twitted about your connection with the League. . . . If the conversation gets too bad, you can knock the man down or threaten to do so, but Mrs Dawson is not in a position to thus deal with her slanderers.[92]

Many feminists were also concerned about social respect – or rather, respectability. They looked aghast at heterosexual free unions of women amongst their own ranks in the fear that the scandal of impropriety would harm the women's cause. According to Sylvia Pankhurst, Elizabeth Wolstenholme, inspired by Mary Wollstonecraft and aware of the disabilities suffered by married women, entered a free union with Ben Elmy in the early 1870s. However, once pregnant, 'there was much fluttering in the suffrage dovecotes' and she was finally induced to marry.[93] The pressure did not stop here however. In December 1875 Mrs Millicent Fawcett wrote to Mrs Wolstenholme Elmy (now formally married) asking her to resign her secretaryship of the Married Women's Property Committee on the grounds that 'the prospects of the women's movement will be very materially affected by what you do at the present time. . . . What happened before you were married has been and is a great injury to the cause of women'.[94] (Fortunately Mrs Wolstenholme

Elmy took no notice and she went on to be the main force behind the Married Women's Property Act of 1882.)

We might have expected such attitudes amongst feminists to have shifted by the 1890s. By the late 1880s, feminist hostility towards free unions was still apparent, however. For example, certain women in the radical Men and Women's Club (and these women were feminist) opposed the proposed membership of Marx's daughter Eleanor precisely because she was living openly in free union with Edward Aveling.[95] By the 1890s, Millicent Fawcett, for one, was still opposed to non-marital relations. In her 1891 introduction to Mary Wollstonecraft's *A Vindication of the Rights of Women* in reference to the group to which Wollstonecraft belonged, she commented: 'one is sickened for ever . . . of the subject of irregular relations'.[96] Feminist lack of interest in the famous 'free love' Lanchester case in 1895 clearly indicated the continuity of such ambivalence, even hostility.

It is unclear how many women actually called themselves 'new women' in this period. Edith Lanchester identified herself as one and she certainly epitomized the image. She was aged 24, middle class, had an honours degree in science from London University, was an ex-teacher (fired for 'advanced opinions') now working as a clerk, she was a feminist, a socialist prominent in the Social Democratic Federation, a close friend of Eleanor Marx and firmly against marriage. In 1894 she had stood as a socialist candidate for the London School Board. In 1895 she decided to live openly with a railway clerk, James Sullivan. When her family heard of her plans they were so horrified that they arranged for a Dr Blandford (a specialist in mental diseases) to come to her lodgings in Battersea and certify her 'insane'. 'Over-education', according to her father, was the cause of her insanity. To the doctor, her 'insanity' was manifested in her obvious seeking of 'social' suicide: the choice to enter a 'free union'.[97] She was forcibly dragged by her brothers and father to a private lunatic asylum. Sullivan, with the help of colleagues, applied for *habeas corpus*. Support and wide publicity were organized through 'Lanchester meetings' and press reports, and three days later she was released. From then until his death she lived in a free union with Sullivan.[98]

The Social Democratic Federation had not backed Edith Lanchester's actions (although several individual members gave her their support). The Federation's leader Hyndman deplored her action on the grounds that its identification of socialism and free love would alienate the working classes. Unsurprisingly the Legitimation League rallied to Edith's defence and helped to organize the 'Lanchester meetings'. As far as Oswald Dawson was concerned: 'she now ranks . . . with the advance guard to whose lot falls the burden in the battles of sexual freedom'.[99] Feminists were less enthusiastic. *The Woman's Signal*, while granting that she was clearly an intelligent and sane young woman, did not support her actions. 'She appears to have been misled by the example of Mr Grant Allen's theoretical "Woman Who Did".' (Allen's notorious novel *The Woman Who Did* concerned a woman who chose to bear an illegitimate child.) *The Woman's Signal* continued: 'It is natural enough that this decision should cause great distress to her parents, who . . . are old enough to know the terrible and life-long martyrdom which their daughter would bring upon herself by such conduct.' However, while they could 'fully sympathise with the position of her father', they did not approve of his use of the lunacy laws, which they argued were in need of immediate reform. Indeed their interest in the case rapidly became one of interest in this latter issue, rather than the question of a woman's right to self-determination.[100]

If we compare the Lanchester case with the Clitheroe incident, we become aware of the *boundaries* of feminist interest in a woman's self-determination.[101] Interestingly, *The Woman's Signal* starts its article on Edith Lanchester by citing a connection between the two cases:

> Not since the famous case of Mrs Jackson, whose husband abducted her and carried her to his house by force, has there been so extraordinary a story as that of Miss Lanchester.[102]

If it was so extraordinary, why were feminists not more interested? The two cases were very different in many respects, but both involved the issue of a woman's right to control her own person, and both dealt squarely with the issue of what constituted legitimate sex and legitimate marriage. Both the cases involved a woman's right to freedom – at the most immediate level, a right to *habeas corpus*, more generally, a right to control her own person. In the Jackson case, Emily acted in defiance of the assumed legal 'ownership' her husband had over her. Edith also acted in defiance of the convention that a woman should be tied to a man through his legal ownership of her. She claimed the right to her own person in terms of the right to choose her (male) sexual partner outside the confines, and for women, the subordination of legal marriage. Both cases involved challenges to the institution of marriage: one a challenge to marital law, to the legality of the enforcement of conjugal rights, the other a challenge to the desirability of marriage *per se* and the dominant belief that a sexual union outside marriage was beyond the pale. Both also involved challenges to a man's right to constrain a woman's freedom: in the Jackson case, the husband's right, backed by common law; in the Lanchester case, the father's right, backed by a medical man and his use of the insanity laws. But of course it is the difference between the two cases – one a challenge to the *terms* of marriage, the other an adoption of a heterosexual *alternative* to marriage – that gives the clue to feminist indifference. As I have been arguing, most feminists did not embrace free love with any enthusiasm, given both its connotations of promiscuity and its believed vulnerability for women.

Concluding Thoughts

In conclusion I should like to pose three questions. Firstly, how are we to summarize the main threads of the 1890s feminist reflections on marriage and sex? Secondly, how did these feminist ideas contribute to the feminism of the early twentieth century, in particular to the suffrage movement? Thirdly, how are we to make sense of the various contradictions raised in these debates?

This chapter has been arguing that in the 1890s the rights of married women over their own person started to be voiced. This entailed a demand for the right to say 'no' both to non-consensual sex within marriage and to involuntary childbearing. Many feminists began to demand that marital sex – its form and frequency – be no longer dictated by the husband but by the wife, or be agreed upon by mutual consent. In the place of undesired sexual intercourse and involuntary motherhood, feminists developed new ideas of a sexual relationship based on love not lust, and a maternity that was spaced and voluntary. These new feminist notions of sex and motherhood were often idealized and spiritualized, differentiated from many women's actual experience of unpleasant sexual encounters and painful, endless maternity. Yet despite feminists' disillusionment with the practice of marriage, very few opted for thé alternative of free unions. Indeed their hostility to both non-marital heterosexual relations and to artificial birth control indicated their fear that such options would *increase* the weight of male control.

The ideas developed amongst feminists in the 1890s concerning their desire to transform male sexual behaviour within as well as outside marriage, forged the basic tenets of their notion of an equal moral standard. Such a notion was *central* to the heightened suffrage struggle of the early 1900s. 'There is nothing in the feminist programme about which the feminist feels so keenly as the double standard of morality', reflected suffragist Ethel Snowden in 1911; 'the last and greatest demand of the women's movement is a woman's absolute right over herself after marriage'.[103] The 'new woman' fiction had played an important part in 'speaking out' on male sexuality. By the early twentieth century there was a move from exploring the issue primarily via a fictional form to dealing with it through factual tracts. In relation to venereal disease, for example, the 1900s witness a number of feminist articles that dealt with the problem head-on, drawing unselfconsciously on medical figures and references and making no attempt to distance themselves from the topic via a fictional narrative. The most (in)famous of such writings was Christabel Pankhurst's 1913 *The Great Scourge*, with its rousing slogan: 'Votes for women, chastity for men'.[104]

I made mention above of certain contradictions raised in the debates over sex and marriage. I was referring especially to the co-existence of a critique of marriage and a hostility to free union. I would suggest that at the heart of these contradictions there lay a tension between on the one hand a liberal feminist personal rights philosophy, with a stress on a woman's right over her own person, her right to *choose*, and her claim to equality with men, and on the other, a social purity feminism, with a desire for a changed standard of morality which not only demanded a change in *male* sexual behaviour, but also necessitated highly 'moral' sexual behaviour in women. In recognizing the sexual vulnerability of women, such morality spoke of *difference* in women's experience of sexuality and of procreation. With the greater awareness of the sexual dangers of marriage – the risk of venereal disease, of undesired sex, of incessant pregnancy – there was little reason to suppose that a non-marital relationship with a man would lessen such dangers. A new kind of relationship was desired, one based on love, equality and respect; only when that ideal was realizable, let alone realized, could free-love unions be seen as viable in the here and now. In answer to the cry of some free lovers that women as well as men needed the freedom to seek their own sexual pleasure, many feminists replied that it was sexual dangers which needed immediate attention, their existence challenging the idea of sexual 'freedom' being any *real* freedom for women at all.

These tensions remain with us today. It is salutory to learn that we are not the first to be aware of the dilemmas facing women who seek both sexual pleasures and protection from sexual danger. Feminists in the 1890s tried to explore these tensions, and their writings still give us much food for thought.

6

Party Political Women: A Comparative Study of Liberal Women and the Primrose League, 1890–1914

Linda Walker

That women were to become immersed in the hitherto sacrosanct world of male party politics on a sustained basis was not immediately apparent in the early 1880s. Women were drawn into party work initially for pragmatic rather than feminist reasons. The extension of the franchise through the Reform Act of 1884 and the Corrupt Practices Act of 1883 which forbade the payment of canvassers encouraged party organizers to reconsider their electoral strategies. The emergence of political associations for women in this period should therefore be seen against a backcloth of a changing party system and the development of an organizational network which harnessed the energies of party workers. Organizations provided identity and direction for political newcomers, tapping women's potential in the form of a wide range of electioneering skills, and securing for the politicians their voluntary co-ordinated labour in the constituencies, labour which needed no reward other than a hearty vote of thanks.

As the earlier chapters of this book have indicated, the thread of political action through women's lives before the later Victorian period more usually occurred outside mainstream party politics. Political action was often the result of community or family involvement – for example, working-class community protest during the franchise reform years 1815-20, middle-class commitment to Radical causes such as the Anti-Corn Law League and the women's suffrage movement, and a tradition of political work in certain landed families, such as Lady Dorothy Nevill's in Norfolk.[1] This kind of wider activity enabled some women to gain a political education within a limited sphere – many of these women and their daughters pioneered political party work in the newly emergent women's associations in the 1880s and after.

The evolution of women's role in politics in the late nineteenth century extended a long if somewhat irregular tradition of political effort. This role was developed and defined in accordance with the needs of a changing party system and a gradual shifting of the social conventions which restricted the movement of middle- and upper-class women outside the home. Women were drawn into organized party politics in their thousands within a relatively short period of time.

Because they were excluded from the two main party organizations, a situation which did not alter until 1918 – the year of their enfranchisement and eligibility for Parliament – women were channelled into subsidiary associations. Women's Liberal Associations first appeared from about 1880; the Women's Liberal Federation formed in 1887 and its splinter group the Women's National Liberal Association in 1892; the Women's Liberal Unionist Association started in 1888; all were sex-segregated. Tory women were admitted to the Primrose League in 1884 and confined to the Ladies' Grand Council – although in the local Habitations men and women worked together. The two embryonic socialist parties, the Social Democratic Federation and the Independent Labour Party, formed respectively in 1884 and 1893, preached an egalitarian doctrine of eligibility at all levels of the party and so admitted women on equal terms with men (although in practice, women found themselves in a more conventional, subservient role, and their representation on central committees was the exception rather than the rule). When the Labour Party appeared in 1903, it modelled itself on the older-established parties with the result that women sat on the sidelines in the Women's Labour League, begun in 1906. The issue of segregation versus integration is complex and does not lend itself to easy generalizations.[2] Women-only caucuses could provide a sheltered environment for developing skills and safeguarding women's interests – and in the case of the Women's Liberal Federation fostered a feminist consciousness. The Ladies' Grand Council of the Primrose League, on the other hand, was a pale and powerless imitation of the overall Grand Council and a more rigorous political apprenticeship was acquired in the mixed Habitations.

Whatever the characteristics and nature of the various associations, their collective impact was to make women's contribution an essential part of the electoral process, extending into the twentieth century a tradition of political party work which has never been broken. Foremost in establishing this tradition and in propagating an image of selfless, backroom constituency workers were the 'ladies' of the Primrose

League; not far behind them, and less given to self-abnegation, were the more feminist and independent Liberals.

I

The political canvas in the late nineteenth century was being redrawn to accommodate changing fortunes. After decades of consolidating their economic and political power in the industrial and manufacturing towns, the rising middle classes were seeking to consolidate their political identity in the national arena. In terms of the Liberal Party where the middle classes found their natural home and already enjoyed a strong power base in the halls of Westminster, this process took the form of moral rejuvenation – apparent in the moral fervour of Gladstone's Midlothian campaign of 1880, the Home Rule for Ireland issue which regenerated many Liberal Associations some ten years later, and the concern for social reform which began to permeate the left wing of the parliamentary party from the 1890s. The Liberal traditions of radicalism and Nonconformity, their power base acquired in municipal politics, and the need to respond to electoral and social changes were all factors in the development of a national political organization for Liberal women, and to some extent account for the particular characteristics of the autonomous Women's Liberal Associations which began to make their mark in the local constituencies.

Although there existed a Women's Liberal Association in Birmingham as early as 1874, it seems that Liberal women came together in formal groups after the General Election of 1880.[3] Eliza Orme recalled the effect of Gladstone's Midlothian campaign on 'many people, women as well as men, who had been accustomed to hold themselves aloof from party politics' and who then, with Nonconformist consciences awakened, 'took an active share in the struggle'.[4] Gladstone made a special appeal to women at Dalkeith in November 1879:

> open your own feelings and bear your own part in a political crisis like this, we are making no inappropriate demand, but are beseeching you to fulfil a duty which belongs to you, which, so far from involving any departure from your character as women, is associated with the fulfilment of that character, and the performance of its duties.[5]

Small societies calling themselves Women's Liberal Associations were formed in Bristol, York and Darlington in 1880-1 with the object of drawing together women who desired to educate themselves and others in political questions and to assist the Liberal politicians in their localities. In the early 1880s these associations were but a modest beginning. Women otherwise worked individually and upon invitation as members of the men's associations, helping the Liberal cause in the subsequent General Election of 1885.

Their diligent efforts were carefully observed by Sophia Fry, wife of the MP for Darlington and active in her local association. From information collected in correspondence from different parts of the country, she ascertained that more effective communication between women would greatly enhance their efforts. In the spring of 1886 she summoned a meeting of women engaged in political work at her house at Queen Anne's Gate which resulted a year later in the inaugural session of the Women's Liberal Federation on 25 February 1887 at the Metropole Hotel, London. By that time there were forty associations – socially mixed, judging by the first assembly of delegates which included ladies of rank and wealth, factory hands, board school teachers, wives and daughters of tradespeople and artisans. Many were already engaged in philanthropic work such as the Charity Organization Society, temperance and church societies.[6] Nonconformity prevailed – apparent in the range of issues the Federation championed and in the puritanical wrath which hounded Sir Charles and Lady Dilke once the scandal surrounding his personal life became public. The associations' broad social composition in the early years owed much to lack of rivalry, particularly in the industrial areas where the Primrose League faltered and where the socialist parties had yet to make their mark. By 1895, as the newly formed ILP creamed off the more working-class members, the Women's Liberal Federation, increasingly middle-class, was no longer as socially representative.[7] In the early years the Federation was strongly London oriented and came under pressure to develop closer touch with the majority of its members in the country – for example, by holding meetings in provincial towns. Further decentralization did occur with the formation of Unions of Women's Liberal Associations. The Lancashire and Cheshire, Metropolitan Counties and Sussex Unions were established by 1889.

The first five years were largely devoted to encouraging new associations and attracting women to the Liberal cause – as table 6.1 indicates, with much success. The newly converted activists in the associations required initial guidance, particularly as all members were encouraged to participate as elected officers and to contribute to policy. Some women had experience in suffrage societies and branches of the Ladies' National Association for the Repeal of the Contagious Diseases Acts but the majority were being initiated into a new world of organized

Table 6.1

Year	Number of associations	Total membership
1886	40	10,000
1892	360	75,000
1896	476	82,000
1898	489	69,933
1904	496	66,000
1906	595	81,000
1910	692	104,759
1912	837	133,215
1914	769	115,097

Source: Women's Liberal Federation *Annual Reports*. All total membership figures are approximate. After 1892 some associations chose to affiliate to the Women's National Liberal Association rather than the WLF.

effort as Mary Martin Leake, Secretary of the WLF was careful to stress:

> We are as a sex wholly unaccustomed to the work that results from combination and organization, and, while combining and organizing, we have to train ourselves . . . to carry out these ends while we are actually performing the work.[8]

In towns, a new association would be formed by calling a public meeting, by visiting wives of Liberal sympathisers and by house-to-house canvass. In rural areas Miss Leake suggested cottage meetings and house-to-house visitation as ways to gain support although 'the absolute want of political knowledge amongst women in these remote country districts' and the difficulties of combating the social attractions of the Primrose League made the task considerably harder.[9] Each association decided its programme, established committees and could levy a subscription of 1d to 3d, although the latter was voluntary in the early years in order not to discourage poorer women from joining. The Women's Liberal Associations were therefore more decentralized and less socially hierarchical than Primrose League Habitations. By virtue of being women-only they offered more of their sex an education in political management.

The Federation aimed to shape the opinions of Liberal women and to foster new associations, assisting their growth but not controlling their programmes. The associations were in theory autonomous and therefore free to cultivate ideas and issues. Upon affiliation to the

Federation they could send delegates to the Annual Council Meeting, with the right to forward resolutions, discuss policy and vote officers to the Executive Committee. While members of the latter might call themselves 'servants of the delegates', and modestly deny leadership as did Lady Carlisle in her Presidential acceptance speech in 1894, this was the democratic ideal.[10] In reality the Executive was dynamic, innovative and forceful. It used its London base to press home its policies through Liberal MPs and other national organizations, steered the Annual Council Meeting towards the more radical social and women's issues of the day, and adopted a fighting strategy over suffrage, calling on associations to refuse help to candidates who withheld support. They gave the Federation a reputation for strong feminism and their tactics alienated a minority of members who formed the independent Women's National Liberal Association in 1892. In the long run, however, the Federation did generate the community of ideas and action for which Lady Fry had hoped.

For the Conservative Party, the question of reorganization was given considerable impetus by the Liberal landslide of 1880 and the subsequent widening of the franchise. Certain sections of the party's aristocratic leadership looked to the re-building of a mass-based party which would weld together the gentry in the shires, middle-class Tory leaders in provincial towns and the humble Tory voter. The Primrose League was therefore formed in November 1883 by a group of Tory politicians keen to engage support for their party beyond the traditional Conservative associations and to mould into a compact body the more active and energetic partisans of the newer and more democratic school of Conservatism.[11] Behind its all-encompassing object of maintaining religion, crown and empire, the League conducted propaganda, particularly in rural areas, and recruited supporters who undertook political work amongst the electorate. Members enrolled in Habitations or local units as Knights, Dames and Associates, while the League as a whole was managed by an exclusively male Grand Council in London. Associate members paid much lower dues than Knights and Dames and were drawn largely from the working class. Their inclusion made the League a popular organization and enabled rapid growth.[12] In 1886 the League became somewhat decentralized when Divisional Councils were introduced, consisting of officers and delegates of official Habitations. The entire organization became increasingly complex, even cumbersome, while the Habitations remained efficient, responsive and relatively independent.

Women were admitted to the League in 1884 after pressure from politically interested society hostesses, and a Ladies' Grand Council

Table 6.2

Year	Knights	Dames	Associates	Total number of members	Total number of habitations
1884	747	153	57	957	46
1886	32,645	23,381	181,257	237,283	1,200
1890	60,795	48,796	801,261	910,852	2,081
1900	74,461	64,003	1,380,097	1,518,561	2,380

Source: Compiled from 'Special Supplement on the Primrose League', by Meresia Nevill, *Madame*, 25 May 1901.

was established in March 1885 following a meeting at the London home of Lady Borthwick. Table 6.2 indicates how readily women were accepted by and willing to join the League; they met with encouragement rather than prejudice. Perhaps the growth of Women's Liberal Associations provided a spur, as did Disraeli's blessing in his novels, especially *Endymion*:

> all his good women understood political questions, and devoted their lives and energies to the cause espoused by their husbands and brothers without fee or reward other than the satisfaction of having succeeded.[13]

For an accurate assessment of the practical contribution of women to the League it is useful to consider their place in the organizational structure. The Ladies' Grand Council constituted an aristocratic and wealthy elite. Only Dames could be members – on the annual contribution of one guinea; this was in addition to the Habitation subscription of half a guinea on entrance and half a guinea each year. Of the fourteen women present at the initial meeting to establish the Council, ten were titled and the elected Executive Committee in subsequent years showed a similar exclusivity.[14] Unlike the Women's Liberal Federation, the Council evolved no programme of its own, reflected none of the former's strength of character and defiant stand to force women's suffrage. The Ladies' Grand Council was subservient to the somewhat anodyne pronouncements of the overall Grand Council and therefore adopted a neutral stance on the foremost feminist issue of the day. Janet Robb writes of its 'decorative impotence in contrast to its financial usefulness'.[15] Funds raised were allocated to the coffers of Head Office and the Scottish branch – mostly to cover the cost of distributing literature and sending out lecturers. Anything left over after covering general expenses at the Ladies' Office in Victoria Street was used only then for lectures and the training of canvassers.[16]

Lady Knightley, a member of the Executive Committee, found meetings invariably noisy, ill-managed and subject to personality clashes amongst the titled ladies.[17] Perhaps she was not alone in finding Habitation work far more useful, as membership of the Council was always low. Annual meetings were staid and somewhat desultory –many of the official views about women's role originated here. The Ladies' Grand Council did produce a number of politically astute and very able women – its Honorary Treasurer, Meresia Nevill and Lady Jersey, apparently an excellent speaker – who devoted their time to political work with an eye to the preservation of the traditional influence of the leisured classes and whose idea it originally was to channel the energy of women into electoral support.[18]Clearly, however, the dynamic role that women could play in politics was shown not so much by the Ladies' Grand Council as elsewhere in the Habitations.

Women were frequently instrumental in starting Habitations, particularly in rural areas where such activity became an outgrowth of the usual duties of the gentry. Friends could be recruited as Knights and Dames, local villagers encouraged to join as associates.[19] Lady Knightley described a visit from Lady Wimborne, inviting her to become a Dame:

> It sounds all rubbish – but the objects . . . are excellent – and I can quite believe that the paraphernalia helps to keep Conservatives together; – means, in short, an army of unpaid canvassers.[20]

Lady Knightley gave great time and energy to the League. With her husband she started several Habitations in local districts and was herself Dame President of the Knightley Habitation whose socially mixed membership was 'thoroughly representative – beginning with Colonel Lowndes – and going down to Bagley the chimney sweep'.[21]

An unofficial consensus about women's role in politics quickly emerged within the Primrose League, changing very little over subsequent decades; women's influence was to be indirect – the same was true of the League itself – their duty was to educate themselves and others in political affairs, to assist in electoral work in the constituencies, to be the complement and never the rival of men in politics. The League was always careful to dissociate itself from the militant feminism which characterized the Women's Liberal Federation and delighted in comparing its 'masculine' women with the more womanly Dame.[22]

This limited perception of the role of women in politics was summed up by Lady Jersey at the Annual Meeting of the Ladies' Grand Council in 1890:

We ladies of the Primrose League are not in the least desirous of trenching on any department which does not belong to us; we don't wish to govern the country. Our efforts tend towards two things. We want, so far as lies in our power, to assist in placing men in the Goverment who we think will lead our country in the paths of peace and prosperity – and we want to lead all who come within the sphere of our influence and to bring up our children in those principles of religion and devotion to their country and of patriotism which will make them good men, and, therefore, good citizens.[23]

The notion of woman's proper sphere was thus cleverly elasticated: within the confines of the Primrose League women could retain their womanliness and the mother role; they acquired a political education which could be passed on to their children. Not infrequently were 'mothers of families' exhorted to join the League as this kind of language enhanced its image of propriety.[24] The 'Body Politic' was accordingly 'merely an enlargement of family life'.[25] Moreover, the organizers stressed the good effect of selfless political work on women's characters: it rendered them public spirited and high-minded – more so than charitable activity – and it gave them a sense of duty and responsibility. Lady Knightley of Fawsley in Northamptonshire, a conscientious, striving woman, much concerned about her inner growth, active in the League, the Girls' Friendly Society and the National Union of Women Workers, is typical of those who found virtue and even a religious calling in public affairs. She reflected in her diary:

. . . the semi public life I lead is good – and right – and womanly, and yet it seems as tho I were called to it – both by the position and the powers of speaking and organizing God has given me and by Rainald's liking me to do it.[26]

Such a woman could hardly be straying outside her proper sphere if her work was sanctioned by both God and her husband.

The growth of the Primrose League must be seen against a background of labour organization, agitation and the enfranchisement of agricultural labourers in 1884. The League believed its strength in rural areas would weaken the attempts by Radicals and Labour 'to sow the seeds of class hatred and division' by 'bringing the educated and the ignorant, the wealthy and the poor, into friendly social intercourse'.[27] Hence women's special role: the tradition of district visiting was an established custom in both town and country by which Lady Bountiful assumed a right to enter the homes of the working classes; there women spoke to women across the social divide. The League tapped this tradition for its own purpose, being generally most successful in rural areas where social contact was already established. One Ruling Councillor from a Lancashire town reported difficulty in attracting women members, and suggested that the environment made people 'less suscep- tible to Lady Bountiful who can operate more easily in the quiet and peaceful countryside'.[28] Habitations did vary according to region. The Brighton Dames were middle-class and middle-aged while in the Northern manufacturing towns membership comprised mainly factory workers and artisans.[29]

The Women's Liberal Federation and associations were equally active in attracting new members to their cause. Through leaflets, pamphlets and articles in the *Women's Gazette and Weekly News*, Liberal activists sought to dispel the hesitation of those supporters who could potentially add much to their movement but who feared that involvement in politics meant stepping beyond a woman's proper sphere. Many needed reassurance that politics would not interfere with their domestic duties and was not unwomanly. The arguments used to overcome these doubts did much to shape the language of separate spheres which largely suf- fused the women's movement at least until the First World War. The Liberals stressed that, while taking part in organized politics women should not neglect their domestic duties, but add others:

> Women: your sphere is your home! Yes, but you have a double duty. First of all to your family, and secondly to the wider family, the world of human beings outside, and you fail in one of your most solemn obliga- tions, if you devote yourself solely to your own home and your own children, unmindful of the fact that thousands of poor men and women have no homes, or live in dark degraded homes, and that hundreds and thousands of little children are growing up uncared for, untaught, un- thought of, in slums and alleys or the streets of our great cities.[30]

Another argument, often used, referred to women as mothers and educators of future generations; they were 'bound to try to understand politics, in order that they may teach the children to love liberty and obey law'.[31] Although the supposed claim by the husband of a Midlands WLA member that 'Since my wife took up with politics, it has been a lot jollier at home' was somewhat suspect, it was suggested quite seriously that a mutual interest in politics would strengthen a marriage and promote congenial companionship.[32] This was un- doubtedly a far remove from the more common Victorian assumption that only men should concern themselves with public affairs.

It was, of course, infinitely easier for those with servants to find time for political work in a busy day. Working-class women who in this period were slowly emerging from their long silence to add their voice to the SDF, the ILP and the Women's Co-operative Guild, found it more difficult to combine meetings with domestic duties. The realities of working-class life were not always recognized by those Liberal women who inhabited a more comfortable and well-to-do world. This class divide is aptly illustrated by the following extract in which working-class women are being coaxed to join the new Liberal associations with a vision of rosy domestic contentment that fell far short of the truth:

> [after] the comfortable evening meal [when] the little ones are in bed, and the warm slippers are ready for the husband's weary feet, *then is the opportunity for the work-basket*, and happy is the woman who, while the inevitable stitching goes on, can join with her husband in conversation about matters which are taking place in the wider world around them.[33]

Much of the Liberals' propaganda attempted to raise women's political consciousness by pointing to how laws affected them and their families – laws for the protection of women and children, town and county council regulations over sanitation, housing and public health, laws concerning education and temperance, 'for a law is like the air we breathe: we cannot see it, but its influence penetrates every part of the kingdom, and is powerful for evil or for good, according to its nature.'[34] It was argued that women were particularly subject to unjust laws for 'the law-makers are chosen by both rich and poor men, but by no woman', which could be rectified if women learned to use their influence wisely.[35] The recent Married Women's Property Acts and legislation giving widows the legal right to take care of their own children were but 'two improvements in the Law we owe, chiefly, to the energetic action of women who have long taken an INTEREST IN POLITICS'.[36]

Ireland provided another immediate example of how Liberal women felt bound to alter iniquitous laws and injustice. Josephine Butler suggested that they were outraged by what was happening in Ireland. The inhumane consequences of the Coercion and Crimes Acts 'had touched closely upon their hearts, their maternal feelings, their deepest emotions, their most profound convictions'.[37] Probably many associations were inaugurated largely to redress Irish grievances as the Home Rule question dominated the years 1887 to 1892. The Liberal women's press recorded numerous meetings and published articles testifying to women's vigorous involvement; it roused many women who previously had taken no part in politics. According to Mrs Osler speaking to the Birmingham Women's Liberal Association in 1889:

> The Irish question has done more in the last two or three years to settle definitely the long-contested question of women's mission and women's

place in politics than the patient and laborious efforts of twenty years past had done. It was like the national crisis which in old times had produced a Judith, a Boadicea, and a Joan of Arc. Many women who once personally disapproved of women taking an active part in politics had, during the last few months, not only attended but spoken at meetings on the Irish question.[38]

Many of the Victorian assumptions about women's moral influence on others which had been used to justify their importance to family life and their philanthropic work amongst the poor and the fallen were to underlie their entry into politics. The Liberals were foremost in urging that women had a mission to purify and elevate the moral tenor of public affairs. Hannah Cheetham in a speech to the Southport Women's Liberal Association in 1886 compared the government to a house wherein 'the same sympathy, the same refinement, the same emotional insight, are needed to purify and ennoble the government of that larger home – our country'.[39] It was characteristic of the language of separate spheres that no-one should doubt that women were morally superior to men by reason of 'their higher moral enthusiasm, their preference of righteousness to expediency, their freedom from debasing habits'.[40] The Women's Liberal Federation at its inception had been very conscious of its aim to introduce a new element into politics – which partly explained the emphasis it placed on maintaining a separate identity from that of the men's associations. They were thus free to articulate the women's moral conscience and to introduce their point of view wherever possible. Some cautioned that loss of autonomy might well result in a loss of moral power: 'we are liable at any time to be used as the tool of party politicians for purposes repugnant to our principles and to true womanly feeling'.[41] They hoped to draw into their movement those wives and mothers who by way of their particular place in society were custodians of private virtue:

> we women who work in the field of politics can point to the best of wives and mothers, who, without moving an inch from their high vantage point of domestic duty, can yet further our cause with ability and energy. A good woman will be a true woman wherever she is – in the home circle or on the platform; and we rejoice to think the noble womanhood of England is enlisted on our side.[42]

The scandal surrounding Sir Charles Dilke's personal life which rocked late-Victorian society showed how clearly certain sectors of the women's movement saw their role as custodians of public virtue as well. At the beginning of 1889 a women's committee of protest was formed to challenge Sir Charles Dilke's candidacy as Alderman on the London County Council. A statement with 1,604 signatures, published in the

Women's Penny Paper, was to some extent a who's who of the women's movement and included the names of illustrious Liberals such as Jane Cobden, Elizabeth Garret Anderson, Millicent Fawcett, Elizabeth Blackwell, Louisa Twining, Priscilla Bright McLaren, Eva McLaren, Laura Ormiston Chant and Caroline Ashurst Biggs.[43] The Women's Liberal Federation Executive was sharply divided between those who felt that mere association with Lady Dilke would injure their reputation and who consequently prevented her from reading a paper on trade unions at the annual conference, and those such as Eliza Orme who rallied to her defence. The former faction argued against supporting Sir Charles Dilke's candidature for Parliament in the spring of 1888 with the following justification:

> the W.L.F. . . . consists very largely of ladies whose social position renders it impossible for them to recognise, or even in a distant way countenance, a man in Sir Charles Dilke's position. It also consists very largely of those working women who form the backbone and mainstay of England's Purity, and who speak with English frankness on questions which are of Public Morality. French vices do not find favour with the women of England.[44]

They admonished him to 'Wash your hands first'.[45] The savage campaign launched against the Dilkes revealed the growing strength of the social purity movement in the late nineteenth century, a movement in which several Liberal women such as Laura Ormiston Chant figured prominently. Their activities helped formulate the moral basis of Liberal feminism.

The powerful connection between morality and religion in the Victorian age was well understood. In winning women's participation in politics on moral grounds first, it became easier to correlate the arguments concerning politics and religion. No longer did it hold that the two did not mix in people's lives; they were equally important spheres for women's influence: 'religion is not more important to our spiritual wants than politics to our material wants. . . . Religion tells us we should be helpful one to another, and politics show us how to be helpful, wisely and effectually.'[46]

All the arguments for women's involvement in politics – moral, religious, educational, maternal, legislative – rested on a powerful new notion that was slowly superseding the long-established idea that women should wield influence indirectly, in private, through their male relatives. This new notion was clearly feminist in its implications. Women who wanted to work for the Liberal cause could do so in a way that was open and clear, using direct rather than backstairs influence.

As women, they had a particular point of view to express and a need to safeguard the interests of themselves, their children, the poor and the unfortunate; this could not and should not be done on their behalf by men. To convey this influence they needed to combine and organize as the men had done before them, and the larger the organisation – they believed – the greater their strength and power.

> though woman's quiet influence is a very good thing, her quiet influence *with power behind it* is still better. In union is strength; in organisation is effective force.[47]

> for by union and combination those who are weak become strong, those who are hopeless gain new faith, those who need help obtain the power both of self-help and of helping others.[48]

Liberal women were altogether more muscular in their approach to political organization than the Conservatives. The pioneers who formed the associations and the Federation sensed their power and developed it. The first task was to educate and train the many women who sought to join them; the second was to decide for whom and when this new power should be used.

II

The Primrose League promoted women to positions of responsibility in a political organization where men and women could, unusually, rub shoulders. They were eligible to hold office as Ruling Councillors or Dame Presidents (the titles were interchangeable), to be representatives on Divisional Councils and to act as wardens and sub-wardens for a given area – positions which required business capacity, tact and energy. Dames were encouraged to hold office in their Habitation and many did so. In 1886 in the English and Welsh counties they held 26 per cent of executive positions in local Habitations. The figure varied very much from county to county: from 62 per cent in Cornwall and 51 per cent in Rutland and Cardiganshire to nil in Huntingdonshire and Radnorshire. Although the correlation is not exact, women held a disproportionately large number of executive positions in the most active areas.[49] Some women-only Habitations were formed out of mixed ones in the same locality and were amongst the most powerful in the League, for example, Grantham, Victoria and Croydon.[50]

The social flourishes of the League – the fêtes, soirées and teas – were thought suitable for women's organizing talent because of their social conditioning.[51] But rapid significance was given to their political duties which fell broadly into two general areas: political propaganda, referred to as education, and electioneering. The Corrupt Practices Act of 1883 which forbade the payment of canvassers gave impetus to the engagement of Primrose League members as unpaid substitutes. Lady Knightley remembered canvassing in the 1885 elections as 'an utterly new and strange undertaking' which took her from 'house to house', spending long dreary hours talking to discontented labourers.[52] This political district-visiting formed the basis of women's new political duties in the League, undertaken with much enthusiasm before each General Election and, from 1892, for the elections to municipal and county councils. Women were encouraged to become wardens and subwardens whose work was to supervise canvassers for a certain number of houses, to distribute leaflets and to collate names, addresses and subscriptions.[53] By the mid-1890s a vast army of women volunteers was being mobilized – many on bicycles, thanks to technical modifications which had produced the women's model, a high fashion craze adopted by the well-born and the rich in the summer of 1895, and the formation of the Primrose Cycling Corps – which provoked the Duke of Marlborough to foresee 'the recalcitrant voter being tracked to his lair by a band of enthusiastic and athletic Primrose Dames mounted on bicycles'.[54]

Any apprehensions as to the seemliness of women engaged in such political pursuit had been firmly swept away by the General Elections of 1895 and 1900. Candidate after candidate testified to their usefulness in canvassing, leafleting and clerical tasks, a usefulness born of personal contact, loyalty to the cause and capacity for hard work.[55] W.J. Bull, MP, praised the service rendered by women from the Victoria Dames and Shepherd's Bush Habitations:

> They assembled and addressed 13,000 envelopes, folded 13,000 addresses, addressed another 13,000 envelopes, wrote out 13,000 polling cards, and put them in the second batch of envelopes. Everything was checked, the outvoters were readdressed, and all this was done inside a week . . . willingly done without fee or reward or even a cup of tea.[56]

The remarkable feature of this labour is that it mostly came from a sector of society not noted for its seriousness. Many young debutantes 'in no sense strong-minded' found themselves trailing round the streets of East London 'canvassing ardently for their fathers or their brothers, and speaking repeatedly at public meetings'.[57] The same society women who 'went unattended into lonely neighbourhoods and carried postmen's lanterns to light the path . . . would be shocked to see a woman friend at the theatre at night, alone.'[58] There is a sense here that electoral work was the fashionable thing to do, and with careful nurturing became more widely accepted. Lectures, leaflets, canvassing classes in the constituencies and the Ladies' Grand Council Canvassing Committee perpetuated and improved women's skills as the Edwardian years passed by.

Concomitant with electoral activity was the need for grounding in the political issues of the day – fiscal policies, factory acts and other legislation, municipal and county council concerns. The organizers recognized that women of all classes needed a political education and were concerned to ensure that the Conservative viewpoint prevailed. Consequently, an important part of League work was the instruction of its own members – in drawing-room meetings for Dames, study classes which resembled mothers' meetings begun by the Habitations, and in 1906, an attempt to emulate the women's club movement – social evenings alternating with political discussion. One of the more enterprising ventures was the Ladies' Grand Council Touring Van started in 1892 with a journey through small towns and villages in Bedfordshire and Buckinghamshire, distributing leaflets and making speeches. Like the Clarion Van of the ILP it was considered a great success.[59]

Among the skills which Primrose League women acquired, public speaking was one of the more important and most contentious – not least because it challenged the frontiers of women's place in public. The organization of meetings, acceptance of office in Habitations, even political district-visiting could be done with a low profile and with a sense that women were only extending their domestic managerial role. The public platform, however, placed the speaker firmly in the spotlight of public recognition. Not surprisingly, the Primrose League was ambivalent in its attitude. Unlike the other political parties, which quickly accepted women on the platform, the League was bound by its image of propriety and respectability. Was it womanly? Some thought not.

> Public speaking is manifestly out of our province, so far at least, as the addressing of very large meetings is concerned. Neither by constitution, nor by taste and feeling are we adapted for the part of sharing in the gladiatorial combats of the platform.[60]

Disconcertingly for those who advocated this view, there were a few Conservative women who notably excelled at the art. Lady Jersey opened a Primrose Fete at Fawsley, Northamptonshire before a crowd of two thousand with an 'eloquent speech – thoughtful . . . a peroration worthy of any orator'.[61] She spoke frequently at mixed political gatherings, as did Lady Randolph Churchill, and at Ladies' Grand Council Annual

Meetings alongside her colleagues on the Executive Committee. Public speaking was tremendously difficult for most women in this era. The history of the women's movement is partly the history of individual women, whatever their politics, struggling to shake free of personal inhibitions and Victorian convention. Lady Knightley, used to addressing Girls' Friendly Society meetings, a charitable and therefore womanly exercise, found her talent succumbed to convention in the masculine world of politics. Campaigning for her husband, she longed to speak, but reflected in her diary, 'that I will not do'.[62] It is perhaps important to note that public speaking meant oratory, a particular, stylized form of public address often presented with dramatic and rhetorical flourish, closely associated with the political platform and the debating chambers of Parliament. A graceful way to sidestep a public speech was to read a paper. Many women's organizations in the nineteenth century preferred this more low-key style, as did Primrose League Habitations: their records show that the speaker, sometimes female, invited to address a meeting would then read a paper, followed by discussion and sometimes a resolution. Another alternative, quite acceptable to those who feared the public glare, was to speak simply and directly at smaller, more homely gatherings. Many women thus gained greater confidence and skill.

Women's contribution to the work of the League was set within clearly defined limits. Lady Hardman, Honorary Secretary of the Ladies' Grand Council, expressed the official view in a speech to Upminster Habitation: she hoped that Dames would hesitate to 'enter into public strife and political life' and trusted that they had not 'any intention of becoming a County Councillor, an alderman – or alderwoman (laughter)'.[63] Although this view was quite common in 1889 it would soon seem reactionary. The women's movement was already approving women's candidacy for local government, Board of Guardians and School Board seats and was elated by the election of the Liberals Jane Cobden and Margaret Sandhurst to the London County Council in 1889. The League argued, on the other hand, that it was precisely because women were not involved in the daily run of politics that they had a 'detached understanding of party principles'.[64] The enormous assistance which women rendered to Conservative electoral candidates over the next ten years did nothing to change this argument. When, in 1900, A.J. Balfour suggested that the ladies' great talent was 'persistent plodding and hard work behind scenes', the position of women in the Primrose League was becoming ossified.[65]

A striking difference between Primrose League and Liberal women was the latter's deliberate cultivation of female political power – not simply as canvassers but as voters, candidates and makers of policy. Their practical objectives were fourfold: to improve women's political education, to make sure that women voters used their prerogative in local elections, to encourage women candidates for Poor Law Boards, School Boards, town and county councils and, ultimately, to enhance their claim to the Parliamentary suffrage.

In the associations during the 1890s and after, members moved from social and discussion meetings to concerted action, pushing forward the boundaries of women's public work in their areas. Initially their work bore some resemblance to that of the League – promoting social intercourse and political education among members and taking an active part in all elections. At a conference of northern branches in the autumn of 1888 Mrs J.E. Clark read a paper on 'The Influence of Women's Liberal Associations in Municipal Affairs' in which she suggested that women might do much in the way of canvassing and in bringing voters to the poll. The Federation, Women's National Liberal Association and associations in the localities came to see electoral assistance as an integral part of their work. As had happened in the Primrose League, the introduction of women volunteers helped electioneering become more organized, efficient and effective. Past methods all too often had been slipshod:

> The candidates have started late, the organisation has too often been slack, and the women's opinion and convenience have not been consulted, either in the choice of a candidate or in the method and time of working for him. Now that women's work in politics is becoming organised and definite it is fair to urge that this unsatisfactory state of things should be altered.[66]

From early days, the Women's Liberal Associations went about canvassing in a highly organized and methodical way, stressing the importance of personal house-to-house 'visitation', of placing qualified women on the electoral register and of well-trained canvassers.[67] A.B.H., a contributor to the *Women's Gazette and Weekly News*, pointed out that many voters – lodging house keepers, laundresses, teachers, nurses – read few newspapers, rarely went to meetings and therefore needed a personal visit from someone who would explain the issues, be sympathetic to their troubles and explain the relevance of voting to their private affairs.[68] The Liberals' hard work and persistence did bring rewards. In a survey of one ward over a three-week period, A.B.H. and her WLA had found that out of nearly 300 female voters, 19 were indifferent and would not vote, 28 were indifferent but willing to listen, while 199 were fully determined to vote.

By 1889 York Women's Liberal Association, one of the earliest, had perfected some quite sophisticated methods which others were to emulate. They divided the city into six wards, each in the charge of a WLA ward secretary who gathered a 'band of intelligent, active WLA members familiar with her district'.[69] Concentrating on the women voters in municipal elections, they canvassed to obtain information as to voting intentions and which voters needed transport to the poll. Difficult cases received visits from the secretary or candidate plus special attention throughout the following year.[70] Associations exercised a fair measure of independence as to whom they supported. York WLA set its machine into action only if it deemed the candidate worthy enough – a far cry from the unquestioning subservience of Primrose League Dames. Increasingly over the next two decades, Liberal women, as they realized their power, set test questions for candidates on vice and suffrage. Unfortunate candidates had thus two selection committees to satisfy – the men's and the women's. It was apparently a source of some grievance that the official choosing of a candidate rested with the men's committee alone and this led some women to argue, as did A.W. of York, that to achieve a desirable consensus of the sexes the composition of selection committees should be altered to include women.[71]

The Edwardian years were marked by an increasing sophistication of method and organization as Liberal women sought to consolidate their impact on the party. At the local level they found a circuitous way to influence issues by working through the men's associations in an attempt to reach the National Liberal Federation and its conference debates. At the national level, until women gained the vote and entered Parliament, one of their more effective tactics was, ironically but necessarily, old-fashioned privileged influence through personally known MPs and Cabinet Ministers: Sir Charles McLaren and Corrie Grant, who proved true friends of the women's cause, offered their unofficial services as parliamentary whips on the women's behalf.[72] Less generous were those politicians who recognized the women's usefulness as party workers but refused them their democratic due. The Prime Minister, Asquith, sorely tested their loyalty and patience – to the extent that Elibank, the Liberal Chief Whip, warned him in the autumn of 1910: 'You cannot afford, on the eve of a General Election, to drive the whole Women's Movement into the most bitter opposition nor to weaken and in many cases alienate the support of the most active Liberal women workers.'[73]

Elibank had reason to fear the women's wrath. A pressure group named The Forward Suffrage Union had emerged in 1908 to persuade all Women's Liberal Associations affiliated to the Federation to concentrate their activities on their own enfranchisement.[74] Equally worrying was the rigorous implementation of the policy of test questions on vice and suffrage at recent by-elections. Candidates were interviewed by the Federation area organizer and assessed by the local WLAs as to their support for suffrage and opposition to the state regulation of prostitution. Only after a satisfactory response would a paid organizer and associations then set to work. Liberal women exercised a considerable power and freedom which was based on their organizational autonomy; it led to some startling manoeuvres. In the Wellington division of Somersetshire in June 1911, the Liberal candidate, C. H. Dudley Ward, was refused an organizer because his views on women's suffrage were not considered adequate; the previous year in the Kirkdale division of Liverpool where no Liberal candidate had been adopted, A.G. Cameron, for Labour, who favoured the vote for women and had shrewdly agreed to mention it in his election address, had secured the services of the WLAs in West Toxteth, East Toxteth and West Derby.[75]

III

An assessment of the League's contribution to the women's movement should first of all indicate the discrepancy between the practical advances made in gaining political experience and the curious avoidance of women's issues. There was no attempt at policy-making level to introduce these or other matters of social reform because of the involvement of women.[76] The Ladies' Grand Council in particular adhered to the official party line, and in this respect differed considerably from the experience of Liberal and socialist women. Janet Robb suggests that Primrose Dames were not as feminist as the Liberals, rarely being appealed to through their interest in purely women's questions such as equal pay, the Contagious Diseases Acts and higher education.[77] Liberal, Liberal Unionist and socialist women did tend to be more active in other social causes.

The exception was women's suffrage. Habitations frequently debated the issue, invited National Society for Women's Suffrage lecturers, passed resolutions, and performed playlets with titles such as 'Women's Rights and Men's Wrongs'.[78] Feelings for and against were very strong and Grand Council, afraid of the divisiveness of the issue, authorized official statements to the effect that as women's suffrage was a question of opinion rather than principle it lay outside the scope of the League. Members could hold a private opinion, attend meetings on the subject and sign petitions, but could not attempt to influence the views of candidates or pass resolutions in the Habitations.[79] Women's suffrage was so contentious that it had split the Women's Liberal Federation in 1892, and Primrose League organizers were anxious to avoid a similar occurrence in their own organization. As the League included active supporters for and against the question – Lady Jersey was a member of the Anti-Suffrage League, Betty Balfour belonged to the Conservative and Unionist Women's Franchise Association – this was pragmatic and shrewd. Official pronouncements did not, however, stop the Habitations from engaging in vigorous debate. They continued to invite suffrage speakers and to pass resolutions – many in favour.[80] Nor could the League hide forever from the contradictions of a policy whereby suffragists in the Habitations could find themselves obliged to work for candidates who were against the measure. Lady Balfour exposed this contradiction when she resigned as Dame President of Woking Habitation after Mr McMaster, MP, voted against a Woman Suffrage Bill in the Commons. If he opposed the enfranchisement of women, she argued, he must also be averse to women actively working in politics.[81]

A major vehicle for the developing power of Liberal women was the Annual Council Meeting and Conference which provided a forum for the airing of official Liberal policy and those women's issues which the Federation and associations sought to bring to the forefront of the political stage.[82] In the latter respect these annual gatherings were most unlike those of the Primrose League Ladies' Grand Council and somewhat similar to the Annual Conferences of Labour women in later years. The Federation pioneered the concept of political party meetings whose main purpose was to inject the women's point of view into politics. Although initially, representation came from both all-women and mixed associations, the Federation was quick to tackle the dilemma of whether their annual meeting should be open to men. Foreseeing the dangers of a substantial male presence – male speakers tending to dominate the proceedings, women's issues being pushed to one side – in 1891 the Executive Committee of the Federation decided that the next meeting should be open to women only. Eva McLaren, an active suffragist and feminist, pointed to the success of a recent all-women suffrage demonstration at the Queen's Hall, London and received support from Sophia Fry who remarked that 'a good women's meeting was better than a poor men's one'.[83] Accordingly, at the next Annual Council Meeting the delegates voted to amend the Constitution to ensure that in future all representatives from all associations were women and that representation would be in proportion to the number of women members only:

> While welcoming co-operation on the part of men, we think it impossible to represent the claims of Liberal women if they are representing men. . . . No doubt the ideal position would be for men and women to

work together in one body; we have not got that yet, but we have the Federation to represent the opinions of Liberal women, and it must represent these entirely.[84]

The Conferences covered a wide range of topics: trade unions for women, working conditions, wages and factory acts, education, temperance, housing, free trade, land laws, taxation, matters of public morality, the Contagious Diseases Acts, peace and arbitration, women's suffrage, local government and the appointment of police matrons.[85] Wherever possible, and this applied particularly to domestic issues, they endeavoured to show how women and children were personally affected. The papers presented were detailed and knowledgeable; Liberal women were active in diverse social and industrial organizations and brought much expertise to the Federation. The Conferences bestowed not only a good general political and economic education on its members but became the fulcrum for campaigns and pressure groups, lobbying MPs and giving evidence to government committees on matters concerning women.[86] Such activity became an increasingly viable means of obtaining reform by the turn of the century, and in this sense, the Women's Liberal Federation became an integral part of the women's movement over the next thirty years. The Annual General Meeting sparked ideas and action, enabling Liberal women to contribute, often controversially, to the ideology and practice of feminism.

The outstanding issue of the day was of course that of suffrage, for which all women's organizations had at some point to register their loyalty, neutrality or opposition. For the Liberals it proved troublesome and divisive. From 1887 until 1892 the Federation Executive was carved into two groups, the Progressives and Moderates, the former seeking to make it an official object of the constitution, the latter wishing to adhere to the original position of neutrality.[87]

The Moderates, who included Sophia Fry, Eliza Orme and Mrs Bryant among others, agreed that as the WLF was intended to be a party organization, women's suffrage, which all political parties regarded as a non-party issue, could not be given prominence by inclusion in the official programme.[88] They doubted the wisdom and expediency of unduly pressing their claim for suffrage at a time when the Liberal leaders were facing great difficulties over the Irish Question: 'Let women then sink their own wishes for the present moment, and work for Ireland with heart and hand'.[89] They argued that numerous suffrage societies existed already with energy and influence; by adopting the demand officially, declared Eliza Orme, the WLF would become simply one more.[90] Moreover, the suffrage movement was itself undergoing upheavals as to the kind of franchise to be sought and for whom. It should be noted that the Executive, most of whom were suffragists, comprised women with wide experience in public affairs, whereas the vast majority of members in the associations were only just finding their political feet. Some WLAs were no doubt politically wise on the subject and were affiliated to local suffrage societies, but others were what Miss Ryley of Southport despairingly described as 'apathetic . . . indifferent in the matter which of all others concerns them most vitally'.[91] The Moderates were thus chary of forcing a stand on the uninitiated and feared that by appearing to bully the associations they would lose the support and membership of those who did not share their views.

The Progressives, who included Eva McLaren, Rosalind Carlisle, Laura McLaren, Margaret Sandhurst, Emma Cons and Jane Cobden, desired conversely to see the associations march in the vanguard of the suffrage movement. They believed that if every WLA in the country had 'a rallying force of ten women with convictions' they could play an enormous part in stirring up local public opinion – which would only ripen if the associations treated it as a matter of paramount importance – and here the Federation could take the lead by turning talk into action, by making suffrage an official issue.[92] The Moderates were on the whole well-born, well-known and well-connected to the inner circle of the Liberal Party:

> their role is so brilliant, they have such prestige, are so much respected, and are in appearance so important, that they scarcely see how insignificant women as a class are, and how their refusal to take up our cause adds for the time to our insignificance.[93]

The Progressives understood rather more the impotence of those who watch while others make decisions:

> without a political status all political action is hollow and unreal. We may agitate and call meetings – we may seem influential and be flattered and perhaps made use of, but we do not and cannot affect the legislature one bit. . . . We are only turned into party machines without rights or responsibilities, to canvass for the men our party has chosen to represent them.[94]

The Progressives could argue persuasively that suffrage should be made an official object because it was after all a natural Liberal policy. As Mrs Wynford Phillips argued at the Annual Council Meeting in 1891, it upheld 'the true Liberal principle that taxation and representation must go together. . . . I am a strong suffragist because I am a strong Liberal. . . . I learned my Liberalism from Gladstone and Bright, and I say that we women want the keystone of the vote as men did.'[95] As Eliza Orme was later to reflect, the Progressives were more broadly feminist in their outlook, desiring that the Federation take up those questions which especially pertained to women and which were more moral and social in their nature than political in the ordinary sense of the word.[96] They wished to draw attention to women as a class, not merely as party workers, and were deeply suspicious of those politicians such as Gladstone who made use of their services but wished to silence their demand for representation.[97]

The Progressives waged a staunch campaign and won the day. At the Annual Council Meeting in May 1892, Lady Carlisle proposed and Eva McLaren seconded a successful amendment calling on the Executive Committee to promote the enfranchisement of women. The following year, object two of the constitution was reworded to include the amendment and to signal to all Liberal politicians the women's comprehensive determination to fight for the legislative interests of their sex.[98]

The cost of this divisive struggle was loss of the Moderate faction and a number of associations who set up the Women's National Liberal Association some months later. They continued to do worthy work on behalf of 'the true spirit of Liberalism', spreading political knowledge amongst women and offering electoral assistance in a 'quiet, steady, unobtrusive but persistent way'.[99] By the end of the 1890s the scattered band of exiles had built up a solid, rival network of associations which clearly appealed to women who found the Federation's branch of feminism too strong. The WNLA showed a passive rather than an active interest in women's questions; at the Annual Conferences by the end of the decade speakers such as Emilia Dilke, Gertrude Tuckwell and Margaret Bondfield were invited to give talks on the position of working women, and modest approval of the right to women's suffrage was voiced in the *Quarterly Leaflet*.[100] But there was little encouragement for members to push themselves to the fore of either Liberal politics or the women's movement; that was left to the Federation. The two organizations flourished side by side, without acrimony, content to differ.[101]

As for the Women's Liberal Federation, it promptly became embroiled in yet another dispute as to whether women's suffrage should be made a test question to determine support for candidates at parliamentary elections. There had always been those suffragists who saw the illogicality and inconsistency of working for franchise opponents. Women's political associations had become a universally acknowledged force whose organized labour had the power to decide the fortunes of aspiring MPs. How long, wondered Kate Barrington in a letter to the *Women's*

Penny Paper, would they submit to being 'Political Charwomen'?[102] In 1896 a Union of Practical Suffragists (UPS) was formed within the Federation to persuade members to accept the test question as official policy; they believed that the first aim and duty of a political organization of unenfranchised citizens was to secure political representation.[103] A decade before the Women's Social and Political Union was to make the test question a fighting strategy, the UPS realized its power as a tactical weapon and a challenge to male dominance and authority. They dismissed cries of disloyalty, treachery and the danger of losing the election for the Liberal candidate by their withdrawal of labour: 'Those who have strength can strike' and if the WLF was to say it would not work in future for any parliamentary candidate opposed to women's suffrage until it became part of the party programme, the Liberal leaders and candidates 'would think twice before they throw overboard such a large army of zealous workers'.[104]

In 1902 the Annual Council instructed the Executive 'that the official organiser of the Federation be sent to help those candidates only who would support Women's Suffrage in the House of Commons'. In deference to the Federation's democratic structure, local associations retained their freedom as to whom they helped; in practice, many followed the Federation's corporate stand. The same Council boldly called on the Liberal Party to adopt a simplified policy of 'one person', one vote'; in effect, registered adult suffrage with a three-month residential qualification to replace all others. The Federation proved unable to change Asquith's mind, but significantly influenced many rank-and-file Liberal members. In the first decade of the twentieth century the wider suffrage movement regained sufficient momentum to make the parliamentary franchise a distinct possibility. With their shrewd tactics and progressive call for adult suffrage, Liberal women moved in advance of the changing tide.[105]

IV

In their use of traditional campaign tactics – deputations to the Prime Minister and members of the Cabinet, evidence to parliamentary committees and Royal Commissions, circulars and letters to MPs and newspapers, participation in public meetings and conferences – Liberal women came to share a sense of solidarity with a wide network of feminist organizations who attempted to apply pressure from without. The women's movement was very much a part of that nineteenth-century development whereby interest groups sought to influence the establishment to obtain legislative reform. Working sometimes alone, sometimes in concert with the Women's Co-operative Guild, the Women's Local Government Society, suffrage associations and the National Union of Women Workers, the Liberals applied their energies and organizational strength to the major women's issues of the day – divorce law reform, the National Insurance Bill, labour legislation and, above all, the parliamentary and municipal vote.

As a force in party politics Liberal women's organizations earned a wary respect for their essential spade work at elections; they learned to negotiate the complex maze of party machinery with great skill and a shrewd sense of timing. Perhaps their hallmark was a certain moral arrogance which motivated their efforts and their conviction that women should shape their own political destiny.

Primrose League women distinguished themselves not in the field of policy or ideology but in their practical contribution to politics. People quickly became accustomed to the idea that average women without a political family background could play an active part in the body politic, that they could learn campaigning techniques and exercise executive functions, and that their participation should be seen not as a privilege but as a right.[106] Not only Conservative politicians realized the value of women's work; Liberals and socialists recognized it too by calling on their female supporters to follow the new path trodden by the League. The Women's Liberal Federation noted:

> We may despise or condemn its ridiculous paraphernalia, its appeals to the ignorance and frivolous vanities of women . . . instead of seeking to redress the wrongs and secure the individual rights of women, it indulges in vague and delusive cries of 'The Church', or 'The Empire' . . . it is resolute, spectacular, defiant, and must be met and counteracted by the combined action of Liberal women, systematically promoting political education, and exercising, by independent and self-respecting intercourse, an enlightened and elevating influence.[107]

Millicent Fawcett, prominent in the Women's Liberal Unionist Association, paid tribute to the claim that Primrose Dames had made women a new force in politics and noted: 'It has been the frank and universal admission of successful Conservative candidates that they have been lifted into Parliament by the Primrose League.'[108] Even the Social Democratic Federation in its newspaper *Justice* gave credit to the League for being 'the most powerful political machine in Great Britain. . . . The women are even more active than the men', and in 1897 suggested that canvassing be made illegal.[109]

Certainly the League cultivated a sense of political responsibility where previously none existed, and through its impact on other parties might claim to have 'brought to life, politically, half a nation'.[110] In this respect, its best work was done before 1900. It never evolved beyond the self-imposed boundaries of woman's informal, indirect persuasion in politics. The notion that women gained and retained influence not by their talents but by their charms, that they had 'ten times more influence, and three times as much tongue as any man' was precisely the sort of Victorian cant that feminists were trying to shrug off, not sustain.[111] The argument that women had a special backroom role to play which was based on the traditional qualities of the old rather than the new woman, postponed the day of equality.

7

Women in Council:
Separate Spheres, Public Space

Patricia Hollis

Barbara Leigh Smith Bodichon, friend of Emily Davies and Elizabeth Garrett, wrote in 1866,

> I know of no better means, at this present time, of counteracting the tendency to prefer narrow private ends to the public good than this, of giving to all women, duly qualified, a direct and conscious participation in political affairs. . . . As it is, women of the middle classes occupy themselves but little with anything beyond their family circle. They do not consider it any part of theirs, if poor men and women are ill used in workhouse infirmaries, and poor children ill taught in workhouse schools. If the roads are bad, the drains neglected, the water poisoned, they think it all very wrong, but it does not occur to them that it is their duty to get it put right – they think it is men's business, not theirs, to look after such things. It is this belief, so narrowing and deadening in its influence, that the exercise of the franchise would tend to dissipate. The mere fact of being called upon to enforce an opinion by a vote would have an immediate effect in awakening a healthy sense of responsibility. There is no reason why these women should not take an active interest in all the social questions – education, public health, prison discipline, the poor laws and the rest – which occupy Parliament, and by bringing women into hearty cooperation with men, we gain the benefit not only of their work, but of their intelligent sympathy.[2]

Women needed the vote, argued Barbara Bodichon, to educate them into a moral responsibility for the local and social questions of the day.

In 1889 the anti-suffragist Mrs Humphrey Ward collected signatures for her *Appeal Against Female Suffrage* to show that women did not want the vote. (Though, as Emily Davies tartly remarked, the signatories were not distinguished women, but the wives of distinguished men.)[3] Barbara Bodichon's plea was turned on its head. Since 1870, said the *Appeal*, women had found their way into local government where they could indeed engage in local and social questions, where 'judgement is weighted by a true responsibility and can be guided by experience and the practical information that comes from it'. As voters for or members of School and Poor Law Boards, 'women have now opportunities for public usefulness which must promote the growth of character, and at the same time strengthen among them the social sense and habit'. Women had found an appropriate sphere of service. Since women now had the local or 'domestic' vote, they no longer needed the national or 'imperial' vote, argued Mrs Humphrey Ward. Just because they were effective members of elected local authorities, they had no need to seek service in parliamentary politics. Local government was not to be seen as the road to Westminster, as the suffragists would have it, but as women's parallel path. How far had women walked along that path?

When Barbara Bodichon penned her essay, a few women ratepayers possessed the parish vote, and memory suggested that one or two of them had held parish (and poor law) office in the past. That apart, they were not a presence in local government. By 1889 and Mrs Ward's *Appeal Against Female Suffrage*, the situation had changed beyond recognition. Women had arrived in local government – fifty years before they were to arrive in Parliament.

The Second Reform Act of 1867 had focused the demands of the emerging women's movement on the vote. The speeches and writings of John Stuart Mill in the late 1860s sought the parliamentary vote for women on the same terms as men. This was denied, but Jacob Bright did succeed in 1869 in amending the local municipal register to include women ratepayers. Although the Courts ruled in *Regina v. Harrold* in 1872 that only *unmarried* women ratepayers could exercise the local municipal vote,[4] nonetheless women ratepayer electors formed some 12 per cent to 25 per cent of the municipal electorate by the late 1880s. Bath had 1600 women to 5900 men voters, Sheffield 6000 to 44,900. By 1900, a million women in England and Wales had the local vote: and were sometimes using it to advance temperance, social purity and family values. But although women had the municipal vote, they could not obtain enabling legislation to sit on town councils themselves until 1907.

Local Boards, however, were a different matter. Women were entitled not only to vote but to serve on the new School Boards established by the 1870 Education Act. By 1889 nearly a hundred women were on School Boards; by 1900 their numbers had doubled, and there were few substantial boards without one or two women among their nine to fifteen members. Several women were serving as chairmen. Elizabeth Garrett and Emily Davies, though not much interested in elementary education, had conscientiously sought election to the first London School Board as a public statement and precedent; Elizabeth Garrett had received the highest number of votes cast for any candidate. By 1889 women like Mrs Alice Westlake and Miss Rosamund Davenport Hill in London, Miss Lydia Becker in Manchester, Miss Sturge at Bristol, Mrs Wycliffe Wilson in Sheffield, Mrs Cowen of Nottingham and Mrs Leach of Yarmouth had become senior members of their boards, initiating and implementing policy, chairing committees, making keynote speeches from public platforms and disconcertingly often coming in head of the poll.

Shortly afterwards women began to break into poor law work. It was simply unclear whether women ratepayers were qualified to become guardians, but Miss Martha Merrington quietly stood for Kensington's Board in 1875, and was elected without legal challenge. By 1889 some eighty women were guardians. When the property qualification for guardians was removed in 1894, their numbers rapidly rose and nearly a thousand women were guardians by 1900. Miss Louisa Twining of Kensington, Miss Mary Clifford of Bristol, Miss Elizabeth Lidgett of St Pancras, Miss Agatha Stacey of Birmingham and Miss Brodie Hall of Eastbourne were by then prominent in the official poor law conference circuit, promoting best practice, and helping to reshape the domestic administration of the poor law.

Both suffragists and antisuffragists agreed by the late 1880s, as did most MPs, that women were serving in local government with distinction, even if they drew different lessons from it. For local government was all things to all men and most women. Local women's suffrage committees in Manchester and Bristol had been among the first to run women candidates for School Boards in the 1870s. Local government, they believed, interconnected as it was with national government, would allow women to stake out their citizen claims to a wider political and public life. Every high poll of women electors, every achievement of women members was quoted by suffragists as evidence that women were, in a popular phrase, a 'trained electorate'. For other women, experienced in voluntary and parish work, local government was an avenue by which the dedicated and devoted could offer their lives to Christian and philanthropic service. Those women coming from the Charity Organization Society into poor law work, had even more ambitious aspirations, to rescue and remoralize the urban derelict. For yet others, it was an arena in which to advance pressure group or party fortunes. Professional women with expertise in education, sanitation or medicine naturally followed their work from the voluntary into the public domain. Even anti-suffrage women, with their preference for the quiet of the family circle and their fear that politics would pollute domestic tranquillity, agreed that local government was 'social house-keeping', the school and the workhouse an extended family, the munci-pality and the locality women's parish. Though they themselves might hesitate to come forward, they refrained from sniping at those who did.

Who were these local government ladies? What did they offer? What problems did they face?

They shared a common background. They were at their strongest in and around London where political families and women's societies had their base. They were also active in cities with a strong women's move-ment, based on the suffrage societies and women's liberalism – Bristol, Birmingham, Manchester, Leeds, Nottingham, Bradford – where women often found themselves adroitly incorporated into male liberalism. And until the mid-1890s women were also remarkably visible in the 'spa, sand, spires, spinsters' complex of towns like Brighton and Eastbourne, Oxford and Southport, with an abundant supply of leisured able ladies, abler by far than most of the men in their town's local political life. Not until the later 1890s, with the introduction of parish and district coun-cils, the removal of the property qualification for guardians, and the rise of Labour, did women seek public office in the industrial towns of the North such as Bolton and Salford and the rural counties of Norfolk and the south-west. The dockyard towns and ports hesitated to elect women to anything.

Local government ladies were the wives, widows, daughters and sisters of a town's civic and social elite, of its industrialists and its pro-fessional men; and they had many years of philanthropic work in the roughest part of their towns behind them. In politics usually they were nonconformist, suffragist and liberal, with their menfolk often already on the town council. Even when they were churchwomen and to be found on Tory slates, their policies were seldom distinguishable from the official progressives. They were highly educated, very often graduates, but with money enough not to seek waged work, apart perhaps from writing the occasional Latin grammar, sanitary textbook or nature study guide for children.

School and poor law women came from similar social, political, regional and cultural backgrounds. They did however need different qualifications for office, a technical distinction that was to have a pro-found impact on their policy positions. Any woman, with or without a home or a husband, could stand for the School Board; most were mar-ried with children of their own. Poor law guardians had until 1894 to possess a property qualification, as high as £40 in London. Only the single and the affluent could serve. For School Board purposes, London was divided into eleven vast multi-member divisions. Outside London, School Boards were elected across the whole town, each voter having as many votes as seats and able to plump them for one candidate (a device designed to protect religious minorities). Poor law guardians, in contrast, were elected for those parishes in which they held property. As a result, electoral and ideological considerations interlocked in very different ways.

Because School Board women were not hindered by the need for formal qualification, many women were able to serve. Because education was seen as entirely appropriate work for women, since infants and girls needed a woman's hand, and most teachers were women, many women were willing to serve. With multi-member divisions, women could be adopted to balance a slate; and because electors could plump their votes, women candidates were almost always elected, drawing as they did on the women's vote. By the mid-1870s most of the larger School Boards were run on party lines, as church/chapel confrontations subsided. Any party foolish enough to refuse a place on the slate to a determined woman might find she was elected as an independent, displacing an official candidate, and holding the balance of power. In Manchester, Brighton and Leeds, able Liberal women carved out seats for themselves with the help of the women's vote, and their parties acquiesced. In Birmingham, Dixon and Chamberlain matter-of-factly included one or two women on the slate without fuss. Bristol Liberals were reluctant to include a woman until an independent temperance woman captured one of their seats; thereafter they and the Tories allowed one or two seats to pass down the female line. In Nottingham and Sheffield, women were brought forward to aid party fortunes; Mrs Cowen of Nottingham had to ask voters not to plump for her but to distribute their votes, as otherwise her party would fail to secure a working majority. Women could be too popular. In Bradford, however, the men bullied would-be women candidates to withdraw; they would not, and the situation remained strained for many years until in the later 1890s Margaret McMillan joined the board and won them over.[5] A woman with a strong woman's committee (drawn from liberal and suffrage circles) willing to canvass hard for plumpers, could probably negotiate or blackmail her way on to the official slate if she was determined enough. She could usually count on many women voters plumping all their votes for her; could also look for several votes from clergy, doctors and charitable workers, as well as working men; and could expect friendly 'puffs' from the local press. Whether she was welcomed or resented, depended on the pressures of the local political scene. It was an electoral structure highly advantageous to women.

Poor Law Boards were much harder work. Few women were eligible to stand, even fewer were willing to do so. The work itself was decidedly unpleasant; 'repulsive' was the word that women often used, as they tried to civilize the foul VD wards, clean up senile and incontinent old people, and sanitize evil-smelling and infectious sick wards. Their presence, and temperance, were resented by many inmates, staff and male guardians, who regarded women as trespassers, their very election a criticism of male ways of doing things, an impediment to the dirty jokes and local politicking that occupied members' time at the board. Some of the more spiteful men kept women off the key committees (in Brighton, Bedford and London for example), refused to let them visit the workhouse, and pointedly ignored their every contribution. The parties were somewhat indifferent to poor law elections, for the Unions were not coterminous with parliamentary constituencies, their clients were not electors, and the issues not political, at least until the arrival of Labour brought questions of outdoor relief back on to the agenda. So women stood largely alone. It took considerable courage and strong Christian convictions to stay the course. Though Miss Merrington was elected in 1875, so faltering had women's efforts become by the early 1880s, that a handful of women formed the Women Guardians Society to seek out and support women candidates through the difficult early months on hostile boards.[6] Slowly and by 1889 the worth of women guardians was being grudgingly acknowledged; and the more silent and tactful of them were beginning to overhaul their workhouses.

Not only their reception but their electoral support distinguished poor law from School Board women. Poor law guardians had to possess a property qualification. For women this was usually their home. They therefore stood for and represented the more affluent parishes in which they lived, at considerable geographical and cultural distance from the urban poor. As in addition they had been toughened and trained by the Charity Organization Society and the temperance movement, they endorsed with unusual firmness the principles of 1834. Women guardians were imaginative and compassionate towards workhouse inmates, censorious and harsh towards the outdoor poor. They were often heartily detested, and were among the first to lose their seats after 1894.

Nonetheless, elected ladies, married and unmarried, north and south alike, shared a common cluster of attitudes that marked them off from most male members on School and Poor Law Boards.

The first was their clear view, especially on the part of School Board women, that by standing for public office, they were staking out women's citizen and suffrage rights. They were demonstrating their worthiness – and were often conscientious, diligent and painstaking to a fault, setting themselves higher standards than they would expect of any man, turning in immaculate attendance records, visiting schools, sites and homes which never saw a male member. Many were effectively full-time unpaid public servants, and not a few burnt themselves out in the process. Some, like Elizabeth Garrett or Catherine Rickets of Brighton, Helen Taylor and Annie Besant of the London School Board, Margaret McMillan, or Councillor Maud Burnett of Tyneside, were charismatic candidates, with a flair for public speaking, able to hold an audience in their hand. When they softened their voice, the crowd stilled. Most were skilful committee women, moving the business along with expedition and information, tenacious and even-tempered. Without exception, they were dedicated social workers to the clients in their patch, rustling up school boots, arranging school dinners and holidays, finding a place in a rescue home.

Women were not only exercising their rights, they were also offering their service. The Newcastle Commission of the mid-1860s had shown that most towns lacked sufficient voluntary school places for their children; and that those children who did attend, came intermittently and unwillingly to school. The early School Boards had to engage in a crash building programme, and a crash by-laws policy imposing compulsory attendance, while at the same time extracting compulsory fees. It was perhaps inevitably a numbers game: places, attendances, fees, grants. It was left largely to women members to raise the quality questions, to read the school through the eyes of the child, and to see it as a community of groups with special needs. Women members introduced kindergarten teaching – Mrs Leach passed round samples of the work done by Norwich infants with bricks, sticks, peas and straw, to prod Yarmouth forward.[7] Miss Davenport Hill went off to Sweden to learn hand-and-eye methods, others trained in Froebel practices, and introduced phonetic reading schemes. They protected older girls from 'overpressure' by teachers anxious for them to earn grant, parents anxious for them to earn wages, and needlework inspectors looking for fine examples of fancy seams. Those who opposed corporal punishment were always women members; and Helen Taylor of London and Kate Ryley of Southport in particular earned the hostility of male assistant teachers who believed, with some justification, that women did not understand the day-to-day difficulties of disciplining unruly boys. Women members tried to widen the curriculum so that it nourished the whole child, introducing PE, music, swimming and nature study. Mrs Buckton of Leeds sent children home clutching packets of seeds for their window boxes.[8] And along with many men, they constantly criticized payment by results as substituting instruction for education.

Delinquent and damaged children they made their especial care, coaxing the truant back to school, developing special schooling for those in need. Mrs Surr of the London Board achieved national prominence when she revealed cases of systematic cruelty to children in industrial schools; many a woman member spent her holidays visiting country reformatories, checking on 'her' children, and uncovering abuse.[9] For thirty years women also tried to build up the physical health of malnourished and stunted children, organizing meals, mobilizing their networks to aid invalid children; and demanding better buildings and better facilities for the poorest. Margaret McMillan obtained swimming baths at Bradford, others like Nettie Adler tried to limit child labour, and most women followed Mary Dendy of Manchester and made the education of physically and mentally handicapped children their particular concern.[10] In return, School Board women were often much loved.

Women School Board members were not only child-centred but community-centred. Male members rejoiced at every new three-storey Gothic terracotta building planted in working-class districts, but many women were all too aware that such schools were regarded as coercive and invasive by parents. The regimented classroom discipline, the mechanical rote learning, the compulsory attendance and fees, alienated children and parents alike. Women sought consent. Lydia Becker of Manchester and Annie Besant of London devised schemes for remitting fees;[11] Helen Taylor of London appointed working-class parents as school managers, and tried to make the buildings, books and playgrounds available for community use.[12] Miss Wilkinson of York and Miss Eleanor Smith in Oxford fought hard to build Board Schools so that parents should have a choice in their children's education.[13] Women were among the most insistent that pupil teachers should receive adequate training before they took their place in the classroom; and tried to broaden the curriculum to better fit working-class aspirations. Their task became easier in the 1890s as the second generation of Board School children came to school, as fees were abandoned, as demands for child labour were reduced, and as real wages rose.

No one doubted where the women's priorities lay – with the children and their communities, never with staff or ratepayers. Women were often brought forward as candidates by working men's clubs, worked closely on the board with the solitary working man who was often also part of the Liberal balanced ticket, and were among the first on the boards to back direct labour organizations and the demand for trade union rates.

In 1902 school boards were abolished, to the dismay of the women's movement. Elementary education passed to town and county councils, to which women were not eligible to be elected. When MPs belatedly agreed that women should at least be statutorily co-opted on to all Local Education Authorities, they were recognizing the service women had brought to children's education, even if they were not respecting their rights as elected members.

Poor law women by 1889 could point to a similar record. At the heart of poor relief policy was the workhouse, designed in 1834 to discourage ablebodied men from voluntary idleness, but nonetheless occupied largely by women and children, the old and the sick. Only women guardians could turn 'the house' into a home.

> 'Now it may seem to be a truism to say that where domestic and household management is concerned, there women should have a place and a power of control . . . in the hundreds of large households which are nonetheless such because they are public institutions and not private families'.[14]

If ratepayers 'want some measure of motherly influence in bringing up their hundreds and thousands of neglected children, of womanly experience and sympathy in making arrangements for the sick and old, or in helping other women back into the straight road, or even of domestic knowledge for making the best of the parish money for the comfort of paupers as well as officials, the remedy is in their own hands. They must elect women guardians'.[15] Only women were qualified by expertise, experience, delicacy and compassion to act as the social housekeepers of their community. Women guardians inspected clothes, and found inmates without night clothes, warm clothes or underclothes. They prodded beds, investigated the sanitary arrangements, tasted the food, hired cooks; and uncovered a catalogue of petty miseries, old men and women trying to eat food without cutlery and without teeth, children in 'playrooms' without a single toy. Mrs Evans of the Strand in London found 120 pauper girls sharing five brushes, eight towels and ringworm; Louisa Twining found the frail nursing the infirm.[16]

Many women came into poor law work at the call of Mrs Nassau Senior, appointed by James Stansfeld, president of the Local Government Board, to inspect workhouse girls. Her Report of 1873 found that two-thirds of the girls 'failed' for lack of 'mothering'. Institutionalized, lethargic and listless, they drifted into prostitution or pauperism, unable to hold down any job outside. The only way to rid children of the workhouse 'taint' was to remove them from the workhouse altogether into the foster care of a family or into small community homes with emotional warmth and a kitten before the fire. Women guardians made it their mission to cherish the children of the state, to board them out, find families, homes, training and jobs for them, and thereby break the cycle of deprivation. By the Edwardian years, the Local Government Board was following where women led and urging guardians to remove children from the workhouse into more homely surroundings.

A second cause for concern was the state of the sick wards, dangerous, dirty, noisy; sheets unchanged between infectious patients; sanitation sometimes only a tub in the corner; the sick and dying sleeping in corridors and sheds. Worse even than the physical state of the wards was the lack of any nursing care. Paupers nursed paupers, as far as ignorance, slovenliness, illiteracy or intemperance permitted. Doctors and women visitors joined to demand separate infirmaries and trained nurses. Miss Twining, practical as ever, started an Association to Promote Workhouse Nursing in 1879 which over the next twenty years placed eight hundred nurses in workhouse service, and which pressed the Government into banning the use of pauper nurses except under the supervision of trained head nurses.[17]

Many of the infirm were also the elderly, who lived a minimalist life in the bleak workhouse rooms, furnished with white walls, hard benches and damp stone floors. Women workhouse visitors and guardians brought in cheer, colour and comforts to the elderly: red shawls, curtains, cushions, books and pictures, tea and snuff, the occupational therapy of the Brabazon scheme and music of an evening. Bradford was one of several unions which, pressed by its women members, built sheltered cottages for its elderly where they might brew tea amid their own belongings to their heart's content.[18] Slowly standards of comfort rose in the later 1890s, and stigma receded, as the Local Government Board encouraged Boards to relax their punitive regimes for the elderly.

As with school children, it was a client-centred approach, an insistence that inmates were individuals. As Caroline Ashurst Biggs wrote in 1881, 'It is not pleasant work to which we invite women. . . . But it is emphatically the most womanly work that women of leisure and independence can undertake – the most motherly, the most Christian'.[19] Doctors and inspectors alike agreed that the arrival of women worked a transformation in workhouse life. But that philanthropic emphasis on befriending the individual, which did so much to improve the quality of pauper life, was also to inhibit the ability of women guardians to read the structural nature of much pauperism. By 1889, after all, progressive circles were fiercely debating the demand by unemployed men for public works rather than the workhouse test, and the desire of the elderly for pensions rather than poor relief. Women guardians like Mrs Shaen of Kensington or Miss Sophia Lonsdale of Lichfield continued to insist that outdoor relief was morally dangerous and that pauperism was the inability of the weak-willed and born-tired to say no to drink.[20] As male guardians succumbed to a more relaxed approach to outdoor relief, women guardians remained loyal to Charity Organisation Society and temperance teaching, isolated from working-class communities by their property qualification, and censorious in their style. When in 1894 the property qualification was removed, many did not survive in the changed political atmosphere. They were replaced by working men and married women of more generous views, young women from the Settlement world, and Progressive women run on a party ticket committed to public works, outdoor relief and the end of the old workhouse.

Women had over the years become firmly located in school and poor law work. They had initiated and implemented policy changes to a degree unequalled by most of their male colleagues. Much of what they had stood for had become absorbed into main-line party policies. Whole areas of work had effectively been relegated to their hands. Men continued to construct the buildings, let the contracts, maintain the fabric, employ the male and manual staff, order the supplies, side-step the Local Government Board, and balance the accounts; on School Boards men occasionally argued theology, on poor law Boards they determined the size of out-relief payments. Women meanwhile cared for the inmates of schools, workhouses and cottage homes, appointed female staff, and considered 'the quality questions' of what they were doing. The men had the easier task, dealing with things that could be counted, rather than evaluating what could not. The ablest women did not, however, confine themselves to issues of domestic housekeeping. On School Boards, Miss Rickets of Brighton, Miss Sturge of Bristol and Mrs Buckton of Leeds, to name but three, worked across the whole surface of educational policy, mapping and meeting the full spectrum of educational needs. Within the poor law, Elizabeth Lidgett and Sarah Ward Andrews were serving their turn on Finance Committees in the early 1880s, while other women in time served on buildings and contracts committees, and joined the conference circuit.

A third area of traditional womanly concern, for healthy homes in healthy streets, the public health and sanitary questions of the built environment, had so far eluded them. Since the founding days of the Social Science Association in the late 1850s, local ladies' sanitary committees had preached the virtues of hygiene and carbolic to working-class families. They issued tracts, circulated lecturers, and visited house to house. But formal and structural public health questions – clean water, decent sanitary arrangements, safely lit streets, property in good repair, and the control of nuisances such as slaughter houses, smoke pollution and gross overcrowding – were a matter for vestries within London and for town councils outside. More and more women came to argue that these were also truly women's issues. Yet though the law permitted women to sit on School Boards and had not stopped them sitting on poor law Boards, the Municipal Corporations Act of 1835 permitted no such space. It had referred to 'males' throughout. Women had recovered the ratepayer vote in 1869; they remained ineligible for town council office. The 1835 Act had not, however, applied to London; and in any case London vestries resembled parishes as much as boroughs. Accordingly, a group of women already active in liberal, local government and social purity groups, came together in 1886 to test the law. They decided to run Mrs Charles, a popular Paddington guardian, for Paddington vestry. Her nomination papers were refused by the returning officer but, while the women were deciding what to do next, the old Metropolitan Board of Works collapsed amid charges of corruption, to be replaced by the London County Council. Although the government had not envisaged women becoming county councillors, since it would set a precedent for Parliament, the wording of the Act was still sufficiently ambiguous to be worth the testing.

The women's group reassembled. It was to become the Women's Local Government Society. Annie Leigh Browne was its pivotal figure, helped by her mother, her sister, and her friend Mary Kilgour; Louisa Twining and James Stansfeld were its patrons. The WLGS was a small London liberal upper-middle-class society which worked by lobby and by network. Stoutly feminist, its membership overlapped with the Women Guardians Society, women's liberalism, temperance, social purity, organized philanthropy, women's suffrage, and London Progressive circles. Members' brothers and husbands were often MPs, lawyers or both; and they were married into the Lords, the Local Government Board, the London County Council and London male clubland. It was a tiny, influential and effective society, doggedly testing the law on every doubtful Court decision on the one hand, and bringing forward year after year bills to give full local government rights to women on the other.[21]

During the winter of 1888, the WLGS found two women willing to try to stand for the London County Council (LCC), Richard Cobden's daughter, Jane, and Margaret Sandhurst, the widow of an Anglo-Indian administrator, and after elaborately courteous negotiation, the two gallant LCC divisions of Bow and Bromley were found to be willing to run them, if the WLGS did the work and paid the bills. The receiving officers accepted their nominations, the women sent out election addresses showing how women were needed in every task of the LCC, and early in 1889 they were both triumphantly elected. Emma Cons, manager of the Old Vic and friend of Octavia Hill, was selected as an alderman. Lady Sandhurst promptly devoted her energies to inspecting baby farms, Jane Cobden to children in reformatories, Emma Cons to women inmates of lunatic asylums. Their Progressive colleagues gave them every support and encouragement.

Did this mean that women were in practice eligible for all town and county councils? Margaret Sandhurst's Tory opponent promptly lodged an election appeal. It went to court, she was unseated and he took her place. The other two women were encouraged by the WLGS to duck and weave. Electoral law held that if candidates were not challenged within twelve months, their election however improper was deemed valid. So the women went low-profile and abstained from voting. The Tories refrained from challenging them. When the twelve months were up in February 1890, they resumed active committee membership. Matters came to a head. They could not now be unseated; they could be thwarted. The Tories filed writs for punitive damages, claiming that their votes were invalid. The courts agreed and the women were fined. They had to revert to nonvoting roles, protesting publicly all the while at the insult to womanhood. In February 1892 the triennial elections recurred, and the women had to stand down. No women would now have their nomination papers accepted. Mrs Humphrey Ward remained silent.[22]

It looked as though women were blocked from further advance, excluded from the glittering prizes of town and county councils, confined to specialist precepting boards of a 'domestic' nature. However the Liberals completed the local government reforms of 1888 by introducing in 1894 parish and district councils, on to which women and working men swept in what contemporaries described as 'a rural revolution'.[23] The new councillors sought allotments, appropriated parish charities, established new burial grounds, constructed drainage and sewerage schemes, paved roads and repaired cottages, in addition to their poor law work. A byproduct of the 1894 Act was to allow women to come on to London's vestries. Some vestries – such as Islington and Camberwell – were large and progressive, effectively municipal councils; others were small, sleepy, Tory or corrupt. Alice Busk and Elizabeth Kenney were vestrywomen in one of London's poorest parishes, St George's Southwark, where much of the rotting property was below the sewage outfall and high water mark. The women worked all hours to get property repaired and fumigated, drains rebuilt, infant mortality reduced, and open spaces inserted into the slums.[24] The amount that could be done to improve London's health by fifteen to eighteen women scattered across its vestries was obviously miniscule, yet they were among their most resolute members as well as being the toughest opponents of vestry jobbery, secrecy and incompetence.

By the late 1890s, therefore, women were impressively in evidence within local government, on School Boards and Poor Law Boards, on parish, rural and urban district councils, and on London's vestries. Only the city and county councils eluded them. Then, within a couple of years, achievements that women thought were safely banked, began to slip away. Changes in local government structures, focusing more and more responsibility on the generalist town councils, began to work to women's disadvantage. From 1900, the London Boroughs Act which reformed London's vestries, excluded women from office. In 1902 when town and county councils became the education authorities, women lost their elected status. As Mrs Stanbury, former WLGS secretary, angrily said to an NUWW conference, 'at present the main object of this government was to exclude women as much as possible from taking any part in public life'.[25] If, as seemed possible, government passed poor law work to town councils as well, there would be nothing left to women. The WLGS redoubled its efforts to prise open town and county councils where public work now largely resided, but not until the Liberal victory of late 1905 and a sympathetic Local Government Board president in John Burns, could women recover. After much negotiation, the WLGS bill to admit women to all local government authorities was adopted by the Government. It became law in August 1907, and the women ran their first candidates that autumn.

Seventeen women stood for the borough elections outside London in 1907 (London's borough and county elections did not occur until 1909 and 1910), and six were successful, led yet again by Elizabeth Garrett Anderson, now retired to Aldeburgh on the Suffolk coast.[26] By 1914 they had been joined by such formidable, well-educated and well-connected women as Margaret Ashton of Manchester, Eleanor Rathbone of Liverpool, Ellen Hume Pinsent in Birmingham, Nettie Adler and Susan Lawrence on the LCC, Marion Phillips and Ethel Bentham on Kensington Municipal Borough, many of whom went on to become the first cohort of women MPs after the war. By 1914 some fifty women were serving on borough and county councils in England and Wales, in addition to the seven hundred or so coopted onto the LEAs and other committees.

The women themselves were disappointed that so few of them had broken into the final citadel of local power, after all their struggles. It was difficult. Town councillors needed a property qualification, just as guardians did before 1894, and this limited the field to the single and well-to-do. Local branches of the WLGS found that none of their experienced local government women who were guardians or coopted LEA members qualified. Of those eligible, fewer still were adopted by their parties. Town council seats were in demand from men, who carried the clout of the parliamentary vote as well. There was the further hurdle of election. Most women candidates stood on the left, while local government after 1906 was swinging to the Tories. In addition, it was clear that unlike all previous experience, women candidates polled fewer votes than men, and won by smaller margins. Plumping, of course, was not permitted. Mabel Clarkson was a Coslany guardian; but she could not win the Coslany town council seat in Norwich. Sarah Reddish cost the Bolton Liberals a safe seat.[27] Women put it down to the backlash from suffragette militancy; party managers to the doubts of the electorate that town council business was suitable work for women. Disadvantage was layered on disability. Most women only won town council seats when the electoral conditions approximated to those of School or Poor Law Boards – where there was an all-out election and party managers were seeking a balanced slate; where there were substantial boundary extensions, 'empty seats' and less competition for seats; or when aldermen vacated a safe seat, and majorities were secure.

Undaunted, women insisted that town councils were properly within women's sphere. Though they seemed largely content to leave the management of utilities and highways to men, they recast most of the rest of town council work into the language of family and domesticity. Healthy families needed healthy homes needed healthy streets (and that meant attending to drains, sewers and dung heaps, however unladylike such subjects might first appear). Women members quietly bought textbooks on engineering and took crash courses in sewage farms so that they might demonstrate how private health depended on public health, and how qualified they were to talk on both. Beyond public health they also wanted the provision of urban amenities with women in mind, baths and washhouses, parks and gardens, public lavatories. Chamberlain had sought to embellish the city with handsome boulevards line by prestigious public buildings. Women councillors had a rather different version of town planning, domestic and residential. They favoured the garden suburb, with its cottage gardens and tree-lined streets. Mrs Lees, as mayor of Oldham, led a campaign against ugliness. She cleared some slums, improved others, and built her own garden suburb on the model of Letchworth. Her work was described by a visiting American journalist as 'mothering a municipality'.[28]

The issue that focused women's town council work, above all, was infant mortality, at its worst ever in 1899. Mounting eugenic fears, public
conferences and governmental departmental committees all helped to
put the problem on local councils' agenda. Women workers were, in
their words, determined to stop the massacre of the innocents. To that
end they fought for clean water and pure milk. Miss Sophia Merivale of
Oxford persuaded her local dairy company to 'humanize' milk for small
babies; other women such as Margaret Ashton of Manchester pressed
their councils to follow the example of St Helens and start municipal
milk depots.[29] Women councillors everywhere found themselves super-
vising creches, clinics and schools for mothers. Marion Phillips and
Ethel Bentham copied the Paddington School for Mothers in their
North Kensington ward which served as a model for many. Women
members worked to persuade their LEA to provide school meals and
medical inspection. Mabel Clarkson of Norwich, Mrs Hughes of
Oxford and Maud Burnett of Tyneside called for greater ruthlessness in
clearing slums, greater energy in replacing and repairing property that
otherwise damaged the health of the small child. And through it all they
kept, as Eleanor Rathbone and Margaret Ashton both said, 'a watching
brief' for women's questions: municipal lodging houses for women,
cheap workmen's fares for women, public relief workshops for women
during the pre-war unemployment, all as far as possible on the same
terms as men.[30] Eleanor Rathbone, cheerily admitting that her own
domestic skills were in somewhat short supply, nonetheless supervised
women's sewing and tailoring workshops in style.[31] Few though they
were, marginal in standing, backbenchers in experience, yet almost
without exception women councillors left solid achievement behind
them. The very visibility of women in council ensured that the
women's agenda was not entirely overlooked by men in power.

Local government women held themselves accountable, morally as well
as politically, to a wider concept of community than most of their male
colleagues. Accountable to women, obviously, but – drawing on their
philanthropic inheritance – also accountable to the degraded and
deprived who, as one women member put it, were equally precious in
the eyes of God. So, to education, women brought a sense of the individuality of each child. As guardians, they struggled to mitigate the
punitive forms of the workhouse, and to return as many inmates as
possible to normal life, families and home. On vestries, rural district
councils and town councils, women were far fewer in number and less
prominent. Much of what concerned them, such as the level of infant

mortality, and the need for a more domestic and residential version of town planning, was already part of Progressive thought (to a degree because women had helped to make it so). Yet within the constraints of their numbers, women worked hard to make a reality of Progressive proposals.

Invariably and inevitably, women members spoke the language of separate spheres, the work that only women could do for other women and for children, and with it an insistence that there was in any case so much work for women to do that they had neither need to nor intention of trespassing on male territory. Women members claimed special aptitudes and perceptions for themselves which they could offer in local government service; and they identified special needs among their natural constituency of women and children, the old, the poor and the sick, that were being overlooked or neglected by men. As the *Englishwoman's Review* wrote in 1881, 'In answer to the frequent objection, "I don't like a woman to step into a man's sphere, and be appointed guardian", we might say, "It is really men who have stepped into a woman's sphere – that of dispenser, nurse and teacher of the poor"'.[32] Such language of separate spheres should not be dismissed as necessarily conservative and confining.

Some elected women certainly loathed the public spotlight, but steeled themselves to face election in order to do good. In a different culture they would perhaps have belonged to a Sisterhood. Their motives had nothing to do with women's rights and everything to do with selfless service. They would have been happier working in the private domain, but as such work moved into the public sector, they followed it. If they could avoid the limelight of election they would, waiting for a vacancy, seeking a co-option. Their style was essentially private and retiring; they said little in public; and men approvingly spoke the language of separate spheres on their behalf.

Many other women welcomed the fact that women's work for women was to take place in public. They were proud to be women, unembarrassed by seeking election as a woman for women, and valued the skills they could bring with them. Social work experience, knowledge of domestic management, familiarity with the homes and streets of their town, and the willingness to prioritize public service over other claims on their time, were part of their philanthropic portfolio. In Anna Jameson's evocative phrase, they could offer 'a communion of labour', with its connotations of sacrament, service and commitment, much needed as they saw men struggling to choose the clothes of workhouse children and supervise the housewifery lessons of school girls. They called on and received the help of other public-spirited women in the community, to canvass for them, elect them, and provide professional and philanthropic support.

So women candidates repeatedly made the same two points. Every duty of local government affected the lives of ordinary women and their families. Every task of local government would benefit from the social housekeeping skills that dedicated and experienced women would bring. Their election leaflets set out the functions of their local authority, in checklist fashion, and against each item they would show why women were needed.[33] By the time they had finished, there was little enough left for men exclusively to do, apart possibly from sending out the rate demands, and even there more than one woman prided herself on her head for business and her ability with accounts.

Such women spoke the language of separate spheres, not because they wished to confine and limit their work in local government, nor because they accepted male versions of what local government was about. On the contrary. The language of separate spheres allowed them both to reorientate perceptions about local government, infusing it with more humanistic values, and also to extend the boundaries of what local government did. It permitted women to claim some public space at the expense of men in an unthreatening way, and then to add on a lot more of their own: to bring client groups, such as the physically and mentally handicapped, for example, from the margins into the mainstream of policy consideration; and to integrate into the public sector the voluntary provision of baby clinics, school ambulance services, and the aftercare of workhouse girls.

Other women, rather more cynical or sophisticated perhaps, unashamedly manipulated the language of separate spheres to suit themselves. Margaret Ashton of Manchester, Miss Balkwill of Hampstead, and Mrs Rackham of Cambridge all insisted that women were as well qualified as any man to hold public office on the same terms as men but, sensibly having it both ways, that women were different from men and that therefore their contribution was especially needful. As the (Tory) Miss Balkwill said at a WLGS dinner in 1909, 'Women sat on the councils in the interests of the poorer classes, feeling that the well-to-do could look after themselves better. They went on bodies as citizens and comrades not as women solely'. She then went on, 'Women had opportunities of getting to know the inner life of the community which were not open to the business man'.[34] Women could do everything that men could do, and some extra things as well. They used the language of separate spheres to shield women from unwanted public difficulties, to cover themselves against allegations of competing with men, of being unwomanly and shrill (a useful device as suffragette militancy mounted), and to demand positive discrimination from party agents or the popular vote when it came to obtaining seats. They claimed equal rights and special consideration as 'representative women' at the very same time.

Separate spheres, in other words, could be deployed in either conservative or radical ways. Conservative, in that it reinforced stereotyping of women's nature; supportive, in that it encouraged women to come forward with the confidence that their domestic and family background was as useful and relevant to public service as men's commercial and business experience; and radical, in that it permitted women to claim public space and to expand the contours of what elected authorities were there to do, and for whom they were to do it. Given that the Chamberlain legacy was to read local government as Town Hall Incorporated, and managing utilities as its most interesting enterprise, women's humanistic perceptions of service, care for the individual, and advocacy of family values were a much-needed corrective. Most women, one senses from their speeches, manipulated the language of separate spheres to extract from it and their gender as much mileage as they could, to the palpable irritation of male opponents, who preferred a cleaner and simpler fight.

By highlighting their gender, women invited sexual hostility – though one must be careful not to attribute all the hostility women faced to gender. The unpleasantness met by Mrs Charles on Paddington Vestry or Mrs Ada Salter on Bermondsey Borough Council was clearly political rather than sexual in source.[25] On School Boards, some women were sought out, others were clearly not wanted. It varied from town to town. But because school Board seats were limited in number and much prized, an elected woman was displacing a man. On most boards women were thought to contribute more than they cost; they acquired one or two seats (a healthy 12 per cent to 15 per cent, better than many LEAs today), and thereafter enjoyed equal rights and rather more moral authority than their male colleagues, who in any case remained gentlemen under pressure. Helen Taylor had a rough ride on the London School Board, Kate Ryley on the Birkdale School Board. In both cases the women invited the battles and colluded in the controversy. Annie Besant was just as radical, just as feminist, but encouraged far less aggression towards her.

Poor law women incurred hostility not so much at the point of election (the problem for them there was the property qualification), since seats were rather more plentiful and contests low-key; but on the board itself. It took considerable courage to endure the snubs, smuttiness and cold-shoulder treatment women met on many boards: told in the 1870s that they would be excluded from committees they wanted because their delicate sensibilities would be shocked by lumpen paupers, in the 1880s because they might be too generous with public money to paupers, and in the 1890s because they were too harsh and judgmental to the pauper poor. Yet there were many boards, such as Richmond and Bristol, which were proud of their women members. The sexual politicking was seldom unambiguous. In Leicester, a liberal clergyman persuaded Miss Fullager in the late 1880s to stand for the board. She asked for another women, Miss Else, to join her. By then a Mr North had been selected by the ward committee. He agreed to stand down, but the ward would not then adopt Miss Else. She was forced into an election which she lost.[36] In London when women on certain boards were refused their committees, other men would usually offer to stand down for them, an offer which the women would not accept. For the most part, women won a grudging acceptance – it was seldom more than that – which they achieved by tact, persistence, silence and hard work.

With town councils, the problems were different again: of finding a winnable seat and of winning it once found. Why did so few women succeed in the years before the First World War? Essentially they faced all the disabilities of poor law women, allied to the competition for seats faced by School Board women. Had there been no property qualification for candidates (allowing far more talented women to come forward); had many more women had the municipal vote; had councils adopted triennial elections rather than one-third of their membership out each year (thus allowing a slate in each ward which women might join to balance the ticket); had local government been swinging to the left instead of to the right (allowing Progressive and Labour women to win marginals) and had the whole issue not been bedevilled by suffragette activity; then many more women would have been elected. When in 1919 these conditions did apply, the results were impressive. The number of women holding town and county council seats rose from around 48 in 1914 to 320 in 1919, half of them held in London.[37]

The language of separate spheres not only highlighted the claims of gender and invited sexual hostility in its turn; but it also raised profound problems for women's loyalty, torn three ways as most of them were between loyalty to clients, to women, and to party. Labour women saw no problem. Their clients and their party largely overlapped; and the claims of feminism as such for a Marion Phillips or Susan Lawrence, came a long way behind. They were concerned with women's issues only in so far as the women were working-class women, and their problems those of employment, amenities, or housing. Tory women seemed to find no problem either. They came out of parish and church work and were there to serve the poor. They fell in behind their party on matters of rate aid to voluntary schools or the scale of municipal enterprise, and behind other women in caring for female staff; but their commitment was to their clients. In policy terms, they were soft Progressives in all but label. Liberal women, however, found it very difficult. Liberal local government women were often the founders and natural leaders of their Women's Liberal Associations (indeed it was very often the muscle exercised by WLAs that had forced male caucuses to accept women candidates with more or less grace). When senior male parliamentary Liberals refused to commit the party to women's suffrage on any terms, however, liberal women found themselves pinned. Some, like Miss Sturge of Bristol in the late 1870s, Mrs Cowen of Nottingham in the late 1880s, and Mrs Lees of Oldham in the Edwardian years, were working with a staunch suffragist local liberal party; they were proud to sport a party label, rightly considering that their adoption by the official party was a major stride towards equal rights.[38] Others like Maud Burnett of Tynemouth or Miss Foster Newton of Richmond fudged the issue. They remained liberal, but considered that party labels were irrelevant to local government.[39] They kept free of bad faith by standing as independents, and the local party often acquiesced by not running an official candidate against them. A few, like Margaret Ashton of Manchester or Kate Ryley of Southport, resolved the tension by holding fast to liberalism but not to the Liberal Party.[40] They stood as independents, not primarily to keep politics out of local government, but because they chose the women's constituency over party loyalty. In the temperate advice of Jane Brownlow, writing the WLGS handbook in 1911, 'If possible a woman should stand as an independent candidate. The work she is going to do is not to advance any political party, but to benefit the community, with special regard to the needs of women, children and those who are helpless'.[41] The logical conclusion was the Women's Municipal Party, formed in 1913 by the Duchess of Marlborough which attracted Eleanor Rathbone of Liverpool and several WLGS women, to run women candidates irrespective of party. It disappeared after the War.[42]

Mirror-image difficulties faced Liberal Party managers, pressed by women to relinquish a safe seat (and they were in short supply) without receiving in return their loyalty. Yet if a woman ran as a spoiling candidate, she could let in a Tory. In the view of the caucus, women had neither the parliamentary vote to be worth the wooing nor the electoral appeal with municipal voters to be worth the having. Party managers, anxious to advance their party's fortunes, regarded local government women with little enthusiasm and wished they would go away.

They could not, would not. Back in 1881 Mrs Ethel Leach, wife of a Yarmouth ironmonger had joined her School Board. Within a few years, she introduced kindergarten teaching and a pupil training centre, and raised the school leaving age. She organized school dinners, banned home lessons, limited corporal punishment, reformed the board's industrial school. Almost singlehandedly, she brought a small, isolated, reactionary and sectarian Board into line with Progressive thought. In 1894 she was also elected to the Poor Law Board; and after managing to sack the woman-hating clerk to the board, she introduced a new infirmary, child care, and comforts for the elderly. Now a widow, in 1908 she sought election to Yarmouth Town Council. Her low-key election address spelled out why she sought a council seat.

SUPPORT
MRS LEACH
ON MONDAY NEXT

BECAUSE the Council is now the Educational Authority, and you need a Woman's sympathy and help for your daughters and children.

BECAUSE the Council has to carry out the 'Old Age Pension Scheme,' and the 'Unemployed Workmen's Act,' which affect both men and women.

BECAUSE you need a Woman's tact and sympathy in carrying out the Act for the provision of Meals to necessitous School Children.

BECAUSE women are as much interested as men in the Sanitary condition of the Town; the Housing of the Working Classes, the Paving and Lighting of the Streets; and the welfare of the Borough generally.

BECAUSE she lives in the Ward, is a Large Ratepayer, and interested in the Economical expenditure of the Rates.

BECAUSE you have had 25 Years' experience of her capacity for public work.

For all these reasons she asks you to favour her with your VOTE and CORDIAL HELP to return her to the Town Council.[43]

Her opponent's election manifesto was even simpler: 'whether ladies should be allowed to participate in municipal work'. It was a Tory ward and she lost, but went on after the War, to become a magistrate, a councillor, alderman and mayor. Barbara Bodichon would have approved.

8

'In the Comradeship of the Sexes Lies the Hope of Progress and Social Regeneration'[1]: Women in the West Riding ILP, c.1890–1914

June Hannam

Recalling her first visit to West Yorkshire in 1892 as a young Fabian lecturer, Katharine Bruce Glasier told the Independent Labour Party's Coming of Age Conference in 1914 that she had found an atmosphere of 'swift and eager welcome for every woman comrade and of settled conviction as to the women's equal rights of citizenship with men'. She contrasted this 'fruitful attitude to women' with the more hostile outlook of Glasgow and London.[2]

She was not alone in drawing attention to the sympathetic attitudes of West Riding socialists towards women. Time and again in their reminiscences, socialist pioneers of the 1880s and the 1890s recall the contribution made by women to the movement, the atmosphere of comradeship between the sexes and the discussions held on the 'woman question' in the West Riding. Isabella Ford, a well-known propagandist for independent labour politics in the area, claimed that she had been drawn to the ILP because it was the only party that 'had put women on an equal footing with men'. Writing in 1912 she was eager to dispel any misgivings among suffragists that the Independent Labour Party might fail them. 'When I seem too confident in my belief in the ILP it is because I have keen memories of enthusiastic labour meetings, of long, serious talks and discussions in all parts of England, years ago, on the woman question'.[3]

Attention has often been drawn to the close theoretical links between socialist politics and women's emancipation in different historical periods.[4] The socialist revival of the 1880s and 1890s was no exception.

The question of women's rights was widely debated among socialists at a time when the women's movement was becoming more active, and a common membership ensured a two-way flow of ideas.

The importance of these links, and of women's contribution to socialism, was recognized by Joseph Clayton in one of the first histories of the socialist movement. His experience of the atmosphere and concerns of the ILP, gained as secretary of the Leeds branch in the 1890s, led him to conclude that 'in the early ILP women were a great deal more than mere helpers to men, they were quite literally the co-leaders'. Isabella Ford and others 'not only strove to make the ILP a national organisation, they gave it a tendency to look upon women's suffrage as a reform of vital need, and the equal co-operation of men and women in politics not an ideal but an everyday business'.[5]

It is all the more surprising, therefore, that recent studies have shown little interest in the contribution of women and feminist questions to ILP politics. Henry Pelling draws attention to the 'new woman' from a middle-class background who was attracted to the ILP in the 1890s. He singles out Katharine Conway, Carolyn Martyn and Enid Stacy because of their popularity as speakers, but in doing so gives the impression that they were unique, rather than representative of a much broader group. Moreover, the importance of feminist issues for the policies and tactics of the party, in particular after 1900, is not explored in any depth.

David Howell's more recent study of the ILP adds little to this analysis. He claims that the popular image of the party as placing a significant emphasis on the role of women rests on the popularity of the early female propagandists, but that in reality their prominence was short-lived. Enid Stacy and Katharine Conway were less active after their marriages, while Carolyn Martyn died in the mid-1890s. Howell adds Margaret McMillan and Mrs Pankhurst to his list of prominent women, but argues that the influence of the former was reduced because she concentrated on Bradford politics, while the latter was diverted to the suffrage movement. He concludes that 'some indication of the limited impact of women can be found perhaps in their slight presence at Party conferences'.[6] The study focuses, therefore, on four male leaders to symbolize the character and complexities of the ILP.

This emphasis on the role of male leaders and neglect of feminist issues stems partly from the process of selection, in which only some debates and political activities are considered worthy of attention. It also comes from an institutional approach. Men were far more visible in formal political roles – as trade union leaders, MPs, city councillors and office holders in the ILP. As such their activities were widely reported in the press and highlighted in the autobiographies of fellow labour leaders, and this served to underline the importance of their contribution.

A very different picture, however, is presented by Jill Liddington and Jill Norris in their study of Lancashire working women. They show how industrial experience and trade union organization laid the basis for working women's increasing involvement in socialist and suffrage politics after 1900. These 'radical suffragists' demanded the vote as part of a broader campaign to achieve equality at work and in the home, and they pursued these issues, albeit unsuccessfully, within the labour movement.

Liddington and Norris raise questions of general importance in their study. They suggest that labour and socialist politics had attractions for working women as well as for men, but also show the way in which women's specific needs as a sex could cut across and conflict with class loyalties. Their research also points up the need for such questions to be explored in different local contexts. Lancashire cotton workers were 'by far the highest paid and best organised of all working women' and therefore cannot be seen as necessarily representative.[7] In the West Riding, for example, women were extensively employed in the wool and worsted textile trade and in the ready-made clothing factories of Leeds which grew steadily in number and size after the 1880s.[8] But their trade union organization was weak and their pay was low compared to the cotton workers of Lancashire.

The West Riding, therefore, provides a very different context in which to examine both women's contribution to the growth of independent labour politics and also the extent to which the 'woman question' was raised as an important area of debate in the socialist movement. Although closely related, these two issues are not necessarily the same. Many women who were active in socialist politics did not seek to focus explicitly on women's rights, but their political involvement did pose an implicit challenge to women's identification with the private sphere.

The degree of autonomy and political differences between ILP branches also suggest the need for a local study. The founding conference of the ILP was held in Bradford in 1893 and branches were soon formed throughout the West Riding. The new organization had an uphill struggle to increase membership and to make gains in elections, in particular after the defeats of 1895. Electoral strength was concentrated in Bradford, Halifax, Huddersfield, Dewsbury, Keighley and villages in the Colne Valley. In Leeds, the largest city in the region, the strength of Liberalism on the City Council and the Trades Council meant that electoral success came comparatively late. Nonetheless, Leeds socialists made a vital contribution to the development of a theoretical framework to link sex equality and socialism in the 1880s and 1890s.

Such links arose almost naturally from the broad socialist perspective adopted by members of the Leeds Socialist League in the 1880s. Tom Maguire, Tom Paylor, James Sweeney and others were encouraged by the writings of Edward Carpenter and William Morris to see socialism as a way of life and not just as an external commitment. Carpenter's interest in the nature of masculinity, femininity and sexuality, and his critique of contemporary marriage, led his followers to see sex equality, personal relations and the development of democratic comradeship as a vital element in their struggle for socialism.[9]

The interest of members of the Leeds Socialist League in sex equality was reinforced by their contacts with Isabella and Bessie Ford. The two sisters had grown up in a household steeped in radical liberal causes and support for women's rights. Their father was the Leeds solicitor, John Lawson Ford and their mother, Hannah, was a member of the wealthy Pease family of Darlington. Along with other Quakers of their generation, Hannah and Robert took part in Josephine Butler's campaign against the Contagious Diseases Acts, the movement for women's suffrage in the 1860s and 1870s, and the fight to extend educational provision for women. They were also interested in the education of working women and financed a night school for mill girls in the 1850s.

Isabella and Bessie inherited this interest in women's rights and sympathy with the needs of working women. But they were to depart from their parents' politics, making the transition, along with other young Quakers, from radical liberalism to socialism.[10] In their early twenties they had already begun to question the prevailing emphasis of liberalism on materialism, competition and individual responsibility, but their ideas were given more direction in the mid-1870s when they became close friends with Edward Carpenter. They felt an instant rapport with Carpenter's interest in exploring personal relationships and with his emphasis on correct moral behaviour as a way of achieving the millenium. He introduced them to the writings of Walt Whitman whose *Democratic Vistas* was described by Bessie as 'a great help coming from a long way off'.[11]

Isabella's general interest in women's rights was focused in a more practical way on the needs of working women in the mid-1880s. She was encouraged by Emma Paterson, President of the Women's Provident and Protective League and a family friend, to help organize a society for tailoresses in Leeds, and it was through this work that she first came into contact with members of the Socialist League.[12] This link between socialists and the organization of women workers was strengthened during the labour unrest of 1888 to 1891. Disputes involving women workers played an important part in pushing forward the demand for independent labour politics and in providing the final impetus for individuals such as Isabella and Bessie Ford to become socialists.

Isabella Ford helped weavers in Leeds and Alverthorpe who were among the first to strike. During these disputes she met Ben Turner and Allen Gee, who had been trying to organize textile workers since the early 1880s. Turner lived in Leeds for a short period in 1889, where he joined the Leeds Socialist Society. Both men formed lifelong friendships with the Ford sisters and played an important role in the ILP during the 1890s.[13]

In the context of mounting discontent in the tailoring trade Isabella Ford established the Leeds Tailoresses' Union in October 1889. A few days later 700 machinists employed by Arthur & Co struck to gain a reduction in the charge made for power and remained on strike for several weeks before suffering defeat.[14] Isabella Ford, Maguire, Sweeney and Paylor gave energetic leadership, urging workers to ignore differences of sex, race and skill. They were assisted by other socialists, including Walt Wood, secretary of the Leeds branch of the Gas Workers' Union, Alf Mattison, a young engineer and Ben Turner, as well as by non-socialist members of the Trades Council.

The Tailoresses' strike provided one of the first occasions on which the differences in outlook between the Socialist and Liberal members of the Trades Council were revealed. These differences were exacerbated during the Gas strike of 1890 and for a short time socialists formed a rival group to the Trades Council.

Isabella Ford, Turner, Gee and members of the Leeds Socialist League were also prominent in the Bradford Manningham Mills dispute of 1890 where women workers were again leading participants. The defeat of the strike is usually seen as providing the impetus for the growth of independent labour politics in the area, and by 1893 socialists had gained control of the Bradford Trades Council.[15]

Socialists used the disputes to point out the similarities between Liberal and Tory employers. Fred Jowett, later the leader of the Bradford ILP, claimed that 'in the Lister strike, the people of Bradford saw plainly, as they had never seen before, that whether their rulers are Liberal or Tory they are capitalists first and politicians afterwards'.[16] Isabella Ford's conclusion was similar, but she analysed the strike from the perspective of the woman worker. She found that Liberal employers were as bitter as any others 'against their female employees who dare to join a union'. The tone in which they spoke to women showed that 'sex hatred, or what is even worse, sex contempt on the part of men towards women, was underlying our social structure'.[17]

From the beginning, therefore, West Riding socialists had to take some account of the needs of women workers. The strikes gave them first-hand experience of women's working conditions and many continued to be involved in organizing female workers in subsequent years. Once the excitement of strike action was over, however, it was difficult to recruit tailoresses and textile workers into the unions and by the turn of the century only a small proportion were organized.[18]

This weak trade union membership made it difficult for women workers to exert an influence on the West Riding ILP as an organized group, but individual women were politically active and made a contribution. Although the backgrounds of rank-and-file ILP members are difficult to trace, it is clear that some young, single women were attracted to the party and their political commitment was often reinforced by marriage to fellow socialists. Lizzie Harold of the Lower Briggate ILP was remembered as 'lively and bright, ever ready to be one in the country rambles organised by the young members of the club. They would distribute socialist leaflets in the villages they visited'. She later married Walter Slater, a salesman, who stood for election to the Leeds North East Ward in 1907, and they had 'a hard struggle to maintain decent living conditions'.[19]

Trade unionists, such as Agnes Close, full-time secretary of the Leeds Tailoresses' Union and other members of the all-female committee, also joined the ILP, but most members appear to have been drawn from families active in labour politics. For example, Ben Turner's wife, Elizabeth and her five daughters all joined the Batley ILP, while Walt Wood and his wife acted as joint caretakers of the ILP club at New Briggate, Leeds.

The ILP recruited members of either sex only slowly, but there were enough female members in the 1890s to justify the formation of separate women's groups in some towns. The Leeds West Ward Labour Club formed a Women's Labour Guild in 1893, and in the following year Tom Maguire claimed that in Hunslet, Holbeck and Bramley women were coming 'timidly and tentatively, it is true, but increasingly – with the result that the appearance of the Party is much improved and its social qualities stimulated'.[20]

Separate women's organizations were established both to encourage women to join the ILP and also to give them an opportunity to use their special talents. In 1898, for example, the Bradford Women's Independent Labour Association decided to hold a tea before all party meetings in order to raise funds and to cater for those who worked in town.

Members also became involved in the Clarion Women's Cinderella Association which provided food, clothing and outings for children.

Such activities fell within contemporary definitions of what was appropriate to a woman's sphere and have been used by Howell to suggest that, outside Lancashire, women played largely a supportive and tea-making role.[21] But there is a danger here of underestimating the value of this contribution. The early ILP displayed a missionary zeal in its attempts to 'make socialists' and the social and political sides of the movement were often fused. Socialist Sunday Schools, rambles, picnics and concerts, usually organized by women, helped cement the movement together, attracted members and contributed towards 'the promotion of that spirit of good comradeship which is always present on such occasions'.[22]

Fund-raising was also crucial at a time of limited resources. the Bradford Women's Labour Association, for example, raised money for the local ILP branch and also sent £3 to striking miners in 1898, while the Leeds women's committee saved the local Labour Church by paying off debts on its piano. Financial contributions from middle-class women could also be vital. Bessie and Isabella Ford paid the rent on the ILP premises at New Briggate, cleared debts incurred by Joseph Burgess for the Leeds ILP and provided rented premises for a Women's Trade Union Club in Leeds.

Women were not just to be found behind the scenes in the ILP. They also took a more prominent political role as speakers, journalists, trade union organizers and elected members of public bodies. Not all such women were primarily interested in broad feminist issues, but they shared a commitment to awakening interest in the lives of industrial women, and their presence added to the atmosphere of comradeship between the sexes that was so frequently noted in the West Riding.

Isabella Ford later wrote that women in the ILP 'are consulted, they are listened to, just as much as men; indeed, as in the Society of Friends, women are reckoned of as much value as men, both spiritually and socially'. This gave women greater confidence. 'The women in the Party are not made of submissive, doormat material, and consequently the relationship between them and their mankind is of a more wholesome and cordial nature than is always usual between men and women'.[23] The Ford sisters are mentioned time and again in contemporary reminiscences for the role that they played in creating this atmosphere. They were described as 'Yorkshire's chief women and, with money and service made the movement grow. They were Trojans at the work'. Katharine Bruce Glasier thought that Yorkshire labour leaders were 'very influenced by the companionship which Isabella and

Bessie Ford of Adel bore them in their efforts for full freedom of women and workers'.[24]

Their home at Adel became the meeting place for local socialists from a variety of backgrounds – Maguire, Turner, Mattison, Agnes Close, the Woods and the Priestmans were frequent visitors – as well as a place where West Riding ILP members could meet men and women with a national or international reputation. On his visits to Adel Alf Mattison met, among others, Vernon Lee the author, Mary Anderson the Factory Inspector, Stepniak the Russian exile, Edward Carpenter and the American, Henry Demarest Lloyd.[25]

One of the practical ways in which women could wield political influence, while still denied the vote, was to stand for election to School Boards, Boards of Guardians and other public bodies. They were encouraged to do so by the West Riding ILP and came forward in increasing numbers, although the importance of their work in building up support for social reform and in showing up the inadequacies of the existing political parties has not been fully recognized.

Female candidates were drawn from varied social backgrounds. Mrs Tom Duncan, wife of the secretary of the Leeds Shop Assistants' Union, stood unsuccessfully for the Holbeck Board of Guardians in 1894. Isabella Ford was elected to the Adel Parish Council in 1895, while Miss Dixon, later the wife of the Rev. Stansfield, stood successfully for the Keighley School Board in the mid-1890s. In Bradford Margaret McMillan was elected to the School Board in 1894 and two female ILP members gained a place on the Board of Guardians in 1898 and 1901 respectively: Edith Priestman, a middle-class Quaker and wife of a Labour councillor, and Julia Varley, a mill worker and trade union activist.[26]

Margaret McMillan became well known in the area for her efforts to improve the social, educational and medical provisions for children in Bradford. Her parents had lost their money through business failures in America and, after her father's death, the family moved back to their native Scotland. With the help of her grandparents, Margaret received a boarding school education and became a lady's companion in London. She was drawn to Bradford in 1892 by the possibilities it seemed to offer for the development of a mass movement in favour of social reform and she stayed in the city until 1902.[27]

It has been suggested that Margaret McMillan's influence on the ILP was limited by her involvement in local politics,[28] but her child welfare work placed her at the centre of debates about whether or not social reforms were merely palliatives which distracted socialists from more fundamental changes. Answering her critics she wrote: 'School feeding is, of course, no palliative at all. It is pure socialism – so far as it goes – just as a dewdrop is water so far as it goes. One need not lose sight of that fact merely because one has grasped another – namely, that the drop is not quite so big as the ocean'.[29] Margaret McMillan took her interest in child welfare beyond the confines of Bradford. She wrote numerous articles for the *Labour Leader*, spoke at Annual Conferences in the early 1900s and was a member of the National Administrative Council (NAC).

Patricia Hollis's article in the present volume highlights the way in which women who stood for election to public bodies in the nineteenth century used the language of separate spheres. They sought to claim public space without appearing too threatening, to bring the needs of women and children to the front and to infuse local government with humanistic values. The language of separate spheres was also widely used in the ILP where it was argued by both sexes that women had a special contribution to make in the areas of poor relief, child welfare and education because of their caring role within the family. The *Bradford Labour Echo*, for example, declared that 'the general advent of women into the field of politics is among the most hopeful phenomena of the time', for their position in various departments of public work 'is a symptom of our advancing civilisation'.[30]

On one level the language of separate spheres clearly reinforced the contemporary stereotype of women's special nature but, as Hollis argues, it could also have more radical implications. It gave women the confidence to stand for election to public bodies and encouraged the ILP, along with the women's movement, to argue that women's special attributes should not be confined to the home. For example, when Mrs Stansfield sought re-election to the Keighley Board of Guardians after her marriage she was accused by the local press of 'departing from decent conventions'. The *Bradford Labour Echo* was quick to jump to her defence, using the occasion to warn women of the treatment they could expect from the Liberal press if they dared to maintain their 'individuality'.[31]

Female members of Boards of Guardians and School Boards in the late nineteenth century shared a common interest in the needs of women and children which often came before loyalty to any political group. This led ILP members in cities such as Bradford, where Jowett and other councillors aimed to build a progressive cross-class alliance, to see such women as natural allies. When Edith Priestman, an ILP member of the Bradford Board of Guardians, moved a resolution to rescind the standing regulation which denied out-relief to women with illegitimate children, it was noted in the labour press that 'all the women present voted with our comrades, which gives a glad promise for the future, for what the women decide to be the right thing to do will be done sooner or later'.[32] On the other hand this progressive alliance could break down over more party political issues, for Edith Priestman's second resolution opposing property buying by the Board from members of the Board was less well supported.

Even women most heavily involved in the work of public bodies also took part in broader propaganda for socialism and women's rights. Edith Priestman regularly spoke in support of ILP candidates in municipal and Parliamentary elections, lecturing to branches all over the West Riding on subjects ranging from 'Liberty' and 'Socialism' to a critique of the book *The Roadmender* by M. Fairless. Margaret McMillan supported a limited franchise for women, since 'liberty must always be wrested piecemeal. . . . we have the whole industrial history of the century to show us that appeals to legislative authority must be, at first, tentative'.[33] Jowett remembered her as 'an eloquent and attractive speaker . . . in great demand not only for Bradford meetings, but for meetings in other towns', where she spoke on women's rights, child welfare and socialism.[34]

The priority for other women was the organization of female workers into trade unions. Isabella Ford was president of the Leeds Tailoresses' Union during the 1890s and made strenuous efforts to recruit new members by holding organizing meetings and by helping out in disputes. After 1896 she paid the salary of the full-time secretary and put up the finance for a Women's Trade Union Club which was to provide a meeting place for women workers and a focus for their organization. But the organization of the clothing industry, which created divisions in the labour force, and the low pay of female workers militated against successful trade unionism. Membership remained well below 300 and the union ceased to have a separate existence in 1899.

Isabella Ford also helped the Textile Workers' Union, a mixed-sex organization whose leaders, Turner and Gee, were more sympathetic than most male trade unionists to the needs of working women. The union was affiliated to the Women's Trade Union League and women were encouraged to speak at meetings. Again, the low pay and poor working conditions in the industry made organization difficult among both sexes, although women were even less likely than men to become union members and to take part in its affairs.[35]

The main exception to this was Julia Varley, a Bradford mill worker, who had been influenced as a child by her mother's 'intense interest in politics and social welfare', derived from her great-grandfather's involvement in Chartism.[36] At the age of fifteen, Julia became secretary of the Bradford branch of the union and was soon elected onto the executive of the Trades Council.

For both Isabella Ford and Julia Varley women's suffrage, the struggle for socialism and trade union organization were inextricably linked in their attempts to improve the industrial and social conditions of women workers. Isabella argued time and again that 'trade unions will never flourish amongst women until on election days the female trade union voice can make itself heard alongside of the male trade union voice'. The vote would increase women's industrial status and hence their wages. They had to be made, therefore, to 'understand its connection with every part of their individual lives' and be encouraged to 'undertake the troublesome, difficult tasks of full citizenship'.

Isabella was particularly concerned that women workers should have a say in their own affairs. 'When the working woman does awake and desire her true salvation, she must, as all of us must, work it out for herself. All that can be done by outsiders . . . is to help awaken that desire'.[37] She had an unusual understanding of the way in which industrial work had psychological as well as material effects on women's lives and led to a 'deadening and warping of their humanity'.[38] Tom Maguire revealed similar insights in his series of poems, *Machine Room Chants*, where he pointed to the pressures workgirls faced in combining monotonous factory work with home duties.

When girls go into the factory they are drilled, an' driven an' tried,
An' they want some relaxation away from their own fireside.
It's too much to ask of a woman, pent up all day in the shop,
To take on the duties of home besides, and forever at home to stop.[39]

Both Isabella Ford and Tom Maguire constantly drew attention to the specific problems facing women in the workplace – in particular low pay, fining and sexual harassment. In contrast to the majority of trade union leaders Isabella refused to see the woman worker as a problem. She sought instead to explain women's lack of interest in trade unionism by pointing to their upbringing which equated femininity with submissiveness.[40]

This focus on women's specific needs in the workplace posed difficulties for the ILP. It was one thing to support a general improvement in women's wages and work conditions, but quite another to challenge their secondary status within industry. This raised the question of whether the interests of male and female workers were compatible and whether women's needs as a sex could cut across and conflict with class solidarity. Female speakers and trade union organizers were ambivalent in their views.

Mrs Byles of Bradford, Mrs Ann Ellis of Batley, who had taken a prominent part in the weavers' dispute of 1875 and was described by Turner as 'the recognised women's textile leader for Yorkshire' in the 1880s,[41] Miss Roberts, an Alverthorpe weaver, Isabella Ford and others who helped the Textile Workers' Union in the 1880s and 90s advocated mixed-sex trade unionism as the best way to increase the industrial strength of the woman worker.

Isabella Ford was only too aware of the weak position of the single-sex Leeds Tailoresses' Union and was instrumental in negotiating, first a federation and then an amalgamation between the women's union and the Amalgamated Union of Clothing Operatives (AUCO). But her support for mixed-sex trade unionism co-existed uneasily with her demands that 'work must be paid for as work, not as women's or men's work' and for women's equal access to employment, for these demands brought to the surface the separate interests of male and female workers.

Committee members of the Tailoresses' Union were not wholeheartedly behind the merger with the AUCO, for they feared that women's interests would be lost sight of in a mixed-sex organization.[42] It is significant in this context that Agnes Close did not give her services to the AUCO, but remained attached to the Women's Trade Union Club as a female organizer before emigrating to Canada in 1902. In the pre-war years the AUCO managed to recruit more female members and appointed a number of women organizers, but their loyalty was to the policies of the union rather than to the interests of their sex.

Even the most sympathetic male union leaders continued to see women's position in the workplace as marginal when the interests of male workers appeared threatened. This can be seen most clearly during the depression in the wool and worsted industry which led to lower wages, short-time work and the displacement of male by female workers. In this context union leaders, including Turner and Gee, made the married woman worker a scapegoat for the industry's problems and led an attack on her right to work.

The arguments used against married women working were not simply a response to immediate economic problems, but were deeply rooted in a view of family life in which men were seen as the breadwinners. Turner expressed the ideas of many in the ILP when he claimed that 'it was essential that the father of a house should be the breadwinner and not just have to depend upon the assistance of the children and the wife to get a combined income that would only just pull them through'.[43] In his vision of a socialist future men would earn enough so that their wives could stay at home, released from their double burden of waged work and domestic chores.

Sex equality at home and in the workplace, women's political rights, the nature of family life and the relationship of these issues to socialism were widely debated in the West Riding ILP in the 1890s. An interest in these questions arose from the broad vision of socialism held by many members of the local ILP and was also prompted by the widespread industrial employment of women in the area. Discussion in the branches was encouraged through the speeches and writings of Julia Varley, Edith Priestman, Margaret McMillan, Isabella Ford and Tom Maguire, as well as by female speakers from outside the region.

Isabella Ford had a weekly column in the *Leeds Forward* which she wrote with wit and humour. Topics covered ranged from descriptions of work conditions in match factories to women's involvement in international political movements. Commenting on the high mortality rates among men in France, she noted that 'in medical journals one reads that much of this feeble vitality among Frenchmen is due to the lives of dissipation they so generally lead. It is a comfort to find that sometimes evil doesn't pay!' The underlying theme of all her pieces was that 'everywhere women have greater cause to cry for vengeance than men have, and that is why even for a peaceful revolution such as trade unionism or socialism, the presence and influence of women is absolutely indispensable'.[44]

It was women's role within the family which caused most controversy within the West Riding ILP and helped to shape attitudes towards the 'woman question' as a whole. Discussions on the question gained a sense of immediacy from the growing fears of male textile and clothing workers that the cheap competition of female labour was undermining their industrial position. Only a few speakers, therefore, were critical of the prevailing emphasis on women's natural identification with domesticity and child care. Enid Stacy, a popular national speaker who frequently visited the West Riding in the 1890s, called for greater equality within marriage, the right to choose whether or not to have children, political rights and freedom for women as workers.

Of the more local speakers it was Tom Maguire and Isabella Ford who sought to analyse the relationship between class and sex oppression and to link women's inequality in the home with that in the workplace. Maguire, for example, suggested that men did not encourage their female relatives to join a union because they were used to being serviced by their wives: '*My* Sarah Jane must stay at home and make *my* home comfortable for *me*! What is a wife for!'[45]

Isabella Ford had an unsentimental view of family life. She was 'heartily tired of hearing so much abuse of the married woman worker' who, with a low income, poor housing and being often subject to involuntary motherhood could hardly be blamed if she neglected home and children.[46] She did not challenge the idea that women were the best suited to care for children. What she did argue against was women's inequality in the home which resulted from economic dependence and political subjection. This made the man into his wife's oppressor, 'for they stand in a false position of inequality towards each other, and that falseness spreads, as a fungus spreads its evil growth, into their relationship to others'.[47] She could see no reason why women should be confined by the domestic sphere or why their role within the home should mean an unequal position in the workplace.

These views were not shared by the majority of speakers who took family life and marriage as a theme, in particular after 1900. Katharine Bruce Glasier's most popular lecture in the West Riding in the early 1900s, later produced as a pamphlet, was 'Socialism and the Home'. Edna Penny from Sheffield, the wife of the Labour agent, discussed marriage and the home in her lecture, 'A Woman's View of Socialism', given to several local branches, while Daisy Halling, an actress, toured the area in 1908 speaking on 'Socialism and Family Life'.

All these speakers had a sentimental view of the mother's role within the family and, in the context of a growing public interest in the 'strength of the race', were keen to emphasize the importance of motherhood. They strongly denied that socialism would mean free love and the end of family ties, a question often asked by members of the audience at socialist meetings. On the contrary Edna Penny argued that it was the capitalist system, with its sweated wages and inadequate housing, that led to undernourished children and undermined family life. Only socialism would free women and their children for 'it was no good talking about "Home Sweet Home" until we were quite sure that everybody had got a home'.[48]

The predominance of male union leaders in the West Riding ILP, the fears of their union members and the weakness of female industrial workers ensured that this more sentimental view of family life prevailed among West Riding socialists and served to prevent any real challenge to the sex division of labour in the workplace and in the home.

Underlying these views was the assumption that there was a harmony of interests between men and women who faced the common enemy of capitalist exploitation. The involvement of entire working-class families in labour politics reinforced this and encouraged male leaders to refer patronizingly to the 'silent sacrifice' of their wives.[49]

Little evidence remains about the attitudes of the wives themselves, although many must have shared Hannah Mitchell's resentment of the young men she met in the ILP who were earnest about women's rights, but still expected her to make the tea.[50] Tensions between women's domestic duties and their political activism appear less frequently in the reminiscences of middle-class women who were cushioned to some extent by domestic servants.

In the 1890s the ILP held wide-ranging debates on the social and economic position of women. The needs of the working-class woman were emphasized and links drawn between trade union organization, women's suffrage and socialism as the way to achieve her emancipation. After 1903 the demand for the vote became paramount. A single-sex issue was now placed at the top of the political agenda, and it became a focus for all the conflicts between class and sex loyalties and between male and female workers which had been simmering beneath the surface of the ILP for so long.

At first the agitation for women's suffrage went hand in hand with the agitation for socialism. A revival in the suffrage campaign took place initially among women textile workers in Lancashire who linked the vote with an improvement in working conditions. Mrs Pankhurst and other members of the Manchester ILP were encouraged by the response of women workers to set up a new organization, the Women's Social and Political Union (WSPU), to fight for the vote in a more energetic way than the older suffrage societies. They frequently made the journey across the Pennines to speak on women's suffrage, but still combined this with more general socialist propaganda. Christabel Pankhurst, for example, spoke to the Huddersfield ILP in 1906 on 'The Unemployed Question', 'Women in the Labour Movement' and 'Votes for Women'.[51]

Yorkshire women workers also showed an interest in the vote. One suffrage petition was signed by 33,184 Yorkshire female textile workers in 1902, while another, which Agnes Close helped to take round in 1903, was signed by 8,600 West Riding tailoresses.[52] This early interest failed, however, to develop into a mass movement of support. Weak trade unionism and low pay meant that women lacked an organizational base and perhaps the confidence to engage in sustained political agitation. Nonetheless, the suffrage campaign encouraged many women to take a more active role in the ILP and helped to attract new female members to the party.

Ethel Annakin and Mary Gawthorpe were typical of the self-supporting young women, often employed in white-blouse and professional occupations, who made up the rank and file of the ILP in these years. They were based in Leeds, where the connections between socialist and feminist politics had always been strong. Ethel Annakin, a schoolteacher, was beginning to establish a reputation as an ILP and suffrage speaker when she married Philip Snowden in 1905. Along with her close friend Isabella Ford she persuaded him to support a limited franchise for women.[53]

Mary Gawthorpe provides another example of a schoolteacher who joined the ILP and then the suffrage movement. She was introduced to socialist politics by her boyfriend, a Leeds compositor, and was soon active in the Dewsbury Road Socialist Institute, eventually becoming vice-president of the Leeds ILP. She was described as 'all fire and quick response, a flash of energy' and was a popular speaker, standing on concrete stumps at the Cross Flatts, Bramley to put forward her message.

Mary developed an interest in women's suffrage when her work for the Lord Mayor's Child Relief Fund convinced her that women were powerless to wield any influence without the vote. She came to the attention of Isabella Ford when she wrote to the local press to protest about the arrest of Annie Kenney and Christabel Pankhurst at the Manchester Free Trade Hall in 1905, and was drafted immediately onto the committee of the Leeds Women's Suffrage Society.[54]

Mary's propaganda work in 1905 and 1906 provides a perfect example of the way in which socialist and feminist politics were fused at this time. She spoke on socialism and on women's suffrage to branches of the ILP, the Co-operative Guild, the Women's Labour League (WLL) and to trade union and suffrage groups thoughout the West Riding. Her autobiography recalls the excitement of these years. 'Back to Leeds, the week following was packed with meetings, the camp stool meetings, so called because such stools were sold or could be hired for a penny at these open air gatherings, were going strong. . . . The Tailoresses' meeting of that week and a meeting for organizing printers' operatives were outstanding events'.[55]

Mary spoke at the latter alongside Mrs Tom Duncan, Councillor Macrae of the Leeds Labour Representation Committee, Isabella Ford and Teresa Billington, a founder member of the WSPU and an ILP organizer. They aimed to increase trade unionism among women, to seek affiliation to the LRC and to promote support for women's suffrage. Similar meetings were held elsewhere in the county. At Huddersfield 'socialist women . . . were always having big meetings and demonstrations of still more ambitious nature, with grand singing of Edward Carpenter's noble hymn, "England Arise"'.[56]

A large women's meeting, organized by female members of the ILP, was held in the Huddersfield Town Hall in March 1906. At the meeting Mary Gawthorpe argued that socialism stood for the emancipation of women as well as men, Teresa Billington linked socialism to an improvement in wages, while Katharine Bruce Glasier spoke of the way in which socialism meant the end of exploitation and the possibility of co-operation between the sexes.[57] Women's increasing involvement in the ILP appears to have actually revived some branches, including those at Halifax and North Brierley.

The links between the labour movement and the suffrage movement were also explored at a more theoretical level in Isabella Ford's little-known pamphlet, *Women and Socialism*, published by the ILP in 1904. By this time Isabella was one of the leaders of the party, sitting on the NAC between 1903 and 1907, and was able to exert an influence on the extent to which the party paid attention to women's rights.

In the pamphlet she argued that the labour and women's movements were inextricably linked because each arose from economic dependence and the nature of property ownership. They complemented each other: the Labour Party kept the economic side to the front and the women's movement ensured that the 'moral regeneration of society' which socialism stood for would not be forgotten. Isabella believed that political freedom would bring economic freedom by raising women's industrial status and hence increasing the chance of effective trade unionism. It would also mean a new relationship for men and women in the family, based on justice. From the basis of this more equal home life women could influence laws on divorce, marriage and child custody which 'press most heavily on the lives of poor women'.[58]

In these years the West Riding ILP supported not only the aims of the WSPU, but also its methods, which were largely confined to the disruption of meetings, and no hard and fast lines were drawn between suffrage groups. As a member of the Leeds WSS, Mary Gawthorpe heckled Parliamentary candidates and declared that she was ready to go to prison for the cause. Walt Wood attended a meeting at Morley to put a question to Asquith on votes for women. He had a fight with stewards who tried to pull him out. 'Mrs Wood was also pulled down, but, as Walt adds proudly, "Not before she had broken her umbrella over three of their heads"'.[59]

The arrest of the Manchester suffragettes in 1905 was widely condemned in the West Riding. An ILP manifesto in support of the imprisoned women was signed by twenty-three female members in Halifax, twenty-one in Harrogate, twenty-seven in Milnsbridge, twelve in Yeadon, fourteen in Keighley and by smaller numbers elsewhere in the county. These figures compare well with centres of support for women's suffrage, such as Nelson with twenty-two signatories.[60]

By 1907, however, it had become more difficult to combine labour and suffrage politics. At successive Annual Conferences the Labour

Party refused to endorse a resolution in favour of a limited franchise for women and gave support instead to the principle of adult suffrage. It was argued that a limited measure would enfranchise largely middle-class women, and that this would be detrimental to the Labour Party during elections and would not help working women.

The ILP did give support to a limited franchise on the grounds of principle at the Annual Conference of 1905, but the changing political tactics of the WSPU strained the loyalties of its ILP supporters. At the Cockermouth by-election of 1906 the WSPU campaigned against the Liberal candidate, but refused to give positive backing to Robert Smillie who was standing for the ILP. The suffragettes claimed that the labour movement did not take the women's cause seriously and that it was time for women to put the interests of their sex before class loyalty.

ILP women who were not members of the WSPU were also worried about the party's commitment to women's suffrage. Smillie had given an ambivalent answer when asked about his views on a limited franchise. This prompted Isabella Ford and Margaret McMillan to write to their fellow NAC members to express concern that Smillie's views had not been made clear before he had been adopted as a candidate. They argued that anyone who hesitated on this could not be a 'sincere socialist . . . and in order to prevent the party losing the support of such of us, during election times, we would very much like this course to be adopted'.[61]

In the event many leading women in the West Riding ILP, such as Isabella Ford and Ethel Snowden, decided to give a full-time commitment to the suffrage campaign and 'laid aside for the time all other political questions, leaving socialism to take care of itself until women had been granted the Parliamentary franchise'.[62] They worked from within the constitutionalist NUWSS and Isabella always sought to foster links between the National Union and the ILP. Ethel Snowden, however, resigned from the ILP in 1909 because two members of the NAC were declared adult suffragists. Others, such as Mary Gawthorpe, worked for the WSPU which severed its connections at a national level with the labour movement and became increasingly hostile to it.

The suffrage campaign diverted many women, and some men, from their work for the ILP. On the other hand, the splits between the labour and women's movements at a national level were not necessarily reflected locally. Here the boundaries between feminist and socialist politics remained fluid, and many rank-and-file members of the West Riding ILP continued to campaign for women's suffrage from within a broad framework of labour politics.

In contrast to Lancashire, the National Union was never able to gain a firm basis of support among working women in Yorkshire, who had little experience of organizing together in trade unions, and it tended to retain a sedate, middle-class image. For many individual ILP members who became active suffrage workers it was the WSPU, with its roots in the labour movement and its emphasis on direct action, that had most appeal. Several ILP members were among the eleven Yorkshire working women arrested in a WSPU raid on the House of Commons in 1907, including Julia Varley, her sister Pattie Barrett, described as a weaver, and Mrs Mary Alice Taylor, a member of the Halifax Board of Guardians and the wife of a Labour councillor. In Leeds Marie Foster, a tailoress and member of the negotiating committee of the AUCO, Lily Escritt and her father Robert, vice-president of the Leeds LRC, were all suffragettes. Similar examples can be found in other West Riding towns.

Women continued to be popular as speakers and often combined socialist and suffrage propaganda. Katherine Bruce Glasier, Margaret McMillan and Daisy Halling were frequent visitors to the West Riding, while Mrs Despard and Ethel Snowden took time out from their suffrage work to further the cause of socialism in the area. A younger generation of local speakers also came forward.

Hannah Burgess, a Bradford weaver and the daughter of Joseph Burgess, spoke to local branches on 'The Relationship of Man to the Planet' and 'Millionaires'. In addressing the Halifax Socialist Sunday School in September 1909 she reminded her audience of 'The Crimes of the Present Government' which had welcomed the Tsar, kept black people in chains and refused votes for women in order to keep them in subjection. When the NUWSS Pilgrimage for women's suffrage passed through Yorkshire, Hannah addressed many of the meetings with 'great brilliance'.[63]

After 1906 the Women's Labour League provided a base for ILP members who wished to focus on women's issues. Local groups were often small and drew their members from the families of labour activists or from women in white-blouse and professional occupations. The main aim of the League was to involve women in politics, both to help the Labour Party win elections and to increase pressure for social reforms. It campaigned to increase women's representation on public bodies, and a much larger number of female candidates were successful in the pre-war years.

The League also raised women's suffrage within the labour movement, and resolutions of support were passed by trade unions, ILP branches and Trades Councils in the West Riding. The women's cause was given even greater publicity once the Labour Party and the

PICTURE AND PORTRAITS OF THE DAY

MISS JULIA VARLEY,
the Bradford suffragette, who received a nasty fall outside the House of Commons on Wednesday night, and was afterwards committed for several days. She is a prominent Socialist and Trade Unionist, and is well known as a lecturer and speaker on labour and social topics.

MRS. PATTIE BARRETT
is a sister of Miss Varley, and is now undergoing fourteen days' imprisonment for "demonstrating" at St. Stephen's. She is employed by the Bradford Guardians as a visitor to underfed school children.

MRS. MARY ALICE TAYLOR,
another imprisoned suffragette, is the wife of Councillor Taylor, of Halifax, and herself a member of the Board of Guardians, and a grandmother. She and her husband have long been active workers in the interests of Trade Unionism and the I.L.P., and Mrs. Taylor played a prominent part in the recent tram strike in Halifax.

Three of the eleven Yorkshire working women arrested during a raid by the Women's Social and Political Union on the House of Commons in 1907.

NUWSS formed an electoral alliance in 1912. This led to numerous articles on women's suffrage and the need for women's participation in politics in the local labour press. NUWSS members were in great demand as speakers and the campaign for women's suffrage was given a prominent place at May Day rallies. As the Suffrage Pilgrimage passed through the West Riding it was reported that the importance of women's work in the area and the friendliness of the men's unions meant that speakers had 'secured a sympathetic hearing'.[64]

The suffrage campaign could cause divisions, however, if it involved criticism of the Labour Party. The League, for example, put loyalty to the Labour Party first and tended to avoid issues which raised the possibility of a 'sex war'. Nonetheless, some WLL groups and members were less willing than others to subordinate women's specific needs to the cause of labour unity.

Members of the East and North-East Leeds WLL, drawn from the East Leeds ILP, were also members of the WSPU and particularly keen to pursue women's specific interests. They debated whether mothers should receive an endowment from the state to make them economically independent and took a strong line on women's suffrage. At the League's Annual Conference of 1914 Mrs Geldart and Mrs Hunter, both from the East Leeds group, moved a resolution that Labour MPs should refuse to support any further legislation until women had the vote. Only three delegates voted in favour.

Conflicts over dual membership of the WLL and the WSPU came to a head in 1913. Members of the East and North-East WLL joined other WSPU women in heckling Phillip Snowden when he came to Leeds to speak on militarism. Jeannie Arnott, secretary of the Leeds Central WLL and the wife of an engineer and Labour councillor, was quick to condemn their actions. She argued that members of the WLL were expected to support Labour candidates and that this was incompatible with membership of the WSPU. Mrs Dightam, secretary of the East Leeds group disagreed, defending her actions on the grounds that the Labour Party had fallen away from its ideals in refusing to support sex equality. The debate continued in the press for many weeks, only to lose significance with the outbreak of war.[65]

Throughout this period, therefore, women campaigned for the vote from within the West Riding ILP, even if it meant conflicts with both male and female members. Support for women's suffrage grew steadily within the labour movement as a whole, but the emphasis on political equality could be seen as diverting attention from women's unequal role in production and in the home. Bornat, for example, argues that because Yorkshire suffrage activists were nearly all members of the

ILP, 'the containment of a women's issue within labour politics may have had the effect of neutralizing women's special concerns'. She suggests that in contrast to Lancashire the suffrage issue in the West Riding 'retained a purely political profile' and failed to link the vote with changes in sex roles at the workplace.[66]

This argument can be accepted up to a point. It was usually suggested that women should have the vote in order to increase their interest and role in labour politics. Edna Penny's speech to a large meeting in Halifax provides a typical example. In keeping with ILP ideas as a whole, she emphasized the importance of political action to achieve social and economic change. 'She wished she could get the women of the country to understand the vital necessity of taking an interest in politics. . . . mothers of the working classes only bore children that they might be enslaved later by the children of another class. . . . socialism alone would free them and their children'.[67]

Women were seen as crucial for the building of a new society because of their caring qualities, which had been nurtured within the family. The series of articles on the woman worker in politics written for the *Bradford Pioneer* by Marion Phillips, general secretary of the WLL, were based on the ideology of separate spheres which predominated in the ILP: 'Labour politics aim at better homes, and women must take part, because they know what homes should be and their experience must help to find the way of nation-building in the future'.[68] Similar arguments were also put forward by the NUWSS and contributed to the close working relationship that developed between the ILP and the National Union in the pre-war years.

The vote was not, however, seen in purely political terms by members of the West Riding ILP. In the 1890s and early 1900s Tom Maguire, Isabella Ford and Julia Varley had all linked the vote with higher wages and improved working conditions for women workers. Julia Varley told a meeting of working women that 'we work shoulder to shoulder with men in the mills and in the councils of the workers; why should they deny us the right to help to choose the men who make the laws that govern the workers'.[69]

After the labour-suffrage alliance of 1912, references to the relationship between the vote and an improvement in women's industrial status became increasingly common in the speeches of Labour councillors, MPs and trade union leaders. Councillor Foster of Leeds, for example, argued that when democracy arrived men and women could 'shape the conditions of their lives. . . . it would then be no longer possible . . . for the woman industrial worker to be demeaned in her status and stipend because she was a woman'.

Such speeches failed, however, to share the concern of earlier feminists, such as Tom Maguire and Isabella Ford, to explore the relationship between sex and class oppression in the workplace and in the home. They were based on the assumption that 'in the coming battles women and men of the working classes will have common interests. They will work for a common cause, march hand in hand to conquer fairer worlds than they have yet seen'.[70]

Such rhetoric glossed over the very real conflict of interest between the sexes in the workplace which became apparent during the labour unrest of the pre-war years. The unrest led to an increase in women's participation in unions and in the number of female trade unionists in the West Riding. Such women often became active in labour and socialist politics. Emily Tate, an organizer for the AUCO, was an ILP member and leader in the Socialist Sunday School movement. Miss Holmes and Bertha Quinn, both on the AUCO branch committee in Leeds, were delegates to the Leeds Trades Council after 1912. Bertha was appointed a full-time organizer in 1915. She was elected to the Leeds Board of Guardians in 1918 and stood as a Labour Party candidate in the West Ward municipal elections in 1920. In 1913 she moved a resolution of protest against the Cat and Mouse Bill on behalf of the AUCO. She said that she had had great pleasure in 'throwing a boot at Mr Redmond', a supporter of the Bill, when he had visited Leeds.[71]

Female trade union activists, however, tended to support women's suffrage only in so far as it formed part of Labour Party policy and usually put labour unity above the specific interests of their sex. In 1913, for example, the AUCO managed to secure higher minimum rates of pay for tailoring workers, but accepted a clause that employers would be complying with the agreement as long as seventy per cent of their female workers received the new rate. It was widely believed that the percentage clause had been accepted to safeguard the men's agreed rates and that women workers would be worse off.

Discontent was expressed in the correspondence columns of the local press. One female worker, calling herself 'Justice', thought that men should have gone on strike to get a better rate for women. She argued that women were at a double disadvantage because of their sex and class, with men ready 'to exploit women of their own class'. Both male and female union organizers refuted these allegations. Bernard Sullivan, a member of the negotiating committee, argued that 'there is no sex war in the economic field, but there is a class war which demands the whole of the energy and activity of the workers, irrespective of sex or creed, in one camp, if they wished to attain a fuller and higher life'. Emily Tate suggested that it was the women's own fault if they had not gained more: 'all the bitterness and hatred in me is reserved for the men – aye and the women too – of the master class, who have oppressed my class for centuries'.[72]

Isabella-Ford joined in the controversy. She reminded the AUCO that the Tailoresses' Strike in 1889 had inspired the men to organize. She had always advocated mixed-sex trade unions, but was aware that women's interests could be neglected. They were rarely consulted, and yet the percentage question 'affects women and should be decided by women'. She showed once again why the vote had become such an important issue for her: 'It is a matter of deep regret to me that, owing to the long struggle for the vote (the only weapon of real, effective and permanent use), I am unable to work for trade unionism for women as I have done formerly. Men's unions will never be really strong until women's unions are strong; and women's unions will always be weak and powerless until women are voters.'[73]

Isabella's faith that political equality would pave the way for co-operation between the sexes allowed even her to sidestep the obvious conflict that existed at the workplace. Along with many others in the women's movement and the ILP, she was carried away by the excitement of the labour-suffrage alliance in which the interests of women and the interests of the labour movement seemed to be at one.

From the outset the ILP had had to grapple with the conflicts between the specific interests of women as a sex and its overall emphasis on the need for unity between men and women of the working class. Attitudes to these issues were complex. It was not simply the case that women's needs were lost sight of because the ILP was a mixed-sex organization. Even Isabella Ford, who always kept the interests of female workers to the front, thought that the best way to gain women's emancipation was by co-operation between the sexes and the achievement of a socialist society. For a brief period the suffrage campaign placed sex comradeship above class loyalty, but ultimately this was to prove unsatisfactory for most ILP women. They could not ignore for long the question of what the vote would be used for, which was to prove divisive after 1918 for the women's movement, and showed considerable relief once the alliance of 1912 brought the labour and women's movements back together.

The ILP failed in the end to challenge in any fundamental way women's unequal position in the workplace and in the home. The predominance of male trade unionists in the West Riding ILP, the weakness of female workers and the deeply rooted commitment to a family life in which women were at the centre helps to explain this. But the women's movement also played a part through its growing emphasis on political equality as the key to women's emancipation. This enabled the ILP to support its female members and their right to take part in public life, while leaving untouched the sexual division of labour.

Despite these weaknesses, the West Riding ILP did make a contribution to women's rights at both a practical and a theoretical level. As Clayton notes, it provided a way for 'working-class women trade unionists and the wives and sisters of ILP men' to become 'of political account, especially at election times. The entrance of women into politics was the work of the Socialists in general and of the ILP in particular'.[74] At a more theoretical level, members of the ILP engaged in debates around the relationship between feminism and socialism which raised questions that remain unresolved in the labour movement today.

Notes

Place of publication is London unless otherwise stated. All places of publication are given for nineteenth-century and earlier works.

Introduction

1 Some of the excellent recent work on the suffrage movement includes: Andrew Rosen, *Rise up Women! the militant campaign of the Women's Social and Political Union 1903-14* (Routledge and Kegan Paul, 1974); David Morgan, *Suffragists and Liberals. The Politics of the Woman's Movement in Britain* (Basil Blackwell, Oxford, 1975); Martin Pugh, *Electoral Reform in War and Peace 1906-18* (Routledge and Kegan Paul, 1978); Brian Harrison, *Separate Spheres: the Opposition to Women's Suffrage in Britain* (Croom Helm, 1978); Jill Liddington and Jill Norris, *One Hand Tied Behind Us. The Rise of the Women's Suffrage Movement* (Virago, 1978); Leslie Parker Hume, *The National Union of Women's Suffrage Societies* (Garland, New York, 1982); Brian Harrison, 'Women's Suffrage at Westminster 1866-1928' in Michael Bentley and John Stevenson (eds), *High and Low Politics in Modern Britain: ten case studies* (Oxford University Press, Oxford, 1983).
2 Michelle Zimbalist Rosaldo, 'Woman, Culture and Society: A Theoretical Overview', in Michelle Zimbalist Rosaldo and Louise Lamphere (eds), *Woman, Culture and Society* (Stanford University Press, Stanford, 1974) p. 37.
3 For a most effective discussion of this distinction see: Jean Bethke Elshtain, *Public Man Private Woman. Women in Social and Political Thought* (Martin Robertson, Oxford, 1981). See also Elizabeth Fox Genovese, 'Property and Patriarchy in Classical Bourgeois Political Economy', *Radical History Review* 4 (1977), pp. 36-59.
4 For a discussion which points specifically to the parallels between the paternal authority of landlords, employers and philanthropists, and the patriarchal authority of a father within the family, see David Roberts,

Paternalism in Early Victorian England (Croom Helm, 1979). Other political historians who have written extensively of such political patterns include: T. J. Nossiter, *Influence, Opinion and Political Idioms in Reformed England: case studies from the North-east, 1832–74* (Harvester, Brighton, 1975); D.C. Moore, *The Politics of Deference: a study of the mid-nineteenth century political system* (Harvester, Brighton, 1976).

5 On John Stuart Mill see Elshtain, *Public Man, Private Woman*, pp. 132–46; Susan M. Okin, *Women in Western Political Thought* (Princeton University Press, Princeton, 1979), ch. 9; Julia M. Annas, 'Mill and the *Subjection of Women*', *Philosophy*, 52 (1977), pp. 179–94; Susan Mendus, 'The Marriage of True Minds: the ideal of marriage in the philosophy of John Stuart Mill', in Susan Mendus and Jane Rendall (eds), *Images of Women: the Victorian Legacy* (Methuen, forthcoming).

6 See the stimulating debate between: Ellen Dubois, Mari Jo Buhle, Temma Kaplan, Gerda Lerner, and Carroll Smith-Rosenberg, 'Politics and Culture in Women's History: A Symposium', *Feminist Studies*, 6 (1980), pp. 26–63; also Tony Judt, 'A Clown in Regal Purple: Social History and the Historians' *History Workshop* 7 (1979), pp. 66–94; Patricia Hilden, 'Women's History: the second wave', *Historical Journal*, 25 (1982), pp. 501–12.

7 Sally Alexander, 'Women, class, and sexual difference', *History Workshop*, 17 (1984), p. 135.

8 M. Segalen, *Love and Power in the French Peasant Family. Rural France in the Nineteenth Century* (Blackwell, Oxford, 1983).

9 E. P. Thompson ' "Rough Music": le charivari anglais', *Annales ESC* 27 (1972), pp. 285–312.

10 J. F. C. Harrison, *The Second Coming. Popular Millenarianism, 1780–1850* (Routledge and Kegan Paul, 1979); Clarke Garrett, *Respectable Folly: Millenarianism and the French Revolution in France and England* (Johns Hopkins University Press, Baltimore and London, 1975).

11 Deborah Valenze, *Prophetic Sons and Daughters. Female Preaching and Popular Religion in Industrial England* (Princeton University Press, Princeton, NJ, 1985).

12 Malcolm Thomis and Jennifer Grimmett, *Women in Protest 1800–1850* (Croom Helm, 1982), pp. 88–103.

13 Dorothy Thompson, *The Chartists. Popular Politics in the Industrial Revolution* (Wildwood House, Aldershot, 1986) pp. 120–52; David Jones, 'Women and Chartism', *History* 68 (1983), pp. 1–21.

14 Barbara Taylor, *Eve and the New Jerusalem. Socialism and Feminism in the Nineteenth Century* (Virago, 1983) pp. 212–16: Mary Wollstonescraft, *Vindication of the Rights of Woman* ed. Miriam Kramnick (Penguin, Harmondsworth, 1982).

15 Dorothy Thompson, 'Women and nineteenth century radical politics: a lost dimension' in Juliet Mitchell and Ann Oakley (eds), *The Rights and Wrongs of Woman* (Penguin, Harmondsworth, 1976).

16 Jane Lewis, 'The Working Class Wife and Mother and State Intervention,

1870-1918', in Jane Lewis (ed.) *Labour and Love. Women's Experience of Home and Family* (Blackwell, Oxford, 1986); Ellen Ross, '"Fierce Questions and Taunts": Married Life in Working Class London, 1870-1914', *Feminist Studies*, 8 (1982), pp. 575-605 and 'Survival Networks: Women's Neighbourhood Sharing in London before World War I', *History Workshop Journal*, 15 (1983), pp. 4-28.

17 Dorothy Thompson, *The Chartists*, pp. 336-9.

18 Leslie Mitchell, *Holland House* (Duckworth, 1980) pp. 15-38.

19 Patricia Jalland, *Women, Marriage and Politics, 1860-1914* (Oxford University Press, Oxford, 1986) pp. 234-6.

20 F. K. Prochaska, *Women and Philanthropy in Nineteenth Century England* (Oxford University Press, Oxford, 1980) pp. 107 and 174.

21 Margaret Oliphant, *Hester* (1883, reprinted Virago, 1984); *Kirsteen. The story of a Scotch Family seventy years ago* (1890, reprinted with an introduction by Merryn Williams, Dent, 1984).

22 Catherine Hall, 'The early formation of Victorian domestic ideology', in S. Burman (ed.), *Fit Work for Women* (Croom Helm, London and Canberra, 1979); Jane Rendall, *The Origins of Modern Feminism: Women in Britain, France and the United States 1789-1860* (Macmillan, 1985), ch. 3; Prochaska, *Women and Philanthropy in Nineteenth Century England*, Introduction; and see Gail Malmgreen's introduction as editor to her *Religion in the Lives of English Women 1760-1930* (Croom Helm, 1986).

23 Alan Gilbert, *Religion and Society in Industrial England. Church, Chapel and Social Change* (Longman, 1976), pp. 40-1.

24 F. K. Prochaska, 'Women in English Philanthropy, 1790-1830', *International Journal of Social History*, 19 (1974), pp. 426-45.

25 Alex Tyrrell, '"Woman's Mission" and Pressure Group Politics in Britain (1825-1860),' *Bulletin of the John Rylands Library*, 63 (1980), p. 194-230.

26 Prochaska, *Women and Philanthropy in Nineteenth Century England*, ch. V.

27 See, for instance, Frances Finnegan, *Poverty and Prostitution. A study of Victorian York* (Cambridge University Press, Cambridge, 1979), ch. 6.

28 See Lee Holcombe, *Wives and Property. Reform of the Married Women's Property Law in Nineteenth Century England* (Martin Robertson, Oxford, 1983).

29 Liz Stanley, 'Feminism and Friendship in England from 1825 to 1938: the case of Olive Schreiner', in *Feminism and Friendship*, Studies in Sexual Politics, 8 (Department of Sociology, University of Manchester, Manchester, 1985-6); Martha Vicinus, *Independent Women. Work and Community for Single Women, 1850-1920* (Virago, 1985).

30 Lilian Faderman, *Surpassing the Love of Women. Romantic Friendship and Love between Women from the Renaissance to the Present Day* (Women's Press, 1985).

31 Jalland, *Women, Marriage and Politics*, p. 90.

32 Ibid, pp. 91-2.

33 D. C. Coleman, *Courtaulds. An Economic and Social History* (Oxford University Press, Oxford, 1969), 2 vols, Vol. I, pp. 205-8.

34 Paul McHugh, *Prostitution and Social Reform* (Croom Helm, 1980), p. 170.

35 Robert Moore, *Pit-men, Preachers and Politics. The effects of Methodism in a Durham mining community* (Cambridge University Press, Cambridge, 1974), p. 146.

36 Olive Banks, *Becoming a Feminist. The Social Origins of 'First Wave' Feminism* (Wheatsheaf, Brighton, 1986) p. 44.

37 Barbara Caine, 'Family history as women's history: the sisters of Beatrice Webb', *Feminist Studies*, 12 (1986), pp. 294–319.

38 Thomis and Grimmett, *Women in Protest*, pp. 96–7; Rendall, *Origins of Modern Feminism*, Plates 10 and 11, p. 363n.

39 Elizabeth Gaskell, *North and South* (1855, reprinted Penguin, Harmondsworth, 1970), p. 110.

40 Taylor, *Eve and the New Jerusalem*, p. 229.

41 David Vincent, *Bread, Knowledge and Freedom. A study of nineteenth century working class autobiography* (Methuen, 1981), p. 44 'In very few instances do they (the autobiographers) seem to have regarded their sweethearts and wives or any other women as equal partners in the search for reason and truth which occupied so much of their lives and autobiographies'.

42 Elizabeth Roberts, *A Woman's Place* (Blackwell, Oxford, 1984), ch. 2.

43 E. Showalter, *A Literature of Their Own. British Women Novelists from Bronte to Lessing* (Virago, 1978), ch. III.

44 Sally Mitchell, *The Fallen Angel: chastity, class and women's reading 1835–1880* (Bowling Green University Popular Press, Bowling Green, Ohio, 1981) pp. 23–30.

45 Lady Eastlake, '*Vanity Fair* and *Jane Eyre*,' *Quarterly Review*, Dec. 1848, pp. 153–85.

46 Tyrrell, ' "Woman's Mission" ', p. 230.

47 Olive Anderson, 'Women Preachers in Mid-Victorian Britain: some reflections on feminism, popular religion and social change', *Historical Journal*, XII (1969), pp. 467–84.

48 K. McCrone, 'The National Association for the Promotion of Social Science and the Advancement of Victorian Women', *Atlantis* (Canada) 8 (1982), pp. 44–66.

49 Frances Mary Sterling to Ray Strachey, n.d. Fawcett Library autograph collection, Vol. 1N.

50 See Judith Walkowitz, *Prostitution and Victorian Society. Women, Class and the State* (Cambridge University Press, Cambridge, 1980); Paul McHugh, *Prostitution and Social Reform* (Croom Helm, London, 1980).

51 For different treatments of this movement, see Prochaska, *Women and Philanthropy in Nineteenth century England*, ch. VI; Sheila Jeffreys. *The Spinster and her Enemies. Feminism and Sexuality 1880–1930* (Pandora, 1985), chs 1, 3, 4.

52 For differing views again see Jeffreys, *The Spinster and her Enemies*, pp. 93–4; Les Garner, *Stepping Stones to Women's Liberty. Feminist Ideas in the Women's Suffrage Movement, 1900–1918* (Heinemann, 1984), ch. 5.

53 Martin Pugh, *The Tories and the People 1880–1935* (Blackwell, Oxford, 1985).

54 Steven C. Hause with Anne R. Kenney, *Women's Suffrage and Social Politics in the French Third Republic* (Princeton University Press, Princeton, NJ, 1984).

55 Judy Lown, 'Not so much a factory, more a form of patriarchy: gender and class during industrialisation' in Eva Gamarnikow et al. *Gender, class and work* (Heinemann, 1983); Patrick Joyce, *Work, Society and Politics. The culture of the factory in late Victorian England* (Methuen, 1982), p. 115.

56 See the recent discussions of this difficult question by Joanna Bornat, Ellen Mappen and Deborah Thom, in Angela V. John (ed.) *Unequal Opportunities. Women's Employment in England 1800–1918* (Blackwell, Oxford, 1986).

57 Gail Braybon, *Women Workers and the First World War* (Croom Helm, 1981), ch. 3.

58 Gareth Stedman Jones, 'Working-class culture and working-class politics in London, 1870–1900: Notes on the remaking of a working class', in *Languages of Class: Studies in English Working-class History 1832–1982* (Cambridge University Press, Cambridge, 1983).

59 Lilian Lewis Shiman, '"Changes are Dangerous": Women and Temperance in Victorian England', in Malmgreen (ed.) *Religion in the Lives of English Women*; Moore, *Pit-men, Preachers and Politics*, pp. 141, 146.

60 Jean Gaffin, 'Women and Co-operation' in Lucy Middleton (ed.) *Women in the Labour Movement. The British Experience* (Croom Helm, 1977); Raymond Dale Sutton, 'Co-operation and the Poor, 1890–1908', MA thesis, University of York, 1985.

61 Jill Liddington and Jill Norris, *One Hand Tied Behind Us. The Rise of the Women's Suffrage Movement* (Virago, 1978); Jill Liddington, *The Life and Times of a Respectable Rebel. Selina Cooper (1864–1936)* (Virago, 1984), pp. 191–2.

Chapter 1 Cottage Religion and the Politics of Survival

1 Outstanding examples of historical treatments of working-class women's struggle for political rights include Dorothy Thompson, 'Women and Nineteenth-Century Radical Politics: A Lost Dimension', in Juliet Mitchell and Ann Oakley (eds), *The Rights and Wrongs of Women* (Penguin Books, Harmondsworth, 1976), pp. 112–48; Barbara Taylor, *Eve and the New Jerusalem* (Virago, 1983), and, for a later period, Jill Liddington and Jill Norris, *One Hand Tied Behind Us* (Virago, 1978).

2 See, for example, the suggestive discussion of women and religion in Jane Rendall, *The Origins of Modern Feminism: Women in Britain, France and the United States, 1780–1860* (Schocken, New York, 1984), ch. 3, esp. pp. 91–3. For a different emphasis, see Martha Vicinus, *Independent Women: Work and Community for Single Women, 1850–1920* (Chicago University Press, Chicago, Ill., 1985), ch. 2.

3 For a fuller discussion of female preaching in this context, see Deborah M. Valenze, *Prophetic Sons and Daughters: Female Preaching and Popular*

Religion in Industrial England (Princeton University Press, Princeton, N.J., 1985).

4 Marxist historians have disagreed over this point. The literature is enormous; for a critical view of the role of Methodism in working-class culture, see E. P. Thompson, *The Making of the English Working Class* (Vintage, New York, 1968), esp. pp. 38–51. Other important discussions include E. J. Hobsbawn, *Primitive Rebels* (Norton, New York, 1965), ch. 8, and 'Methodism and the Threat of Revolution', in *Labouring Men* (Weidenfeld and Nicolson, 1964), pp. 23–33; for a recent interpretation, see G. S. Jones, 'From Mesmer to Fourier: The Cosmological Framework of Early Socialism', unpublished paper.

5 Dorothy Thompson, 'Women in Nineteenth-Century Radical Politics', pp. 138, 115.

6 Taylor, *Eve and the New Jerusalem*, esp. ch. 8.

7 G. S. Jones, 'Rethinking Chartism', in *Languages of Class: Studies in English Working Class History, 1832–1982* (Cambridge University Press, Cambridge, 1983), pp. 90–178. For a highly suggestive discussion of women and radical politics, see Sally Alexander, 'Women, Class and Sexual Difference', *History Workshop Journal* 17 (1984), pp. 125–49.

8 David Vincent, *Bread, Knowledge and Freedom: A Study of Nineteenth-Century Working Class Autobiography* (Europa, 1981), esp. p. 8.

9 See Margaret R. Somers, 'The People and the Law: The State, the Family, and Rural Industry in English Working Class Formation', Ph.D. Harvard University, 1986.

10 E. P. Thompson, 'The Moral Economy of the English Crowd in the Eighteenth Century', *Past and Present* 50 (1971), pp. 76–136, esp. pp. 90–1; Elizabeth Fox-Genovese, 'The Many Faces of Moral Economy: A Contribution to a Debate', *Past and Present* 58 (1973), pp. 161–8.

11 The new principles of political economy enjoyed popularity with commercial farmers; see Arthur Young's *Annals of Agriculture*, 1784–1815. For analogous changes in legal relations, see P. S. Atiyah, *The Rise and Fall of Freedom of Contract* (Clarendon Press, Oxford, 1979), esp. pp. 399–400.

12 'Women and the Family Economy in Eighteenth-Century France', *French Historical Studies* 9 (1975), pp. 1–22.

13 William Blackstone, *Commentaries on the Laws of England*, (1769; new edn., 1857), I, p. 471.

14 On images of working women, see Leonore Davidoff, 'Class and Gender in Victorian England', in Judith L. Newton, Mary P. Ryan, and Judith R. Walkowitz (eds), *Sex and Class in Women's History* (Routledge and Kegan Paul, 1983), pp. 16–71; see also Nina Auerbach, *Woman and the Demon: The Life of a Victorian Myth* (Harvard University Press, Cambridge, Mass., 1982), esp. ch. 5.

15 *Letters from England* (London, 1814 edn.), vol. 2, p. 47, quoted in E. P. Thompson, 'The Moral Economy of the English Crowd', p. 116.

16 E. P. Thompson, 'The Moral Economy of the English Crowd', pp. 115–16; see also Temma Kaplan, 'Female Consciousness and Collective Action: The Case of Barcelona, 1910–1918', *Signs* 7 (1982), pp. 545–66, esp. p. 548.

17 Quotes come from 'Memoir of Mrs Susanna Pickles', *Primitive Methodist Magazine*, 1850, pp. 262-6, and 'Memoir of Mrs Mary Taphouse', Ibid., 1846, pp. 386-7; see also D. Valenze, 'Pilgrims and Progress in Nineteenth-Century England', in Raphael Samuel and Gareth Stedman Jones (eds), *Culture, Ideology and Politics* (Routledge and Kegan Paul, 1983), esp. pp. 116-18.

18 Philip Fisher, *Hard Facts: Setting and Form in the American Novel* (Oxford University Press, New York, 1985), p. 102.

19 James Obelkevich discusses the relationship of religion to the transformation of rural society for a later period in *Religion and Rural Society: South Lindsey, 1825-1875* (Clarendon Press, Oxford, 1976).

20 Valenze, *Prophetic Sons and Daughters*, esp. ch. 5.

21 Most of the biographical information regarding Mary Porteus's life is taken from Rev. John Lightfoot, *The Power of Faith and Prayer Exemplified in the Life and Labours of Mrs Mary Porteus* (London, 1862); see also *Primitive Methodist Magazine*, 1861, pp. 520-3.

22 Lightfoot, *Mary Porteus*, pp. 10-13.

23 Ibid., pp. 14-15.

24 Ibid., pp. 20-1.

25 Ibid., pp. 23-5. On typical patterns of shifting employment within domestic service, see Theresa McBride, *The Domestic Revolution* (Holmes and Meier, New York, 1976), p. 74.

26 Lightfoot, *Mary Porteus*, pp. 27-9.

27 Ibid., p. 29.

28 Ibid., pp. 35-6, 42, 50-1. For a similar pattern of mutuality among working-class women, see Ellen Ross, 'Survival Networks: Women's Neighbourhood Sharing in London before World War II', *History Workshop Journal* 15 (1983), pp. 4-27; see also Elizabeth Roberts, 'Working Wives and Their Families', in Theo Barker and Michael Drake (eds), *Population and Society in Britain, 1850-1980* (Batsford, 1982), pp. 140-62.

29 Hugh Bourne, *A General Collection of Hymns and Spiritual Songs, For Camp Meetings, Revivals, &c.* (Bingham, 1819), no. 13.

30 'Remarks on the Ministry of Women', reprinted in John Walford, *Memoirs of the Life and Labours of the late venerable Hugh Bourne*, ed. W. Antliff (London, 1855), pp. 172-3.

31 Ibid., pp. 175, 176-7.

32 Lightfoot, *Mary Porteus*, p. 72.

33 Ibid., pp. 72-3.

34 'On the Ministry of Women', *Primitive Methodist Magazine*, 1821, pp. 180-1.

35 *Primitive Methodist Magazine*, 1821, pp. 190-2. 'Written originally by the Wife of W. O'Bryan'.

36 See Taylor, *Eve and the New Jerusalem*, pp. 131, 171-2.

37 Lightfoot, *Mary Porteus*, p. 73.

38 Ibid., pp. 72, 76.

39 Ibid., pp. 79-80.

40 Ibid., p. 81; printed in *Primitive Methodist Magazine*, Oct 1824.

41 Carolyn Bynum, 'Fast, Feast, and Flesh: The Religious Significance of Food to Medieval Women', *Representations* 11 (1985), pp. 1–25.

42 Lightfoot, *Mary Porteus*, p. 85.

43 See Ross, 'Survival Networks'; on women and relational definitions of moral identity, see Ruth L. Smith, 'Feminism and the Moral Subject', in Barbara Andolsen, Christine Gudorf and Mary Pellauer (eds), *Women's Consciousness, Women's Conscience* (Winston Press, Minneapolis, Minn., 1985), pp. 235–50; Ruth L. Smith and Deborah M. Valenze, 'Mutuality and Marginality: Liberal Moral Theory and Women in Nineteenth-Century England', forthcoming, *Signs*.

44 On the intersection of material hardship and bereavement, see Vincent, *Bread, Knowledge and Freedom*, pp. 58–9; see also Thomas Laqueur, 'Bodies, Death, and Pauper Funerals', *Representations* 1 (1983), pp. 109–31.

45 Lightfoot, *Mary Porteus*, pp. 68–71; 90–3.

46 For an illuminating discussion of this concept, see Rachel Adler, 'A Mother in Israel: Aspects of the Mother Role in Jewish Myth', in Rita Gross (ed.), *Beyond Androcentrism* (Scholars Press, Missoula, Montana, 1977), pp. 237–68.

47 For a critique of the economic needs established by this definition of human nature, see Leszek Kolakowski, *Main Currents of Marxism* (Oxford University Press, Oxford, 1981), vol. 1, p. 413, quoted in Michael Ignatieff, *The Needs of Strangers* (Viking, New York, 1985), p. 150.

48 A definitive treatment of communities of middle-class women can be found in Martha Vicinus, *Independent Women*.

49 Ignatieff, *Needs of Strangers*, p. 13.

Chapter 2 Woman, Work and Politics in Nineteenth-Century England: The Problem of Authority

1 For a recent summary of the legal position of married women in mid-nineteenth-century Britain, see Lee Holcombe, *Wives and Property. Reform of the Married Women's Property Law in Nineteenth-Century England* (Martin Robertson, Oxford, 1983).

2 Marilyn S. Butler, *Maria Edgeworth, a Literary Biography* (Oxford University Press, Oxford, 1972).

3 For her measures of coercion of the tenantry during a key election, see Michael C. Hurst, *Maria Edgeworth and the Public Scene* (Macmillan, 1969) p. 78 and passim.

4 An interesting and thought-provoking discussion of this question is Jean Bethke Elshtain, *Public Man, Private Woman. Women in Social and Political Thought* (Martin Robertson, Oxford, 1981).

5 I have been told that in parts of the Adirondacks women still refer to work done outside the home as 'public' work.

6 *A poem descriptive of the Manners of the Clothiers, written about the year 1730* (copy in Leeds Reference Library).

7 Mary Thale (ed.), *The Autobiography of Francis Place, 1771–1854* (Cambridge University Press, Cambridge, 1972), p. 124.

8 Robert Crowe, *The Reminiscences of Robert Crowe, the Octogenarian [sic] Tailor* (New York, n.d. [1902?] reprinted Garland, New York, 1986) p. 10.

9 John Bedford Leno, *The Aftermath* (Leno, London, 1892, reprinted Garland, New York, 1986) p. 30.

10 *Newcastle Weekly Chronicle*, 20 February 1869. [My attention was drawn to this fascinating article entitled 'The Artisan and his Club' by Keith McClelland.]

11 Dorothy Thompson, 'Women and Nineteenth Century Radical Politics: A Lost Dimension', in Juliet Mitchell and Ann Oakley (eds), *The Rights and Wrongs of Women* (Penguin, Harmondsworth, 1976). For women in the Chartist period, see ch. 7 of my *The Chartists* (Temple Smith, 1984); D. J. V. Jones, 'Women and Chartism', *History* 68 (1983) pp. 1–21. Malcolm I. Thomis and Jennifer Grimmett, *Women in Protest, 1800–1850* (Croom Helm, 1982) lists a number of additional public actions by women in the early years of the century.

12 For two interesting accounts of working-class family life and of the place of women in particular, see the work of Ellen Ross, ' "Fierce Questions and Taunts": Married Life in Working Class London 1870–1914', *Feminist Studies* 8 (1982) pp. 575–605, and Carl Chinn, 'The Anatomy of a Working-Class Neighbourhood, West Sparkbrook 1871–1914', (Unpublished Ph.D., University of Birmingham, 1986) ch. 10, pp. 164–74 and passim.

13 For an account of the 1854 and 1855 riots and a discussion of the sigificance of this kind of activity in the nineteenth century, see H. I. Dutton and J. E. King, 'Not the Last Food Riots: England in 1854 and 1855' in J. E. King and O. Westall (eds), *Innovation and Labour during British Industrialization, a Celebration of the Life and Work of Harry Dutton* (Huntingdon Publishers, Cambridge, 1985).

14 Swift, 'Food Riots in mid-Victorian Exeter, 1847–67', *Southern History*, 2 (1980) pp. 101–27.

15 *Hansard*. 3rd series, vol. CCXV, p. 1200 (1873).

16 Mrs J. Stewart, *The Missing Law: A Woman's Birthright* (London, 1869), p. 16.

17 A. V. Dicey, *Law and Public Opinion in England* (2nd edition, Macmillan, 1962) p. 384. See the whole of Dicey's Lecture XI, part 11, for an explanation of how the law relating to married women's property actually worked before 1870, and also for his comment that the same kind of situation existed in relation to divorce – i.e. that in spite of the legal inequalities, rich women, by the use of private acts of Parliament, could avoid the disadvantages under which less well-off members of their sex suffered.

18 Cornholme W. E. A. branch, *Shore in Stansfield, A Pennine Weaving Community 1660–1750* (Cornholme, 1986).

19 M. K. Ashby, *Countrywomen's Occasions* (Truex, Oxford, 1974), pp. 18–19.

20 Charlotte Bronte, *Shirley* (Penguin reprint, Harmondsworth, 1974), p. 377 and passim.

21 Cecil Woodham-Smith, *Florence Nightingale* (Fontana, 1964), p. 46.

22 Nigel Cross, *The Common Writer: Life in Nineteenth Century Grub Street* (Cambridge University Press, Cambridge, 1985) ch. 5, pp. 164–203.

23 Fabian Tract No 93, *Women and Councillors* (1900) p. 1.

24 Ibid., p. 3.

25 [Hannah More], *Coelebs in Search of a Wife* (5th edn, London, 1809), Vol. 2, pp. 20-1.

26 F. K. Prochaska, *Women and Philanthropy in Nineteenth Century England* (Oxford University Press, Oxford, 1980).

27 For a hilarious account of the 'Mendikity Society' in action, seen from the receiver's end, see the autobiography of J. J. Bezer in David Vincent (ed.) *Testaments of Radicalism* (Europa, 1977) pp. 184-6.

28 Prochaska, *Women and Philanthropy in Nineteenth Century England*, Appendix 1.

29 *Stamford Mercury*, 7 Jan 1820. For this and other references to the *Stamford Mercury*, I am indebted to Rex C. Russell.

30 Ben Brierley, *Home Memories and Recollections of Life* (London, 1886) p. 6.

31 *Stamford Mercury*, 3 Jan. 1845.

32 e.g. '. . . the poor of the parish of Broughton are allowed to go to Manby twice a week for the broken victuals of the establishment; by which many a humble dwelling is filled with good things', *Stamford Mercury*, 10 Jan 1840.

33 Harriet and John Stuart Mill, 'The Enfranchisement of Women', *Westminster and Foreign Quarterly Review*, 55 (July 1851), pp. 289-311.

34 Alex Tyrrell, '"Woman's Mission" and Pressure Group Politics in Britain 1825-60', *Bulletin of the John Rylands Library* 63 (1980), pp. 194-230.

35 Verses on the death of Eliza Lynn Linton by Sir Walter Besant (1898), cited in G. S. Layard, *Mrs Lynn Linton* (Methuen, 1901), p. 142.

36 Extract from the Journal of Anne Lister of Shibden Hall, Halifax, from selection printed in *Halifax Courier and Guardian*, 1926-1929. A full transcription of the Journal is now in preparation.

37 See e.g. Journal entries for 5 May 1835, 2 June, 8 July, and 23 July 1837.

38 Sir William Napier, *The Life and Opinions of General Sir Charles James Napier* (London, 1857), Vol. I, p. 467.

39 Jessie Stewart, *Jane Ellen Harrison* (Merlin Press, 1959), p. 120.

40 For Florence Nightingale's career, Cecil Woodham-Smith, *Florence Nightingale*. For Miss Nightingale's complaint about women, see pp. 296-8.

41 *Newcastle Weekly Chronicle*, 24 Feb 1866.

42 E. S. Beesly, 'The Social Future of the Working Classes', *Fortnightly Review*, n.s. V (1869), p. 359.

43 *Queen Victoria's Journal*, 8 June 1846, cited in Robert Rhodes James, *Albert Prince Consort* (Hamish Hamilton, 1983) p. 168.

Chapter 3 'A Burning Zeal for Righteousness': Women in the British Anti-Slavery Movement, 1820–1860

1 Helen Blackburn, *Women's Suffrage: A Record of the Women's Suffrage Movement in the British Isles with Biographical Sketches of Miss Becker*

(Williams and Norgate, 1902), pp. 14ff, and Ray Strachey, *The Cause: A Short History of the Women's Movement in Great Britain* (G. Bell and Sons, 1928), pp. 40-3, and 'The Emancipation of Women', *Westminster Review* 128 (1887), pp. 163-73 indicate the anti-slavery antecedents of feminism; Rosamund Billington, 'The Women's Education and Suffrage Movements, 1850-1914: Innovation and Institutionalization' (unpublished PhD thesis, University of Hull, 1976), especially chs 2 and 3, deals with the origins of feminism in radical reform. The large literature on women in American abolitionism is apparent throughout these footnotes. James Walvin (ed.), *Slavery and British Society 1776-1846* (Macmillan, 1982), pp. 61-3 was one of the few accounts to emphasize women's involvement in British abolitionism until the recent study by Kenneth Corfield, 'Elizabeth Heyrick: Radical Quaker', in *Religion in the Lives of English Women, 1760-1930*, ed. Gail Malmgreen (Croom Helm, 1986) pp. 41-67.

2 Charles I. Foster, *An Errand of Mercy: The Evangelical United Front 1790-1837* (University of N. Carolina Press, Chapel Hill, 1960), and Ford K. Brown *Fathers of the Victorians: The Age of Wilberforce* (Cambridge University Press, Cambridge, 1961), pp. 317-60 indicate the range and operations of the societies. For women see F.K. Prochaska, *Women and Philanthropy in Nineteenth Century England* (Oxford University Press, Oxford, 1980), pp. 1-94; Alex Tyrrell, '"Woman's Mission" and Pressure Group Politics in Britain (1825-60)', *Bulletin of the John Rylands Library*, 63 (1980-1), pp. 194-230. *Home Missionary Magazine*, 4-10 (1823-9) gives details of the work of women in one organization, the Congregational Home Missionary Society.

3 Jemina Thompson, *Memoirs of British Female Missionaries; With a Survey of the Condition of Women in Heathen Countries* (London, 1841). This surveys the careers of women missionaries from the late eighteenth century and contains a key essay, 'The Importance of Female Agency in Evangelizing Pagan Nations', pp. XIII-XIV, from which the quotations come.

4 Prochaska, *Women and Philanthropy*, pp. 1-72; Brown, *Fathers of the Victorians*, pp. 332-8; Keith E. Melder, *Beginnings of Sisterhood: The American Woman's Rights Movement, 1800-1850* (Schocken Books, New York, 1977), pp. 39-42.

5 Prochaska, *Women and Philanthropy*, pp. 25-33; Eugene Stock, *The History of the Church Missionary Society* (Church Missionary Society, London, 1899), vol. 1, pp. 74 and 140.

6 Prochaska, *Women and Philanthropy*, pp. 25-7 and 69; J.P. Grant (ed.), *Memoir and Correspondence of Mrs Grant of Laggan* (London, 1844), vol. 2, pp. 194ff and vol. 3, pp. 134ff gives many letters from a woman familiar with benevolent work on both sides of the Atlantic, active in 'female societies', but nervous of the less 'congenial' aspects of their work.

7 Elizabeth Isichei, *Victorian Quakers* (Oxford University Press, Oxford, 1970), pp. 1-65; Sara W. Sturge, *Memoir of Mary Lloyd of Wednesbury* (Privately printed, 1921), pp. 30-4; M.G. Jones, *Hannah More* (Cambridge University Press, Cambridge, 1952), pp. 82-90.

8 *Account of the Receipts and Disbursements of the Anti-Slavery Society for the Years 1823, 1825, & 1826 with a list of subscribers* (London, n.d.).

9 *Account of the Receipts and Disbursements*, 1825, p. 6; *Ladies' Anti-Slavery Associations* (n.p., n.d.), especially p. 5.

10 *Ladies' Anti-Slavery Associations*, p. 5; Elizabeth Heyrick, *Appeal to the Hearts and Consciences of British Women* quoted in Corfield, 'Elizabeth Heyrick', p. 52.

11 Ms Minute Book of the Birmingham Ladies' Society for the Relief of Negro Slaves (1825–52), Birmingham Reference Library; Sturge, *Memoir of Mary Lloyd*, pp. 30–1.

12 Ms Minutes Birmingham Ladies' Society, 16 Nov 1826–10 Apr 1827; *Annual Reports of the Female Society for Birmingham, West Bromwich, Wednesbury, Walsall and Their Respective Neighbourhoods for the Relief of the British Negro Slaves* (Birmingham, 1826–30); *First Annual Report of the Ladies' Association for Salisbury, Calne, Melksham, Devizes and Their Respective Neighbourhoods* (Calne, 1826) cited in Ms Minutes Birmingham Ladies' Society, 16 Nov 1826.

13 This is based on *Annual Reports* and Ms Minutes cited above in notes 11 and 12. For the men's society see Ms Minute Book of the Birmingham Anti-Slavery Society (1826–59), vol. 1, Birmingham Reference Library.

14 *Second Annual Report of the Female Society for Birmingham*, Abstract of Cash Accounts; *Account of Receipts and Disbursements*, 1827 and 1828, pp. 9 and 14; Ms Cash Book of the Ladies' Negro's Friend Society (1825–51), Birmingham Reference Library. Some ladies' societies themselves suffered a decline in support during the late 1820s; see N.B. Lewis, 'The Abolition Movement in Sheffield, 1823–1833', *Bulletin of the John Rylands Library*, 18 (1934), pp. 380–3.

15 Ms Minutes Birmingham Ladies' Society; *Second Annual Report of the Female Society of Birmingham*.

16 *Account of Receipts and Disbursements*, 1830 and 1831. Many of these societies in small towns like Beverley and Bridlington have left little trace. They contributed a few pounds to the national society and bought £6–£7 worth of literature.

17 *Annual Reports of Sheffield Female Anti-Slavery Society* (Sheffield, 1827–30). *An Appeal to the Christian Women of Sheffield from the Association for the Universal Abolition of Slavery* (Sheffield, 1837) gives a brief history of women's anti-slavery work in the city up to that date. See also Ms Minute Book of the Sheffield Female Anti-Slavery Society, John Rylands Library, University of Manchester and Lewis, 'The Abolition Movement in Sheffield', pp. 377–92.

18 *Account of Receipts and Disbursements*, 1830 and 1831; Corfield, 'Elizabeth Heyrick', p. 50 notes the patronizing tone of some male abolitionist leaders like George Stephen.

19 This is based on Ms Minutes and Cash Books of the Birmingham Ladies' Society and Ms Minutes of Sheffield Female Society cited above.

20 *Ladies' Anti-Slavery Associations*, pp. 1–2 and an *Address on Free Labour*

Sugar (London, 1825) are typical of the huge propaganda on the subject. Corfield, 'Elizabeth Heyrick', pp. 42ff is particularly good on this issue.

21 Ms Minutes Birmingham Ladies' Society, 8 Sept 1825 and 26 Nov 1829; *Fourth Annual Report of the Ladies' Association for Salisbury, Calne, Melksham, Devizes* . . . (Calne, 1829); Circular from James Heywood, Great Eastcheap, London, offering wholesale and retail free labour sugar, John Rylands Library, English Mss 742.

22 Ms Minutes Birmingham Ladies' Society, 26 Nov 1829.

23 *Second Report of the Female Society for Birmingham* . . . *For the Relief of British Negro Slaves* (Birmingham, 1827); *Ladies' Society for the Relief of Negro Slaves: Card Explanatory of the Society's Work Bags and Albums* (n.p., n.d.); Sturge, *Memoir of Mary Lloyd*, p. 30.

24 Albums survive in the Birmingham Reference Library and the Local History Collection of the Hull Central Library.

25 Elizabeth Heyrick, *Immediate not Gradual Abolition of Slavery; or an Inquiry into the Shortest, Safest, and Most Effectual Means of Getting Rid of West Indian Slavery* (London, 1824).

26 Although some historians like Rice and Davis, cited below, have argued that Heyrick's pamphlet had limited impact, it quickly went through three printings and was circulated by the national Anti-Slavery Society. See Corfield, 'Elizabeth Heyrick', pp. 47-8.

27 Corfield, 'Elizabeth Heyrick', p. 49; Benjamin Lundy, *The Life, Travels and Opinions of Benjamin Lundy* (Philadelphia, 1847), pp. 216 and 306; Anon., *A Brief Sketch of the Life and Labours of Mrs Elizabeth Heyrick* (Leicester, 1862), pp. 17-18; Louis Billington, 'British Humanitarians and American Cotton, 1840-1860', *Journal of American Studies*, 11 (1977), pp. 313-14.

28 Corfield, 'Elizabeth Heyrick', pp. 45-6; *Second Report of the Sheffield Female Anti-Slavery Society* (Sheffield, 1827), pp. 3 and 6; Ms Minutes Birmingham Ladies' Society, 8 Apr 1830.

29 David Brion Davis, 'The Emergence of Immediatism in British and American Antislavery Thought', *Mississippi Valley Historical Review*, 49 (1962), p. 221; C. Duncan Rice, *The Scots Abolitionists 1833-1861* (Louisiana State University Press, Baton Rouge, 1981), p. 38.

30 Ms Minutes Birmingham Ladies' Society, Apr 1831; *Report of the Agency Committee of the Anti-Slavery Society* (London, n.d.).

31 Ms Minutes Birmingham Ladies' Society, 14 Apr 1835; *Three Years Female Anti-Slavery Effort in Britain and America: Being a Report of the Proceedings of the Glasgow Ladies' Auxiliary Emancipation Society, Since Its Formation in January, 1834, Containing A Sketch of the Rise and Progress of the American Female Anti-Slavery Societies* (Glasgow, 1837).

32 Tyrrell, ' "Woman's Mission" ', pp. 212-13; R. Coupland, *The British Anti-Slavery Movement* (Thornton Butterworth, 1933), p. 137; *Hansard's Parliamentary Debates* 3 ser., vol. 18, 1833, p. 372. William Wilberforce opposed women 'stirring up petitions' as unsuitable for the female character 'as delineated in scripture', but his view was ignored: see Robert Isaac Wilberforce and Samuel Wilberforce, *The Life of William L. Wilberforce*

(London, 1838), vol. 5, pp. 264-5. Billington, 'Women's Education and Suffrage', pp. 408-69 and 503-36, shows the development of women's later political activity.

33 Roger Anstey, 'Parliamentary Reform, Methodism and Anti-Slavery Politics, 1829-1833', *Slavery and Abolition*, 2 (December 1981), pp. 211-23; Philip Wright, *Knibb 'The Notorious': Slaves' Missionary 1803-1845* (Sidgwick and Jackson, 1973), pp. 93-133; David Hempton, *Methodism and Politics in British Society* (Hutchinson, 1984), pp. 208-11.

34 *Liberator* (Boston, Mass), 8 Jan to 19 Nov 1831; Ms Minutes Birmingham Ladies' Society, 23 Dec 1830; Fred Landon, 'Captain Charles Stuart, Abolitionist', *Western Ontario History Nuggets*, No. 24 (1956), pp. 1-20; Gilbert H. Barnes and Dwight L. Dumond (eds), *Letters of Theodore Dwight Weld, Angelina Grimké Weld and Sarah Grimké* (D. Appleton-Century, New York, 1934), vol. 1, pp. xx and 28-74; P.J. Staudenraus, *The African Colonization Movement, 1816-1865* (Columbia University Press, New York, 1961), pp. 201-23.

35 George Stephen to Anne Knight, 14 Nov 1834, Knight Papers, Friends House Library.

36 *Liberator*, 7 Jan 1832; see also Wendell P. and Francis J. Garrison, *William Lloyd Garrison. The Story of His Life Told by His Children* (Century Co., New York, 1885-9), vol. 1, pp. 1-140 and especially 127-37.

37 *Liberator*, 1 Dec 1832; Melder, *Beginnings of Sisterhood*, pp. 57-61; Otelia Cromwell, *Lucretia Mott* (Harvard University Press, Cambridge, Mass., 1958), pp. 48-51; Blanche Glassman Hersh, *The Slavery of Sex: Feminist-Abolitionists in America* (University of Illinois Press, Urbana, 1978), pp. 6-17. Hersh shows how the American movement used many of the arguments and symbols of the British women abolitionists during these pioneer years.

38 *Appeal to Christian Women of Sheffield*; Ms Minutes Birmingham Ladies' Society; *Annual Reports of the Birmingham Ladies' Negro's Friend Society* (Birmingham, 1834-6).

39 Louis Billington, 'Some Connections Between British and American Reform Movements, 1830-1860' (unpublished MA thesis, University of Bristol, 1966), pp. 43-4; *Three Years Female Anti-Slavery Effort*; Rice, *Scots Abolitionists*, pp. 30-79; Anna M. Stoddart, *Elizabeth Pease Nichol* (London, 1899), pp. 100-50.

40 Tyrrell, '"Woman's Mission"', p. 213

41 Stoddart, *Elizabeth Pease Nichol*, pp. 149-60; *Report of the Sheffield Ladies' Association for the Universal Abolition of Slavery*; a petition for 1838 is in the John Rylands Library, University of Manchester.

42 Sheffield Ladies' Association for the Universal Abolition of Slavery: Resolutions, 13 March 1838 and letter to the Men's Committee, in John Rylands Library, University of Manchester.

43 The general history of the anti-slavery movement at the time is thoroughly covered in Billington, 'Some Connections', pp. 104ff; also see Howard Temperley, *British Anti-Slavery, 1833-1870* (Longman, 1972), pp. 191-205;

and Betty Fladeland, *Men and Brothers: Anglo-American Anti-Slavery Cooperation* (University of Illinois Press, Urbana, 1972), pp. 221-56.

44 Edwin W. Small and Miriam R. Small, 'Prudence Crandall, Champion of Negro Education', *New England Quarterly*, 17 (1944), pp. 506-29; *Liberator*, 13 Sept 1833; Clare Taylor, *British and American Abolitionists. An Episode in Transatlantic Understanding* (Edinburgh University Press, Edinburgh, 1974), p. 22; *Slavery in the United States of America. An Appeal to the Friends of Negro Emancipation Throughout Great Britain* (Edinburgh, 1833).

45 Taylor, *British and American Abolitionists*, pp. 28-33; *Three Years Female Anti-Slavery Effort*, pp. 10-12.

46 Ms copy of Captain Stuart's letter of 28 Jul 1834 in Rhodes House Library, Oxford; Barnes and Dumond, *Weld-Grimké Letters*, vol. 1, pp. 130-1 and 353; Carroll Smith-Rosenberg, *Disorderly Conduct: Visions of Gender in Victorian America* (Knopf, New York, 1985), pp. 109-28; Melder, *Beginnings of Sisterhood*, pp. 58-9.

47 Billington, 'Some Connections', pp. 49-50; Ms Minutes Birmingham Ladies' Society, 14 Apr 1835; C. Duncan Rice, 'The Anti-Slavery Mission of George Thompson to the United States, 1834-1835', *Journal of American Studies*, 2 (1968), pp. 13-31. Rice quotes the *New York Courier and Inquirer* which ridiculed members of the Glasgow Female Emancipation Society as 'canting old women', 'the old pussy-cats of Glasgow', and 'Miss Lucretia McTabb and a bevy of old maids' for financing Thompson's mission.

48 *Report of the Sheffield Ladies' Association for the Universal Abolition of Slavery* (Sheffield, 1839); *Three Years Female Anti-Slavery Effort*; Stoddart, *Elizabeth Pease Nichol*, pp. 149ff; Taylor, *British and American Abolitionists*, pp. 61-6; Melder, *Beginnings of Sisterhood*, p. 72. For violent hostility to women's activity in the anti-Contagious Diseases Acts campaign see Josephine E. Butler, *Personal Reminiscences of a Great Campaign* (Horace Marshall & Son, 1910) especially pp. 27ff, and for hostility to women suffragists, Billington, 'Women's Education and Suffrage', pp. 487ff and 727ff.

49 *Appeal to Christian Women of Sheffield*. The tone of many of these societies is indicated by Mary Rawson's publication of *Hymns For Anti-Slavery Prayer Meetings* (London, 1838).

50 Stoddart, *Elizabeth Pease Nichol*, pp. 149-50; *Darlington Ladies' Anti-Slavery and British India Society Report* (Darlington, 1840); Taylor, *British and American Abolitionist*, pp. 66-71; Barnes and Dumond, *Weld-Grimke Letters*, vol. 1, pp. 349-53.

51 Benjamin Quarles, 'Sources of Abolitionist Income', *Mississippi Valley Historical Review*, 32 (1945-6), pp. 71-3.

52 Barnes and Dumond, *Weld-Grimké Letters*, vol. 1, p. 407; George Thompson, *Slavery in America: a Reprint of an Appeal to the Christian Women of the Slave States of America by Angelina Grimké of Charleston, South Carolina, with Introduction, Notes, and Appendix* (London, 1837); Gerda Lerner, *The Grimké Sisters from South Carolina: Pioneers for Woman's Rights and Abolition* (Schocken Books, New York, 1971), pp. 138-43.

53 Taylor, *British and American Abolitionists* and Barnes and Dumond, *Weld-Grimké Letters*, print part of Elizabeth Pease's correspondence. More letters can be found in the Garrison and Weston Papers, Boston Public Library and Weld-Grimké Mss, William L. Clements Library, University of Michigan. For Anne Knight see Gail Malmgreen, 'Anne Knight and the Radical Subculture', *Quaker History*, 71 (Fall 1982), pp. 100-13.

54 Harriet Martineau, 'The Martyr Age of the United States', *Westminster Review*, 32 (1839), pp. 1-59; Maria Weston Chapman (ed.), *Harriet Martineau's Autobiography* (Smith, Elder, London, 1877), vol. 2, pp. 29-60; R.K. Webb, *Harriet Martineau: A Radical Victorian* (Heinemann, 1960), pp. 134-74.

55 Billington, 'Some Connections', pp. 55-96. Elizabeth Pease became very concerned at the conservatism of American Friends and investigated this through her American correspondents. See sources cited in n. 53 above and Elizabeth Pease, *The Society of Friends in the United States – Their View of the Anti-Slavery Question* (Darlington, 1840).

56 *An Appeal to the Ladies of Great Britain in Behalf of the American Slave by the Committee of the Glasgow Female Anti-Slavery Society* (Glasgow, 1841); Stoddart, *Elizabeth Pease Nichol*, pp. 149-50.

57 Corfield, 'Elizabeth Heyrick', pp. 51-2.

58 Lerner, *Grimké Sisters*, pp. 165-82; Katherine Du Pré Lumpkin, *The Emancipation of Angelina Grimké* (University of North Carolina Press, Chapel Hill, 1974), pp. 94-154.

59 Melder, *Beginnings of Sisterhood*, p. 75; Barnes and Dumond, *Weld-Grimké Letters*, vol. 1, pp. 386-92.

60 Smith-Rosenberg, *Disorderly Conduct*, pp. 110ff discusses the radical attack by some American women, from the mid-1830s, on sexual exploitation of all kinds. Their British counterparts confessed there was greater reluctance to advocate 'moral purity' in Britain. See *Advocate of Moral Reform* (New York), 1835-45, which contains Anglo-American correspondence; also the *Female's Friend* (London), 1846.

61 Melder, *Beginnings of Sisterhood*, pp. 95-112; Hersh, *Slavery of Sex*, pp. 20-35; Barnes and Dumond, *Weld-Grimké Letters*, vol. 1, pp. 414-19. For the campaign against women preachers see Louis Billington, '"Female Laborers in the Church": Women Preachers in the Northeastern United States', *Journal of American Studies*, 19 (1985), pp. 378-80.

62 Maria Weston Chapman, *Harriet Martineau's Autobiography*, vol. 3, pp. 194-5. The split is well covered in Billington, 'Some Connections', pp. 99-108; Fladeland, *Men and Brothers*, pp. 263-73; Lawrence J. Friedman, *Gregarious Saints: Self and Community in American Abolitionism, 1830-1870* (Cambridge University Press, Cambridge, 1982), pp. 43-95.

63 Fladeland, *Men and Brothers*, pp. 257-73; Rice, *Scots Abolitionists*, pp. 81-107; F.B. Tolles (ed.), 'Slavery and "The Woman Question": Lucretia Mott's Diary of her visit to Great Britain to Attend the World's Anti-Slavery Convention of 1840', *Journal of the Friends' Historical Society*, Supplement No. 23 (1952). Taylor, *British and American Abolitionists*, pp. 91-111 and

Louis Ruchames and Walter M. Merrill (eds), *The Letters of William Lloyd Garrison* (Harvard University Press, Cambridge, Mass., 1971–3), vols 2 and 3 contain much Garrisonian correspondence.

64 Tolles, 'Slavery and "The Woman Question"' where Mott provides a good picture of the radical milieu. A.H. Abel and F.J. Klingberg, *A Sidelight on Anglo-American Relations, 1839–1855* (Association for the Study of Negro Life and History, Lancaster, Pa., 1927) presents documents of the anti-feminist party.

65 Stoddart, *Elizabeth Pease Nichol*, and Malmgreen, 'Anne Knight', indicate the pressure that Pease and Knight came under from more conservative Friends. By 1841 the influential Quaker Joseph John Gurney was depicting the Garrisonians in the worst light and suggesting that their views on the rights of women and other questions threatened 'the more fundamental principles of civil, social and domestic order'. See Joseph John Gurney, *A Journey in North America Described in Familiar Letters to Amelia Opie* (Norwich, 1841), pp. 108–9.

66 Tolles, 'Slavery and "The Woman Question"', pp. 53–79; Ruchames, *Letters of Garrison*, vol. 2, pp. 654–76.

67 Barnes and Dumond, *Weld-Grimké Letters*, vol. 2, p. 847.

68 Tolles, 'Slavery and "The Woman Question"', pp. 62–78; *Memorial of Sarah Pugh, A Tribute of Respect From Her Cousins* (Philadelphia, 1888), pp. 22–30.

69 Tolles, 'Slavery and "The Woman Question"', p. 40. The Garrison Papers, Boston Public Library, and the Anti-Slavery Collection, Rhodes House Library, Oxford, contain many letters by Stuart and about his campaign, and copies of his printed circulars. A specimen is printed in Barnes and Dumond, *Weld-Grimké Letters*, vol. 2, pp. 858–60.

70 Ms Minutes Birmingham Ladies' Society, April 1842; Ms Minute Book of the Bristol and Clifton Ladies' Anti-Slavery Society, 17 Sept 1840 and 4 Mar 1841, Dr Williams Library, London.

71 Mary Rawson to Elizabeth Pease, Sheffield, 5 Feb 1841, Garrison Papers, Boston Public Library. Mary Rawson had been invited to the World's Convention but her status as 'visitor not delegate' was emphasized in the invitation; see John Scoble to Mary Ann Rawson, London, 18 May 1840, in Rawson Papers, John Rylands Library.

72 John A. Collins, *Right and Wrong among the Abolitionists of the United States With an Introductory Letter by Harriet Martineau* (Glasgow, 1841). Billington, 'Some Connections', pp. 138–44, and Rice, *Scots Abolitionists*, pp. 99–114, indicate the divisive consequences of Collins's visit. A sample of his correspondence with friends and enemies is printed in Taylor, *British and American Abolitionists*, pp. 118–56.

73 *Eclectic Review* (London), Aug 1840; Rice, *Scots Abolitionists*, pp. 112–13; Taylor, *British and American Abolitionists*, pp. 143–52.

74 *Appeal . . . in Behalf of the American Slave by Glasgow Female Anti-Slavery Society.* See also *First Annual Report of the Glasgow Female Anti-Slavery Society* (Glasgow, 1842).

75 Ms Journal of Henry Clarke Wright, 1 Aug 1845 in Boston Public Library. Wright was an ultra-radical reformer and friend of Elizabeth Pease, Anne Knight and other radical British women; see Billington, 'Some Connections', and Lewis Perry, *Childhood, Marriage and Reform: Henry Clarke Wright, 1790-1870* (University of Chicago Press, Chicago, 1980).

76 See, for example, the letter from R.D. Webb to Maria Weston Chapman, Dublin, 20, 11 mo., 1841, printed in Taylor, *British and American Abolitionists*, pp. 156–7; also see Billington, 'Some Connections', pp. 135–44.

77 R. Thompson, 'The *Liberty Bell* and Other Gift Books', *New England Quarterly*, 7 (1934), pp. 154–68; Mary Carpenter, 'Offerings of English Women', *Liberty Bell* (Boston, 1845), pp. 238–42; Quarles, 'Sources of Abolitionist Income', pp. 71–4; Taylor, *British and American Abolitionists*, pp. 333–7.

78 Tolles, 'Slavery and "The Woman Question"', p. 49. Mott attempted to call a public meeting for women in London, but was supported only by Pease, Knight, and a few others. For more on British women as drudges see Lucretia Mott to Maria Weston Chapman, Dublin, 29, 7 mo., 1840, printed in Taylor, *British and American Abolitionists*, pp. 103–4.

79 Sarah Pugh, another American feminist visiting London in 1840, emphasized how difficult Englishwomen seemed to find breaking out of their subordinate position; see Sarah Pugh to Richard Webb, London, 2, 7 mo., 1840, in Garrison Papers, and *Memorial of Sarah Pugh*, pp. 26–7.

80 Tyrrell, '"Woman's Mission"', pp. 213–21.

81 Malmgreen, 'Anne Knight', pp. 107–8; Taylor, *British and American Abolitionists*, pp. 182–97; Barbara Taylor, *Eve and the New Jerusalem: Socialism and Feminism in the Nineteenth Century* (Virago, 1983), pp. 265–75; Joseph Barker's magazines, *The Christian* (London), 1845–7, and *The People* (Wortley, nr Leeds), 1849–50, contain information on American Garrisonians and their British feminist allies; see especially *The People*, 2 (1850), p. 315 for a letter on 'The Rights of Women' by Anne Knight, and Barker's comments.

82 See, for example, Margaret New to Maria Weston Chapman, London, 7 Sept 1841, and C.S. Toll to same, Birmingham, 7 Jan 1844, printed in Taylor, *British and American Abolitionists*, pp. 177–8 and 210–11. New described her friend Mrs Toll as one of the few women in England with sufficient moral courage to challenge the 'fearful state of bondage' in which British women languished.

83 Ms Minutes Birmingham Ladies' Society and *Annual Reports* of the society.

84 Billington, 'Some Connections', pp. 175–219; Rice, *Scots Abolitionists*, pp. 115–50; Douglas Charles Stange, *British Unitarians Against American Slavery: 1833–65* (Fairleigh Dickinson University Press, Rutherford, N.J., 1984), pp. 82–3.

85 Taylor, *British and American Abolitionists*, pp. 314–20. John Campbell, the fiery Congregationalist editor, published numerous attacks on Garrisonianism; see for example, *Christian Witness*, Sept and Oct 1846 and a reply, *The 'Christian Witness' examined on the Defamatory Charge of Infideli-*

ty Against William Lloyd Garrison (London, n.d.). *Liberator,* 13 April 1849 and 13 May 1850, contained reports on Women's Rights and Anti-Sabbath conventions, typical of radical causes which alienated British evangelicals.

86 *Anti-Slavery Cause* (Glasgow), 1850, and J.B. Estlin, *Reply to a Circular Issued by the Glasgow Association for the Abolition of Slavery Recommending a Discontinuance of British Support for the Boston Anti-Slavery Bazaar* (Paris, 1850); Taylor, *British and American Abolitionists,* pp. 342-8, prints the *Anti-Slavery Cause* and the resolutions and correspondence of the Edinburgh Ladies' Society.

87 Rice, *Scots Abolitionists,* p. 157; C. Peter Ripley (ed.), *The Black Abolitionist Papers* (University of North Carolina Press, Chapel Hill, 1985), vol. 1, pp. 185-9.

88 The Ladies' Society was an offshoot of the British and Foreign Anti-Slavery Society and its Minute Book is in the Anti-Slavery Collection, Rhodes House Library, Oxford. See also *Report of the Ladies' Society to Aid Fugitives from Slavery* (London, 1855). The animus between the Garrisonians and some fugitive slaves is indicated in Ripley, *Black Abolitionist Papers,* vol. 1, pp. 417-20, and Taylor, *British and American Abolitionists,* p. 412.

89 Benjamin Quarles, *Frederick Douglass* (Atheneum, N.Y., 1969), pp. 87-8, 91-5 and 103-7; Nancy A. Hewitt, *Women's Activism and Social Change: Rochester, New York, 1822-1872* (Cornell University Press, Ithaca, 1984), pp. 141-150; Ripley, *Black Abolitionist Papers,* vol. 1, pp. 225-6; Julia Griffiths (ed.), *Autographs for Freedom* (Auburn and Boston, 1853-4 and London, 1853). Little seems known about Julia Griffiths. Elihu Burritt met her and Douglass in Rochester, N.Y., in 1850 and described her as 'a colored lady from London'; see Ms Journal of Elihu Burritt, 27 Feb 1850, City Library, New Britain, Conn.

90 Billington, 'Some Connections', pp. 229-35; Ms Minutes Bristol and Clifton Ladies' Society, 1842-6; Fanny Tribe to L.A. Chamerovzow, Bristol, 13 Jan 1851, Anti-Slavery Collection, Rhodes House Library, Oxford.

91 Stange, *British Unitarians,* p. 102.

92 Ms Minutes Bristol and Clifton Ladies' Society, 13 Feb and 6 Mar 1851.

93 *Bristol Examiner,* Jan. 1850, and Aug. and Sept. 1851.

94 *Special Report of the Bristol and Clifton Ladies' Anti-Slavery Society during the eighteen months from Jan. 1851 to June 1852 with a statement of the Reasons of its Separation from the British and Foreign Anti-Slavery Society* (London, 1852); Ms Minutes Bristol and Clifton Ladies' Society, 11 Sept 1851 to 19 Feb 1852; Taylor, *British and American Abolitionists,* pp. 382-3.

95 *Memorial of Sarah Pugh,* pp. 54-81; Rice, *Scots Abolitionists,* pp. 166-7. There are many letters from Sarah Pugh to Mary Estlin in the Estlin Collection, Dr Williams Library, London, and in the Boston Public Library.

96 See collections cited in previous note and *Memorial of Sarah Pugh,* pp. 88-136, and p. 97. Radical women like Pugh explained lack of enthusiasm for women's rights amongst British reformers by important differences between Britain and America. Mary Estlin explained to Maria Weston Chapman that few in Britain understood that in America sex and

colour, rather than property and class, presented barriers to legal and political rights. In Britain the oppressions of women merged with those of oppressed men. See Mary Estlin to Maria Weston Chapman, 10 Jan 1853, Estlin Papers, Boston Public Library.

97 The free produce movement is covered more fully and documented in Billington, 'British Humanitarians and American Cotton' and 'Some Connections', Appendix; Burritt's Ms Journal, 13 Aug 1851, reports Anne Knight and Mrs H.M. Tracy from Ohio, advocating women's rights 'with a good deal of zeal . . . [and] much ability' at an Olive Leaf Circle Festival.

98 F.J. Klingberg, 'Harriet Beecher Stowe and Social Reform in England', *American Historical Review* 43 (1938), pp. 542–52; G.A. Shepperson, 'Harriet Beecher Stowe and Scotland', *Scottish Historical Review*, 32 (1953), pp. 40–60; Temperley, *British Anti-Slavery*, pp. 224–6; Billington, 'Some Connections', pp. 256–9; *Memorial of Sarah Pugh*, pp. 78–80.

99 Rice, *Scots Abolitionists*, pp. 178–86; Taylor, *British and American Abolitionists* pp. 386–97.

100 *Anti-Slavery Advocate* (London), 1852–61.

101 *Anti-Slavery Advocate*, Jan 1855; Stange, *British Unitarians*, pp. 152–3.

102 For Parker Pillsbury see his *Acts of the Anti-Slavery Apostles* (Cupples & Co., Boston, Mass., 1884) and Louis Filler, 'Parker Pillsbury: An Anti-Slavery Apostle', *New England Quarterly*, 19 (1946), pp. 315–37. The *Vegetarian Messenger* (Manchester), 6, 1856, 62–5 reports Pillsbury's address on universal reform, including women's rights, and *Anti-Slavery Advocate*, Oct 1854 to Feb 1855 reports his British lecture tour.

103 H. McLachlan, 'A Liverpool Lady's Journal a Century Ago', *Transactions of the Unitarian Historical Society* 11 (1955–8), p. 12; *Pennsylvania Freeman* (Philadelphia), 20 Oct 1853.

104 *Anti-Slavery Advocate*, June 1854; Taylor, *British and American Abolitionists*, p. 414.

105 Anne Tribe to L.A. Chamerovzow, Kingsdown, Bristol, 5 Dec 1853, in Anti-Slavery Collection, Rhodes House, Oxford.

106 Rice, *Scots Abolitionists*, pp. 158–61; Taylor, *British and American Abolitionists*, pp. 396–8; *Report of the Edinburgh Ladies' New Anti-Slavery Association for the years 1856 and 1857* (Edinburgh, 1858).

107 *Anti-Slavery Advocate*, June 1858 and June 1860.

108 Isabella Lucy Bird, *Aspects of Religion in the United States* (London, 1859), pp. 72–92 and especially p. 83, from which the quotation comes; see also Isabella Lucy Bird, *The Englishwoman in America* (University of Wisconsin Press, Madison, 1966), reprint of 1856 edn. with introduction and notes by Andrew Hill Clark; and Anna M. Stoddart, *Life of Isabella Bird* (John Murray, 1908), pp. 42–4. For Garrisonian reply see *Anti-Slavery Advocate*, July 1860.

109 Barbara Leigh Smith Bodichon, *An American Diary* (Routledge and Kegan Paul, 1972), ed. Joseph W. Reed Jr, especially p. 63.

110 Taylor, *British and American Abolitionists*, pp. 429–35; *Anti-Slavery Advocate*, Sept and Oct 1858.

111 Billington, 'Some Connections', Appendix, pp. xxix-xxxix; Ripley, *Black Abolitionist Papers*, vol. 1, pp. 447-52; R.J.M. Blackett, *Building an Anti-Slavery Wall: Black Americans in the Atlantic Abolitionist Movement 1830-60* (Louisiana State University Press, Baton Rouge, 1983), pp. 162-94.

112 William L. Andrews (ed.), *Sisters of the Spirit: Three Black Women's Biographies of the Nineteenth Century* (Indiana University Press, Bloomington, 1986), pp. 50-160 reprints the 1846 edition of Zilpha Elaw's *Memoirs* which describes her preaching tour in England. William Crafts, *Running a Thousand Miles for Freedom or the Escape of William and Ellen Crafts from Slavery* (London, 1860) and Ripley, *Black Abolitionist Papers*, throw some light on black women in British anti-slavery circles.

113 Key documents on Remond are in Ripley, *Black Abolitionist Papers*, vol. 1, pp. 435-73. The *Anti-Slavery Advocate*, Mar 1859 to Feb 1861 contains reports of her lectures. Her career is outlined in Ruth Bogin, 'Sarah Parker Remond: Black Abolitionist from Salem', *Essex Institute Historical Collections*, 110 (April 1971), pp. 120-50, and Dorothy B. Porter, 'Sarah Parker Remond, Abolitionist and Physician', *Journal of Negro History*, 20 (July 1935), pp. 287-93.

114 Ripley, *Black Abolitionist Papers*, vol. 1, pp. 462-3; *English Woman's Journal* (London) 7, 1861, pp. 269-75; Matthew Davenport Hill (ed.), *Our Exemplars, Poor and Rich* (London, 1861), pp. 276-86.

115 Ripley, *Black Abolitionist Papers*, vol. 1, pp. 435-46. Remond spoke on the platform on the plight of slave women, but kept her franker comments for women's meetings. Women lecturers had already appeared on temperance platforms, for example see Jane Rendall, *The Origins of Modern Feminism: Women in Britain, France and the United States* (Macmillan, 1985), p. 256 for Clara Lucas Balfour. Women suffrage lecturers were still a novelty and subject to ridicule and abuse in the 1860s; see Rosamund Billington, 'Ideology and Feminism: Why the Suffragettes Were "Wild Women"', *Women's Studies International Forum* 5, (1982), pp. 663-74.

116 Ripley, *Black Abolitionist Papers*, vol. 1, pp. 469-73; Billington, 'Some Connections', pp. 338-43.

117 *Anti-Slavery Advocate*, July 1853 and Jan 1854; Thomas L. Nichols, *Forty Years of American Life* (London, 1874), p. 372; Douglas A. Lorimer, *Colour, Class and the Victorians: English Attitudes to the Negro in the Mid-Nineteenth Century* (Leicester University Press, Leicester, 1978), pp. 45-68 and 131-61.

118 *Frederick Douglass' Paper* (Rochester, N.Y.), 31 Aug 1855 and following issues contain 'Letters from the Old World' by Julia Griffiths, reporting her progress. For evangelical approval of Julia Griffiths and condemnation of Garrison see, for example, *British Standard*, 27 May and 25 Nov 1859.

119 Billington, 'Some Connections', pp. 334-5 cites ephemeral printed appeals and reports from local women's anti-slavery groups to aid Frederick Douglass; see also Blackett, *An Anti-Slavery Wall*, pp. 114-17.

120 Philip Foner, *Life and Writings of Frederick Douglass* (International

Publishers, N.Y., 1953-5), vol. 2, pp. 498-9; Joseph A. Borone, 'Some Additional Light on Frederick Douglass', *Journal of Negro History*, 38, (1953), pp. 216-17.

121   James Oliver Horton, 'Freedom's Yoke: Gender Conventions Among Antebellum Free Blacks', *Feminist Studies*, 12 (Spring 1986), p. 71.

122   *An Appeal to the Clergy from the Sheffield Ladies' Anti-Slavery Association* (March 1857). Garrison disliked Douglass's appeal as a 'Christian' abolitionist; see Ruchames, *Letters of Garrison*, vol. 4, p. 391.

123   Taylor, *British and American Abolitionists*, pp. 475-8.

124   Ms Minute Book of the Birmingham and Midland Freedman's Aid Society, 1864-5, includes pamphlets, circulars and newspaper cuttings; Christine Bolt, *The Anti-Slavery Movement and Reconstuction: A Study in Anglo-American Cooperation 1833-77* (Oxford University Press, 1969) contains much information on women but ignores the gender implications of her own data.

125   *Memorial of Sarah Pugh*, pp. 110-36 contains a good selection of her letters to Mary Estlin and others, discussing the American women's suffrage movement, social purity and women's progress since 1840. Paul McHugh, *Prostitution and Victorian Social Reform* (Croom Helm, 1980), pp. 163ff, especially 170-1, indicates women's importance in the social purity movement and states that the biggest influence on the Ladies' National Association for the Repeal of the Contagious Diseases Acts was Garrisonian abolitionism. Many of the women mentioned, including Eliza Wigham and Mary Estlin, were prominent in abolitionism.

126   For an interesting analysis of this separation of spheres see Catherine Hall, 'Gender Divisions and Class Formation in the Birmingham Middle Class 1780-1850', in Raphael Samuel (ed.), *People's History and Socialist Theory* (Routledge and Kegan Paul, 1981), pp. 164-75.

127   This is discussed at length in Rosamund Billington, 'Victorian Values: Women – Highest or Lowest Sphere', to be published in Eric Sigsworth (ed.), *Victorian Values*, Manchester University Press, forthcoming.

Chapter 4   'A Moral Engine'? Feminism, Liberalism, and the *English Woman's Journal*

I should like to thank the Mistress and Fellows of Girton College, Cambridge, for permission to quote from papers held at Girton College, and Kate Perry for all her help on the Girton archives. Jacquie Matthews' careful reading and critical comments were greatly appreciated. I should also like to acknowledge gratefully financial assistance from the J. B. Morrell Foundation for the Study of Toleration.

Abbreviations: BRP – Bessie Rayner Parkes; BLSB – Barbara Leigh Smith Bodichon; *EWJ* – *English Woman's Journal*; PPG – Parkes Papers, Girton College, Cambridge; BCG – Bodichon Collection, Girton College, Cambridge.

1 *Saturday Review*, 10 April 1858, pp. 369–70; George Eliot to Sara Sophia Hennell, 2 March 1858, Gordon S. Haight (ed.), *The Letters of George Eliot*, 6 vols (Oxford University Press, 1954), II, pp. 437–9; Bessie Rayner Parkes, 'The Use of a Special Periodical', *Alexandra Magazine and Englishwoman's Journal*, I (Sept 1865), p. 258.

2 On the mid-nineteenth-century movement see Lee Holcombe, *Victorian Ladies at Work. Middle Class Working Women in England and Wales, 1850–1914* (David & Charles, Newton Abbot, 1973), ch. 1, and *Wives and Property. Reform of the Married Women's Property Law in Nineteenth Century England* (Basil Blackwell, Oxford, 1983). For Mill and 'liberal feminism', see: Julia Annas, 'Mill and the *Subjection of Women*', *Philosophy*, 52 (1977), pp. 179–94; Zillah Eisenstein, *The Radical Future of Liberal Feminism* (Longman, New York, 1981) pp. 113–44; Jean Bethke Elshtain, *Public Man, Private Woman. Women in Social and Political Thought* (Basil Blackwell, Oxford, 1981) pp. 132–46; Susan M. Okin, *Women in Western Political Thought* (Princeton University Press, Princeton, 1979) ch. 9. On the *English Woman's Journal*, see Pauline A. Nestor, 'A New Departure in Women's Publishing: *The English Woman's Journal* and *The Victoria Magazine*', *Victorian Periodicals Review*, 15 (1982), pp. 93–106, and for women's participation in NAPSS, Kathleen E. McCrone, 'The National Association for the Promotion of Social Science, and the Advancement of Victorian Women,' *Atlantis* (Canada) 8 (1982), pp. 44–66.

There is an excellent unpublished thesis by Diane Mary Chase Worzala, 'The Langham Place Circle: the beginnings of the organized women's movement in England, 1854–70', Ph.D., University of Wisconsin-Madison, 1982, consulted after writing this essay.

3 On Joseph Parkes and the Parkes family, see William Thomas, *The Philosophic Radicals. Nine Studies in Theory and Practice, 1817–41*, (Oxford University Press, Oxford, 1979), ch. 6, and Jessie Buckley, *Joseph Parkes of Birmingham* (Methuen, 1926). There is material on Bessie Rayner Parkes in the memoir by her daughter Marie Belloc Lowndes, *'I Too Have Lived in Arcadia'. A record of love and of childhood* (Macmillan, 1941). Barbara Leigh Smith Bodichon's family background is traced in Sheila Herstein, *A Mid-Victorian Feminist, Barbara Leigh Smith Bodichon* (Yale University Press, New Haven and London, 1985). See also Jacquie Matthews, 'Barbara Bodichon: Integrity in Diversity (1827–91)' in Dale Spender (ed.), *Feminist Theorists. Three Centuries of Women's Intellectual Traditions* (Women's Press, 1983). For the Courtauld-Taylor family connection, and their religious, philanthropic and political work, see D.C. Coleman, *Courtauld's. An Economic and Social History*, 2 vols (Oxford University Press, Oxford, 1969), Vol. I, especially ch. X.

4 For the early friendship of the two women, see my 'Friendship and Politics: Barbara Leigh Smith Bodichon (1827–91) and Bessie Rayner Parkes (1829–1925)', in Jane Rendall and Susan Mendus (eds) *Images of Women: the Victorian Legacy* (Methuen, forthcoming); Lilian Faderman, *Surpassing the Love of Women. Romantic Friendship between Women from the Renaissance to the Present* (Women's Press, 1985), especially pp. 147–230; Martha Vicinus,

Independent Women. Work and Community for Single Women 1850–1920 (Virago, 1985) pp. 15–18 and passim.

5 BRP to Samuel Blackwell, n.d., PPG, Vol. IX/12.

6 BRP to Samuel Blackwell, 28 July 1854, PPG, Vol. IX/6.

7 On this campaign, see Holcombe, *Wives and Property*, chs 4–5.

8 Anna Jameson to BRP, 2 Mar 1858 and 10 Dec [n.y.], PPG, Vol. VI/23, and 40.

9 Little is known of Matilda Hays. See the references in Patricia Thomson, *George Sand and the Victorians* (Macmillan, 1977); Haight (ed.), *Letters of George Eliot*, Vol. II, p. 438; Joseph Leach, *Bright Particular Star. The Life and Times of Charlotte Cushman* (Yale University Press, New Haven and London, 1970); Faderman, *Surpassing the Love of Women*, pp. 220–5. In one of Hays's novels, *Adrienne Hope* (2 vols (London, 1866)), there are clearly autobiographical references both to her relationship with Charlotte Cushman and to her work for the *English Woman's Journal.*

10 BRP to BLSB, 10 Aug and 11 Sept 1855, 24 July 1856, PPG, Vol. V/70, 77, and 81.

11 Mary Merryweather, *Experiences of Factory Life: being a record of fourteen years at Mr Courtauld's silk mill at Halstead in Essex.* Third edition. Much enlarged with a preface by Bessie Rayner Parkes (London, 1862); BRP to Mary Merryweather, 26 Jan 1857, PPG, Vol. VI/72.

12 BRP, 'A Review of the Last Six Years', *EWJ*, XII (Feb 1864), pp. 363–5; I have located the *Waverley Journal* only for the issues 9 Aug 1856 to 10 Jan 1857 (in Glasgow University Library), and 1 to 15 Jan 1858 (British Newspaper Library, Colindale).

13 *Waverley Journal*, 5 and 16 Oct 1856, 10 Jan 1857; BRP, 'Review of the Last Six Years', *EWJ*, XII, p. 364.

14 *Waverley Journal*, 1 Nov 1856, 10 Jan 1857; Haight (ed.), *Letters of George Eliot*, Vol. II, p. 365n; Joseph Parkes to BRP, 12 Feb 1857, PPG, Vol. II/57.

15 BRP, 'Review of the Last Six Years', *EWJ*, XII, p. 364; Anna Jameson to BRP, 2 Aug 1857, PPG, Vol. VI/22.

16 BRP to BLSB, 14 May 1857, PPG, Vol. V/84; Charles Mitchell, *The Newspaper Press Directory . . . for the year 1858* (London, 1858) p. 130.

17 BRP to BLSB, 14 May 1857, PPG, Vol. V/84; *Waverley Journal*, 1 Jan 1858; BRP to Hatty Hosmer, 30 Dec 1858, PPG, Vol. IX/33; George Eliot to BRP, 1 Sept 1857, Haight (ed.), *Letters of George Eliot*, Vol. II, pp. 379–80.

18 BRP, 'Review of the Last Six Years', *EWJ*, XII, p. 364; *Experiences of Factory Life* by M.M. reprinted from the 'Waverley', a working woman's journal (London, 1857). These are written in the form of seven letters addressed to 'Dear B.' between 30 June and 10 Sept 1857.

19 *Waverley Journal*, 1 and 15 Jan 1858; BRP, 'Review of the Last Six Years', *EWJ*, XII, p. 364.

20 BRP to Mary Merryweather, 26 Jan 1857, PPG, Vol. VI/72; BRP to BLSB, 19 May 1857, PPG, Vol. V/85.

21 BRP, 'The Ladies Reading Room', 14 Jan 1860, unidentified newspaper cutting, PPG, Vol. XI/33.

22 All information on the English Woman's Journal Company is taken from the file in the Public Record Office, BT 41 227/1274; for early limited liability legislation and its requirements see H.A. Shannon, 'The coming of general limited liability', in E. Carus-Wilson, *Essays in Economic History*, 2 vols (Edward Arnold, 1954).

23 For Samuel Courtauld's interest in such activities, and acquaintance with BRP, see: Haight (ed.), *Letters of George Eliot*, Vol. II, p. 69n; Sir Stephen Courtauld, *The Huguenot Family of Courtauld*, 3 vols (privately printed, London, 1957-67), Vol. III, pp. 115-16, 121; *Courtauld Family Letters, 1782-1900*, 8 vols (Bowes & Bowes, Cambridge, 1916), Vol. VIII, pp. 3838-41. For James Vaughan, see Joseph Foster, *Men at the Bar . . .* (London, 1885), p. 480, and for William Strickland Cookson, *Solicitor's Journal*, 21 July 1877, which points to his work for the Law Amendment Society, the NAPSS and the Society for the Promotion of the Employment of Women.

24 BRP, 'The Opinions of John Stuart Mill', *EWJ*, VI (Sept 1860), p. 10. I have identified this article and a number of others as by BRP, on the basis of its inclusion in her *Essays on Woman's Work* (London, 1865). Some have been identified from information in the Parkes Papers. The article on Mill probably represents past joint discussions between Barbara Leigh Smith and Bessie Parkes, PPG, Vol. I/4/12, entry for 4 Nov 1849, and Herstein, *Barbara Leigh Smith Bodichon*, p. 18.

25 See Charles C. Osborne, *Anna Maria Helena Comtesse de Noailles* (Wightman & Co, 1928); Elizabeth Blackwell, *Pioneer Work for Women* (Dent, 1914 edition), pp. 172-80.

26 BRP, 'The Ladies Reading Room', 14 Jan 1860, PPG, Vol. XI/33; BRP to BLSB, 19 Oct 1859 and 8 Jan 1860, PPG, Vol. V/92 and 95. On Theodosia Lady Monson, see Haight (ed), *Letters of George Eliot*, Vol. II, pp. 82-3; *The Complete Peerage . . .* by G.E. Cokayne, edited by H.A. Doubleday and Lord Howard de Walden (St Catherine's Press, 1936), Vol. IX, pp. 72-3.

27 BRP to BLSB, 5 and 30 Jan 1859, PPG, Vol. V/86 and 87.

28 Jessie Boucherett, 'Adelaide Anne Procter', *EWJ*, XIII (March 1864), p. 18; Emily Davies, 'Family Chronicle', pp. 210-11, 214, 217, 244-5, Davies Papers, Girton College, and 'Report of the Northumberland and Durham branch of the Society for Promoting the Employment of Women', *EWJ*, VIII (Dec 1861), pp. 223-6.

29 BRP, 'Review of the Last Six Years', *EWJ*, XII, p. 364: Elizabeth Eiloart can be identified as the 'present editor' from BRP to BLSB, 18 Nov 1863, PPG, Vol. V/123.

30 Emily Davies, 'Family Chronicle' pp. 262-4; Adelaide Anne Procter to BRP, Thursday afternoon [1862], PPG, Vol. VIII/28; BRP to BLSB, Sept 1862, PPG, Vol. V/115.

31 BRP, 'The Use of a Special Periodical', *Alexandra Magazine*, I (Sept 1865), pp. 257-9 and 'Review of the Last Six Years', *EWJ*, XII, pp. 363-6.

32 BRP to BLSB, 5 Jan 1858 and 13 Sept 1859, PPG, Vol. V/ 86 and 90; BLSB to George Eliot, 26 April 1859, and George Eliot to BLSB, 5 May 1859, Haight (ed.), *Letters of George Eliot*, III pp. 56-7, and 63-4.

33 BRP, 'The Profession of the Teacher', *EWJ*, I (March 1858) p. 11; *idem*, 'What can Educated Women Do?', *EWJ*, IV (Jan 1860), p. 298.

34 'A West End Housekeeper', 'Open Council', *EWJ*, VIII (Oct 1861), pp. 138-9; 'Open Council' (Nov 1861), pp. 205-10; 'West End Housekeepers', (Dec 1861), pp. 249-54; BRP, 'A Year's Experience in Woman's Work', *EWJ*, VI (Oct 1860), pp. 115-16. I owe the suggestion that this was a planted letter to Jacquie Matthews.

35 BRP, 'What can Educated Women Do?', *EWJ*, IV (Jan 1860), p. 296.

36 Jessie Boucherett, 'On the Obstacles to the Employment of Women', *EWJ*, IV (Feb 1860), pp. 361-75; BRP, 'On Printing', *EWJ*, IV (Dec 1859), p. 275.

37 'Society for Promoting the Employment of Women', *EWJ*, V (Aug 1860), pp. 394-6.

38 Emily Faithfull, 'The Victoria Press', *EWJ*, VI (Oct 1860), pp. 121-6; 'Alban', 'Training Schools for Female Servants', and 'The Training of Female Servants', *EWJ*, III (March and May 1859), pp. 1-6, 145-151; 'Open Council', *EWJ*, IV (Oct 1859), pp. 137-8, and many other contributions.

39 BRP, 'Domestic Life', *EWJ*, II (Oct 1858), pp. 73-82; 'What can Educated Women Do?', *EWJ*, IV (Jan 1860), pp. 292-3.

40 Jessie Boucherett, 'The Temperance Movement and Working Women', *EWJ*, XI (May 1863), pp. 176-80.

41 BRP, 'The Condition of Working Women in England and France', *EWJ*, VIII (Sept 1861) pp. 1-9; 'Notices of Books', *EWJ*, VIII (Sept 1861), pp. 61-9.

42 BRP, 'The Balance of Public Opinion in Regard to Woman's Work', *EWJ*, IX (July 1862), pp. 340-5; Emily Faithfull, 'Open Council', *EWJ*, X (Sept 1862), pp. 70-1.

43 Jessie Boucherett, 'Causes of the Distress among Single Women', *EWJ*, XII (Feb 1864), pp. 300-9.

44 See, for instance, the review of Emily Shirreff, *Intellectual Education* . . . (1858) in *EWJ*, I (July 1858), 'Notices of Books', pp. 341-53.

45 'Female Education in the Middle Classes', *EWJ*, I (June 1858), pp. 217-27; BRP, 'Colleges for Girls', *EWJ*, II (Feb 1859), pp. 361-74.

46 BLSB, 'Middle-Class Schools for Girls', *EWJ*, VI (Nov 1860), pp. 168-77; Jessie Boucherett, 'Endowed Schools, their Uses and Shortcomings', *EWJ*, IX (March 1862), pp. 20-9.

47 'The Society of Arts Examinations', *EWJ*, I (July 1858), pp. 326-32; 'Female Education in the Middle Classes', *EWJ*, I. p. 176; 'University of London', *EWJ*, IX (April 1862), pp. 119-20; 'London University', *EWJ*, X (Oct 1862), pp. 123-4; 'University Local Examinations', *EWJ*, X (Nov 1862), pp. 191-205; 'Examinations of the Society of Arts', *EWJ*, X (Jan 1863), pp. 289-99; 'The University of London and the Graduation of Women', *EWJ*, XI (June 1863), pp. 270-8.

48 'A Suggestion for the Daughters of the Middle Classes', *EWJ*, V (Mar 1860), pp. 49-53; 'E.R.', 'Remunerative Work for Gentlewomen', *EWJ*, V (Nov 1862), pp. 183-9.

49 *EWJ*, II (Oct 1858), pp. 116-18, and correspondence, II, pp. 209, 280, 426; Isa Craig, 'An Interesting Blue Book', *EWJ*, VII (June and Aug 1861), pp. 217-24, 376-84.

50 Though Moncure D. Conway argued for co-education from American experience in an interesting article, 'Antioch College', *EWJ*, XII (Dec 1863), pp. 217-28.

51 Anna Mary Howitt, 'A House of Mercy', *EWJ*, I (Mar 1858), pp. 13-27; Mary Howitt to BRP, 10 Nov. [n.y.], PPG, Vol. VII/25; BRP, 'Domestic Life', *EWJ*, II, p. 75; Joseph Parkes to BRP, 6 Oct 1858, PPG, Vol. II/64, and Anna Jameson to BRP, 14 Oct [1858], PPG, Vol. VI/35.

52 Anna Jameson, *Sisters of Charity . . . and the Communion of Labour*, second edition (Boston, 1857; Hyperion, 1976 reprint), p. 172, quoted in S.R.P, 'The Details of Woman's Work in Reform', *EWJ*, III (June 1859), p. 217.

53 Mary Carpenter, 'Women's Work in the Reformatory Movement', *EWJ*, I (July 1858), pp. 289-95; Louisa Twining, 'The Workhouse Visiting Society', *EWJ*, I (Aug 1858), pp. 361-7; Frances Power Cobbe, 'The Preventive Branch of the Bristol Female Mission', *EWJ*, VIII (Nov 1861), pp. 144-51; Maria Rye, 'A Night in Westminster', *EWJ*, II (Dec 1858), pp. 265-70.

54 BRP, 'The Ladies Sanitary Association', *EWJ*, III (April 1859), pp. 73-85.

55 Mary Merryweather, 'Cottage Habitations', *EWJ*, IV (Oct 1859), pp. 73-82.

56 'The Second Annual Report of the Ladies' National Association for the Diffusion of Sanitary Knowledge', *EWJ*, III (Aug 1859), pp. 380-8; BRP to BLSB, 8 Jan 1860, PPG, Vol. V/95.

57 'Park and Play-Ground *versus* Gin-Palace and Prison', *EWJ*, I (July 1858), pp. 306-18; 'Notices of Books', *EWJ*, VIII (Jan 1862), pp. 335-46; Jessie Boucherett, 'The Temperance Movement and Working Women', *EWJ*, XI (May 1863), pp. 176-80.

58 BRP, 'La Soeur Rosalie', *EWJ*, IV (Sept 1859), pp. 152-63, (Dec 1859), pp. 227-35, (Jan 1860), pp. 298-311; BRP, 'Madame Luce, of Algiers', *EWJ*, VII (May 1861), pp. 157-68, (June 1861), pp. 224-36, (July 1861), pp. 296-308; BRP, 'Madame Marie Pape-Carpentier', *EWJ*, VIII (Jan 1862), pp. 298-307.

59 BRP, 'From Paris. - No II', *EWJ*, V (June 1860), pp. 259-69; BRP to unknown correspondent, n.d. [1875?], PPG, Vol. X/34.

60 Matilda Hays, 'Florence Nightingale and the English Soldier', *EWJ*, I (April 1858), pp. 73-80; A.R.L, 'Organization', *EWJ*, Vol. VI (Jan 1861), pp. 330-9. On 'sisterhoods' in mid-Victorian England, see Vicinus, *Independent Communities*, ch. 2.

61 'Open Council', *EWJ*, V (June 1860) p. 284, (July 1860), p. 354; 'Open Council', *EWJ*, VI (Dec 1860), pp. 282-4.

62 BRP, 'On Nursing Past and Present', *EWJ*, X (Feb 1863), pp. 381-92.

63 Rev. J.S. Howson, 'The Official Employment of Women in Works of Charity', *EWJ*, IX (Aug 1862), pp. 361-4.

64 *Saturday Review*, 10 April 1858, pp. 369-70; 12 Nov 1859, pp. 575-6.

65 *Saturday Review*, 10 April 1858, pp. 369-70; 'The "Saturday Review" and the "English Woman's Journal". The Reviewer Reviewed', *EWJ*, I (May 1858), pp. 201-4.

66 Jessie Boucherett, 'Obstacles to the Employment of Women', *EWJ*, IV (Feb 1860), p. 372; Emily Faithfull, 'Women Compositors', *EWJ*, VIII (Sept 1861), p. 38; BRP, 'Special Meetings at Glasgow and Edinburgh with regard to the Industrial Employment of Women' *EWJ*, VI (Nov 1860) pp. 154-7.

67 Jessie Boucherett, 'Causes of the Distress among Single Women', *EWJ*, XII (Feb 1864), pp. 406-9; J.T., 'Our Tradeswomen', *EWJ*, XIII (May 1864), pp. 145-51.

68 BRP, 'What can Educated Women Do?', *EWJ*, IV (Jan 1860), p. 297.

69 BRP, 'The Opinions of John Stuart Mill', *EWJ*, VI (Sept and Nov 1860), pp. 1-11, 193-202.

70 M.A., 'Outline of a Plan for the Formation of Industrial Associations among Workwomen', *EWJ*, VI (Oct 1860), pp. 73-6; Emily Davies, 'Family Chronicle', 4 June 1861, p. 217, Girton College, and BRP to BLSB, 12 Jan 1862, PPG, Vol. V/112; BRP, 'Women and Co-operation', *EWJ*, XII (Feb 1864), pp. 368-76; Ellen Barlee, 'Institution for the Employment of Needlewomen', *EWJ*, V (June 1860), pp. 255-9.

71 'Political Economy and Christianity', *EWJ*, XII (Jan 1864), pp. 289-96; Emily Davies to BLSB, 14 Jan 1863, B313, BCG.

72 BRP to BLSB, 5 and 30 Jan, 3 and 5 Nov 1859, PPG, Vol. V/ 86,87, 93.

73 BRP to BLSB, 8 Jan 1860, 8 Dec 1861, and 1 April 1862, PPG, Vol. V/95, 108, 114.

74 Sarah Lewin to BLSB, Jan 1863, and Emily Davies to BLSB [Jan 1863], BCG, B307, 308.

75 Emily Davies to BLSB, 3 and 28 Dec 1862 and 3 Jan 1863, BCG, B302, 303 and 305.

76 P.R.O., BT 41 227/1274.

77 BRP to BLSB, 8 Jan 1860, 30 Mar, 19 April 1861, and 21 Aug [n.y.], PPG, Vol. V/95, 102,104,158.

78 Joseph Parkes to BRP, 24 Sept 1858, PPG, Vol. II/63; Emily Davies to BLSB, 3 Dec 1862 and 3 Jan 1863, BCG, B302, 305; BRP to BLSB, 8 Dec 1861, PPG, Vol. V/108.

79 *Saturday Review*, 7 Jan 1860; BRP to BLSB, 8 Dec 1861 and 22 Jan 1862, PPG, Vol. V/108,113.

80 Emily Davies to BLSB, 3 Jan 1863, BCG, B305; BRP to BLSB, 19 April 1861, PPG, Vol. V/104.

81 BRP to BLSB [1863] PPG, Vol. V/121; BRP, 'A Review of the Last Six Years', *EWJ*, XII (Feb 1864), p. 366.

82 Emily Davies to BLSB, 3 and 8 Jan 1863, BCG, B305,B306.

83 Adelaide Procter to BRP [1862], PPG, Vol. VIII/24.

84 Emily Davies to BLSB, 14 Jan 1863, BCG, B309.
85 Emily Davies to BLSB, 3 Dec 1862, BCG, B302, and 12 Mar 1863, B313; Emily Davies, 'Family Chronicle', pp. 337-8.
86 BRP to BLSB, 7 April 1864, PPG, Vol. V/131; Emily Davies to BLSB, 8 Jan 1863, BCG, B306.

Chapter 5 The Married Woman, the 'New Woman' and the Feminist: Sexual Politics of the 1890s

1 For example, see Andrew Rosen, *Rise up Women! The Militant Campaign of the Women's Social and Political Union 1903-14* (Routledge and Kegan Paul, 1974), pp. 9-13.
2 Ray Strachey, *The Cause* (Virago, 1978), p. 282.
3 Ibid., pp. 282-8.
4 See Gillian Kersley, *Darling Madame: Sarah Grand and Devoted Friend* (Virago, 1983).
5 See Lucy Bland, 'Marriage Laid Bare', in Jane Lewis (ed.) *Labour and Love. Women's Experience of Home and Family 1850-1940* (Blackwell, Oxford, 1986); Judith Walkowitz, *Prostitution and Victorian Society. Women, Class and the State* (Cambridge University Press, Cambridge, 1980).
6 See Jenni Calder, *Women and Marriage in Victorian Fiction* (Thames and Hudson, 1976); Gail Cunningham, *The New Woman and the Victorian Novel* (Macmillan, 1978); Elaine Showalter, *A Literature of Their Own, British Women Novelists from Bronte to Lessing* (Virago, 1977); Patricia Stubbs, *Women and Fiction* (Harvester, Brighton, 1979).
7 Mary Haweis in her 1894 address to the Women Writers Dinner in Rev. H.R. Haweis (ed.) *Words to Women: Addresses and Essays* (London, 1909), pp. 70-1, quoted in Showalter, *A Literature of Their Own*, pp. 182-3.
8 For example, see *Shafts* I (25 Feb 1893) p. 268 for a review of Sarah Grand, *The Heavenly Twins*, and *Shafts* III (April, June and July 1895) for a lengthy and highly praising review of Mona Caird, *The Daughters of Danaus* (London, 1894).
9 See, for example, the interview with Mona Caird in *Women's Penny Paper (WPP)* 11 (28 June 1890).
10 For example, Caird approvingly quoted Grand's 'Ideala' in *The Morality of Marriage* (London, 1897).
11 Martha Vicinus, *Independent Women. Work and Community for Single Women, 1850-1920* (Virago, 1985), p. 5.
12 Ibid., p. 12.
13 Sarah Grand in *The Young Girl* (1898-9), quoted in Deborah Gorham, *The Victorian Girl and the Feminine Ideal* (Croom Helm, 1982), p. 2.
14 See interview with Caird, *WPP* 11(28 June 1890).
15 Mona Caird, 'Marriage', *Westminster Review (WR)* 130 (Aug 1888), pp. 186-201.
16 'Ideal Marriage', *WR* 130 (Nov 1888), pp. 617-36; 'The Morality of

.riage', *Fortnightly Review* 47 n.s. (March 1890), pp. 310–30; 'A Defence of the so-called "Wild Women"', *Nineteenth Century* 31 (May 1892), pp. 811–29.

17 See Harry Quilter (ed.), *Is Marriage a Failure?* (London, 1888).

18 Edith Ward, *Shafts* I (3 Nov 1892), p. 2.

19 Letter from 'Knowledge', *Shafts* I (28 Jan 1895), p. 205.

20 'Ignota', 'Judicial Sex Bias', *WR*, 149 (Mar 1898), pp. 279–88.

21 See articles by Mona Caird, and see Millicent Fawcett, 'The Emancipation of Women', *Fortnightly Review* 50 n.s. (Nov 1891), pp. 673–85.

22 For example, see Wolstenholme Elmy, *Shafts* V (March 1897), p. 87.

23 Caird, *WR* 130 (Nov 1888), pp. 617–36.

24 *Shafts* II (April 1894), p. 234.

25 See Elizabeth Chapman, 'The Decline of Divorce', *WR* 133 (April 1890), pp. 417–34.

26 Caird, *WR* 130 (Aug 1888), pp. 186–201.

27 Lady Kathleen Caffe, 'A Reply from the Daughters', *Nineteenth Century* 35 (Mar 1894), pp. 437–42.

28 Elizabeth Chapman, *Marriage Questions in Modern Fiction* (London, 1897), p. 208.

29 Caird, *WR* 130 (Aug 1888), p. 198.

30 Alma Gillan, *Shafts* II (Mar 1894), pp. 229–30.

31 P.M. Bromley, *Family Law* (Butterworths, 1981), p. 110.

32 'Ignota', *WR* 149 (Mar 1898), pp. 279–88.

33 Ibid.

34 R. v. Jackson *Law Reports*, 1 Q.B. (1891), p. 671.

35 See Sylvia Pankhurst, *The Suffragette Movement* (1931, reprinted Virago, 1977).

36 Quoted in Sylvia Pankhurst, *The Suffragette Movement*, p. 95.

37 E. Wolstenholme Elmy to Mrs McIlquaham, 21 Mar 1891, British Library (BL) Add. Mss. 47,449.

38 E. Wolstenholme Elmy to Mrs McIlquaham, 2 Apr 1891, BL. Add. Mss. 47,449.

39 Mrs Wolstenholme Elmy, *The Decision in the Clitheroe Case and its Consequences* (Manchester Guardian, 1891); *4th and Last Report of the Women's Emancipation Union* (Congleton, 1899), p. 1.

40 *Fourth and Last Report of the WEU*, pp. 1–2.

41 *WEU 1891–1899: an Epitome of 8 Years Effort for Justice to Women* (Congleton, 1899).

42 Fourth and Last Report of the WEU, pp. 1–2.

43 E. Wolstenholme Elmy to Mrs McIlquaham, 26 Apr 1891, BL. Add. Mss. 47,449.

44 E. Wolstenholme Elmy to Mrs McIlquaham, 26 Nov 1895, BL. Add. Mss. 47,450.

45 Ibid.

46 Blanche Leppington, 'Debrutalisation of Man', *Contemporary Review*, 67 (May 1895), p. 742.

47 Quoted in Gail Cunningham, *The New Woman and the Victorian Novel* (Macmillan, 1978), p. 67.
48 George Egerton, 'Virgin Soil', *Discords* (1894, reprinted Virago 1983) p. 155.
49 G.B. Shaw, *The Quintessence of Ibsenism* (Constable & Co, 1926), pp. 87–8.
50 Showalter, *A Literature of Their Own*, p. 206.
51 Quoted in Norma Clarke, 'Feminism and the Popular Novel in the 1890s', *Feminist Review* 20 (1985), pp. 81–94.
52 Quoted in Gillian Kersley, *Darling Madame*, p. 70.
53 Ibid., p. 15.
54 Ellis Ethelmer, *Women Free* (WEU, Congleton, 1893), pp. 100–1.
55 Mona Caird, 'Results of the non-enfranchisement of women', *WR* 133 (Mar 1890), pp. 231–9.
56 Mona Caird, *WR* 31 (May 1892), p. 88.
57 Mona Caird, *Daughters of Danaus*, p. 187.
58 *Saturday Review*, 8 June 1895.
59 For example, see Ethelmer, *Woman Free*.
60 George Egerton, *Discords*, p. 157.
61 Quoted in Cunningham, *The New Woman and the Victorian Novel*, p. 69.
62 Sylvia Pankhurst, *The Suffragette Movement*, p. 31; Sheila Jeffreys, *The Spinster and her Enemies. Feminism and Sexuality 1880–1930* (Pluto Press, 1985) p. 29.
63 E. Wolstenholme Elmy to Mrs McIlquaham, 10 Sept 1891, BL. Add. Mss. 47,449.
64 Sylvia Pankhurst, *The Suffragette Movement*, p. 31.
65 Ellis Ethelmer, *The Human Flower* (Congleton, 1894), p. 43.
66 See some of Egerton's short stories, and see Florence Dixie, *Gloriana, or the Revolution of 1900* (London, 1890).
67 Egerton, *Discords*, p. 248.
68 E. Wolstenholme Elmy, *Woman and the Law* (WEU, 1894) p. 10.
69 B. Leppington, *Contemporary Review* 67 (May 1895), pp. 725–43.
70 Sarah Grand, *Lady's Realm* (1898) quoted in Kersley, *Darling Madame*, p. 101.
71 Egerton, 'Virgin Soil', *Discords*, p. 155.
72 Ethelmer, *Life to Woman* (Congleton, 1896), p. 66.
73 E. Wolstenholme Elmy, *Woman and the Law*, p. 6.
74 *Shafts* II (Sept 1894), p. 314.
75 'Ignota', *WR* 152 (July 1899), p. 69.
76 *Shafts* V (Nov 1897), pp. 301–2.
77 E. Wolstenholme Elmy, *Woman and the Law*, p. 6.
78 See Anna Davin, 'Imperialism and Motherhood', *History Workshop* 5 (1978), pp. 9–65.
79 'A trained nurse' in Quilter (ed.), *Is Marriage a Failure?*, p. 142.
80 Eleanor Keeting, *Shafts* III (July 1895), p. 61.
81 Effie Johnson, 'Marriage or Free Love?' *WR* 152 (July 1899), p. 96.
82 'Matrimonial Failure' in Quilter (ed.), *Is Marriage a Failure?*, p. 267.
83 *Moral Reform Union 4th Annual Report* (1886).

84 Oswald Dawson (ed.) *The Bar Sinister and Licit Love* (London, 1895), p. 1.
85 Ibid., p. 8.
86 Gerald Moore, *The Adult* 2 (Sept 1898).
87 *The Adult* 1 (June 1897), p. 4.
88 George Bedborough, *The Adult* 1 (Oct 1897), p. 47.
89 *The Adult* 1 (June 1897), p. 4.
90 *The Adult* 1 (Oct 1897), p. 47.
91 Mary Reed, *The Adult* 2 (Aug 1898), p. 204.
92 Dawson (ed.), *The Bar Sinister*, pp. 228-9.
93 Sylvia Pankhurst, *The Suffragette Movement*, p. 31.
94 Millicent Fawcett to E. Wolstenholme Elmy, 10 Dec 1875, Fawcett Library.
95 Men and Women's Club, minutes and correspondence, Pearson Collection, University College London, and see Bland, 'Marriage Laid Bare', in Lewis (ed.) *Labour and Love.*
96 Quoted in Constance Rover, *Love, Morals and the Feminists* (Routledge and Kegan Paul, 1970), p. 53.
97 Dr Blandford argued that if she had been contemplating ordinary suicide, a certificate would have been signed without delay, and that social suicide was no different. *The Lancet,* however, disagreed, pointing out that whilst an attempt at suicide was a penal offence, 'living together' unmarried was not. See Dawson (ed.), *The Bar Sinister*, pp. 368-9, 378-9.
98 See Yvonne Kapp, *Eleanor Marx*, 2 vols (Virago, 1979), Vol. 2, p. 621.
99 Dawson (ed.), *The Bar Sinister*, p. 307.
100 *The Woman's Signal* 31 Oct 1895, p. 280.
101 Since making this comparison I have discovered that David Rubinstein's *Before the Suffragettes* (Harvester, Brighton, 1986) ch. 5 also makes a comparison between the two cases, but for different ends.
102 *The Woman's Signal,* 31 Oct 1895, p. 280.
103 Ethel Snowden, *The Feminist Movement* (Collins, 1911).
104 Christabel Pankhurst, *The Great Scourge and how to end it* (E. Pankhurst, 1913).

Chapter 6   Party Political Women: A Comparative Study of Liberal Women and the Primrose League, 1880-1914

I would particularly like to thank the staff of the British Library, Colindale, and the Fawcett Library for their assistance, and the Women's Liberal Federation for access to their records.

1 For a full account of the Primrose League and the role of the political hostess see Martin Pugh, *The Tories and the People 1880-1935,* (Blackwell, Oxford, 1985), ch. 3 'Women and Conservative Politics'.
2 For a discussion of this issue see Melville Currell, *Political Woman* (Croom Helm, 1974).
3 Letter from Julia Smith, *Women's Penny Paper*, 10 Nov 1888.
4 Eliza Orme, *Lady Fry of Darlington* (London, 1898), pp. 107-8.

5 Ibid., p. 110.
6 Ibid., pp. 112-24.
7 C.S. Bremner, 'The Great Woman Question', *Woman's Signal*, 13 June 1895.
8 'The Organization and Work of Women's Liberal Associations', *Women's Gazette and Weekly News*, 15 Aug 1891.
9 Ibid. Mrs Bayley speaking at the Birmingham WLF Conference on 'Work in County constituencies', *Women's Gazette and Weekly News*, 17 Nov 1889.
10 Report of the Annual Council Meeting, *Woman's Signal*, 3 May 1894.
11 Ralph Nevill (ed.), *The Reminiscences of Lady Dorothy Nevill*, London, 1906, p. 286.
12 Janet Robb, *The Primrose League 1883-1906*, (New York, 1942), p. 50.
13 *A Short History of the Primrose League*, by a member of the staff, (London, 1887), p. 5.
14 Lady Borthwick, 'English Women as a Political Force', *Primrose League Gazette*, 15 Oct 1887.
15 Robb, *Primrose League*, p. 112.
16 *The Ladies' Grand Council*, pamphlet published by the Executive Committee, 1908.
17 Diaries of Lady Knightley of Fawsley (Louise Mary), 11 May 1888, 22 Apr 1887, Northamptonshire Record Office.
18 Editorial, *Primrose League Gazette*, 8 Oct 1887.
19 'What Dames of the League can do.' Circular from Head Political Department, Primrose League, n.d., British Library (BL) Collection.
20 Knightley Diaries, 12 May 1885.
21 Ibid., 6 Apr 1887.
22 Meresia Nevill, 'Special Supplement to the Primrose League', *Madame*, 25 May 1901.
23 *Primrose League Gazette*, 24 May 1890.
24 Leaflet no. 181, Primrose League, n.d., BL Collection.
25 *Primrose League Gazette*, 8 Oct 1887.
26 Knightley Diaries, 5 Aug 1888. Sir Rainald Knightley was her husband.
27 *Primrose League Gazette*, 10 June 1893.
28 'How Habitations are Worked', *Primrose League Gazette*, 1 Jan 1896.
29 Robb, *Primrose League*, p. 61.
30 Mrs Wynford Phillips, *An Appeal to Women*, Westminster Women's Liberal Association Leaflet, *c.*1890, Fawcett Library (FL) Collection.
31 U.M.G., *Why Should Women Care for Politics*, Warwick and Leamington Women's Liberal Association Leaflet, *c.*1890, FL Collection.
32 H.P.H., *Women and the State*, Warwick and Leamington Women's Liberal Association Leaflet, *c.*1890, FL Collection. Lady Dilke's address to the Fulham WLA reported in the *Women's Gazette and Weekly News*, 9 Mar 1889.
33 H.P.H., *Women and the State*.
34 *Why Should Women Take an Interest in Politics?*, Bristol Women's Liberal Association Leaflet, *c.*1890, FL Collection.
35 Ibid.

36 *Why Women Should Take an Interest in Politics*, WLF Leaflet, *c.*1890, FL Collection.
37 Josephine Butler speaking to the Portsmouth Women's Liberal Association, 11 Apr 1888, *Women and Politics*, WLA Leaflet, FL Collection.
38 Quoted in 'Irish home rule and women in politics', *Women's Gazette and Weekly News*, 30 Mar 1889.
39 Miss Cheetham, *Speech delivered at a meeting of the Southport Women's Liberal Association*, 8 Nov 1886, Southport WLA Pamphlet, FL Collection.
40 Rev. W. Tuckwell, *Combine! Combine! Combine! An Appeal to Women*, Warwick and Leamington WLA Leaflet, *c.*1890, FL Collection.
41 H.S. Cheetham, 'Protest from a Member of the Southport Women's Liberal Association', *Women's Penny Paper*, 1 June 1889.
42 Miss Cheetham's Speech to Southport WLA.
43 'Women's Protest Against Sir Charles Dilke', *Women's Penny Paper*, 2 Feb 1889.
44 *Women's Penny Paper*, 25 May 1889.
45 Ibid.
46 M.A.Y., *A Few Thoughts of a Woman on Religion and Politics*, Warwick and Leamington Women's Liberal Association Leaflet, *c.*1890, FL Collection.
47 Miss Cheetham's *Speech at the Southport WLA*.
48 Mrs Wynford Phillips, *An Appeal to Women*.
49 Information provided by Michael Wills from his own research on 'The Primrose League 1883–1914'.
50 The 1886 Report of the Ladies' Grand Council shows that 57 out of some 400 Habitations were women-only. Robb, *Primrose League*, p. 113.
51 'Coaxing versus Caucussing in Feminine Politics', *Primrose League Gazette*, 1 Apr 1896.
52 Knightley Diaries, 29 July, 3 Aug, 21 Sept 1885.
53 'How our Habitation is Worked in the Metropolis', *Primrose League Gazette*, 2 Dec 1895.
54 Tony Osman, *The New Cyclist*, London 1982, pp.18–20. Report of the Grand Habitation Business Meeting, *Primrose League Gazette*, 1 June 1898.
55 See letters from candidates to the *Primrose League Gazette*, Aug 1895 and Nov 1900.
56 *Primrose League Gazette*, 1 Nov 1900.
57 'Women in Elections. What an American Thinks of her English Sisters', *Primrose League Gazette*, 1 Nov 1900.
58 Ibid.
59 Report of the Ladies' Grand Council Annual Meeting, *Primrose League Gazette*, 14 May 1892.
60 Mrs Courtenay Lord, wife of the Ruling Councillor of Burnaby Habitation, Birmingham, quoted in *Primrose League Gazette*, 19 Nov 1887.
61 Knightley Diaries, 23 Sept 1887.
62 Ibid., 29 June 1886.
63 'Women in Public Life. Lady Hardman on County Councilloresses', *Women's Penny Paper*, 1 June 1889.

64 Sir Algernon Borthwick, MP, speaking at the annual meeting of the Ladies' Grand Council, *Primrose League Gazette*, 1 Jan 1900.

65 'What "The Times" says about the Primrose League', *Primrose League Gazette*, 1 Jan 1900.

66 Editorial, *Women's Gazette and Weekly News*, 5 Oct 1889.

67 A.W. 'Municipal Work in York', *Women's Gazette and Weekly News*, 23 Nov 1889.

68 A.B.H., 'Women Voters'.

69 A.W., 'Municipal Work in York'.

70 In York there were 1,888 women voters out of a total of 11,808 on the municipal register. Ibid.

71 A.W. noted that in two wards in York where women had been elected members of the Liberal 400 they took part in the selection process. Ibid.

72 WLF, *Annual Report for 1904*. WNLF Executive Committee Minutes, 10 June 1910.

73 Quoted in David Morgan, *Suffragists and Liberals* (Blackwell, Oxford, 1975), p. 70.

74 *The Suffrage Annual and Women's Who's Who* (London, 1913), p. 35.

75 WNLF Executive Committee Minutes, July and Oct 1910, June 1911.

76 *A Short History of the Primrose League*.

77 Robb, *Primrose League*, p. 127.

78 Ibid., p. 125.

79 *Primrose League Gazette*, 13 Feb 1892. *Authoritative Statement on the Question of Women's Suffrage*, issued by the Ladies' Grand Council of the Primrose League with the approval of Grand Council, Primrose League, October 1909, *Primrose League* Leaflet, LSE Collection.

80 *The Enfranchisement of Women: An Ancient Right, a Modern Need*, paper read by Mrs McIlquham to the Bedminster (Bristol) Champion Habitation, 11 Dec 1891, Women's Emancipation Union Pamphlet, BL Collection. 'Habitation Notes', *Primrose League Gazette*, 1 Jan 1894. *Women's Place in Politics*, address given by Mrs Mitchell, Dame President of the Llanfrechfa Habitation to the Talbot Habitation, 20 Apr 1903, Pamphlet, Museum of London Collection.

81 'Two Points of View', *Primrose League Gazette*, Sept 1910.

82 From 1891 the Annual General Meeting comprised two parts: the Annual Council Meeting which controlled the Executive, and the Conference – a discussion and debating body with no voting power.

83 Report of the WLF Executive Committee Meeting on 30 Apr 1891, *Women's Gazette and Weekly News*, 15 May 1891.

84 Report of the WLF Annual Council Meeting, 27 May 1891, *Women's Gazette and Weekly News*, 15 June 1891.

85 WLF *Annual Reports*.

86 Ibid.

87 Eva McLaren, *The History of the Women's Suffrage Movement in the Women's Liberal Federation*, WLF Pamphlet, 1903.

88 Paper read by Mrs Fry at the Darlington Conference, 'Relation of the

Women's Liberal Federation to the Suffrage Question', *Women's Gazette and Weekly News*, 30 Nov 1889.

89 Miss Garratt of the Kennington WLA, 'Women's Suffrage as a Present Political Object', *Women's Gazette and Weekly News*, 14 Mar 1891.

90 Eliza Orme, 'A Clear Issue', *Women's Gazette and Weekly News*, 15 Aug 1891.

91 Paper read by Miss Ryley to the WLF Conference at Birmingham, *Women's Gazette and Weekly News*, 12 Jan 1889.

92 Ibid.

93 'Letter from a suffrageite of seventeen years standing. The Associations and Women's Suffrage', *Women's Gazette and Weekly News*, 14 Sept 1889.

94 Ibid.

95 Mrs Wynford Phillips speaking at the Annual Council Meeting, *Women's Gazette and Weekly News*, 15 June 1891.

96 Eliza Orme, *Lady Fry of Darlington*, p. 130.

97 *A Letter from the Right Hon. W.E. Gladstone, M.P. to Samuel Smith, M.P., 'Female Suffrage'*, Pamphlet, Fawcett Papers, Manchester Public Library. The Liberal Party Head Office issued a circular 'warning candidates not to allow Liberal women on their platforms lest they take the opportunity of advocating W.S.' [women's suffrage]; 'Point to make about W.S.,' Handwritten Memo, June 1892, Fawcett Papers, Manchester Public Library.

98 Eva McLaren, *The History of the Women's Suffrage Movement,*, p. 101. The amendment to the constitution was as follows: 'To promote just legislation for women (including the Local and Parliamentary Franchise for all women, married, single or widowed, who possess any of the legal qualifications which entitle men to vote) and the removal of all their legal disabilities as citizens.'

99 Women's National Liberal Association, *Quarterly Leaflet*, 15 June 1897.

100 WNLA, *Quarterly Leaflet*, 1895-9.

101 The WLF and WNLA amalgamated in 1919 after the first instalment of suffrage was granted, becoming the Women's National Liberal Federation.

102 'What are Men without the Vote?' *Women's Penny Paper*, 17 Aug 1889.

103 Letter from Anna Priestman, 'Union of Practical Suffragists', *Shafts*, Jan 1897.

104 M. Taylor, *To the Delegates of the Women's Liberal Federation*, WLF Leaflet, 8 June 1896, FL Collection.

105 For further discussion of women Liberals and the suffrage campaign see Rosamund Billington, 'Women, Politics and Local Liberalism: from "Female Suffrage" to "Votes for Women"', in *The Journal of Regional and Local Studies*, vol. 5, no. 1, Spring 1985; Nicola R. Mills, 'The Formation and Development of the Women's Liberal Federation and its Contribution to the Suffrage Movement 1886-1918', M.A. Dissertation (CNAA), Thames Polytechnic, 1986.

106 'Women's Work in the Primrose League', Mrs Van Raalte, *Primrose League Gazette*, Aug 1903.

107 Quoted in Robb, *Primrose League*, p. 9.

108 Address by Mrs Fawcett to the students of Bedford College quoted in *Primrose League Gazette*, 15 Oct 1887.
109 *Justice*, 23 June 1890. SDF Annual Report for 1897.
110 'Women and Politics', *Primrose League Gazette*, 1 Aug 1900. Robb, *Primrose League*, p. 137.
111 'Coaxing versus Caucussing in Feminine Politics', *Primrose League Gazette*, 1 Apr 1896. George Lane-Fox, Vice-Chancellor of the Primrose League, quoted in 'How Women Wield Political Influence', *Primrose League Gazette*, 2 July 1894.

Chapter 7 Women in Council: Separate Spheres, Public Space

1 This essay is drawn from my *Ladies Elect: Women in English Local Government 1865-1914* (Oxford University Press, 1987), to which I would refer readers for further information and detailed sources.
2 Barbara Bodichon, *Reasons for and against the Enfranchisement of Women* (London, 1866).
3 *Nineteenth Century* 25 (June 1889), pp. 781-7; E. Davies to Miss Manning, 17 May 1891, quoted in Barbara Stephen, *Emily Davies and Girton College* (Constable & Co, 1927), p. 348.
4 By that ruling, married women who had property which might otherwise qualify them, were regarded as *femes covert*, whose legal rights were merged with those of their husbands. By 1900, qualified women ratepayers were voting in town and county council elections, for parish, vestry, rural and urban district councils, for School and Poor Law Boards.
5 For Bristol, *Western Daily Press*, 16-22 Jan 1877, 19 Jan 1880; for Nottingham, *Nottingham Daily Express*, 19-27 Nov 1883; for Bradford, *Bradford Observer*, 8 Nov 1882, 21 Nov 1888, 8 Nov 1897.
6 Society for Promoting the Return of Women Guardians, *Annual Reports*.
7 Mrs Leach, *Yarmouth Times*, 5 Feb 1881.
8 Mrs Buckton, *School Board Chronicle* (*SBC*) 10 Apr 1875, 28 June 1879.
9 Mrs Surr, *SBC*, 19 Mar 1881.
10 Margaret McMillan, *Bradford Observer*, 3 and 6 Aug 1897; H. Adler, 'Children and wage earning', *Fortnightly Review*, 73 (May 1903); for Mary Dendy, H. McClachlan, *Records of a Family 1800-1935* (Manchester University Press, Manchester, 1935) pp. 135-84; *Woman's Signal*, 21 June 1898.
11 *SBC*, 2 Nov 1872; 18 May 1889; *National Reformer*, 9 Feb 1890.
12 *SBC*, 28 July, 10 Nov 1877, 27 July 1878, 17 July 1880.
13 *SBC*, 22 Oct 1892; *Oxford Chronicle*, 16 Mar 1872.
14 L. Twining, 'Women as public servants', *Nineteenth Century*, 28 (Dec 1890), pp. 950-8.
15 'Are More Women Guardians Needed?', *Englishwoman's Review* (*EWR*), 20 (Mar 1889), pp. 97-102.

16 Mrs Evans, *Richmond Times*, 6 Apr 1889; L. Twining, *Workhouses and Pauperism* (London, 1898).

17 Workhouse Infirmary Nursing Association, *Annual Reports*.

18 *Woman's Signal*, 18 July 1895.

19 'The duty of being a poor law guardian', *EWR*, 12 (15 Feb 1881), pp. 67–70.

20 Mrs Shaen, Mrs Lonsdale, National Union of Women Workers (NUWW) Conference *Annual Report* for 1895, pp. 153–62.

21 Women's Local Government Society (WLGS), *Annual Reports* and *Minutes* (38 volumes). Its inner circle included Elizabeth Lidgett and Sarah Ward Andrews of the Women Guardians Society, Eva McClaren of temperance and women's liberalism, Mrs Sheldon Amos, a suffrage and purity worker, and at its head the Countess of Aberdeen, and Lady Strachey.

22 This account is drawn from the *Women's Penny Paper* (*WPP*) 18 and 25 May 1889; *EWR* 20, (15 June 1889); *WPP*, 14 June and 1 July 1890; *Women's Herald*, 9 May 1891; WLGS Minute Books. Outside London, Mrs McIlquaham stood for Gloucestershire CC, and Mrs Massingberd for Lincolnshire CC.

23 R. Heath, 'The Rural Revolution', *Contemporary Review*, 67 (Feb 1895), pp. 182–200. One hundred and fifty women were immediately elected as rural district councillors.

24 A. Busk, 'Women's Work on Vestries and Councils' in Rev. J. Hand (ed.), *Good Citizenship* (London, 1899).

25 *NUWW Occasional Papers*, Jan 1902.

26 The others were Edith Sutton, of Sutton Seeds, Reading; Mrs Woodward, hotel owner of Bewdley near Kidderminster; Miss Sophia Merivale, dean's daughter, Oxford; Miss Dove, headmistress at High Wycombe; and on a by-election, the wealthy widowed Mrs Lees at Oldham.

27 Sarah Redditch, *Bolton Journal*, 25 Oct 1907. Mabel Clarkson, election ephemera, Colmon and Rye Library, Norwich.

28 H. McDowell, 'Mothering a Municipality', *The Designer*, Feb 1891, p. 227. See also the Lees Collection, Oldham.

29 Oxford Sanitary Aid Association Reports, 1908–9; 'Municipal Milk', *Fabian Tract* 122 by F. Lawson Dodd, 1905.

30 'Women Councillors', *The Englishwoman*, VII (Sept 1910), pp. 121–5.

31 Liverpool Distress Committee 1906, 1910 Annual Reports.

32 *EWR*, 15 Feb 1881.

33 See e.g. Eleanor Smith at Oxford 1871, Ruth Homans for the London School Board 1897, Maud Burnett for Tynemouth 1910; and the WLGS series of leaflets, 'Why women are wanted on. . .'. See also Mrs L. Mallet, 'Shall women be eligible to serve on County Councils?' (1896) reprinted in P. Hollis (ed.) *Women in Public 1850–1900* (Allen and Unwin, 1979), pp. 268–72.

34 M. Ashton, *Woman Citizen* (Dec 1937) p. 11; *Manchester Guardian*, 30 Oct 1907; Miss Balkwill, *Report of Anglo-Japanese Congress* (1910), p. 11; Mrs Rackham, *The Englishwoman*, XXI (Feb 1914), pp. 145–9; Miss Balkwill,

WLGS dinner speech 1909, cutting in the Lees collection, Oldham, L. 151.

35 *London* 1 Apr 1897; *Southwark Recorder*, 12 and 19 Nov 1909, 6 May 1910, 8 Nov 1910.

36 *EWR*, 15 Apr 1889.

37 *WLGS Annual Reports* 1914-15, 1919-20. In 1914 there were in England and Wales 1546 women guardians of whom 200 were RD councillors; 15 UD councillors, 48 town and county councillors; 679 co-opted LEA members, 1032 co-opted Insurance committee members; 289 co-opted members of Mental Deficiency Committees and a handful on library committees.

38 Miss Sturge, *Western Daily Press*, 14 and 19 Jan 1880; Mrs Cowen, *Notts. Daily Express*, 19-27 Nov 1883; Mrs Lees, *Oldham Standard*, 15 Nov 1907, *Oldham Evening Chronicle*, 19 Nov 1907.

39 Maud Burnett, *Shields Daily News*, 9 Oct 1909, 22 Oct 1910; Jenny Foster Newton, *Richmond Times*, 21 Mar 1888.

40 M. Ashton, *Manchester Guardian*, 15 Oct 1908; Kate Ryley, letter to Eva McClaren, *WLA Southport Minute Books*, 27 Oct 1899.

41 J.M.E. Brownlow, *Women's Work in Local Government* (David Nutt, 1911), pp. 4-5.

42 *The Wants of the Women's Municipal Party* (1913).

43 *Yarmouth Mercury*, 31 Oct 1908.

Chapter 8 'In the Comradeship of the Sexes Lies the Hope of Progress and Social Regeneration': Women in the West Riding ILP, c.1890–1914

1 *Labour Leader*, 9 Jan 1913, Special Suffrage Supplement. Editorial.

2 Ibid., 9 Apr 1914.

3 *Common Cause*, 19 Sept 1912.

4 For example, see S. Rowbotham, *Hidden from History* (Pluto, 1973) and B. Taylor, *Eve and the New Jerusalem: Socialism and Feminism in the Nineteenth Century* (Virago, 1983).

5 J. Clayton, *The Rise and Decline of Socialism in Great Britain, 1884-1924* (Faber & Gwyer, 1926), pp. 84-5.

6 H. Pelling, *Origins of the Labour Party* (Oxford University Press, Oxford, 1966), p. 155. D. Howell, *British Workers and the Independent Labour Party, 1886-1906* (Manchester University Press, Manchester, 1983), p. 335.

7 J. Liddington and J. Norris, *One Hand Tied Behind Us: The Rise of the Women's Suffrage Movement* (Virago, 1978), p. 262. See also J. Liddington, *The Life and Times of a Respectable Rebel: Selina Cooper, 1864-1946* (Virago, 1984.

8 In Leeds women formed 61.1% of the labour force in textiles and 67.6% in tailoring in 1911. *Census of England and Wales for 1911* (PP 1913, LXXIX).

9 For a discussion of Carpenter's views, see S. Rowbotham and J. Weeks, *Socialism and the New Life: The Personal and Sexual Politics of Edward*

Carpenter and Havelock Ellis (Pluto, 1977). For the Leeds Socialist League, see E.P. Thompson, *William Morris: Romantic to Revolutionary* (Merlin, 1977), part 3.

10 Bessie was born in 1848 and Isabella in 1855. Their close cousin was Edward Pease, a founder member of the Fabian Society.

11 Letter from Bessie Ford to Walt Whitman, 16 Feb 1875 (Feinburg Collection, Library of Congress, Washington D.C.).

12 Emma Paterson attempted to set up all-female benefit societies in the provinces in the 1880s, usually among dressmakers, tailoresses and printers. For Isabella Ford's first meeting with the Socialist League, see Alf Mattison's Diaries, Notebook 1, Brotherton Library, University of Leeds.

13 The organization of wool and worsted workers is described in B. Turner, *Short History of the General Union of Textile Workers* (Labour Pioneer and Factory Times, Heckmondwike, 1920).

14 For a detailed account of the strike, see J. Hendrick, 'The Tailoresses in the Ready-Made Clothing Industry in Leeds, 1888–99' (unpublished MA dissertation, University of Warwick, 1970).

15 For example, see K. Laybourn, 'The Manningham Mills Strike: Its Importance in Bradford History', *Bradford Antiquary*, XLVI (1976), C. Pearce, *The Manningham Mills Strike, Bradford Dec. 1890 – April 1891* (University of Hull, Occasional Papers no. 7, 1975), and E.P. Thompson, 'Homage to Tom Maguire', in A. Briggs and J. Saville (eds), *Essays in Labour History, Vol. 1* (Macmillan, 1960).

16 Quoted in Laybourn, 'The Manningham Mills Strike', p. 7.

17 I.O. Ford, 'Why Women Should be Socialists', *Labour Leader*, 1 May 1913.

18 For the weakness of textile trade unionism, see J. Bornat, 'Lost Leaders: Women, Trade Unionism and the Case of the General Union of Textile Workers, 1875-1914', in A. John (ed.), *Unequal Opportunities: Women's Employment in England, 1880-1918* (Blackwell, Oxford, 1986). For tailoresses, see Hendrick, 'Tailoresses in Ready-Made Clothing'.

19 J. Badlay, *50 Years' Service to Labour* (Leeds, n.d.).

20 *Labour Leader*, 26 May 1894.

21 Howell, *British Workers*, p. 335.

22 *Bradford Labour Echo*, 29 July 1899.

23 *Common Cause*, 19 Sept 1912.

24 B. Turner, 'Looking Backwards', *Socialist Review*, XXIII, no. 125 (Feb 1924), pp. 66–7 and *Labour Leader*, 9 Apr 1914.

25 Alf Mattison's Diaries, Notebook I, Brotherton Library, Leeds.

26 The local press provides numerous examples of women who stood successfully as ILP candidates.

27 For an account of her life, see D'Arcy Cresswell, *Margaret McMillan: A Memoir* (Hutchinson, 1948).

28 Howell, *British Workers*, p. 334.

29 M. McMillan, 'The Food Depot "At Home"', *Labour Leader*, 13 Mar 1908, p. 172.

30 *Bradford Labour Echo*, 22 Apr 1899.

31 Ibid., 25 March 1899.

32 Ibid., 13 Aug 1898. Similar instances can be found in other ILP branches. In Huddersfield, for example, regret was expressed when Miss Siddon decided not to stand again for the Board of Guardians after 31 years' service, for she had always taken a 'prominent and progressive part', especially towards the care of children and young women. *The Worker*, 22 Mar 1913.

33 *Woman's Herald*, 7 May 1892.

34 F. Brockway, *Socialism Over Sixty Years: The Life of Jowett of Bradford* (George Allen & Unwin, 1946), p. 61.

35 For more details, see Bornat, 'Lost Leaders', pp. 219-24.

36 J. Woollcombe, 'Julia Varley: A Lifelong Campaigner', *The Gateway*, vol. 111, XIV (June 1930) in the Varley Collection, Hull University.

37 I.O. Ford, *Industrial Women and How to Help Them* (Humanitarian League, c.1900).

38 *Humane Review*, 2 (1901-2), p. 198.

39 T. Maguire, 'The Old Order Changeth', *Machine Room Chants* (Labour Leader, 1895).

40 *Women's Trade Union Review* (Jan 1900).

41 B. Turner, *Short History of the General Union of Textile Workers* (Heckmondwike, *Labour Pioneer and Factory Times*, 1920), p. 119.

42 *Leeds Weekly Citizen*, 12 June 1914, and I.O. Ford, *Women and Socialism* (ILP, 1904), p. 6.

43 *Yorkshire Factory Times*, 1 Apr 1904.

44 *Leeds Forward*, Sept and Oct 1898.

45 *Labour Chronicle*, 6 May 1893.

46 I.O. Ford, 'In Praise of Married Women', *Labour Leader*, 2 Sept 1904, p.262.

47 I.O. Ford, *Women and Socialism* (ILP, 1906), p. 3.

48 E. Penny, 'Women and Politics', *Halifax and District Labour News*, 10 July 1909. For examples of similar views, see E. Girdlestone, 'Objections to Socialism Answered', *Bradford Labour Echo*, 7 May 1898; 'The Hand That Rocks the Cradle - Demands a Vote', *Bradford Pioneer*, 19 Sept 1913.

49 B. Turner, 'Looking Backwards', p. 72.

50 H. Mitchell, *The Hard Way Up* (Virago, 1977), ch. 3.

51 For details of the campaign in Lancashire, see Liddington, *Life and Times*, chs. 9 and 10. Christabel's speeches are noted in *The Worker* (Huddersfield), 19 Jan 1906.

52 Ford, *Women and Socialism*, p. 16.

53 E.S. Pankhurst, *The Suffragette Movement* (Virago, 1977), p. 203.

54 M. Ogden White, 'Miss Mary Gawthorpe', Archives of New York State Women's Suffrage Party, and M. Gawthorpe, *Up Hill to Holloway* (Traversity Press, Penobscot, Maine, 1962), p. 205.

55 Gawthorpe, *Up Hill*, p. 221.

56 Ibid., p. 232.

57 *The Worker* (Huddersfield), 23 Mar 1906.

58 Ford, *Women and Socialism*, p. 10. The ILP published this revised version in 1906.

59 *Labour Leader*, 9 Feb 1906.

60 *Manifesto to the Women's Social and Political Union* (ILP, 1906).
61 Letter to Francis Johnson, 28 Oct 1906. Johnson collection, London School of Economics.
62 Clayton, *Rise and Decline of Socialism*, p. 156.
63 *Halifax and District Labour News*, 18 Sept 1909 and *Common Cause*, 11 July 1913.
64 *Common Cause*, 18 July 1913.
65 *Leeds Weekly Citizen*, 21 Nov, 5 and 26 Dec 1913, 9 Jan 1914. Mrs Dightam was the wife of the vice-president of the East Leeds LRC.
66 Bornat, 'Lost Leaders', p. 218.
67 *Halifax and District Labour News*, 10 July 1906.
68 M. Phillips, 'The Working Woman in Politics. Article 1', *Bradford Pioneer*, 26 Sept 1913.
69 *Bradford Daily Argus*, 15 Feb 1907.
70 *Bradford Pioneer*, 5 Dec 1913.
71 *Leeds Weekly Citizen*, 1 Aug 1913.
72 Ibid., 12 and 26 Dec 1913, 9 Jan 1914.
73 Ibid., 16 Jan 1914.
74 Clayton, *Rise and Decline of Socialism*, p. 84.

Index

Index by Janet Shuter